THE DRAMATURGY OF THE SPECTATOR

Italian Theatre and the Public Sphere, 1600–1800

The Dramaturgy of the Spectator

Italian Theatre and the Public Sphere, 1600–1800

TATIANA KORNEEVA

UNIVERSITY OF TORONTO PRESS
Toronto Buffalo London

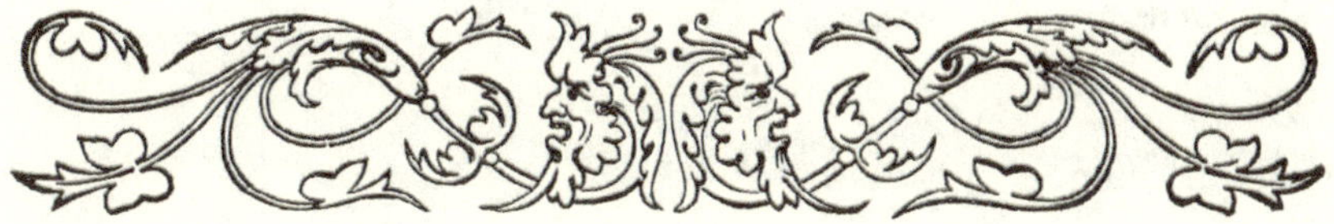

Toronto Buffalo London
utorontopress.com

ISBN 978-1-4875-0535-6

Toronto Italian Studies

Library and Archives Canada Cataloguing in Publication

Title: The dramaturgy of the spectator: Italian theatre and the public sphere, 1600–1800 / Tatiana Korneeva.
Names: Korneeva, Tatiana, author.
Series: Toronto Italian studies.
Description: Series statement: Toronto Italian studies | Includes bibliographical references and index.
Identifiers: Canadiana 20190067160 | ISBN 9781487505356 (hardcover)
Subjects: LCSH: Theater audiences – Italy – History – 17th century. | LCSH: Theater audiences – Italy – History – 18th century. | LCSH: Theater audiences – Italy – Psychology – History – 17th century. | LCSH: Theater audiences – Italy – Psychology – History – 18th century. | LCSH: Spectators – Italy – History – 17th century. | LCSH: Spectators – Italy – History – 18th century. | LCSH: Italian drama – To 1700 – History and criticism. | LCSH: Italian drama – 18th century – History and criticism.
Classification: LCC PN2672.A84 K67 2019 | DDC 792.0945—dc23

Vintage fleuron found on thegraphicsfairy.com

This book has been published with the assistance of the DramaNet project, funded by the European Research Council.

University of Toronto Press acknowledges the financial assistance to its publishing program of the Canada Council for the Arts and the Ontario Arts Council, an agency of the Government of Ontario.

Canada Council for the Arts
Conseil des Arts du Canada

Funded by the Government of Canada
Financé par le gouvernement du Canada
Canada

Contents

Acknowledgments vii

Chronology of Italian Theatre, 1600–1800 ix

Introduction 3

1 How Theatre Invents the Public Sphere 16

2 The Privileged Visibility of the Viewer 44

3 The Politics of Spectatorship 69

4 Public Emotions and Emotional Publics 91

5 Playwrights Fight Back 115

6 Liberty and the Audience 142

Epilogue 177

Notes 185

Bibliography 225

Index 251

Acknowledgments

One of my greatest pleasures in finishing this book is having the opportunity to acknowledge the many institutions and individuals whose assistance has been invaluable during its long period of gestation. The research for this project was supported by "Early Modern European Drama and the Cultural Net (DramaNet)," which was funded by the European Research Council Advanced Grant Project and was directed by Professor Joachim Küpper at the Freie Universität Berlin from 2010 to 2016. I am also grateful for the financial support I received during the last stages of writing and rewriting from the Eurias Junior Fellowship at the Institute of Advanced Studies of the Alma Mater Studiorum – Università di Bologna and the Fritz Thyssen Stiftung.

This research would not have been possible without access to the primary materials held by many libraries and archives in Italy and elsewhere, and I warmly thank their staff for generous help over the years. In particular, I thank the expert staff of the Philologische Bibliothek at the Freie Universität Berlin, the Biblioteca del Museo Correr, the Biblioteca Nazionale Marciana, and the Sezione musica of the Biblioteca del Dipartimento delle Arti at the Università di Bologna.

Portions of this book were presented at various meetings: of DramaNet (at the project's international conferences in 2012, 2013, and 2016), the International Society for Eighteenth-Century Studies, the Renaissance Society of America, the British Society for Eighteenth-Century Studies, the American Association for Italian Studies, and the Associazione per gli Studi di Teoria e Storia Comparata della Letteratura. I wish to thank my hosts, respondents, and audiences at these venues for having helped define and sharpen the focus of this project.

I have profited from the incisive comments of a number of specialist readers and owe a great debt to Joachim Küpper, whose advice, constructive criticism, insightful comments, and continual support as a mentor have accompanied me throughout the years. This monograph also relies heavily on knowledge shared by scholars from many other fields of learning. Special thanks go to Lorenzo Bianconi, Igor Candido, Bruno Capaci, and Piermario Vescovo, for reading early drafts of this study and for providing invaluable suggestions for its improvement. For their generous help with scholarly matters large and small, I wish also to thank Stephanie Elsky, Ari Friedlander, Blair Hoxby, Piero Lucchi, Kirill Ospovat, and Cristina Savettieri. Many friends have aided my endeavours, provided countless gestures of support at crucial times, and asked thought-provoking and penetrating questions. I am profoundly grateful to Roberta Colbertaldo, Cristina David, Maraike Di Domenica, Agnes Kloocke, Alessandra Origgi, Alessandro Serretti, Daniele Vecchiato, and Alexander Winkler. My gratitude is due to Amyrose McCue Gill of TextFormations for her professional competence and for her valuable assistance with the editing of this book and the translation from Italian. Also, I thank the two anonymous readers of my manuscript who contributed to the manuscript's final shape through their helpful critiques and recommendations. Finally, my profoundest thanks go to my parents for their love and constant encouragement over the years.

Early versions of chapters 1, 2, and 3 appeared in *Politics and Aesthetics in European Baroque and Classicist Tragedy*, edited by Jan Bloemendal and Nigel Smith (Leiden-Boston: Brill, 2016): 260–93, *"Goldoni avant la lettre": Esperienze teatrali pregoldoniane (1650–1750)*, edited by Javier Gutiérrez Carou (Venezia: lineadacqua, 2015): 503–12, and *Dramatic Experience: Poetics of Drama and the Public Sphere(s) in Early Modern Europe and Beyond*, edited by Katja Gvozdeva, Tatiana Korneeva, and Kirill Ospovat (Leiden and Boston: Brill, 2016): 140–71, respectively. An earlier and much different version of my fourth chapter was published in Italian in *Italian Studies*, 70.1 (2015): 92–116. I am grateful to these publishers for their generous permission to republish these essays in my book; all previously published material has been thoroughly revised and reshaped.

Chronology of Italian Theatre, 1600–1800

1600	*Euridice* (libretto by Ottavio Rinuccini and music by Jacopo Peri and Giulio Caccini is performed in Florence to celebrate the wedding of Henry IV and Maria de' Medici.
	Emilio de' Cavalieri's *Rappresentazione di Anima, et di Corpo* is performed in Rome.
1606	Giacinto Andrea Cicognini is born in Florence.
1630	The Accademia degli Incogniti is founded in Venice.
1637	The first public playhouse, Teatro San Cassiano, opens in Venice, with *L'Andromeda* by Benedetto Ferrari and Francesco Manelli.
1640s	The opera industry in Venice enjoys remarkable economic growth and more openings of public theatres catering to a paying audience: Teatro Santi Giovanni e Paolo (1639), Teatro San Moisè (1640), and Teatro Novissimo (1641).
1641	Cicognini's *Don Gastone di Moncada* is performed at the Teatro della Dogana (also known as Baldracca) by a troupe of professional comic actors.
1644	Cicognini's *La caduta del gran capitan Belissario sotto la condanna di Giustiniano imperatore* is performed at the Teatro della Dogana by the Compagnia degli Affezionati.
1646	Cicognini's *Celio* is performed at the Teatro della Dogana by a troupe of professional comic actors.
	Cicognini departs Florence for Venice, where he pursues a career as a librettist for musical dramas.
1649	Cicognini's *Giasone* (with music by Francesco Cavalli) is performed at the Teatro San Cassiano in Venice.
	Cicognini dies in Venice.

1675 Scipione Maffei is born in Verona.
1690 The Accademia degli Arcadi is inaugurated in Rome. Members, including Giovanni Maria Crescimbeni, Gian Vincenzo Gravina, and Ludovico Muratori, turn to antiquity and to Petrarch in order to reform poetry and poetic drama.
1707 Carlo Goldoni is born in Venice.
1713 Maffei's *Merope* is performed in Modena by a theatre company directed by Luigi Riccoboni and Elena Balletti.
1720 Carlo Gozzi is born in Venice.
1723–5 Maffei's collection *Teatro italiano o sia scelta di Tragedie per uso della scena* is published in Verona.
1734 Goldoni encounters, in Verona, the company of Giuseppe Imer, who engages him as "poeta teatrale" for the Teatro San Samuele in Venice.

Goldoni's *Belisario* is performed by Giuseppe Imer's company at the same theatre.
1737 Goldoni is offered the position of director at the Teatro San Giovanni Grisostomo, owned by the nobleman Michele Grimani.
1738 *Momolo cortesan* (published as *L'uomo di mondo*, Goldoni's first "comedy of character" with the part of protagonist entirely written out) is performed in Venice.
1743 Goldoni's *La donna di garbo* (the first comedy written as a fully elaborated script) is composed; it premieres in Livorno in 1747.
1743–8 Goldoni's reform of Italian comedy begins.
1745 Goldoni's *Il servitore di due padroni* is commissioned by actor and impresario Antonio Sacchi.
1747 The Accademia dei Granelleschi is founded in Venice.
1748 Goldoni contracts with impresario Girolamo Medebach to work at the Teatro Sant'Angelo.

Goldoni's activity as a librettist of comic musical dramas begins.
1749 Vittorio Alfieri is born in Asti.
1749–50 Goldoni's reform enters its crucial year, which includes an intense polemic with Pietro Chiari.
1750–1 Goldoni's *sedici commedie nuove* in the reformed style enjoy a glorious season performed at the Teatro Sant'Angelo theatre in Venice with *Il teatro comico* (1750) as the first title.

1750–5 Goldoni's works are published with printer Giuseppe Bettinelli.

1751 Gozzi composes his first comedy, *Le gare teatrali*, a metatheatrical play about the Goldoni–Chiari rivalry that reveals Gozzi's desire to take part in it.

1753 Goldoni's work begins at the Vendramin brothers' Teatro San Luca, the biggest and the most important theatre in Venice.

Maffei composes *De' teatri antichi e moderni.*

1755 Maffei dies in Verona.

1761 Carlo Gozzi's *L'amore delle tre melarance* is performed at the Teatro San Samuele in Venice.

1761–77 Goldoni's works are published with printer Giambattista Pasquali.

1762 The last comedies written by Goldoni in Italy are performed at the Teatro San Luca: *Una delle ultime sere di carnovale* and *La bella verità.*

Goldoni departs to work for the Comédie Italienne in Paris.

1764 Goldoni composes *Il genio buono e il genio cattivo* for the Comédie Italienne.

1767 Goldoni's *Il genio buono e il genio cattivo* is performed by Girolamo Medebach's company at the Teatro di San Giovanni Grisostomo in Venice.

1771 Goldoni's *Le bourru bienfaisant* is performed at the Comédie Française in Paris to great acclaim.

1772 Gozzi publishes *Il ragionamento ingenuo e storia sincera dell'origine delle mie dieci fiabe teatrali.*

1772–4 Gozzi's ten *Fiabe teatrali* (written and performed in 1761–5) first appear in printed form in the Venetian Colombani edition.

1775–80 The first period of tragedies by Alfieri: *Filippo* (1775), *Polinice* (1776), *Antigone* (1776), *Agamennone* (1776), *Oreste* (1776), *Virginia* (1777), *Don Garzia* (1777), *La congiura dei Pazzi* (1777), *Maria Stuarda* (1778), *Rosmunda* (1779), *Timoleone* (1779), and *Ottavia* (1779).

1777–87 Alfieri composes *Della tirannide.*

1778–86 Alfieri composes *Del principe e delle lettere.*

1780 Gozzi writes his autobiography, *Le memorie inutili* (published 1797).

1780–9 The second period of tragedies by Alfieri: *Agide* (1784), *Merope* (1782), *Saul* (1782), *Mirra* (1784), *Sofonisba* (1784), *Il Bruto primo* (1786–87), and *Il Bruto secondo* (1786–87).

1783	Alfieri's tragedies are published in the two-volume Giuseppe Pazzini Carli edition in Siena.
	Alfieri composes *Risposta al Calzabigi* following the disputes that arose after the publication of the first volume of Alfieri's tragedies.
1784–7	Goldoni publishes his *Mémoires.*
1785	Alfieri composes *Parere sull'arte comica in Italia.*
1787–90	Alfieri writes his *Vita scritta da esso.*
1788	Alfieri drafts *Parere sulle tragedie.*
1788–95	Goldoni's complete works are published by Antonio Zatta in Venice.
1789	Alfieri's tragedies are published by Didot in Paris.
1793	Goldoni dies in Paris.
1796–9	France invades and occupies the Italian peninsula.
	An intense period of theatrical reforms begins in an attempt to diffuse the concept of "national theatre"; public theatres become more common spaces for urban sociability.
1797	The Republic of Venice capitulates to Napoleon in the wake of French revolutionary expansion.
1798	The Treaty of Campoformio cedes Venice from France to the Habsburg Empire.
1804	Gozzi publishes *La più lunga lettera di risposta che sia stata scritta inviata da Carlo Gozzi a un poeta teatrale italiano de' nostri giorni* in an edition by Zanardi; this is the last detailed analysis by Gozzi of his dramatic works.
1803	Alfieri dies in Florence.
1806	Gozzi dies in Venice.

THE DRAMATURGY OF THE SPECTATOR

Italian Theatre and the Public Sphere, 1600–1800

Introduction

The Theatre Public and the Public Sphere

Shortly after Carlo Goldoni arrived in Bologna in 1752, he was taking his coffee at a shop in front of the church of San Petronio when he overheard a conversation among some locals, who did not recognize him. The Bolognese knew that the playwright was coming to their city and were gossiping about his reform of Italian theatre. Unhappy with certain aspects of his reform, they reproached him for abolishing *commedia dell'arte* masks from his plays. Rather than being offended or discounting their critiques as uninformed, Goldoni writes in his autobiography that he listened carefully and in fact treasured the opinions – however counter to his own – of the citizens of Bologna, a city that had become a testing ground for new and innovative theatre productions and that boasted competent, well-educated spectators.[1] Indeed, according to Goldoni's *La bella verità* (*Beautiful Truth*, 1762), the Bolognese theatre-going public consisted of "Uomini dotti, […] Dame perspicasissime, e […] Cavalieri eruditi" ("learned men, […] exceedingly shrewd women, and […] erudite gentlemen").[2] In this meta-theatrical musical drama, which stages the vicissitudes of a theatre company, a singer claims that "[n]on v'è nel mondo / Chi conosca il teatro, / E sappia quel che a' buoni attor bisogna, / Più della dotta mia cara Bologna" ("there is no one in the world / who knows the theatre better, / and knows better what is needed by good actors, / than my dearest, learned Bologna").[3] Prior to the 1700s, spectators often went to the theatre in boisterous and uncritical crowds, primarily to be entertained.[4] In the panorama of mid-eighteenth-century Italian theatrical life, however, Bologna's more learned audiences were the rule, not the exception. Other Italian cities, including Naples, Rome,

Florence, Genoa, Milan, and Venice, had an equally highly developed culture of theatre-going – with equally thoughtful and critical audiences. The question is: How did the theatre-going public in Italy come to consist of skilled critics of music and theatre, champions of public and political debate, and astute adjudicators of theatrical writing and performance? In short, how did Goldoni's coffee-shop detractors – regular Bolognese citizens – come to hold opinions worthy of the attention and respect of one of the greatest playwrights in Europe?

This is a book about how Italian theatre consciously adjusted to the emergence of a new kind of spectator that became central to society, politics, and culture from the mid-seventeenth through the eighteenth centuries. By tracing the evolution of the Italian theatre public alongside the theatrical innovations and communication techniques that were developed by playwrights, theorists, and critics in order to manipulate the relationship between spectator and performance, this study reveals the origin of an important shift in our understanding of audience as both theoretical concept and historical phenomenon. More specifically, this volume moves beyond the investigation of spectatorship per se to explore and analyse its reflexive relationship with social and cultural politics in Italy, especially as they concern sovereignty, structures of power, and the emergent public sphere. I argue that playwrights devoted sustained attention to spectators, directly addressing them and compelling them to take on specific roles as viewers, thereby turning audience members into free-thinking critical agents who would become explicitly central to theatrical – and eventually political – theory and practice.

My investigation begins around the time the first public playhouses were established in Italy, when theatre began to distance itself from its institutional frameworks of court, aristocratic salon, and academy. Between 1600, when the first opera, *Euridice*, was performed in Florence, and the 1630s to 1640s, when the Teatro della Dogana provided access to both royals and a heterogeneous paying audience, and the first public theatres opened in Venice, the theatre became a commercial enterprise. This transformation of theatrical performance from a court ceremony into a spectacle for a socially diverse, paying audience happened thanks to the Florentine dramatist and librettist Giacinto Andrea Cicognini (1606–49, chapter 1), his imitators (chapter 2), and the Veronese marquis Scipione Maffei (1675–1755, chapter 3). Performances of these playwrights' works constitute the first stage of evolution of the complex relationship that came increasingly to bind audience and drama together over the course of the eighteenth century – a relationship that had a significant impact on the dramatic works of Carlo Goldoni (1707–93, chapter 4), Carlo Gozzi (1720–1806, chapter 5), and Vittorio Alfieri (1749–1803, chapter 6). I contend that for each of these playwrights the relationship between author and audience was crucial to their dramaturgy and that this relationship was a driving force for Italian theatre reform. Theatre, moreover, became an important site for the creation of a political public sphere in seventeenth- and eighteenth-century Italy and a vital catalyst for the advent of participatory spectatorship. To explore these phenomena, this study confronts a series of questions: How were ancient myths rewritten to suit the new political concerns of contemporary audiences? How were allegorical associations used to suggest links between figures of power in the plays and audience members attending them? How did playwrights seek to involve spectators via the action onstage, and what innovations in acting techniques and staging practices were developed in the process? How did public response, in turn, influence the production and circulation of dramatic works? In the following six chapters, the analysis of recurrent motifs offers a faithful historical reconstruction of how these playwrights turned the theatre into a space where theatre-goers came into contact with aesthetic and political ideas. This book argues, therefore, that this period saw a change in the self-conception of spectators and demonstrates how theatre called into being an adjudicating public able to judge the validity of not only theatrical but also political "truths" on the basis of the argument placed before them.

Audiences have always been vital to performance and thus a primary concern of playwrights attempting to create a strong connection between the self-contained artificial reality of the stage and the experience of the spectator. The theatre-going public in Italy, however, has never been examined by scholars in a systematic and interdisciplinary way: to date there exist no comprehensive studies on the formation and evolution of the role of the spectator over the course of the two "golden" centuries of Italian dramatic literature. This book addresses this lack by investigating seventeenth- and eighteenth-century spectatorship via a fully comparative approach that employs a broad range of theoretical methods developed by literary scholars, cultural historians, sociologists, and political philosophers. Given that no cultural institution indexed public sentiment more widely and vividly than did theatre, I draw upon Jürgen Habermas's classic *Strukturwandel der Öffentlichkeit* (*The Structural Transformation of the Public Sphere*) of 1962.[5] Anchoring his work in the historical context of France, Germany, and England at the end of the seventeenth and beginning of the eighteenth centuries, Habermas reconstructed the emergence and development of the modern or bourgeois public sphere (*bürgerliche Öffentlichkeit*). This new public sphere, he argued, grew out of a series of social and cultural transformations, including the institution of new networks of communication; the development of new systems for circulating news; and the birth of new forms of socialization such as coffee houses, literary societies, theatres, and salons. Habermas imagined this new collective entity as "the sphere of private people come together as a public," in which, by means of "rational public argument," citizens discuss and take positions on measures enacted by government.[6] The Habermasian public sphere, in other words, is a symbolic, social, and cultural space outside state institutions and within which public opinion is formed.

Italy, politically fragmented into city-states, dominated by Habsburgs in the north and Bourbons in the south, was a sovereign site of public opinion distinct from other early modern European states. This was thanks in part to the numerous literary academies that created a substantial reading public during the mid-seventeenth century. A century later, with the advent of the periodical press and the opening of new channels for private communication such as coffee houses, salons, and bookshops, the Italian public was particularly well informed about contemporary political events and actively participated in public discourse. Despite Italy's belated political unification, Italian regions and cities became citadels of public opinion on social, political, and artistic matters.[7]

Post-Habermasian studies of the public sphere have both expanded the relevance of the Habermasian framework to other geographical and chronological contexts and encouraged, among scholars of early modernity, an increased awareness of the role of public opinion.[8] In collaboration with the recent work of theatre studies scholars and intellectual historians that explores the impact of theatre on the formation of public opinion,[9] this book investigates the role played by Italian theatre in shaping the emergent intellectual and social figure of the public. For this reason, the terms employed throughout my study to refer to spectatorship include "audience" (member), "spectator," "theatre-goer," and "the public." The first three I employ interchangeably as synonyms for the group of observers who gathered together to watch a certain live theatrical performance; from this group I exclude both readers and critics, who are distinguished from spectators by their response to theatrical performances. It is, however, the last term – "public" – that will prove the most important, since my purpose is to pinpoint the complex dynamics that turn theatre into a "potential catalyst of making various publics and counter-publics"[10] and that simultaneously transform audiences (of theatrical performances) into blueprints for a more abstract category of political and social phenomena, namely that of the public(s) and of the public sphere(s).[11] This book claims, therefore, that seventeenth- and eighteenth-century Italian theatre not only coincided with and mirrored the transition from the representative to the modern "authentic" public sphere (to borrow Habermas's phrase) but was also both its forerunner and its active agent.

Despite the fact that a good deal of recent historical research has addressed public opinion, as Robert Darnton reminds us there remains a "fuzziness surrounding the very idea of public opinion,"[12] and we still do not know how it operated in practice. With this in mind, it is perhaps timely to investigate the operations of public opinion against the backdrop of the specific cultural environment of mid-seventeenth- and eighteenth-century Italy. This book thus also interacts with Reinhart Koselleck's theory of modernity, which was developed in his 1959 volume, *Kritik und Krise. Ein Beitrag zur Pathogenese der bürgerlichen Welt* (*Critique and Crisis: Enlightenment and the Pathogenesis of Modern Society*). This important study offers a genetic theory of modern society that both complements and broadens Habermas's conceptualization of the public sphere by offering a political interpretation of the origin and function of public opinion. Koselleck's conception of the Enlightenment as a moral process is useful for understanding how playwrights created a spectator who could be a politically engaged public judge of both dramatic works and social and political matters. Drawing on Habermas and Koselleck, this study sketches a trajectory of the convergence and eventual conflation of the role of the spectator with the role of the expert and learned critic. As is suggested by my title, *The Dramaturgy of the Spectator*, I argue for the relocation of the spectator from a kind of implied and implicit presence – and purely hypothetical agency – that the playwright needed to please, seduce, affect, teach, and instruct, to a genuinely engaged and thoughtful subject at the very forefront of the practice of dramaturgy.

In order to highlight the many and complex interactions among dramatic practice, the public sphere, and symbolic power structures, this study also engages with a wide variety of critical traditions that reveal early modern drama as a prototypical mass medium crucial for cultural signification and exchange. These include new historicism (Stephen Greenblatt), examinations of early modern sovereignty (Walter Benjamin and Louis Marin), discussions of power structures (Michel Foucault and Giorgio Agamben), studies on court society (Norbert Elias), and art historical conceptualizations of the relationship between spectator and art (Michael Fried).

Recent years have witnessed the publication of a number of studies on early modern spectatorship, especially in England and France. This book contributes to and productively departs from recent work on the emergence of spectators as important agents of change during the Enlightenment period, in particular Paul Friedland's *Political Actors* (2002) and Jeffrey Ravel's *The Contested Parterre* (1999). By juxtaposing the theory and practice of eighteenth-century drama with forms of political thought before and during the French Revolution, Friedland documents how and why politics became intimately intertwined with theatre. Ravel provides an assessment of the social composition of the audience and of theatre-goers' behaviour – as well as of their reactions to performances, which he sees as symptomatic of changes in French political culture. This volume not only brings another chronological bookend and geographical space into the conversation but also answers two key questions that these studies raise but do not address: When and how do spectators metamorphose from a supposedly uncritical mass of early modern theatre-goers to a measured, Enlightenment audience of experts and critics? How did the public acquire the right to legitimize artworks by determining their success or failure? I argue that dramatic works themselves contain much – but not all – of the evidence needed to understand what their audiences expected and experienced, and which strategies playwrights developed to communicate with their publics. The nuanced close readings of plays and theatrical writings that follow revise our understanding of how playwrights constructed texts, how actors performed roles, and how critics reviewed performances in the transition from early modern to Enlightenment Italy.

Two more recent books with which this volume enters into dialogue are Joseph Harris's *Inventing the Spectator: Subjectivity and the Theatrical Experience in Early Modern France* (2014) and Logan Connors's *Dramatic Battle in Eighteenth-Century France: Philosophes, Anti-Philosophes, and Polemical Theatre* (2012). Like Harris, I reconstruct the profile and characteristics of the spectator from theoretical statements on theatre, but my interest extends to contemporary practice and the material conditions of performance. Like Connors, I am interested in theatrical performance and the formation of political opinion, but my focus is on how dramatists used stage devices to influence spectators rather than on playwrights' attempts to influence spectators before they entered the theatre. My work also builds upon Blair Hoxby's *What Was Tragedy?* (2015), which provides an assessment of the early modern poetics of tragedy and emphasizes the importance of emotions in drama. This book extends these reflections, bringing them to bear on a broader range of genres. The approach here is *inter*generic: I examine literary and historical accounts of the spectator's role and of audience responses in genres ranging from tragedy, tragicomedy, and comedy to surviving documentary fragments by and about the people who wrote, performed, and watched Italian theatre of the period. Early modern theatre audiences in Italy attended a wide range of performances from *commedia dell'arte* and comedies to tragedies and tragicomedies, and of course to *opere serie* and *buffe*. The public that patronized comedies and tragicomedies differed from audiences of tragic spectacles for the simple reason that the content of comedic repertoire (arias from a *melodramma giocoso*, for instance) was easier to grasp than were the moral messages declaimed in the recitatives, for example, of tragedies, which were often based on classical or mythological subjects. Roughly speaking, therefore, the public for comedies and tragicomedies was larger and included attendees from the lower social classes, while tragedy audiences were more cultivated and often of higher social status. This class and educational distinction between the publics of different genres of theatrical performances only begins to be elided in the nineteenth century, when tragedy and opera audiences (particularly of composers like Giuseppe Verdi and Gaetano Donizetti) begin to merge. In our earlier period, therefore, the intergeneric approach – and the taking into consideration of a variety of theatrical genres – allows the discussion and examination of the full spectrum of Italian publics in all their variety.

As noted above, *The Dramaturgy of the Spectator* shows how, over the course of the two "golden" centuries of Italian dramatic literature, playwrights gradually transformed the theatre into a space where their publics could discuss authority and where theatre-goers were invited to think through political issues, thus rendering a vast citizenry into a social actor of primary importance and influence. Whereas existing studies of early modern spectatorship similarly depict theatre as an important tool of public-making, they tend to present this process as unidirectional: playwrights shaped and manipulated their publics, not the other way around.[13] This study reveals a more complex and fraught process by which publics were, indeed, produced by and within theatre: as spectators became central to more and more dramaturgical and theatrical processes – from playwriting and staging to criticism and practice – they established their will over the dramatists whose plays catered to them.

Yet at the same time, it is playwrights' growing interest in the subjectivity of their audiences, in the psychology of their spectators, and in theatregoers' emotional engagement with performances that brought Italian playwrights of this period into their own.

This book undertakes six interrelated case studies that together aim to offer a sense of historical progression – and of the diachronic evolution of the critically productive spectator – while allowing the close analysis of specific texts and writers. Since each playwright's approach and works raise a distinct set of questions, each of the case studies that follow engages a different set of questions and employs a tailored set of theoretical tools. Despite the individual uniqueness of our six primary dramatists, the interconnectedness of these playwrights and their works is evidenced by their relationships to spectatorship, their use of common motifs and allegories, and the stage devices and dramatic techniques that they learned from one another.

Chapter 1 begins with an examination of the political theatre of Giacinto Andrea Cicognini, one of the most significant playwrights and librettists of the entire Italian Seicento. Taking as a case study one of Cicognini's most dramatically effective and widely performed works, *Il Don Gastone di Moncada* (*Don Gaston of Moncada*, 1641), this chapter addresses two fundamental questions. First, how is sovereignty portrayed in dramas written and performed during the transition from absolutist court theatre to public playhouse? Second, how do the aesthetics of power and the dramatic treatment of royalty change when a playwright attempts to satisfy not only the prince-as-patron but also the collective desires of the increasingly large and heterogeneous audiences of public playhouses, academies, and religious confraternities? Cicognini effects the historical transition from what Habermas termed the "representative" public sphere (in which monarchs represented their unchallenged sovereignty to quiescent subjects) to the bourgeois public sphere (in which private individuals came together to confront and problematize political authority). By exposing the monarch's position in the play as precarious and by showing the king's subjects assuming his kingly role – by making spectators watch onstage characters move from *subjecta* to reasoning individuals – the playwright taught his audience how to analyse statecraft and perform power. Cicognini's poetic and political design was thus aimed at making his audience realize its own importance to – and influence on – social, theatrical, and political life, and at instilling in his spectators the notion of their own absolute power. The great success of this drama suggests that it indeed exercised a shaping influence on the formation of rational and active spectatorship and reveals that features of the "mature" Habermasian bourgeois public sphere existed well before the Enlightenment. In this sense, Cicognini's play can be considered a theatrical precursor to and catalyst of this societal change.

Cicognini's remarkable popularity in print and the adaptability of his texts to different theatrical contexts – which rely on the dramatist's attention to public response – made it easy for authors and editors to borrow his name to ensure the success of their own productions. Chapter 2 explores the influence of Cicognini – or, more precisely, the Cicogninian dramatic mode – on the theatrical practice of Carlo Goldoni. By comparing the tale of the legendary captain Belisario as treated by pseudo-Cicognini (an anonymous imitator of the famed playwright) in his *La caduta di gran capitan Belissario sotto la condanna di Giustiniano imperatore* (*The Downfall of the Great Captain Belisarius under the Rule of Emperor Justinian,* 1661) and by Goldoni in *Il Belisario* (*Belisarius,* 1734), this chapter investigates how pseudo-Cicognini's construction of the relationship between spectator and performance anticipates that of Goldoni. Whatever the identity of *La caduta*'s author, his play strictly reflects Cicognini's analysis of both statecraft and stagecraft, allowing us to trace the earlier dramatist's influence on Goldoni. *La caduta* creates an analogy between stage characters and spectators through repeated references to the sense of sight. But if the act of beholding is also an act of understanding and judging, then, on a meta-theatrical level, pseudo-Cicognini's construction of the specular relationship between characters and spectators invited the latter to become attentive critics whose cultural knowledge allowed them to make informed judgments. Goldoni's rewriting reveals how, on the one hand, he adopted pseudo-Cicognini's refined strategies of communication with his public. At the same time, all of the changes Goldoni made in his rewriting of the myth (altering the mode of expression from tragic to tragicomic; deepening the psychological complexity of the characters – thereby reinforcing the identification between audience and *dramatis personae* and staging Popolo, the collective character of the people)[14] were determined by his intention to offer spectators a role as active participants in the plot of the play. The discovery of pseudo-Cicognini's influence on Goldoni's strategies of communication with his public allows us to trace the historical evolution of the public's increasing centrality to dramatic practice. This process begins with Cicognini's and his imitator's recognition of spectator centrality for performance effectiveness and concludes with Goldoni's placement of public opinion at the forefront of the theatrical enterprise – and, therefore, with the inclusion of the spectator in the theatrical and in the socio-political spheres.

Chapter 3 is devoted to Scipione Maffei's *Merope* (1713), which had instant success with both critics and the broader European public. Via an investigation into the tragedy's political dimension and an examination of its figures of sovereignty, I show how the Veronese playwright created an audience capable of making critical judgments about what was represented onstage. By representing two antithetical models of governance – one negative, embodied by the tyrant Polyphontes, and one positive, that of the more enlightened Merope – Maffei called into being an adjudicating spectator capable of real-world political analysis. Ultimately, this chapter analyses how Maffei's idea of public sovereignty was communicated to theatre-goers through the figure of Aegistus, whose gradual achievement of a new identity (from shepherd to king) allegorizes the people's – the public's – social redemption. This unmasking of the play's political allegories not only makes evident the impact of Maffei's work – and of theatrical practice in general – on the production of a new critical self-awareness in his audiences; it also reveals how Maffei's citizen-spectator anticipates Jean-Baptiste Dubos's *Réflexions critiques sur la poésie et sur la peinture* (*Critical Reflections on Poetry and Painting*, 1719), which for the first time attributed absolute centrality to the public's judgment.

Chapter 4 explores the dramatic works and writings of Carlo Gozzi, taking as a case study his fairy-tale play *L'amore delle tre melarance* (*The Love of the Three Oranges*, 1761). The allegorical association of the Venetian theatre public with the comedy's protagonist prince – the political antithesis of a republican citizenry – offers a reflection on the role audience response played in eighteenth-century theatre practice and dramatic criticism. Through an analysis of the motif of the melancholic sovereign that catalyses the play's action, analogies become apparent between Gozzi's ideas about the function of theatrical entertainment and Dubos's *Réflexions critiques*, which established that works of art should be evaluated by their effect on spectators. Dubos's insights appear to have influenced Gozzi and provide an explanation for his allegorical equation of spectator and prince: the playwright espoused the idea that an audience's response should exercise an aesthetic and cultural authority previously reserved only for a monarch. Last but not least, this chapter challenges the long-standing critical attitude according to which Gozzi is considered a conservative-minded playwright, revealing him instead to be a progressive intellectual and a most original theorist of theatre.

At this point, one might wonder whether Venetian theatre of the later Settecento attempted to reassert its own artistic and political authority over increasingly influential theatre-goers who claimed to be the preeminent critics of drama. As spectators became a critical force, playwrights sought to influence and exploit them in printed and performed debates over political ideologies and theatrical theories. Focusing on how these new spectators – as potentially powerful decision makers – asserted their will on playwrights, thereby changing dramatic production, chapter 5 examines how actor performance practices shifted and playwright innovations developed in response to spectator demands. These issues come to the fore in Carlo Goldoni's *Il genio buono e il genio cattivo* (*The Good Genie and the Evil Genie*, 1767), a meta-theatrical fairy-tale comedy that contains the playwright's reflections on his reform of comic theatre and thus on the relationship between an author and his public. This play, which was written in Paris as a response to Gozzi's theatrical fables and was staged in Venice, permits an exploration of how it was possible to write a play that responded to the public's horizon of expectations in two different nations and thus two distinct theatrical cultures. *Il genio buono* is entirely focused on the audience and engenders a theatrical experience of collective collaboration in which the spectator is an active participant in the onstage action. To construct a new and different relationship between spectator and stage, Goldoni put into practice stage techniques, suggestions on performer management, and rehearsal practices that were developed by his predecessor, the Neapolitan court dramatist Domenico Barone. At the same time, he drew on Denis Diderot's reflections on the use of *tableaux* and pantomime as a means of intensifying the emotional involvement of the audience. This chapter analyses the Barone-Diderot-Goldoni triangulation in order to demonstrate how plays, performance practices, and theories of drama functioned, circulated, and assumed transnational dimensions.

Chapter 6 concludes the book with an investigation of the complex relationship between Vittorio Alfieri, a founder of modern Italian theatre, and his public of spectators. Alfieri's dramas are poised at the cusp of the transformation of court theatre into public, civic, and political theatre; his theoretical reflections on theatre usher in the formation of the spectator as a critical figure at the end of the eighteenth century. In his theatre, the public have a decidedly active role: it is no coincidence that Alfieri claims for himself the merit of having made the character of the people a real protagonist of his plays – an active character who speaks his own lines rather than, as was the contemporary norm, remaining mute if not actually invisible (preface to *Il Bruto secondo, The Second Brutus*). At the same time, Alfieri presents himself as an author without a public who writes for "the dead people" (*Vita – Memoirs*, IV.17). In his *Risposta al Calzabigi* (*Reply to Calzabigi*, 1783), he explains that an informed and engaged public does not yet exist in provincial and ignorant Italy, and that the spectator still needs to be taught how to be an active interlocutor. Alfieri thus addresses his dramatic works instead to "the future people of Italy" (preface to *Il Bruto secondo*), stating that it is necessary for the relationship between public, author, and actors to be not only theatrical but also social and political. His notion of the public, therefore, is complex and problematic. This indefinable nature of the audience, which includes present and future generations, real and fictional figures, leads the playwright to explore the political sense of the word "public." This is particularly evident in *Il Bruto primo* (*The First Brutus*, 1786–9), a play in which Roman history provides a model of free citizenship and the public acquires even more prominence than it did in the plays of Alfieri's predecessors, coming to be defined as a self-determined group of citizens that is no longer a subject but a "sovereign people." Alfieri's conception of theatre was as a collaborative project created by all who participated in it, and his construction of the performance as an act that explicitly returns the spectators' gaze confirms them as rational thinking subjects. Through the lens of Alfieri's writings for and about theatre, this chapter traces the cultural, social, and political circumstances that determined the emergence of the modern public and the evolution of authorial strategies of communication that playwrights sought to use in order to influence and respond to their publics.

The epilogue depicts the major stages of transformation that the concept of "the public" underwent during the period under discussion, suggesting that the later seventeenth and eighteenth centuries present a picture of uniquely powerful processes of public-making that transformed audiences into a public – that is, a critical community coherent in attitudes and expectations with a legitimate role to play in evaluating the products of artistic practice. During the long century stretching from the establishment of the first public playhouses to 1789 (the year Habermas indicated as the political triumph of public opinion),[15] playwrights came to understand that the gauge of true success for performance is based not on adherence to prescriptive dramatic rules, but rather on audience response. The growing necessity of appealing to spectator judgment, as well as an awareness that audience members needed to be taught about theatre-going, required dramatists to develop new ways of communicating with their publics and to generate new strategies for responding to audience horizons of expectation. The rise of a theatrically educated, aware, and critical public, therefore, simultaneously brought about innovations in dramaturgical techniques and helped create the role, as it were, of the modern playwright – encouraging, rather than hindering, playwrights' self-assertion and expression. It is thus the dialectical relationship between spectator and dramatist that enabled each to bring the other into existence at the end of the eighteenth century in Italy.

1 How Theatre Invents the Public Sphere

Giacinto Andrea Cicognini and the New Audience

The figure at the heart of any investigation into the transformation of spectatorship that occurred during the historical transition from court to public playhouse in Italy must be the playwright Giacinto Andrea Cicognini (Florence 1606 – Venice 1649). Cicognini's dramatic production stands at the intersection of courtly performance, of theatre produced by members of learned academies, and of entertainment that was only just starting to become professionalized. His drama thus represents a fruitful forum for reflecting on the fundamental paradigm shift in dramaturgical practice that took place during the first half of the seventeenth century: in Cicognini, we have a playwright who tries to satisfy not only princely and noble spectators, but also a socially diverse, paying audience that avidly attends the new public playhouses.

A brilliant and productive playwright and librettist – author of some forty-five prose tragedies, *commedie regie e politiche*, and sacred dramas, as well as of four opera librettos – Cicognini was a man of remarkable theatrical pedigree and a courtier *par excellence*.[1] From his earliest years, he was closely tied to the Medici court: introduced to the court at the young age of seven, he soon came to be employed as a page boy, thanks to the special interest his godmother, Grand Duchess Christine of Lorraine (1565–1636), took in him.[2] Under her patronage, Cicognini graduated from the University of Pisa with a degree in law, and after his father's death decided to pursue a career as a writer while earning his living at court as an *Ufficial d'Onestà* (an officer of the Florentine Office of Decency). By autumn 1646, Cicognini had moved to Venice[3] and was participating in the cultural activities of the Accademia degli Incogniti

(Academy of the Unknowns), "which functioned as an unofficial seat of political power."[4] It is not surprising, therefore, that many of his plays' plots involve political situations and feature themes touching on kings, royal ministers, courtiers, and the relationships between prince and subjects – sovereign and individual will. Well known for adapting and reworking Spanish *comedias* of the *Siglo de Oro* for the Italian stage,[5] Cicognini often set his plays at the Spanish court – as is the case, for example, with *Le gelosie fortunate del principe Roderigo* (*The Lucky Jealousies of Prince Roderigo*), *Il principe giardiniero* (*The Gardener Prince*), and *Il Don Gastone di Moncada* (*Don Gastone of Moncada*). The socio-political environments of other European courts also appear in his oeuvre: Norway in *L'Adamira, overo La statua dell'honore* (*Adamira, or the Statue of Honour*); Portugal in *L'innocente giustificato* (*The Absolved Innocent*); England in *La moglie di quattro mariti* (*The Wife with Four Husbands*); Sardegna in *Il tradimento per l'onore* (*A Betrayal for the Sake of Honour*); and Poland in *La vita è un sogno* (*Life Is a Dream*). Sometimes the courts in Cicognini's dramatic works are mythological (e.g., *Il Giasone*, one of the most enduringly popular and influential operas of the entire Seicento), historical (e.g., *Gli amori di Alessandro Magno e di Rossane – The Love of Alexander the Great and Roxane*), exotic (e.g., *L'Orontea*), or even biblical (e.g., *La Mariene ovvero Il maggior mostro del mondo – Mariene, or the Greatest Monster in the World* and *La Iuditta – Judith*). His characters include highborn princely protagonists as well as low-ranking *commedia dell'arte* or *gracioso*-like figures, but even the latter belong without exception to aristocratic court culture. The court as a state in miniature, as a centre of decision making and governance, as a stage for royal and aristocratic representation, and as a social network thus permeates Cicognini's dramatic production at a most profound level. Across the full spectrum of his political plays we see a playwright exploring different forms of governance and princely conduct, exposing the unavoidable conflicts that arise between ethical behaviour and *raison d'état*,[6] and engaging with political practice as well as with seventeenth-century theories of statecraft.[7]

Statecraft and Stagecraft

It is vital to recognize that the Florentine and Venetian political and cultural context profoundly influenced artistic activities. In Medicean Florence, the arts flourished by way of a multi-layered network of patronage, at the forefront of which was the Medici grand ducal court. Equally significant in their support and production of the arts were Florentine learned academies and religious confraternities. By the seventeenth century, the Medici court had become a leading centre for the elaboration of new figurative styles in literature, painting, and sculpture; the city was also renowned for its lavish theatrical entertainments and for the spectacular festivals it organized for marriages, coronations, and visits by foreign diplomats. Indeed, it has been argued that the Medici court's most striking contribution to European culture was its staging of large-scale theatrical plays and its commissioning of new kinds of artistic expression, such as opera and ballet.[8] The high point of the 1589 festivities for the wedding of the Grand Duke of Tuscany Ferdinando I (1587–1609) to his French cousin Christine of Lorraine (Cicognini's godmother), for instance, was the performance of Girolamo Bargagli's comedy *La pellegrina* (*The Woman Pilgrim,* music in part by Jacopo Peri, 1561–1633), with *intermedi* (interludes), in the Teatro degli Uffizi.[9] During Ferdinando I's reign, Florence achieved a prominent position in international affairs, as is demonstrated by a political event that would place a Medici family member at the very pinnacle of European society: the wedding of Ferdinando I's daughter Maria de' Medici to King Henry IV of France in 1600. The Florentine marriage celebrations brought together musicians and dramatists with the Medici family itself; the resulting spectacles were incredibly costly, grand, and elaborate – they represented an essential aspect of the Medici politics of prestige.[10] In political terms, these wedding festivities were of course the result of diplomatic manoeuvres on the part of Ferdinando I to further liberate Florence from Spanish domination, but their artistic and cultural significance is enormous. Ottavio Rinuccini's *Euridice* (with music by Jacopo Peri and Giulio Caccini, 1551–1618) was performed for wedding guests at the Palazzo Pitti. This innovative work introduced a new style of theatrical entertainment to Florence – indeed, to the world – and is the first opera to survive complete.[11]

The next revolutionary event in the development of dramatic genres and theatrical life in Europe was the opening of the first public playhouse, the Teatro San Cassiano, in Venice in 1637. With the theatre's staging of *L'Andromeda* (music by Francesco Manelli, libretto by Benedetto Ferrari), opera was exported to a republic where there was no equivalent tradition of musical or theatrical performances at court or in private elite residences. This new dramatic genre thus became immediately accessible to a cross-section of the Venetian population. During the first third of the 1600s, Venice's resistance to the ecclesiastical interference of Rome, its status as a refuge for Europeans fleeing the Thirty Years' War, and its unique urban layout and architecture made it a city where the theatrical arts could prosper. From the moment commercial theatres in Venice opened their doors, opera became a uniquely Venetian phenomenon that was linked not only to Carnival pleasures but above all to the "myth" of Venice, which relied on an idealized notion of *La Serenissima*'s social and civic tranquillity as derived from its unique constitution. When the political and economic power of "the most serene republic" faded a century later, the myth of the city had shifted from the stability of its political configuration to the vitality of its public and theatrical life.[12]

What makes Cicognini's drama an appropriate body of work through which to analyse this shift in specific relation both to changes in dramaturgical practice and to the evolution of spectatorship that began in the early 1600s is his versatility. Cicognini had a remarkable ability to adapt himself and his writing to the rapidly growing demand for professional entertainment that arose out of the ravenous theatrical market of the first commercial playhouses in Venice and their audiences. Indeed, precisely during his Venetian period (which represents the high point of his artistic career), Cicognini brought about the successful "encounter between tragedy and musical drama"[13] that was to shape the genre of opera over the next several hundred years. His plays thus permit us to explore a fundamental set of questions, beginning with how sovereignty is portrayed in dramas that represent a way station in the decisive transition from absolutist court theatre to commercial playhouse, and how audiences became increasingly astute members of a politically engaged public sphere.

Taking into account the intense engagement of Baroque drama with the socio-political life of the communities in which (and for which) it was written, as well as its function as a harbinger – and then diffusive mechanism – of changing political attitudes, we might also seek to uncover the import of Cicognini's tragedies for seventeenth-century audiences both within the local traditions of Italian theatre and on a larger European stage. By approaching Cicognini's political plays as a product of the supply-and-demand forces of the marketplace and with the active influence of his spectators in mind, we learn a great deal about the public's taste in theatre that will help answer two additional questions.[14] First, how did their performance of sovereignty and the aesthetics of power make Cicognini's plays appeal to different kinds of audiences – and, therefore, make them portable across Italy and even Europe?[15] Second, what was it about Cicognini's writing for theatre that caused his plays to remain phenomenally popular into the eighteenth century?

A Theatre Venue and Its Public

The following analysis begins to lay bare the relationship between the theatrical stage and the political culture it served by focusing on one of Cicognini's political tragedies, *Il Don Gastone di Moncada.*[16] Written during his Florentine period (though published in 1658, posthumously, as were almost all of his works), it was staged at the Teatro della Dogana (also called the Teatro della Baldracca) in Florence in 1641. This theatrical venue and the company that performed the play pinpoint the position of Cicognini's dramatic production within the fluid passage from court theatre to public playhouse. Active for almost an entire century, from 1576 to 1653, the Teatro della Dogana was the official seat for touring *comici dell'arte* troupes that came through Florence. Also known as "Stanzone delle Commedie" ("the big room of comedies"), the playhouse was a large space with a slightly raised stage and at least two rows of box seats. Situated inside the Uffizi Palace, the theatre was connected to it by a private secret passage in order to ensure that the Grand Dukes and their guests could come to watch performances incognito.[17]

The Teatro della Dogana was owned by the Florentine Customs office and thus came under the jurisdiction of the grand ducal administration. Medicean princes established a commercial relationship with actors, serving simultaneously as their patrons and their impresarios, and benefitting from full control over the activities and repertoires of local and visiting theatrical companies.[18] The audiences that attended the theatre were heterogeneous and included princes and their guests; members of the court and noble families; and merchants and a lower-class paying audience.[19] The Teatro della Dogana was thus an important venue in Florence for the public commercialization of courtly entertainment that gradually took place as theatre began to distance itself from the framework of courts, intellectual circles, and confraternities.

Cicognini's *Il Don Gastone* was played to an enthusiastic house by a company of professional comic actors at the Teatro della Dogana.[20] We learn in the author's preface to *Il Celio* (a sequel to the play commissioned by Leopoldo de' Medici in 1645)[21] that the audience at *Il Don Gastone*'s première consisted of both elite and common theatre-goers, and that the play was "all'universale così gradito" ("enjoyed a great deal by all").[22]

Subsequently, as Nicola Michelassi and Salomé Vuelta García have pointed out, "Cicognini's play was performed in Florence in the most diverse theatrical spaces: from religious confraternities to public theatres, from noble academies to private houses." In 1642 it was performed at the theatre of the confraternity of Vangelista by members of the Accademia degli Instancabili, and in 1645 it was revived at the confraternity of the Arcangelo Raffaello.[23] In 1657 it was staged again at the Teatro della Dogana by professional players; in 1677 it was performed as *L'amico traditor fedele, ovvero Don Gastone* at the Teatro del Cocomero by members of the Accademia degli Infuocati; and in 1705 it appeared at the villa of the nobleman Giuliano Ulivieri in Fiesole.[24] The range of theatrical venues (from private to public and paying) at which Cicognini's play was performed reflects his ability to construct a dramatic work that appealed to a wide range of audiences, from courtly to common.

Il Don Gastone, in sum, was one of Cicognini's most often staged plays in grand ducal Florence during the rule of Ferdinando II (1621–70) and of Cosimo III de' Medici (1670–1723). It was also by far one of his best-travelled and dramatically effective works.[25] Though it is undoubtedly the case that "[i]ts success was due to the perfect equilibrium between the subject matter of the work and its scenic efficacy,"[26] I suggest that the popularity of *Il Don Gastone* also has to do with its representation of sovereignty.

A Mixed Tragedy for a Mixed Audience

Il Don Gastone is set in Spain and takes place during the rule of the corrupt and decadent tyrant Don Pietro Rè d'Aragona. Don Gastone of Moncada, who is retired from public court life, lives happily with his loving, faithful wife, Donna Violante, and devotes his leisure time to hunting. This peaceful existence is disrupted when the king and Don Merichex di Buccoì, a nobleman exiled for having avenged a family dishonour, arrive at Don Gastone's duchy. The host welcomes the newcomers, generously offering Don Merichex his protection and hospitality. In the meantime, the king meets Donna Violante and becomes immediately infatuated with her. Ignoring the lady's resistance to his advances, the king hatches a plot to pursue her further by inviting the couple and Don Merichex to return with him to the Aragonese court. Although his attempts to seduce Donna Violante continue to be rebuffed, King Pietro persists in his determination to possess her: in exchange for restoring Don Merichex's honour, the king requires that Don Merichex arrange the exile of his new friend Don Gastone as well as an amorous encounter between the lust-filled king and Donna Violante. Don Merichex, after debating with himself over the right course of action, appears to obey entirely the king's commands: he tells Don Gastone that he is to be exiled by the king and orchestrates the murder of the couple's son, Celio, in order to weaken further Donna Violante's resistance to her unwanted royal suitor. Don Merichex in fact goes even further than the king demands by inviting Don Gastone and Donna Violante to a farewell dinner during which they are served their dismembered son. Finally, Don Merichex succeeds in arranging the long-desired encounter between the king and Donna Violante. Only at the end of the play do the characters (and the spectators) learn that Don Merichex had only feigned his execution of the tyrant's orders and did not in fact betray his friend Don Gastone: Celio is still alive and the king spent a night not with Donna Violante but with his neglected wife. In the end, Don Merichex's shrewd manipulation of appearances leads the king to better understand his obligations to his people and re-establishes domestic and political order.

Fausta Antonucci suggests that *Il Don Gastone*'s sources are three plays by Pedro Calderón de la Barca, Lope de Vega, and Tirso de Molina.[27] With Calderón's *Gustos y disgustos son nada más que imaginación* (*Pleasure and Displeasure Are No More Than Imagination*, 1638), Cicognini's drama shares the motif of a king's inappropriate desire for a married noblewoman. Unlike *Gustos y disgustos*, however, *Il Don Gastone* places much more emphasis on the problem of power, on opposition to tyranny, and on the courtier's relationship to the prince. As for his other potential sources, Cicognini may have derived the motif of the faithful noblewoman's resistance to the tyrannical king from Lope de Vega's *La corona merecida* (*The Merited Crown*, 1603) and the motif of friendship between two noblemen – as well as its political meaning – from Tirso de Molina's *Cómo han de ser los amigos* (*How Friends Should Be*, 1612). *Il Don Gastone* also recalls the early dramatic works of Guillén de Castro because of its gravity and its moral and political implications. While *Il Don Gastone* clearly embraces sequences, situations, and plot lines taken from several Spanish *Siglo de Oro comedias*, Antonucci argues that the problems structuring Cicognini's play are absent from these sources.[28] In contrast with them, Cicognini gives centre stage to reflections on tyranny and thoroughly integrates discussions of politics with the play's action. *Il Don Gastone* thus resonates with the political themes of its age: the theatricality of royal power; the overriding importance of appearances at court; the courtier's relationship to the prince and to other courtiers; the discourse on civility; and the art of dissimulation.

There is, in fact, good reason to believe that Cicognini's decision to modify the plot lines of the plays on which he drew so as to emphasize the political significance of his narrative was neither random nor casual.

The political resonance of *Il Don Gastone* is heightened by its tragicomic form[29] – which, in an Italian context, was itself politically charged if not actively politically dangerous, as it offered an alternative to existing systems of government.[30] Indeed, Giambattista Guarini, who set a foundational precedent with the publication of *Il pastor fido* (*The Faithful Shepherd*, first printed 1589), defended the genre of pastoral tragicomedy, with its controversial social mingling of the upper and lower classes, by comparing it to the mixed political form of the republic, asking rhetorically, "E perché non può farlo la poesia, se la politica il fa?" ("Why cannot poetry make the mixture, if politics can do it?": *Compendio della poesia tragicomica*, 1601).[31] By deploying the tragicomic form, Cicognini was thus deliberately elaborating a new aesthetics for a tragic genre that was suited to a mixed audience – a genuine cross-section of the population – that could (and did) identify in complex and bespoke ways with the social and political conflicts portrayed upon the stage.

To return for a moment to Cicognini's dramaturgical models, it should also be pointed out that the sententious discourses of the characters, the violent *coups de théâtre*, and the vivid horrors of the banquet scene – in which Gastone and Violante are served the blood and heart of their murdered son – recall some aspects of Senecan tragedy, as revived by Giovan Battista Giraldi.[32] The particular prominence given to suspense, the *inganno a lieto fine* (twist with a happy ending), and the play's untroubled resolution all echo the innovative form of the *tragedia di lieto fine* created by Giraldi, who justified tragic plots with happy endings, claiming that "[s]i debbono nondimeno far nascere gli avvenimenti di queste men fiere tragedie in guisa che gli spettatori tra l'orrore e la compassione stiano sospesi insino al fine, il qual poscia riuscendo allegro gli lasci tutti consolati" ("[events] should come about in such a way that the spectators are suspended between terror and pity until the end, which, with a happy outcome, should leave everyone consoled").[33] Though Cicognini's play is also tragicomic, it does not conform exactly to Giraldi's mixed-mood form of tragedy (which depicts the virtuous characters' escape from their tragic fate as well as the evil characters' downfall), since *Il Don Gastone* ends happily for the villain as well as for the protagonists.

Cicognini's play, then, is a product of intense cultural exchange and an assemblage of different sources, genres, and dramatic models ranging from Spanish *comedias* and the native Italian tradition of *commedia dell'arte* to Giraldi's *tragedie a lieto fine.* In fact, it is the very heterogeneity of Cicognini's source material that enables his ambivalent portrayal of both sovereignty and tyranny. At the same time as he was influenced by them, however, the playwright seems to have drawn on this wide range of sources in order to unsettle and, indeed, depart radically from them. *Il Don Gastone* is critical throughout in its representation of royal sovereignty, and yet its outcome is entirely forgiving of the villainous king. We might easily expect otherwise, since Pietro d'Aragona is characterized as a tyrant right from the start. In act I, scene 1 – even before the audience has its first glimpse of the king – we hear several comments, mostly negative, about his character. The first of these is by Scappino, a servant of Don Gastone,[34] who explains to another secondary character that although he has never seen the king in person, it is better to stay away from him: "lo star lontano da lui, è vn star lontano dal Diauolo, perche di Rè non hà se non il nome, l'opere son da bestia, e da Tiranno" ("to stay far away from him is to stay far away from the Devil, because he has nothing of a King about him but the title – his deeds are those of a beast and of a Tyrant," I.1).

Later in act I, Don Gastone (reproaching Scappino for not having recognized Don Merichex as a nobleman, and thus failing to greet him properly upon his arrival) is also indirectly critical of the king's tyrannical rule: "Oue imparasti la Dottrina della Tirannide? Se nella Reggia d'Aragona fosti ammaestrato in così fatti errori, sappi, che la mia Ducea è luogo solo oue s'essercita la pietà" ("Whence have you learned the Doctrine of Tyranny? If you were instructed in such errors at the Court of Aragon, know that my Duchy is a place where one employs only respect," I.3). In the words of Donna Violante, the king's court is a "ricetto dell'empietà, scuola d'Inferno" ("vessel of impiety, a school of Hell," II.17) where, according to Scappino, "il pauimento scott[a], e [...] l'aria [è] contagiosa" ("the floor is scorching and [...] the air is pestiferous," II.16). The king of Aragon clearly stands for an absolutist monarchy gone terribly wrong: he is driven by impulse; he craves sex and enjoys the reckless pursuit of pleasure; he is indifferent to the rights of his subjects; and he is ruled by blind *libido dominandi* – the principal characteristic of tyrants great and small. And yet this decadent and destructive king is permitted to redeem himself completely at the end of the play, when he discovers that Don Merichex's *lieto inganno* has set right the king's private life and, consequently, the affairs of the state.

Far from being mere *diletto,* then, Cicognini's drama is highly politically charged. And yet it is difficult to disentangle mid-Seicento commonplaces about tyranny, bad governance, and court corruption from what I view as a specifically Cicogninian treatment of royalty. The following pages will investigate this interpretive challenge in order to show how images of Baroque kingship change when Cicognini attempts to satisfy not only the prince-as-patron and privileged theatre-goers but also the collective desires of an increasingly large market and the socially diverse audiences of public playhouses, academies, and religious confraternities.

The King in Love

Given that Cicognini's attitude towards his sources was to minimize his dependence on and flaunt his departure from them – and that, as a result, comparing his play with its sources does not help us unravel the ambiguities inherent in its portrayal of sovereignty – it may be useful to consider *Il Don Gastone* within the specific institutional framework of the court. From the Quattro- to the Settecento, after all, the court was the fundamental building block of the European political system and functioned simultaneously as a platform for monarchical representation and for political negotiation. Cicognini's play may be essentially a court-centred drama, but it also marks the transition from court to public theatre. German social historian Norbert Elias's theoretical model of court society and his account of the civilizing process and the genesis of bourgeois modernity can thus provide a promising point of entry for our investigation.

The central thesis of *Über den Prozess der Zivilisation* (*The Civilizing Process*, 1939) is that court society constitutes an important step along the path from feudal to modern state society and from a society based upon physical force to one characterized by the restriction of raw emotional expression, by the control of affect, and by the virtue of self-discipline – precisely the dictates of early modern court etiquette.[35] Elias argued that the processes of state formation and of "courtification" (especially as expressed in the absolutist states of seventeenth- and eighteenth-century Europe),[36] the growth of administrative infrastructure, and the centralization of taxes and the use of force limited violence between feudal lords – and in turn resulted in an increased demand for the restraint of aggressive, emotional, and sexual drives, as well as for the refinement of manners.[37] Indeed, Elias maintained that manuals on the education of princes and manners books – which he saw as catalysts of the "civilizing process" – imposed increasingly severe standards of control over impulse and fashioned individuals who would fit within social structures by instilling in individuals "a compulsion to check one's own behaviour."[38] Elias's observation is confirmed by (among countless others) a brilliant Baroque moralist, Baltasar Gracián, who claimed in his *Oráculo manual y arte de prudencia* (*The Art of Worldly Wisdom*, 1647) that "[n]o ai mayor señorío que el de sí mismo, de sus afectos, que llega a ser triunfo del alvedrió" ("no mastery is greater than mastering yourself and your own passions: it is a triumph of the will," aphorism 8).[39] He also pointed out that "[s]ea uno primero señor de sí, y lo será después de los otros" ("if one is master of oneself, one will then be the master of others," aphorism 55).[40] It is Elias's contention that the management and control of emotion (*Affektbeherrschung*) and the ability to conceal one's true feelings thus functioned simultaneously as an expression and a confirmation of differences in status and power.[41] In other words, the absolutist court (the setting in which, according to Elias's scenario, the transformation of the individual's emotional life was most profound) required that its members uncouple the outward display of their feelings from their inner emotional state.

Personal interactions within court society were thus characterized by the norms of "court rationality" – that is, by a balance "between short-term desires and emotional needs, and the longer-term consequences of human action."[42] What Elias's landmark analysis of the historical development of self-surveillance makes clear is that the aristocratic court was marked by an almost complete absence of the distinction between public and private life, since one's private feelings came to be turned to the profit and advantage of one's public life.

The framework provided by Elias's hugely influential study permits me to offer a preliminary explanation as to why the king in Cicognini's play is characterized as a tyrant. Building on Elias's insight into the courtly bonds closely connecting social and power relations, on the one hand, and interpersonal interactions between individuals with distinct personalities and dispositions, on the other, I would suggest that Pietro d'Aragona is defined as a tyrant because he is ruled by unbridled emotion and the reckless pursuit of pleasure. Indeed, in describing his feelings after encountering Donna Violante for the first time, the king demonstrates clearly that, far from being motivated by the norms of "court rationality," he is ruled by passion and self-interest:

> Venni, viddi, e persi, venni à far preda, e fui predato, viddi quella beltade, che in vn punto m'accese, arse, & incenerì, persi, ò Cielo, persi il core, è potente vn Rè, dà la vita, e la toglie, mà più potente è la bellezza, che toglie la vita sì, mà per miracolo d'amore la può ridonare; son morto, ò miei fidi, tutti gli Scettri, tutte le Monarchie non mi possono rauuiuare, mà la beltà di colei è l'vltimo rimedio all'amoroso mio male. (I.10)

> I came, I saw, and I was conquered; I came to be a predator and was preyed upon; I saw that beauty which, in an instant, inflamed, burned, and incinerated me; I lost – Oh Heaven! – I lost my heart! A King is powerful, he gives life and he takes it, but yet more powerful is beauty which, yes, takes life, but because of the miracle of love can also give back life. I am dead, oh my faithful subjects! Neither all the Sceptres nor all the Kingdoms can revive me – naught but her beauty is the final cure for my love-suffering.

It is Pietro's neglect of the core principle of the interdependence of social structures and human interactions – as well as his willingness to seek base pleasure at the expense of his courtiers' honour – that mark him as a despot. This is especially evident when the king uses words most often confined to the political sphere and to war (his "venni, viddi, e persi, venni à far preda," of course, explicitly recalls Julius Ceasar's "veni, vidi, vici"), relocating them within the sphere of private emotion.

The bellicose metaphors, the love-as-war trope, and Pietro's frivolity might remind us of another Baroque ruler compromised in his integrity, namely the King of the Strong Fortress from Giambattista Basile's fairy-tale collection *Lo cunto de li cunti* (*The Tale of Tales,* 1634–6), which was written around the same time as *Il Don Gastone.* In the tenth story of the first day ("La vecchia scortecata," "The Old Woman Who Was Skinned," which is one of the most provocative tales from Basile's masterpiece), the King of the Strong Fortress falls in love with the voices of two hideous old hags and becomes convinced that they are young women. Duped by the falsely engineered beauty of the finger the sisters showed him through a keyhole, he convinces one of them to sleep with him. After discovering her true appearance, however, he throws her out of the window into the branch of a tree beside the king's castle. While she is still hanging in the tree, a troupe of passing fairies transform her into a beautiful young maiden – of precisely the type she had earlier pretended to be – and the king, convinced once more of her real beauty, takes her as his wife. The other sister, envious of this good fortune, attempts to make herself as beautiful as her sister, but instead flays herself and dies. Here again we have a frivolous monarch who is completely oblivious to his political duties and absorbed instead in activities badly suited to his royal and public status – for example, fantasizing about his mysterious lovers under their windows:

> Tanto che le vecchie, che s'erano poste 'n tuono e 'ngarzapellute de l'afferte e 'mprommesse de lo re, pigliattero consiglio de non se lassare perdere sta

accasione de 'ncappare st'auciello che da se stisso se veneva a schiaffare drinto a no codavattolo. Accossì, quanno no iuorno lo re faceva da coppa la fenestra lo sparpetuo, le dissero da la serratura de la porta co na vocella 'n cupo, ca lo chiù gran favore che le potevano fare, fra otto iuorne, sarria stato lo mostrarele schitto no dito de la mano.

Lo re, che comme sordato pratteco sapeva ca a parmo se guadagnano le fortezze, non recosaie sto partito, speranno a dito a dito de guadagnare sta chiazza forte che teneva assediata, sapenno ancora essere mutto antico: "piglia ed addemanna." Perzò, azzettato sto termene perentorio de l'ottavo iuorno pe vedere l'ottavo miracolo de lo munno, le vecchie fra tanto non fecero autro sarzizio che, comm'a speziale che ha devacato lo sceruppo, zucarese le deta, co proposeto che, iunto lo termene dato, chi de loro avesse lo dito chiù liscio ne facesse mostra a lo re.

The old women, who had begun to put on airs and grow bold as a result of the king's offers and promises, resolved that they would not waste the opportunity to nab this bird, who was about to fly into the snare all by himself. And so, when the king was ranting and raving above their window one day, they told him through the keyhole in a tiny little voice that the greatest favor they could do would be to show him, in eight days time, just one finger of their hand. *The king, who as a practiced soldier* knew that *fortresses are conquered little by little,* did not refuse this solution, hoping to conquer finger by finger this stronghold that he was *keeping under siege,* since, besides, he knew very well that an ancient proverb said "first take and then ask." And so once he had accepted this final deadline of the eighth day by which to see the eighth wonder of the world, the old women's sole activity became sucking their fingers like a pharmacist who has spilled syrup, with the plan that when they reached the established day, whoever had the smoothest finger would show it to the king. (My italics.)[43]

The grotesque effect of this passage is achieved by Basile's juxtaposing the heroic rhetoric of high lyric tradition with the base and ugly objects of the king's desire. There is a strong affinity between Cicognini's comic description of King Pietro's lack of moderation and Basile's hypertrophic and parodic portrayal of the fairy-tale King of the Strong Fortress. Both monarchs are oblivious to their royal duties and are instead engrossed in activities that are unsuited to the affairs of state that should occupy them. These affinities with Basile's fairy-tale king denigrate Pietro, whose emotional excesses serve to reinforce his negative characteristics. Indeed, his claim that he alone has the right to possess a woman who, in fact, belongs to another man ("à me solo è lecito il desiderarla, e conseguirla, perche lice all'Aquila sola fissarsi al Sole"; "only I am permitted to desire her and to pursue her, because only an Eagle can look straight at the Sun," I.10), reveals that Pietro is unable to suppress his own self-interest for the greater good of the community and that he prioritizes his individual pleasure above the interests of his subjects.[44] The process of pursuit reveals the dangerous and seductive power a prince possesses, namely the power to follow his passions without fear of opposition or sanction:

> Sono il Rè, ò son l'ombra? Son Vassallo, ò Signore? Più dunque potrà l'ostinazione d'vna femina, che la mia autorità? Don Merichex, già che il sangue del figlio vcciso non fu bastante à piegare l'animo di Donna Violante, adoprisi pur la violenza, così felicitando me se stesso in Amore, farò anco conoscere à lei che vn Rè è Padrone della vita, dell'honore, e dell'arbitrio ancora. (III.8)

> Am I King or shadow? Am I Vassal or Lord? Is the stubbornness of a woman more potent than my authority? Don Merichex, given that the blood of her murdered son was not enough to subdue the soul of Donna Violante, let us resort to further violence. Thus by making myself happy in Love I will also make her learn that a King is the Master of life, of honour, and even of will.

If court society, to continue to employ Elias's sociological perspective, was based on "courtly rationality" as well as on the absence of a distinction between private and public life, we might suggest that Cicognini's king is a tyrant precisely because he allows his private feelings to overwhelm his public role: the sovereign's uncontrolled and undisciplined private body here takes centre stage, illustrating by analogy the ineptitude of a body politic under tyrannical control.

The King's Failed Performance

Alongside Elias's account of the rationalization of human conduct (one aspect of the "civilizing process") it is worth considering his theoretical model of early modern European courts, which he had elaborated some years earlier in *Die höfische Gesellschaft* (*The Court Society*).[45] Elias argued that the growth of civilization and the establishment of the court as a socio-political configuration did not easily pacify the previously autonomous and often violent élite. Instead, these changes transformed social, economic, and political confrontations that had in earlier times been won or lost by means of brute force into symbolic struggles in which both weapons and spoils were replaced by political acts. This new kind of representation meant that political gains and losses came simultaneously to be substitutions for and external manifestations of violence. In contrast to bourgeois-capitalist societies (where the exercise of power revolves around the acquisition of economic capital), in early modern royal courts the exercise of power required the acquisition of symbolic capital – namely status and prestige.[46] Court members were therefore engaged in continuous small-scale competitive manoeuvring for social advantage, power, and prestige in their efforts to secure or protect their status. This meant that king and courtiers were interdependent, as each used the other to reaffirm his (or her) position within a strict hierarchical order. Court ceremonies and etiquette were the vehicles for expressing this interdependence: the king employed them as a means of emphasizing his unique position and his social distance from his courtiers, who employed the same performative events and behavioural practices as a means of displaying their own status within court hierarchies. Commenting on Elias's model, Robert van Krieken explains that, "in court society, individual existence and identity were profoundly *representational* – they consisted of how one exhibited one's position and status to everyone else, and this process of exhibition and performance was highly competitive and constantly fluctuating."[47] In other words, the successful conduct of courtly life depended upon the offstage equivalent of theatrical role-playing.

A brief comparison with Baldassarre Castiglione's often reprinted and much translated *Il libro del cortegiano* (*The Book of the Courtier*, 1528), a major contributor to the "civilizing process," illustrates the point. The *Cortegiano* emphasizes the importance to the courtier of appearances and of making a good impression ("imprim[ere] la bona opinion di sé," I.16).[48] Castiglione was well aware that, by presenting his readers with an image of the perfect courtier, he was instructing them in the art of wearing different masks – of "dressing in" the psychological garb of other people – on different occasions ("vestirsi un'altra persona," II.19). The *Cortegiano* thus teaches its readers to produce and maintain an image of themselves that allows (indeed encourages) others to view it as a continuous aesthetic performance. For Castiglione, the ideal courtier was never unmasked.[49]

In a similar vein, the little-known Italian moralist Don Pio Rossi (1581–1667), an aristocratic friar from Piacenza, observed in his moral lexicon, *Il convito morale* (*The Moral Banquet*), "utilissimo a chi legge, scrive, insegna, governa, Impera" ("most useful to he who reads, writes, teaches, governs, and Rules"), that

> Questo è vn secolo d'apparenza, & si va in maschera tutto l'anno. Pur che altri appara, non si cura d'essere da douero. [...] Pare hoggidì, che chi non sà adulare, mordere, e simulare, che chi non sà auuanzare con la depressione, e sorger con la sommersione altrui, vaglia nulla: sia nulla.[50]

> This is an age of appearances, and one wears a mask every day of the year. As long as one appears otherwise, one does not take care to be so in fact [...]. It seems that, these days, he who does not know how to flatter, snipe, and feign; he who does not know how to advance by pushing others down and to rise by means of submerging others, is worth nothing: is nothing.

As Elias notes, then, the royal court developed increasingly performative and theatricalized codes of behaviour that demanded mastery from its members. It can thus be defined as a society of performance – a cultural and political arena of continual self-dramatization before one's peers, inferiors, and superiors. In the words of Jeroen Duindam, "the absolute ruler and the nobility unknowingly acted out a *tableau vivant* of the civilizing process."[51] In this institutional configuration, where self-representation was crucial for both obtaining and retaining power, good manners, hospitality, politeness, and gift-giving became the primary gestures of that power.

An action that illustrates Elias's formulations about the sociology of power relations at court appears in the very first act of Cicognini's drama, where the king attempts to bestow honours upon Don Gastone and Don Merichex. Here, however, the social and commercial exchange (or gift-giving) is reversed – it is the king's subject, Don Gastone, who gives his sovereign a considerable sum of money, not vice versa:

> Conseruo in questa Ducea gran quantità d'oro, quale appresso di me infruttuoso rimane, pur troppo mi è noto, che nelle passate guerre l'Errario Regio fu in parte suiscerato del suo tesoro, supplico la M. V. si degni per mano d'vn suo seruo riceuere in tributo vn mezo million d'oro, che con douuta humiltà le presenta il più fido Vassallo della sua Corte. (I.12)

> In this Duchy I have set aside a large amount of gold – which, in my keeping, remains unproductive. Unfortunately, it is known to me that during the recent wars the royal treasury was plundered of part of its wealth. I beg of Your Highness that he deign to receive, from the hand of one of

his servants, a gift of half a million in gold, which with all due humility is presented to Him by the most faithful Vassal of his Court.

It is not that subjects never gave gifts to their patrons: on the contrary, courtiers who could not offer a worthy gift to the prince would not go far.[52] This scene, however, is revealing in that it highlights how this sovereign's gestures and actions (which, according to Elias, should mark him as a unique individual entitled to hold power over his courtiers) fail to impress his peerless status upon his subjects. For Elias, gift-giving confirms a power imbalance between dependent and superior – and, far from representing a purely economic exchange, affirms the exchangers' status, identity, and credibility. Here, however, Don Gastone's gesture puts an end to the patron-dependent relationship, since the king entirely fails to perform appropriately the ritual of gift and counter-gift. Indeed, rather than produce a gift in return, the king immediately passes Don Gastone's gift to Don Merichex, clearly demonstrating that he cares little about the well-being of his impoverished state. Indeed, this scene presents us with a subject who is a better caretaker of his kingdom than is his king.

Though apparently incapable of exchanging gifts in the usual, accepted manner, the king still recognizes his obligation to reciprocate Don Gastone's gift in some form. He thus attempts to confer an honorific title of senior horse master upon Don Gastone's six-year-old son in exchange (I.12). The king's ability to reciprocate is thwarted, however, when Don Gastone explains Pietro's error in attempting to grant this honour to a child:

D. GAST.: Fauore al certo non meritato, ma vaglia a dire il vero, ò Signore, come potrà così tenera mano reggere il freno di bizzaro destriero? come potrà Celio mio con fanciullesco fianco premerli il dorso? questo è honore, che a sperimentato Caualiero s'aspetta, questa è carica, che all'adolescenza, non che alla puerilità si adatti; Il zelo del buon seruitio di V. M. m'innanimisce a parlare con disinteressata libertà.

RÈ: Fingo, che anco a gl'infanti non si conferiscono honori; Chi adunque giudicareste habile a tale carica?

D. GAST.: Già che mi chiede V. M. dico, che giudico proportionata la carica al valore di D. Merichex.

RÈ: Sia adunque D. Merichex nostro Caualarizo maggiore. (I.12)

D. GAST.: This is certainly an unmerited favour – it is worth telling the truth, my Lord – how will such a soft hand control the reigns of a crazed steed?

How will my Celio, with his child's hips, press upon the horse's flank? This is an honour hoped for by a young Knight; this is a duty better suited to a young man than to a child. The zeal of Your Highness's good servant spurs me to speak with impartial liberty.

RÈ: I imagine that one doesn't confer honours upon an infant. Who, therefore, would you judge able to take on this charge?

D. GAST.: Since you have asked me, Your Highness, I say that I judge the task in proportion to the valour of D. Merichex.

RÈ: D. Merichex, then, will be our Senior Horse Master.

In Eliàs's scenario, as we have seen, the mechanism by which power operated in early modern court societies was representational in character and was thus heavily dependent on the extent to which others recognized it. What makes Pietro d'Aragona a poor monarch, therefore, is that he fails to represent himself properly to his subjects and to deal appropriately with his courtiers' questioning of his social superiority. Pietro here explicitly contributes to an all-but-complete reversal of power in soliciting and then deferring to Don Gastone's judgment above the king's own. The court in *Il Don Gastone* thus becomes an arena in which power is continuously renegotiated – but not to the king's advantage, though at times by his own hand.

Elias's insights into the centrality of theatricality to the construction of successful social and political agency in the early modern court can productively be brought into conversation with recent critical assessments of early modern political thought that suggest that Baroque rulers regularly displayed their power theatrically. Stephen Orgel and Roy Strong were the first to point out that it was by means of court spectacles and public festivities that princes and the privileged élite exhibited their prominent status and attempted to reinforce their self-mythologizing via ostentatious displays, the parading of political power, and splendid spectacles.[53] Jean-Marie Apostolidès has compared the role of the king to that of an actor in a heroic drama, in which courtiers were at once audience and secondary players,[54] and Stephen Greenblatt has explored the theatrical means by which English Renaissance rulers and historical figures created their "selves."[55] Indeed, the oft-quoted response of Queen Elizabeth to a parliamentary petition for the execution of Mary, Queen of Scots ("we princes [...] are set on stages, in the sight and view of all the world dulie observed; the eies of manie behold our actions"), epitomizes what Greenblatt has called "the whole theatrical apparatus of royal power" and the dependence of Elizabethan power "upon its privileged visibility."[56] According to Louis Marin's compelling study of the semiotics of French absolutism in *Le portrait du roi*, the representation of sovereignty in Baroque political regimes involved the theatricalization of public action and its resulting effects.[57] Even Jürgen Habermas, working within a different framework and distinguishing between the forms of publicity that set the early modern period apart from the eighteenth century, suggested in a somewhat similar vein that the exercise of sovereignty involved the public display of power before the people. Monarchs and their peerage "represented their lordship not for but 'before' the people" ("repräsentieren ihre Herrschaft, statt für das Volk, 'vor' dem Volk").[58] A sovereign thus established his authority via a mode of public self-representation that rendered the invisible source of his political power visible in physical – bodily – form, a type of ceremonial representation that marked the body of the lord with what Habermas calls the mystical "aura" of his own authority. It is worth noting that the English and French monarchies were, however, scarcely different from any other monarchy during almost any historical era in their reliance on the application of the arts of theatre to the projection of kingship.[59]

These critical perspectives complicate Elias's picture of court society and shed light on the fact that when politics, like all the world, was a stage, Baroque princes saw themselves on a rostrum before spectators and understood themselves and their activities in terms of the theatricality of their roles. In light of these broader insights, the specific scenes in *Il Don Gastone* of the king's lack of self-control and his subjects' absent recognition of his authority – not to mention the numerous other critiques he receives – suggest that one of his failings is ineffective role-playing. There are yet other aesthetic criteria for the performance of sovereignty, however, that Cicognini's king of Aragon fails to satisfy.

The Importance of Being Dishonest

The most influential phenomena to contribute to and reflect on the increasingly performative codes of behaviour in early modern political regimes were, according to Elias, courtesy manuals and advice books for princes. One of the cornerstones of social and power relations at court was self-control; the other governing principle – upon which contemporary manners books rather insisted and which was closely connected to both the manipulation of appearances and the theatricality of political behaviour – was the art of dissimulation. Indeed, the sixteenth and seventeenth centuries have been known as "the age of dissimulation," a feature of the period that figures prominently in contemporary courtesy books and in literature on politics and statecraft (perhaps because, as we have seen, politics during the same period took on a decidedly theatrical dimension).[60] In fact, the decade of the 1640s – precisely when Cicognini's play was first performed – saw the climax of the debate over dissimulation and its correlative, simulation.[61]

Of course, Niccolò Machiavelli had already argued (in the famed eighteenth chapter of his 1513 *Il principe* – *The Prince* – a book that has been a *vademecum* for tyranny ever since) that a prerequisite for the virtuous prince was the ability to manipulate appearances. Machiavelli asked his prince to play his part with care; to lie yet to seem to tell the truth. A ruler, he insisted, must be strong like a lion and clever like a fox, and a key element of this cleverness is the ability to be a "gran simulatore e dissimulatore" ("great feigner and dissembler").[62] A politician may be successful while entirely lacking in admirable qualities, "ma è bene necessario *parere* di averle" ("but it is very necessary that he *seem* to have them," my italics).[63] Dissimulation had thus long been thought of as an inescapable element of the political life.

Many Seicento works on dissimulation extended this Machiavellian principle beyond the conduct of princes to that of other members of the body politic. What had originally been a characteristic of princely conduct thus became the standard *modus operandi* (or, to quote Castiglione, the *regula universalissima,* or universal rule) of other groups within the state apparatus.[64] Jon Snyder has pointed out that, "as a practice of self-censorship, dissimulation assisted those who sought not to reveal or disclose anything of their own interiority, but were at the same time intent upon not uttering any untruth to others."[65] He further explains that "[d]issimulation at court was a supremely self-conscious art of producing an image of oneself for others through language, gesture, and action, among other things, even if such a representation was intended to disclose little or nothing about the courtier's true intentions."[66] Castiglione's courtiers famously named this principle of hypocrisy-by-design, coining the neologism *sprezzatura* – that is, a certain cultivated nonchalance: a masking artifice that makes everything appear spontaneous and effortless.[67]

But if, for Castiglione's courtiers, engagement in a kind of theatrical self-presentation (both simulative and dissimulative) was the convention of a gracious court game, in the new historical constellation of Seicento Italy, wearing masks and disguises became an indispensable ingredient of life for other members of the political élite: courtiers, secretaries, bureaucrats, counsellors, ambassadors, and spies. Indeed, Paolo Sarpi

(1552–1623), a counsellor to the Venetian Republic and a political practitioner and theorist, openly recommended hypocrisy, describing himself as a chameleon that takes on the colour of its surroundings:

> Ego eius ingenii sum, ut, velut Chamalaeon, a conversantibus mores sumam; versum, quos ab occultis, et tristibus haurio, invitus incordio: hilares et apertos sponte ac libere recipio: personam coactus fero; licet in Italia nemo sine ea esse possit.

> My character is such that, like the Chameleon, I imitate the behaviour of those amongst whom I find myself. Thus if I am amongst people who are reserved and gloomy I become, despite myself, unfriendly. I respond openly and freely to people who are cheerful and uninhibited. I am compelled to wear a mask. Perhaps there is nobody who can survive in Italy without one.[68]

If we read the king's behaviour in Cicognini's play against the backdrop of Machiavelli's and Castiglione's recommendations to princes and courtiers as well as of Sarpi's self-portrait, another reason for *Il Don Gastone*'s representation of the sovereign as dissolute becomes apparent: the king rejects the cardinal rule of highly theatricalized courtly etiquette, the *ars simulandi et dissimulandi.* In the gift-exchange scene discussed above, the king – irritated by Don Gastone's spontaneous act of generosity that is, apparently, devoid of personal ambition – claims to dissimulate:

> Superbo è D. Gastone, la sua humiltà è la superbia stessa, convien *simulare.* Accetto in buon grado il vostro dono, e perche ne vediate gl'effetti, ecco che ne dispongo, come Padrone; dono à D. Merichex il mezo millione con altrettanto appresso. (I.12, my italics)

> [Aside] D. Gastone is proud, his humility is pride itself – it is fitting to *feign.* [To D. Gastone] I willingly accept your gift; so that you can see its effect, see how I dispose of it, as a Lord: I give to D. Merichex the half million with the same eagerness.

With these words, Pietro d'Aragona openly acknowledges theatrical artifice, whereas a skilled dissimulator does exactly the opposite, announcing nothing and allowing no one to know for sure whether a mask is or is not being used. This king, in contrast, signals his own role-playing, pointedly exposing the mechanisms of theatre at work and reminding the audience of the circumstances of performance. In a society in which each member is an actor who pursues strategies of covert action and theatrical deception, Cicognini's king exhibits Castiglione's *disgrazia dell'affettazione*, the cardinal sin of affectation.[69]

The king's inability to rely on his skills as a dissimulator and on his dramatic self-representation becomes even more apparent when we see not only that he does not (or cannot) properly perform his royal role but also that he makes his subjects play his role instead. At the outset of the play, for example, when Pietro first arrives at Don Gastone's duchy, he asks his servant to pretend to be a king in order to deceive Scappino and to discover why Don Gastone had fled the court for the country. Later in the play, unable to seduce Donna Violante by threat or by force, he commissions Don Merichex to arrange her seduction. During the next two acts of the play, therefore, the king shows a dispositional antipathy to appearing before his subjects and increasingly becomes a mere spectator of a well-staged performance that is orchestrated almost entirely by Don Merichex.

The eclipsing of the king as a model royal figure is particularly evident when we compare him to this courtier character, a man skilled at wearing masks and at prudently simulating and dissimulating. Don Merichex is a hero with a particularly theatrical vision of reality who sees himself and others as dramatic fictions defined by outward appearances. His performative sense of life is immediately apparent: when introducing himself to Don Gastone for the first time, he describes his prior life as a *tragedia*, thus portraying himself as a self-aware actor in his own drama. Don Merichex's "sad history of [his] woeful mishaps" (I.4) displays a radical conviction that Baroque man was not just similar to a character on the theatrical stage – he was in fact identical to an actor onstage and viewed both himself and the world as a theatrical fiction.[70]

When receiving the king's orders to exile Don Gastone and to arrange the seduction of Donna Violante, Don Merichex is torn between his loyalty to his friend and to his prince:

> Oh Dio, ed a qual segno son io ridotto? ò devo mancar al giuramento dato al Rè, ò tradire nell'honore l'amico, se io voglio osseruare, come Caualiero, e forza ch'io manchi, come traditore; non posso preparare la cura alle dolcezze di Sua Maestà, ch'io non fabrichi la tomba della riputatione di D. Gastone. (II.9)

> Oh God, to what act am I reduced? Either I must break my oath to the King or betray my friend's honour. If I want to keep my oath, like a Knight,

I am forced to break faith, like a traitor; I cannot attend to His Majesty's pleasures unless I build a tomb for D. Gastone's reputation.

He thus struggles to make ethical sense of the issues and to act with both justice and humanity:

O tormentato Don Merichex: in qual tenebroso laberinto ti sei ciecamente condotto? S'io penso alla promessa fatta al Rè, sento inuitarmi all'osservanza; s'io mi ricordo dell'obligationi con D. Gastone, mi sento sconsigliare, il giuramento mi sforza, il tradimento mi respinge, l'autorità Reggia mi comanda l'amicitia non lo comporta, mancar di fede al Rè non posso; machinar contro l'honore di D. Gastone non deuo, l'essere spergiuro mi spauenta, tradir l'amico mi vitupera: oh promessa, oh tradimento, ò giuramento, ò amicitia, ò Rè, ò Don Gastone, ò fierissimi tiranni dell'anima mia, così mi tormentate? così m'affliggete. (II.9)

O tormented Don Merichex! Into what shadowy labyrinth have you blindly allowed yourself to be led? If I think of the promise I made to the King, I feel compelled to keep it; if I recall my obligations to D. Gastone, I feel advised against it. The oath binds me, the betrayal repels me, the authority of the State commands me, friendship does not permit it, I cannot break faith with the King, I must not conspire against the honour of D. Gastone, becoming a liar frightens me, betraying a friend vilifies me. Oh promise, oh betrayal, either oath or friendship, either King or D. Gastone, oh haughtiest tyrants of my soul, how you torment me! How you afflict me!

While this audience-directed, emotionally charged soliloquy reveals the internal conflict of the character, his subsequent actions show an extraordinary mastery of self-dramatization. Indeed, his thoughts and feelings remain completely inaccessible both to other characters and to the play's spectators until the very last scene. His actions thus put into practice Pietro Bembo's advice from the second book of Castiglione's *Cortegiano*, which states that nothing should ever be said unless it has been well thought through beforehand and that one should never trust anyone, not even a dear friend, to the extent that he "communicate without reservation all one's thoughts to him."[71]

Don Merichex is a complex character who is conscious of the degree to which the inner self reflects the outer, public self in its daily interactions with one's sovereign and fellow courtiers. Indeed, he reminds himself, "[r]iccordati, che nelle attioni si deue pensare al fine, e che il mancar di fede al Rè hà per fine l'honor dell'amico, e che osseruarui fede ha per scoppo le sue vergogne" ("remember that, with regard to one's actions, one must think of the end result, and that breaking faith with the King has as its end the honour of a friend, and that keeping faith has as its outcome that friend's shame," II.9). In addition to his status as savvy central character and his vital role as problem-solver, Don Merichex is a stage manager, a role through which his character comes to compete with that of the king, and through which the performance of an onstage courtier comes to echo and challenge the "performance" that is state ritual. Don Merichex, in fact, is always in control of the monarch's movements on stage, as well as of the entries and exits of the other characters. Contrary to what we might expect, given the title of the play, Don Merichex – not Don Gastone – is thus the true protagonist of Cicognini's drama.

Yet another aspect of theatricalization in Baroque political regimes is the dependence of princes on their audiences. Indeed, Don Pio Rossi emphasized "vivere una vita da teatro" ("living a theatrical life") among the miseries that accompany the greatness of princes, because the great are always "alla veduta d'un mondo di spettatori" ("in the view of a world of spectators").[72] As David Scott Kastan has observed, "[a] spectacular sovereignty works to subject its audience to – and through – the royal power on display, captivating, in several senses, its onlookers. But this theatrical strategy of what Stephen Greenblatt has called 'privileged visibility' carries with it considerable risks. Significantly, it makes power contingent upon the spectators' assent."[73] The monarch must, in other words, continually play to his subjects, exposing himself to solicit their admiration and showing that he takes seriously his responsibility to represent performatively – theatrically – his unique status and peerless power as evidence of his ability to lead. As Marcel Hénaff, Jean-Louis Morhange, and Marie-Line Allen write perceptively in their keen and convincing analysis of the theatricality of royal power,

> power must never be separated from the display of its legitimacy, from the show of its greatness and splendor. In this way, power confesses its dependence upon those for whom the show is designed. If it has to convince and seduce, it is because it no longer is taken for granted. This distinguishes it from an order based upon the sacred, which asks for nothing and has nothing to prove, but is on the contrary that which founds and legitimizes. By staging itself, power admits that it is subjected to judgment, to evaluation by a public opinion whose support it must secure.[74]

The numerous critiques of Pietro d'Aragona's rule by other characters reveal that *Il Don Gastone* is not merely an expression of aesthetic concern about the centrality of theatricality to the construction of successful social and political agency. Instead, what makes this king a tyrant is his inappropriate liberation from the restraints of popular opinion: he does not care about the response of his audience. Scappino (who, despite being a lower-class character, demonstrates a good deal of moral wisdom) makes a revealing comparison between the king and his master (Don Gastone) that underlines the king's indifference to popular opinion:

> Don Gastone è persona honorata, il Rè d'Aragona non hà altro pensiero, che compiacere à sè stesso. Don Gastone è Caualiero d'azzioni Illustri, il Rè è solo Rè di nome, ma perche pure è il Rè, e mescolando l'autorità Reggia con la Tirannide, e *facendendosi vn decotto al fuoco delle opinioni del Mondo* scema due terzi dell'huomo da bene, e dell'altro terzo se ne caua vn siroppo di furfante. (I.7, my italics)

> Don Gastone is an honourable person; the King of Aragon has no other thought than to please himself. Don Gastone is a Knight of Illustrious Actions, the King is only King in name, but precisely because he is King and confuses the authority of the State with Tyranny, and, *if he were brewing himself a tisane from of the opinions of the World,* he would discard the two-thirds coming from virtuous men and obtain his syrup from the other, good-for-nothing third.

When Scappino, after having discovered that he had been speaking to the king in disguise, asks Pietro d'Aragona to forgive him for having spoken so improperly, the king replies that "[i] grandi non curano l'ingiurie de buffoni" ("the great do not care about the insults of buffoons," I.8). In addition to his refusal to role-play according to the established rules of courtly etiquette, his inability to manipulate the visual and verbal symbols of power, and his subjects' lack of recognition of his authority, therefore, the king's chief flaw – what, in other words, makes him a tyrant in the eyes of his subjects and of the play's audience – is his indifference to his own public image and to popular opinion of it – and, by extension, of his status and ability as a ruler. If, during the Baroque age, the theatre metaphor was a governing mode of almost all forms of human behaviour – social, political, and aesthetic – Cicognini's king's failing is that he forgets that theatre – and, in particular, the performance of politics – is always dependent on its audience. The theatrical metaphor, therefore, has here ceased to describe political authority.

The Evolving Spectator

Given that early modern theatre was a medium for the circulation of information, ideas, and opinion formation – in particular concerning political institutions and events – what conclusions can be drawn about the explicit or implied meanings of Cicognini's drama for its seventeenth-century audiences? Why did its performance of sovereignty and the aesthetics of power make it appeal widely to different kinds of publics? How can we explain the interest of the eighteenth-century reading public in this court-focused play and the related – and immense – success of *Il Don Gastone* not only on stage but in print? One answer to these questions is that by exposing royal sovereignty as empty, by revealing the monarch's position as precarious, and by showing the king's subjects assuming his role, the play astutely illustrates the historical transition from what Jürgen Habermas termed the "representative" public sphere (in which monarchs represented their authoritative power and unchallenged sovereignty to quiescent subjects) to the bourgeois public sphere (in which private individuals came together to confront and problematize political authority). According to Habermas, the king's subjects under absolutism were not rational and self-conscious – they were passive spectators of a political scene that was orchestrated by the monarch and subjected to the "aura" of his God-given authority.[75] In this scenario, the swapping of roles between king and courtiers in Cicognini's play and the evolution of the latter into genuine political actors can be linked to a decisive event: the emergence of a radically new kind of audience and the establishment of the "authentic" public sphere that embraced private citizens who engaged in rational and critical debate (*öffentliches Räsonnement*) about affairs of state.

Habermas's definition of the public sphere reveals Cicognini's drama to be a sustained illustration of and model for the new public that was just beginning to articulate its distinctiveness from past audiences. By watching onstage characters move from *subjecta* to reasoning individuals and from receivers of regulations to interlocutors with authority, the spectators of *Il Don Gastone* were compelled to experience vicariously a particular kind of identity formation. By empathically identifying with the play's dramatic heroes, who engage critically in public discussions and take on the role of active political actors, audience members were invited to project their own ability to judge matters usually considered arcane mysteries of the state. Even though care must be taken when drawing far-reaching conclusions based upon a single playwright's body of work, this interpretation of Cicognini's drama and the history of *Il Don Gastone*'s reception suggest that the play could well have exercised a shaping influence on the formation of rational and critically active spectatorship. Moreover, Cicognini's drama reveals that features of the "mature" Habermasian bourgeois public sphere were anticipated well before the Enlightenment. *Il Don Gastone* can therefore be considered a theatrical precursor to this societal shift.

From one perspective, then, Cicognini's play called into being critical and active consumers of cultural products. From an alternative perspective, the play is simultaneously symptomatic of how the aesthetics of power and the dramatic treatment of royalty were fashioned with respect to the rise of this new, potentially powerful, and adjudicating public – and in response to this new public's horizon of expectations. Indeed, one can read the happy ending and the final redemption of the king as the playwright's pandering to the audience's dissatisfaction with tragic conclusions.[76] The redemption of the tyrant, however, also implies the success the characters' agency (and, by extension, that of the audience) enjoys in bringing the tyrant to justice and, ultimately, in renegotiating rather than simply accepting the sovereign's monopoly on self-representation.

Il Don Gastone's reliance on the spectator for successful political action and the paramount importance the play assigns to the experience of a receptive subject makes it furthermore possible to locate in Cicognini's theatre the emergence of a dramatic aesthetic that is attentive to public response. This kind of aesthetic – one that is typically associated with eighteenth-century dramatic poetics – in fact emerged earlier: precisely at the moment of transition from court theatre to public playhouse. There have already been numerous attempts to emphasize the centrality of the spectator even before this moment,[77] but it seems that only under the pen of a "transitional" playwright like Cicognini does the aesthetic start to take shape in a practical way on stage.

Ultimately, the interpretation of *Il Don Gastone* undertaken in this chapter reveals that Cicognini's wide appeal to different kinds of audiences – or publics – and his fame well into the eighteenth century was due only in part to his ability to "lusingare colla novità lo svogliato gusto degli spettatori" ("tempt with novelties the listless taste of his spectators")[78] and to his play's dramatic effectiveness, moral resonance, and treatment of sovereignty – one that, unusually, both critiques and affirms the current political regime. Instead, the overriding reason for *Il Don Gastone*'s success across Europe and the principal cause of its adaptability to different theatrical contexts lies in the fact that the play is a true site of public-making: Cicognini's aim was explicitly political and was designed to compel audiences to recognize their own centrality in social, theatrical, and political domains alike, and to raise consciousness among the public that it is, itself, the ultimate repository of both critical and political power.

2 The Privileged Visibility of the Viewer

The *Belisarios* of Pseudo-Cicognini and Carlo Goldoni

In eighteenth-century Italian theatre history, no figure is as crucial as Carlo Goldoni (1707–93), the great Venetian reformer of Italian drama and, as we shall see in chapter 5, of the relationship between playwrights and their audiences. Goldoni could only embark upon his programs of reform, however, by following in the footsteps of the authors who came before him. The corpus of pre-Goldonian writing for theatre contains works and traditions with which Goldoni had come into contact as a young man, and these left an imprint on his dramatic practice both on the page and onstage.[1] This chapter studies the connection between Goldoni and this corpus, tracking the origins of Goldoni's theatre in order to help us more deeply comprehend the processes by which the paradigm for eighteenth-century theatre began to change and to enrich our comprehension of the evolution of the Italian public.

This is no easy task, however, since Goldoni – aware of his role as a dramaturgical revolutionary – was often at pains to misrepresent or to ignore the merits of the playwrights who preceded him, not to mention their impact on his work. For instance, he claimed to have incurred no debts whatsoever to Giambattista della Porta (1535–1615), had little good to say about Girolamo Gigli (1660–1742), and never even mentioned several figures of particularly high status, like Luigi Riccoboni (1676–1753). A noteworthy exception to Goldoni's dismissive attitude towards his predecessors, however, is Giacinto Andrea Cicognini:

> Parmi les Auteurs comiques que je lisois et que je relisois très-souvent, Cicognini étoit celui que je préférois. Cet Auteur Florentin, très-peu connu dans

la République des Lettres, avoit fait plusieurs Comédies d'intrigue, mêlées de pathétique larmoyant et de comique trivial; on y trouvoit cependant beaucoup d'intérêt, et il avoit l'art de ménager la suspension, et de plaire par le dénouement. Je m'y attachai infiniment: je l'étudiai beaucoup; et à l'âge de huit ans, j'eus la témérité de crayonner une Comédie.

Among the comic authors whom I frequently read and re-read, Cicognini had the preference. This Florentine author, very little known in the republic of letters, was the author of several comedies of intrigue, full of whining pathos and common-place drollery: still, however, they were exceedingly interesting: for he possessed the art of keeping up a state of suspense, and he was successful in winding-up his plots. I was infinitely attached to him, studied him with great attention, and, at the age of eight, I had the presumption to compose a comedy.[2]

This reference to Cicognini is not unique. Goldoni describes the composition of his first theatrical work in Cicogninian style with even more detail in his preface to the Bettinelli edition of his works (1750–5): "Cadendomi fra le mani Commedie o Drammi, io vi trovava le mie delizie; e mi sovviene, che sul solo esemplare di quelle del Cicognini in età di ott'anni in circa, una Commedia, qual ella si fosse, composi, prima d'averne veduto rappresentar alcuna in sulle Scene" ("[When] Comedies or Dramas fell into my hands, it was in them that I found my delights; and it happened to me that, using as a model one of [the comedies] of Cicognini, around the age of eight years, I wrote a Comedy, whatever one it was, before I had ever seen one on the Stage").[3]

The episode recounted here is also present in the Italian edition of Goldoni's autobiography that appears in the prefaces to the Pasquali edition of his works (1761–78),[4] in which the tale from his childhood functions as a commentary on the historiated frontispiece that depicts Goldoni as a boy writing his first comedy in his library of dramas. On one of the spines of the volumes that so inspired this *enfant prodige* is the name Cicognini. Considering that Goldoni had some control over the content of this vignette and could personally approve the final draft – and given that the subject matter of the engravings in the first four volumes of the Pasquali edition "assume il compito di una vera e propria 'funzione narrativa' in stretta relazione con quanto viene raccontato all''Autore a chi legge'"[5] ("take on the task of real 'narrative function' in close relationship to what is being recounted within the 'Autore a chi legge'"), it is no stretch at all to suggest that the Cicognini volume represents "quella via, che [lo] ha condotto al Teatro" ("the road that led [him] to Theatre").[6]

For Goldoni, Cicognini was the most fascinating figure among all the other seventeenth-century dramatists from the Florentine school of theatre who have traditionally been considered the Venetian's precursors: the Tuscan playwrights Girolamo Gigli, Jacopo Angelo Nelli (1675–1767), and Giovan Battista Fagiuoli (1660–1742). In an autobiographical jab from volume eight of the Pasquali edition, Goldoni reveals himself to be well aware of the importance Cicognini had for the seventeenth-century theatre scene. The *Memorie italiane* recount that Goldoni dedicated his summer holidays at Chioggia "allo studio delle Commedie. Rilessi tutto il mio *Ciccognini*, e cominciai a conoscere le bellezze, e i difetti di quell'Autore, che se nato fosse nel nostro secolo, avrebbe avuto il talento di far delle cose buone" ("to the study of Comedies. I reread all of my *Ciccognini*, and I began to come to know the beauties and the flaws of that Author who – if he had been born in our century – would have had the talent to do good things"). Goldoni added immediately after: "[l]essi il *Faggiuoli*; vi trovai la verità, la semplicità, la natura, ma poco interesse, e pochissima arte, e i suoi riboboli Fiorentini m'incomodavano infinitamente" ("I read the *Faggiuoli*, and there I found truth, simplicity, nature, but little interest and even less art, and his Florentine bombast was an infinite bother").[7]

Goldoni's preface to *Don Giovanni Tenorio o sia Il dissoluto punito* (1736) also cites Cicognini as an important figure in the Italian dissemination of Spanish *comedia aurea* who merits the claim of having been the first to adapt Tirso de Molina's *Burlador de Sevilla y Convidado de piedra* to Italian theatre as *Convitato di pietra*.[8] This tragicomedy's success inspired Goldoni to reach even higher: recalling *L'honorata povertà di Rinaldo* (Cicognini's remaking of Lope de Vega's *Las pobrezas de Reinaldos*), Goldoni composed his own *Rinaldo di Mont'Albano* (1737). Further instances of Cicognini's influence are numerous. Among the possible sources for *Enrico re di Sicilia* (the 1736 tragedy that permitted the young Goldoni to acquire increased visibility thanks to Venetian performances of the play in honour of Crown Prince of Saxony Friedrich Christian) is Cicognini's *Il maritarsi per vendetta* (1662), the drama "di passione e sangue" ("of passion and blood") that Goldoni had known since childhood.[9] One of the models for his tragicomedy in Martellian verse *Gli amori di Alessandro Magno* (1759), along with versions by Metastasio, Zeno, and Pariati, is Cicognini's melodrama *Gli amori di Alessandro e di Rossane* (1652). The plot of Goldoni's *dramma giocoso* entitled *I portentosi effetti della madre natura* (1752) must have been suggested to him by Cicognini's adaptation (*La vita è un sogno,* 1663) of *La vida es sueño* by Pedro Calderón.[10] *Il vero amico*

(1751), which is famous for having provoked a celebrated polemic concerning plagiarism by Diderot (see chapter 5), could well have been inspired by Cicognini's *Amicitia riconosciuta* (1665). And, finally, it would seem significant that, among the *dramatis personae* in Goldoni's Parisian period *pièce à sentiments, Le inquietudini di Zelinda* (1763–4),[11] there is a character named "Signor Ciccognini *avvocato*" ("Mr. Cicognini, *lawyer*").

Although Goldoni never concerned himself with indicating whether the subjects of his first tragedies and melodramas had already been treated by his influential predecessor, it is impossible to deny or to ignore his imitation of Cicognini – not only in the little play Goldoni wrote at the age of eight or nine but also while he was still an apprentice of composition for theatre and even during the later years of his artistic maturity. The influence of the Florentine on the Venetian playwright's formation, however, remains largely neglected. This chapter, therefore, explores the question of influence and imitation both generally and with specific attention to how Cicognini's construction of the relationship between spectator and stage anticipated and influenced Goldoni's own.

As the previous chapter demonstrates, the extraordinary popularity of Cicognini's plays – whether performed before the court public or before the more heterogeneous audience of the Venetian commercial theatres – is due to his awareness of having to deal with a new communicative reality in the theatre – or, perhaps more accurately, with the existence of an increasingly active, participatory, and critical consumer. Indeed, Cicognini's theatre represents the most striking example of a new dramaturgy that was shaped by the demand for art that sought to institute direct feedback with its audience. For Goldoni, it was precisely the link between author and audience that made his reform project possible, based as it was on the education of spectators in terms of refining their aesthetic taste as well as on the playwright's awareness of his need to satisfy their choices and demands.[12] Both of these dramatists, therefore, were very attuned to the communicative power of theatre; for both, the relationship of their theatrical arts to their recipients constituted the crux of these authors' dramaturgy.

Cicognini, Pseudo-Cicognini, and Goldoni's Beginnings

Before facing directly the question of Cicognini's influence on Goldoni's communicative techniques, it is important to note that Cicognini's texts, at least initially, were destined not for the printing press but for the stage. In fact, his plays were printed only posthumously: given the continued success of his melodrama *Il Giasone*, printers thought that publishing his works would cater to an eager market; they were correct. In fact, the extraordinary triumph of these publishing projects, when met with the lack of new works by Cicognini himself, led to the publication of plays falsely attributed to the popular Florentine simply in order to meet public demand.[13] A huge boom in counterfeit "Cicogninian" editions thus occurred around 1660, peaking three years later. Fortunately, recent studies by Diego Sìmini, Flavia Cancedda, and Silvia Castelli have helped us separate correct from false attributions among this vast corpus, but this was, of course, not the situation for Goldoni: during his lifetime, many works circulated under Cicognini's name.[14] Some of these were entirely spurious or were, at the very least, attributed uncertainly to the Florentine. Cicognini's influence on Goldoni thus extends not only to texts verifiably by his popular predecessor but also to all of the works that were assumed to be his, even though they may have been composed by any number of seventeenth-century authors who imitated him simply in the hopes of producing a bestseller.

The *Caduta del gran Capitano Belissario sotto la condotta di Giustiniano Imperatore* (*Downfall of the Great Captain Belisarius under the Rule of the Emperor Justinian*, performed at the Teatro della Dogana by a travelling theatrical troupe known as *I comici Affezionati*) is from this era of the Cicogninian publishing boom.[15] Initially printed with an anonymous author (Bologna: Pisarri, 1661), the next edition explicitly included Cicognini's name on the frontispiece (Rome: Moneta, 1663). This attribution may have been an editorial choice on the part of a publisher seeking to use the prestige of the Cicognini brand to attract more readers. Indeed, based upon the assessment of Leone Allacci[16] and the claim of authorship made by the Venetian playwright Francesco Stramboli, several scholars (including Bottacchiari, Sanesi, and Grashey)[17] have debated the question of attribution.[18]

This *Belisario* (whose author I will refer to here as pseudo-Cicognini) is among the sources of Goldoni's lauded *Belisario* of 1734 and could very well have been among the works that helped him become more conscious of his role as an author for the stage. The earlier *Belisario*, therefore, is also an important text for tracing the imprint Cicogninian writing left upon Goldoni's strategies of communication with spectators. His *Mémoires* mention that Goldoni's inspiration for *Belisario* came from a "détestable Piece" ("detestable Play") – a *commedia dell'arte* scenario that was brought to his attention by the actor Gaetano Casali (d. 1767), who was employed as a *secondo amoroso* in the company directed by Giuseppe

Imer (1700–58).[19] Even though Goldoni specifies no other sources, it is entirely possible that, as with his other tragicomedies, he had foremost in mind pseudo-Cicognini's tragedy.[20] Indeed, Dietmar Rieger argues that the drama "dev'essere letto in opposizione ad uno scenario [...] che a suo tempo riscuoteva ancora successo" ("must be read against a script that, during its time, was still enjoying huge success").[21] Similarly, Irène Mamczarz observes that Goldoni's play "non è soltanto una stesura del canovaccio, ma un'opera nuova di carattere letterario. [...] L'azione del *Belisario* goldoniano è più logica drammaticamente e più conseguente rispetto a quella dello scenario, ma appare anche più semplice e più lineare" ("is not simply a written version of the [*commedia*] scenario, but is instead a new work of literary character. [...] The action of Goldoni's *Belisario* is more dramatically logical and more consistent with respect to that of the [*commedia*] scenario, but it also seems simpler and more linear").[22]

Goldoni's early play, aside from being the first great success that inextricably linked him to the theatre, already presents a few tangible prefigurations of his theatre reform that was to follow.[23] In their account of *Belisario*'s triumph, the *Mémoires* underline the positive critical reception that the work received in comparison with others being performed at the time; Goldoni writes that he hoped these were an auspicious sign that the play could prove to be "le chemin à une réforme du Théatre Italien" ("the road to a reform of Italian theatre").[24] An analysis of this tragicomedy, therefore, allows us to verify the extent to which Goldoni, in the years before his reform, had already recognized the necessity of founding and focusing it upon the audience's centrality to the entire theatrical experience. This line of inquiry sheds light on the extent of Cicognini's influence on Goldoni and reveals the reasons for the enormous eighteenth-century success of the Florentine's plays both in performance and in print.

From History to Stage

The Belisario theme made its debut in Western literature in 1548 with the epic poem *L'Italia liberata dai Goti* by Giangiorgio Trissino. The legend of the loyal general thus moved from history (the *Storia arcana* by Procopio di Cesarea, secretary and counsellor to General Belisario in the service of Emperor Justinian) to epic poetry, arriving for the first time at the theatre with the *Comedia famosa del Capitan Belisario, y exemplo mayor de la desdicha* (1632) by Mira de Amescua, a Spanish playwright from the school of Lope de Vega. Pseudo-Cicognini's play reproduces, for the most part faithfully, Mira's comedia – although, as Scaramuzza Vidoni has pointed out, it also has a debt to the Italian tragedy by Onofrio degli Onofri entitled *Il Bilissario* (Naples, 1645).[25] The modest literary fame of this glorious general, which emerged in various traditions, rewritings, and adaptations during the Renaissance and Baroque periods,[26] is due to the inherent quality of historical themes that makes them productive stimuli for exploring the pressing issues of modernity: political conflicts at court; the disruption of the social order; the consequences of love and the jealousy of women; the ingratitude of rulers to those in their service; and the unlimited power of the sovereign to punish even his most faithful vassals based upon the slightest suspicion.

The relevance of the Belisario tale (as recounted by pseudo-Cicognini and Goldoni) to these larger themes is immediately evident from its basic narrative. General Belisario returns victorious to Costantinople after having won territory for Emperor Justinian's empire. The emperor's wife, Teodora, resents the general because he had refused her love before she married Justinian; she therefore begins to plan her vengeance. Justinian promotes Belisario to the rank of co-emperor, but Teodora persists in her hatred of the new ruler and uses all the means at her disposal to avenge his lack of interest. She orders three courtiers to kill him, but all three, overcome by his splendid munificence, fail to fulfil their duty. She then attempts to sabotage his love of his betrothed, Antonia, by preventing her not only from greeting the victor upon his return from his conquest of Persia but also from casting even a single glance in his direction and by forbidding her to read his love letter. Finally, Teodora leads Justinian to suspect Belisario of loving her, and he is condemned by his former co-emperor to be blinded as punishment for gazing upon that which he should not. Pseudo-Cicognini's play is a tragedy with a dark end: the protagonist dies. Goldoni, instead, transposes all these intrigues into the genre of tragicomedy such that his version comes to a lighter conclusion: his Belisario, though unable to prevent his undeserved punishment, does not actually lose his life. Instead, blinded and disgraced, he finds a way to make himself useful to both emperor and people by suppressing a revolt against Justinian. Finally, the great general pardons the evildoers who had wronged him, providing one last proof of his generosity.

This plot summary reveals the similarities that link the rewritings of the Belisario tale by pseudo-Cicognini and Goldoni and distinguish them from other adaptations: namely, the importance of the symbolism of sight and of the gaze to the onstage action. Glances of love, of outrage and affliction, of jealousy and ambition, and of devotion and inquiry constitute the *leitmotif* of both these dramas. The glances in question are not only those of the fictional tragic characters, however; they are also, on a meta-theatrical level, the gaze of spectators attempting to understand the complicated twists and turns of the plot. Both of these works can thus be considered "plays of the gaze"; both constitute instances of a poetics of drama *mise-en-scène* that critically reflects upon audience reception. If, as Walter Benjamin affirms, the tragic play of the early modern age is more an allegory than a tragedy, what I would like to demonstrate here is that the *Belisari* of pseudo-Cicognini and Goldoni can be read allegorically as a metaphor for the shift in the role of the theatre public over the seventeenth and eighteenth centuries.

To See and Be Seen

Tracing the glances of pseudo-Cicognini's characters enables us to explore the visual communication that the play establishes with its audience. References to the act of looking are numerous in the tragedy; to provide even a few fruitful initial examples we might note how Antonia and Justinian express their respective love and esteem for Belisario via the gaze. For Antonia, who was ordered by Teodora to hide her feelings for the general, being unable to raise her eyes to her beloved is a most exquisite torment (I.14). Justinian would prefer to lose all his conquered lands than to be prevented from constantly seeing his friend: "io altro di saper non pretendo, altro il mio cor non desidera, e pur ch'io ti miri perdasi non solo l'Affrica, mà tutti i Regni, che tengo, poiche più vale vn'amico leale, che tutto quello, che si possiede" ("there is nothing more I aspire to know, nor anything else my heart desires, and so long as I can look upon you I would lose not only Africa but all the Realms that I hold, because a loyal friend is worth more than everything else one could [ever] own," II.8).[27] Hidden from Teodora's gaze, but watching her attempt to kill his dear friend, Justinian compares the general to his portrait: "Belissario ed Io siam vn'Argo, gli occhi de' quali mentre vna dorme, e l'altra veglia. Questo è il mio ritratto, e vn'altro me stesso, e tu indegna cerchi dar a me stesso la morte?" ("Belisario and I are one Argus with whose eyes, while one sleeps, the other keeps watch. He is my portrait and another one of me, and you, unworthy [woman], attempt to give my own self death?," II.18).

Watching is an act that requires the concentrated focus of a spectator and creates a direct and almost physical, tactile contact between observer and observed. We might thus say that such obsessive recourse to verbs of seeing – "guardare" (to look), "vedere" (to see), "mirare" (to watch), "osservare" (to observe), "specchiarsi" (to gaze at oneself in a mirror) – and such constant use of the symbolism of the gaze constitute a conscious strategy on the part of pseudo-Cicognini that aims at encouraging a mutual gaze between the fictional characters onstage and the spectators in the audience. Just as the *Belisario* protagonists are participants in a spectatorial game of glances whose goal is to discover and comprehend the relationships between events, so too those beyond the fourth wall are invited to become attentive and penetrating observers of the performance that is unfolding before their eyes.[28]

This analogy and reciprocity between the visual experiences of the fictional characters and of the spectators is reinforced throughout the play by a high number of meta-theatrical scenes. Through the use of disguises, the playing of roles assigned and performed (whether voluntarily or no), and the transformation of characters into spectators of a rapidly unfolding tragedy, the play's protagonists themselves act out a theatrical *pièce* in miniature. The roles that they play are numerous indeed. This tragedy within a tragedy is set into motion by the emperor's consort who, as we have seen, orders Belisario's betrothed to hide her love for the hero and to feign coldness towards him (I.7, 10, 14). To celebrate Justinian's birthday, Teodora mounts a theatrical performance of the tale of Piramus and Thisbe, whose love story reproduces the tale of Belisario and Antonia. (To make explicit the parallel, these two characters act in the respective roles of the legendary lovers.) During the rehearsals, Antonia is finally able to reveal to her fiancé that her love for him has remained unchanged and that it is Teodora who is after him for revenge (II.10–11). Belisario pretends to talk in his sleep in order to tell Justinian what the general would not dare tell the emperor awake – that is, that his own consort is the one who is trying to kill Belisario (II.15). Teodora plays the role of seductress with Belisario; with Justinian, however, she is the wrongly seduced innocent (III.2–3). (Belisario's final disgrace is in fact the result of her ability to play these two roles convincingly.) While one character performs his lines, the others inevitably become spectators, and these character-spectators mirror the audience-spectators attending the performance. Teodora, just like an audience member who is invisible to the characters onstage, hides herself in order to spy on Antonia, watching to see how well she follows the order to feign indifference to Belisario (I.15). The emperor and all the court watch Belisario while he pretends to be asleep (II.15); Justinian watches Teodora from his own hiding place when she attempts to assassinate the general (II.16).

All of the characters – but above all the protagonists Justinian, Teodora, Belisario, and Antonia – are thus also spectators who continually seek to decipher the other players' game through the language of their gazes. In the end, even the scene of Belisario's execution is explicitly theatrical.[29] The emperor's command that the general be taken outside the city walls to be blinded and then sent to repent such that all can see (*rimirare*) him constitutes yet another instance of a play within a play (III.12). Moreover disguise, which is of course quite typical of Baroque theatre, has a particularly significant place in this drama. The courtier Leonzio dresses as a pilgrim in order to kill the general on Teodora's orders (I.3). Belisario, watching Leonzio and Narsete try, at night, to kill the traitor Filippo, disguises his voice to save Filippo without being recognized by him (II.5). The function of the meta-theatrical as a discursive strategy in this tragedy is thus that of transforming the theatre into a place of mirrors; of literally making visible the link between stage and spectator; and of thereby reinforcing the identification of real audience member with fictional onstage character.

The incredible success of pseudo-Cicognini's *Belisario* unequivocally testifies to the fact that the seventeenth-century theatre-going public enjoyed watching actors interpret the role of the spectator and seeing their own experience as spectators projected onstage. What was so captivating about this continuous game of mirroring from the point of view of the Baroque spectator?

In the previous chapter's analysis of Cicognini's tragedies (which are, *Il Don Gastone di Moncada* included, centred on life at court), we saw how important performance was for the construction and legitimization of sovereignty and how court society, too, was founded upon the principle of visibility: how the existence of the courtier was dependent on the gaze of the sovereign, which could confer prestige or obliterate status in an instant. Similarly, in pseudo-Cicognini's *Belisario* we see how Teodora's power is made manifest via the gaze. As early as the opening scene, Teodora tells her confidante Camilla that the motive for her revenge on Belisario was the visible demonstration of her power: "se son donna, farò senza pietade; son Regnante, son potente, e saprò castigarlo; voglio quello, che desidero, e *mostrerei* di non esser Imperadrice s'io non mi vendicassi" ("if I am a woman, I will act without pity; I am the [female] Ruler, I am powerful, and I know how to punish him; I want him, he whom I desire, and *I will show myself* to be no Empress if I do not revenge myself," I.1, my emphasis). Her power to rule by the gaze shifts from abstract to concrete with the order that she gives to Antonia not to dare raise her eyes to Belisario (I.15). In contrast, Justinian's precariousness as a ruler and his transformation from good and just monarch to tyrant over the course of the drama is made clear via the metaphor of blindness – the inability to *see* the crimes of true traitors until it is too late.

Even the rise of Belisario manifests itself through the symbolism of the gaze. In the first act, his increase in status occurs before the eyes of the entire court (I.4); in the second act, the climax of his ascent takes place when Justinian orders that coins be minted with his own image on one side and Belisario's on the other (II.17). Since, in court society, power becomes legitimized by recourse to symbols and fetishes, the image of the king on the coin is an explicitly visual expression of his power: the king's watchful eyes, literally moving about the kingdom on its currency, enable him to possess and govern the empire while employing only a single gaze. This scene illustrates, therefore, how the penetration of Belisario's gaze and the extent of its surveillance have become equal to the penetration and reach of Justinian's gaze. As Marcel Hénaff, Jean-Louis Morhange, and Marie-Line Allen observe,

> exercising power was, before anything else, being able to occupy the right locus, and there was only one. That locus was, henceforth, the position from which it was possible to see, because seeing amounted to "controlling" action. It is now easier to understand why the paradigm of perspective was such a powerful one during the fifteenth and sixteenth centuries (first in Italy, then in Europe as a whole); it subjected political practice to the mastery of viewing.[30]

Considering the importance of the gaze in court society, it is clear that Belisario's blinding is also allegorically weighted. At a superficial level, deprivation of sight is simply the punishment that fits the (alleged) crime – a punishment that visually inscribes his crime upon his body. Indeed as Justinian, who believes that Belisario's love letter was addressed to Teodora, not to Antonia, affirms, "Mà assicurati pure, che pagaranno gli occhi ogni fallo, che gl'istessi occhi fecero" ("But be most assured that your eyes will pay for every mistake your same eyes made," III.5) – the mistake, of course, being an imagined turning of Belisario's eyes to meet the gaze of the emperor's consort.[31] Thus Belisario's blinding becomes a performance of punishment and an appropriately symbolic penance for the crime committed. As noted by Michel Foucault, however, "the public execution is to be understood not only as a judicial, but also as a political ritual. It belongs, even in minor cases, to the ceremonies by which power is manifested."[32] At a deeper level of interpretation, then, if the public execution and the deprivation of Belisario's sight metaphorically signify a complete loss of status and power, they are simultaneously manifestations of Justinian's authority.

At this point it becomes clear why spectators would have so much appreciated the meta-theatrical aspect of this Cicogninian drama. If power is realized via the gaze and all else is simply an effect of performance, watching actors – with whom the spectators have established a specular and reciprocal bond – is to reproduce the powerful gaze of the sovereign, and thus to acquire and exercise power that had previously belonged only to the monarch.

But to see means also to understand and to judge: with theatre here becoming a mirrored space, the mirror is the instrument by which observers' gazes are guided to themselves, leading to better self-understanding. Indeed, the protagonist's monologue, which he addresses to the public, shows explicitly that the theatre is simultaneously a space for the exercise of critique. Although his blindness leaves Belisario in a permanent position of inequality with respect to Justinian, it is still possible to read the tragedy's finale as positive in part. This protagonist is a model with whom the spectator is to morally identify; thus his last words hold particular significance:

> *Vdite* mortali, *aprite gli occhi*, e *mirate* estinte quelle luci, che reggere sapeano col suo splendore l'Imperio Romano. *Specchiateui* mortali in questo precipitio, essendo il maggiore, che vn Monarca possi dare ad vn suo fauorito in premio di sua leal seruitù. Non falì giamai vassallo à somità tale di grandezze, garreggiando la mia fortuna con quella di Cesare, ed hora *miri* ogn'vno il fine delle mie glorie, la ricompensa dè miei Trionfi: mà se hauess'io giamai errato, che meritar douessi tanti gastighi te ne renderei gratie ò Cesare; mà quello, che mi tormenta maggiormente; che il valore, e la gloria venghi così malamente premiata. Ditelo voi se giamai *con occhio humano mirasti* simil barbarie. (III.13; my emphasis)

> *Listen*, mortals, *open your eyes*, and *look* at those extinguished lights [eyes], which knew how to govern the Roman Empire with their splendour. *See yourselves mirrored*, mortals, in this downfall, which is the greatest that any Monarch could give to one of his favourites as the prize for his loyal service. No vassal has ever fallen from a higher height of prominence – I am comparing my fate to that of Caesar – and now everyone *sees* the end result of my glories, the compensation for my Triumphs: but if I ever erred such that I merited such punishments, I would give thanks to you, O Caesar; but that

which torments me most is that valour and glory come so poorly rewarded. Speak out if *you have ever seen with human eyes* such barbarities.

Belisario's blindness thus offers him the possibility of attaining another order of sight and of seeing in a new way: he becomes a dis-enchanted spectator, aware and in some way reformed. At the level of political interpretation, Belisario's exhortation can be read as a call to the people to no longer be passive spectators of a political scene orchestrated by a monarch, but instead to become active participants who openly debate and discuss the monarch's choices and decisions. Taking into consideration the close tie between spectator and stage that pseudo-Cicognini created via the symbolism of the gaze and the play's meta-theatrical strategies, this monologue can also be interpreted as the construction of the performance's horizon of reception. At a meta-theatrical level, therefore, Belisario's last words signal a change in the function attributed to the public: they are an appeal to the audience to become an active critic and judge of theatrical works.

Power and Public Space

Given that the legitimacy and stability of royal power are determined by a monarch's flair for patronage of the dramatic arts and by the quality of his performance on the stage of power, it is paradoxical that the only character who has no role in the performance of this play within a play is Justinian. This emperor acts the part of passive spectator, withdrawing from participation in the royal performance – and, therefore, from the exercise of power – and requiring others to interpret his role as ruler. Even as early as the first act, Justinian confesses that he would rather be Belisario than the ruler of his own empire as "più non sia il conquistar vn Regno, che quello poi guadagnato gouernarlo" ("it is less difficult to conquer a Realm than to govern what is earned," I.4). The emperor would readily make Belisario govern on his behalf if he could: "Tù mi conquisti i Regni, de' quali farebbe ragione, ch'io concedessi à te la Monarchia, non che reggerla io, mentre tu pigli, e gouerni in un sol punto" ("You conquered the Realms for me, which should be a reason for me to concede to you the Monarchy, so that I do not rule it myself, but you take it, and rule it from a single point," I.4). Justinian's progressive distancing of himself from imperial governance becomes even clearer in the second act when he tells Belisario: "Diuido ancor l'alloro, e ti circondo quelle tempie, acciò conosca il mondo, che fra noi due non regna, che vn potenza. [...] Già sei Rè de' Romani, e sei padrone assoluto di comandare à me stesso, ed io pronto ad osservare" ("I divide the laurel as well, and encircle your temples, so that the world knows that between us not two but one power reigns. [...] You are already the King of the Romans, and you are an absolute ruler who can command even me, and I am ready to obey," II.18). Like the tyrant king Pietro d'Aragona in Cicognini's *Don Gastone*, Justinian is a sovereign who avoids his royal duty of performative self-representation, voluntarily reducing his role instead to that of inactive observer.

We can therefore conclude that, in this rewriting by Cicognini's emulator, the political significance of the Belisario affair and the play's explicit meta-theatricality converge in order to illustrate the new function of the spectator in the emerging public sphere, which is becoming an increasingly powerful actor on the political and cultural stage. Indeed, the theoretical and political aims of pseudo-Cicognini were similar to those of the Florentine playwright himself: they sought to prompt the public towards a clearer understanding of its centrality in the social, political, and theatrical spheres and to raise awareness of the fact that it is within the spectator, the audience, and the public that the ultimate repository of power resides.

The Ascent to Success

Goldoni's *Belisario* was first performed in Venice on 24 November 1734 at the Teatro San Samuele.[33] The work enjoyed an astounding success: as Paola Luciani writes, "paragonabile soltanto a quello ottenuto anni prima dalla *Merope* di Maffei" ("comparable only to that attained years before by Maffei's *Merope*").[34] Irène Mamczarz notes that it is not difficult to explain why the play was such a triumph in the eyes of its particularly broad audience, affirming that Goldoni appealed to the Venetian public, who were used to the melodramatic atmosphere of carnival, "presentando il fasto della corte reale, la grandiosità dell'ambiente, episodi guerreschi e fantastici" ("by presenting the pomp of the royal court, the grandeur of the surrounds, and scenes of war and fantastical episodes") and "provoca[ndo] facili lacrime di compassione per l'eroe perseguitato, e ugualmente facili sentimenti di gioia, quando la virtù veniva premiata" ("by provoking easy tears of compassion for the ill-starred hero – and, equally easily – feelings of joy when virtue was rewarded").[35] According to Mamczarz, "[con l'intreccio che rimane ancora complicato e inverosimile] il giovane autore vuole attirare l'interesse del pubblico dei gondolieri, raccontando innumerevoli insidie delle forze del male, rappresentate da Teodora e Filippo, contro gli eroi (Belisario e Giustiniano)" ("the young author wanted to attract the interest of the gondolier audience [with a plot that remained complicated and improbable], recounting innumerable intrigues about the powers of evil, represented by Teodora and Filippo, against the heroes Belisario and Justinian").[36] This interpretation of the play's success, however, seems to be overly reductive since, as Maddalena Agnelli observes,

> [i]l giudizio dei gondolieri a teatro diviene espressione dell'opinione dell'intera città di Venezia. [...] I gondolieri esprimono il concetto di teatro eterogeneo in cui le differenze sociali vengono azzerate al cospetto di uno spettacolo che si propone a un pubblico di uguali diritti su di esso.
>
> at the theatre, the verdict of the gondoliers became an expression of the opinion of the entire city of Venice. [...] The gondoliers were a manifestation of a heterogeneous conception of theatre in which social differences were eliminated in the presence of a performance that proposed to its public equal rights [to judge] it.[37]

Goldoni himself, in the *Mémoires* (I, 33–6), constructs a narrative of ascent around *Belisario*'s growing success: first it was read to the abbot who was his travelling companion; then it was paraded around the parish of Casalpusterlengo (which included clergy and peasant laity); then it was taken to Giuseppe Imer's company, which Goldoni encountered in Verona; and finally it had an extraordinary triumph in Venice, where it captivated the full range of the city's diverse audience members.[38] Even at the first reading of the work, Goldoni noted, its audience's appreciation truly cut across society:

> Ma lecture fut extrêmement goûtée. Les trois Abbés, qui n'étoient pas sots, saisirent les endroits les plus intéresans et les plus saillans, et les villageois me prouverent, par leurs applaudissemens, que ma Piece étoit à la portée de tout le monde, et qu'elle pouvoit plaire aux gens instruits comme aux ignorans.
>
> The piece was very much relished. The three Abbés, who were by no means blockheads, distinguished the most interesting and remarkable passages; and the villagers proved by their applause that my work was suited to every capacity and [was] equally capable of pleasing the learned and the ignorant.[39]

Regarding the first Venetian staging of the play, Goldoni later added, "les connoisseurs ne purent pas s'empêcher d'applaudir un ouvrage dont ils connoissoient les imperfections" ("the connoisseurs could not avoid applauding a work whose imperfections were well known to them").[40]

Belisario's success in the face of its diverse public, which ranged from highly educated people to the rough-and-tumble gondoliers, was not due entirely to its spectacular machine apparatuses that are described in an unauthorized Bologna edition.[41] Nor it can be reduced to the skill of the actors who performed the play – although, beyond the aforementioned actor Gaetano Casali, for whom the role of Justinian was tailored, the Imer company consisted of excellent performers.[42] Instead, I would argue, what mattered was the young dramatist's ability to implement a complex system of communication with an audience that was becoming ever more expert in theatre. It is thus timely to turn to the question of to what extent, if any, Goldoni might have learned these mechanisms of communication from Cicognini (or pseudo-Cicognini), who had been able to satisfy the tastes of his aristocratic spectators but was still capable of successfully adapting his works to the demands of the public theatre's paying audiences.

Identification and Transparency

Goldoni's play, like his predecessor's tragedy, is permeated with the symbolism of the gaze, of vision, and of blindness – motifs that link spectator and stage, and that catalyse reflections upon the public's horizon of reception.[43] Indeed, his *Mémoires* spell out one of the reasons for the success of his *Belisario*, positioning the play's appeal in terms of the identification of spectator with character. Goldoni explains that his characters were "des hommes, et non pas des demi-Dieux" ("men and not demi-gods") who "faisoient paroître l'humanité telle que nous la connoissions, et ils ne portoient pas leurs vertus et leurs vices à un excès imaginaire" ("made themselves appear human such that we recognized them [as such] and did not carry their virtues and their vices to a fantastical excess"). As to the stylistic aspect of the play, Goldoni adds that "[s]on style n'étoit pas élégant, ma versification n'a jamais donné dans le sublime; mais voilà précisément ce qu'il falloit pour ramener peu à peu à la raison un public accoutumé aux hyperboles, aux antitheses et au ridicule du gigantesque et du romanesque" ("[his] style was not elegant, and my versification has never been [in] any way sublime; but this was precisely what was requisite to bring back to reason a public accustomed to hyperboles, antitheses, and every thing ridiculously gigantic and romantic").[44]

From within the pseudo-Cicogninian example, therefore, Goldoni discerned the premise for the success of his work: a reduction of distance between the spaces of stage and audience. At the same time, he needed to adapt a work about royalty to the demands of the new theatre market and of its new public; thus, Goldoni's strategy for maximally involving the audience in the action onstage differs from that of his predecessor. As we saw in the passage quoted above, the audience's identification with the characters onstage took place primarily on the level of language and was attained by eliminating hyperbole, antithesis, and the ridiculous.[45] The Italian edition of the memoirs adds yet more information concerning why "la Tragedia è andata alle stelle" ("the Tragedy climbed to the stars").[46] What was indispensable for a *rapprochement* of the play with its Venetian audience was "l'interesse, la verità, e la condotta" ("interest, truth, and conduct") – that is, to make "parlare l'Imperatore ed il Capitano come parlano gli Uomini, e non col linguaggio degli eroi favolosi, al quale siamo avvezzati dalle penne sublimi de' valorosi Poeti" ("the Emperor and the Captain speak as do Men, and not in the language of the heroes of fables, to which we are accustomed from the sublime pens of valorous Poets").[47] Goldoni further characterizes the language of his play thus:

> Volendo io esprimere un sentimento, non ho mai cercato il termine più scelto, più elegante, o sublime; ma il più vero, ed il più esprimente. Veduto ho per esperienza, che la semplicità non può mancar di piacere. Non intendo, quando dico *semplicità*, di far parlare un Imperatore come parlerebbe un Pastore; ma intendo di non far parlare i Sovrani, uomini come noi, con un linguaggio incognito alla Natura.

> When I wanted to express a feeling, I never sought the most choice, elegant, or sublime term; but the truest, and the most expressive. I have seen from experience that simplicity does not have to lack pleasure. I do not mean, when I say *simplicity*, to make an Emperor speak as would a Shepherd; but I intend to not make sovereigns, who are men like us, speak with a language that is unknown in Nature.[48]

Goldoni's strategy thus consists in demonstrating the commonalities among *dramatis personae* and Venetian spectators. Indeed, noble characters in general – whether kings, courtiers, or representatives of the wealthy classes – interested Goldoni little and, if at all, not because of their royal standing but because nobles experience the same feelings as commoners and, indeed, as all human beings.[49] From the perspective of his audiences, even though his protagonists lived through extreme conflict (not everyday events) in a royal (not republican) environment, at least they possessed a psychology that made them not at all unlike contemporary spectators.

Goldoni was also aware that in order for theatre to be an expression of and venue for social change, the fiction onstage must be perceived by the audience as a kind of intimacy among individuals who find themselves in the same existential conditions whether they are on- or offstage. *Belisario*'s characters constantly make themselves transparent to the gaze of the public, justifying themselves and rationalizing their actions. This approach partly explains the modification Goldoni made to pseudo-Cicognini's plot: the later version omits the slower lead-up to the climax of Belisario's political ascent, making him instead co-emperor at the very beginning of act I so that the bulk of the narrative is dedicated to the characters' deep analyses of their own and others' feelings. The best example of Goldoni's eloquent ability to detail and explore his characters' psychology is Justinian, who is here a figure of great emotional complexity. It is particularly significant that Goldoni has the emperor pronounce words that had belonged to Belisario in the seventeenth-century play. It was pseudo-Cicognini's hero who accused Justinian of being blind to the chicanery of the court and who insisted that "la vita humana è vn laberinto di falsità, doue si vede vestita con maschera d'inganni l'inuidia, e vi souenga ancora, che alle volte quello, che si vede, gli occhi lo ingannano" ("human life is a labyrinth of falseness, where one sees envy clothed in a mask of deceit, and also remember that, sometimes, what one sees is a trick of the eyes," III.9). In Goldoni, however, it is Justinian who is first aware that

> Facile troppo è l'ingannarsi, e l'occhio
> Stesso talvolta a traveder conduce.
> Un equivoco detto, o mal inteso
> O mal interpretato, esser potrebbe
> Causa d'un grand'error. (II.10)
>
> It is too easy to be deceived, and the eye
> Itself sometimes leads us to mistake one thing for another.
> A misunderstanding stated, or badly intended
> Or wrongly interpreted, this can be
> The root cause of a great error.[50]

This awareness of the dynamics of court life not only makes Justinian's character richer in Goldoni than in pseudo-Cicognini but also causes the emperor's interiority to reveal itself as a locus of ambivalence and conflict. In the later play, a great deal of importance is attributed to the struggle that Justinian grapples with in private when he imagines himself to have been betrayed by his most faithful subject; there are many scenes in which the emperor finds himself plagued by doubts regarding the alleged guilt of his loyal general.

Although Goldoni's drama is set in an imagined royal court far from the realism of his reformed comedies (which are entirely inscribed within the everyday universe of the public), its spectators could not but identify with the characters onstage. In this way, even this early work by Goldoni suggests the new notion of the bourgeois tragedy.

Un-Tragic Tragedy

The transformation of dramatic language and the deepening of character psychology are not the only changes Goldoni made in his attempt to reinforce the bond between spectator and protagonist in his *Belisario*. Another modification consists of the refashioning, already noted above, of the tragedy's dénouement, which shifts the play's genre to tragicomedy: Belisario, unequivocally the victim in earlier versions, is here revealed instead as a victor. This rewriting also shifts the play's tendency further towards the melodramatic. Goldoni's decision to revise Belisario's tale as a tragicomedy is not coincidental: as Paola Luciani observes, with this change in expressive and narrative mode

> Goldoni pone [...] la tragedia su un piano di maggiore accettabilità per lo spettatore, poiché smorza le tinte più crude e uniforma il racconto evitando ogni eccesso orroroso. Un Goldoni memore di Zeno e di Metastasio molto più che dei principi graviniani, o dell'esempio contiano, opera un incontro di melodramma e tragedia, che in nome dell'efficacia spettacolare trascura, in definitiva, ogni distinzione di genere.

> Goldoni locates [...] tragedy on a level that is more accessible to the spectator, since he softens its rougher aspects and makes uniform its narrative, avoiding all horrifying excess. A Goldoni mindful of Zeno and Metastasio – much more than of the principles of Gravina or of the example of Conti – is working [towards] the encounter of melodrama and tragedy which, in the name of the success of the performance, ultimately neglects every distinction of genre.[51]

Without diminishing the important contributions of Metastasio and Zeno, we must recognize that the first playwright to definitively dissolve the boundary between tragedy and melodrama was Cicognini. Indeed, it was for the "contamination" of tragedy and comedy, of noble and common in his dramas, that Cicognini received a *damnatio* from the *custode generale* of the Academy of Arcadians, Giovanni Maria Crescimbeni (1663–1728),[52] who, in 1700, placed full responsibility for the decline of Italian theatre at the Florentine's feet:

> Giacinto Andrea Cicognini intorno alla metà di quel secolo con più felice ardimento introdusse i Drammi con suo Giasone, il quale per vero dire è il primo, e il più perfetto Dramma, che si truovi; e con esso portò l'esterminio dell'Istrionica, per conseguenza della ver, e buona Comica, e della Tragica stessa; imperciocchè per maggiormente lusingare colla novità lo svogliato gusto degli spettatori, nauseati ugualmente la vista delle cose Comiche, e la gravità delle Tragiche, l'inventor de' Drammi unì l'una e l'altra in essi, mettendo pratica con mostruosità non pià udita tra Re, ed Eroi, ed altri illustri Personaggi, e Buffoni, e Servi, e vilissimi uomini. Questo guazzabuglio di personaggi fu cagione del total guastamento delle regole Poetiche.[53]

> Around the middle of that century, Giacinto Andrea Cicognini introduced Dramas [for music] with his *Giasone*, (which is, to tell the truth, the first and the most perfect Drama to be found), thus leading to the extermination of histrionics [i.e., spoken comedy and tragedy] (that is, of true and good Comedy, and of Tragedy itself) since in searching for novelties that might stimulate the apathetic taste of spectators, who were as nauseated by the vileness of comedy as they were by the pathos of tragedy, this inventor of Dramas [i.e., Cicognini] joined the two together, and with unparalleled monstrosity made Kings and Heroes and other illustrious characters consort with Buffoons and Serfs and the vilest creatures of mankind. It was this hodgepodge of characters that caused the utter ruin of poetic rules.[54]

In fact, as we saw in the previous chapter, after his move to Venice, Cicognini wrote tragicomedies, a genre with great potential for political resonance. Pseudo-Cicognini's *Belisario*, despite its tragic ending, also contains various elements that belong to tragicomedy: misunderstandings, tricks, mistaken homicides (murders that prove not actually to have been carried out), disguises, and startling moments of recognition. The fusion of styles proposed by Cicognini was thus promptly absorbed by his imitators, and indeed pseudo-Cicognini's *Belisario* demonstrates that its author understood that the tragicomic form could satisfy a heterogeneous audience able to identify in complex ways with the social and political conflicts represented onstage.

In his transformation of *Belisario*'s finale from tragic to happy and his propulsion of the plot via the mechanisms of tragicomedy, Goldoni was raiding the treasure chest of techniques that had been cached by sixteenth-century authors, who were among the first to have understood that a reduction in tragic tone was the only way to make a space for the participation of the middle classes – and, therefore, the only way to reach a more expanded audience. As Valeria Pompejano Natoli observes,

> la tragicommedia ha assolto come nessun'altra forma letteraria (o paraletteraria) alla funzione di raccordo fra il potere, attraverso i suoi agenti-autori, e il suo nuovo interlocutore: quel ceto medio produttivo che assorbiva, metabolizzava ed esprimeva consenso. La tragicommedia diventa tribuna di opinioni, strumento di diffusione delle idee, veicolo di mentalità: essa si configura come uno dei primi *media* di massa della cultura europea.

> tragicomedy carries out, as does no other literary (or para-literary) form, the function of connecting with power via its agent-authors and its new interlocutor: that productive middle class that absorbed, metabolized, and expressed approval. Tragicomedy became a forum of opinions, an instrument for the dissemination of ideas, a vehicle for *mentalités*: it amounted to one of the first mass media of European culture.[55]

With the communicative power of tragicomedy and its ability to transmit clear, unambiguous messages in mind, we can now explore what the significance of Goldoni's innovations may have been for Venetian spectators.

The People Onstage

Beyond the use of tragicomedy, another communicative strategy Goldoni adopted at least in part from Cicognini and his followers is the concept of a performance that focuses entirely on its spectators by placing them – or an allegorical equivalent – onstage. Here, the allegorical equivalent of the audience is no longer pseudo-Cicognini's courtiers: spectators find their analogue among the "Guardie" and "Soldati" (Guards and Soldiers) as well as among, as Carlo Gozzi would say, the "minuto popolo" (literally, "small people" – that is, commoners). The "popolo," who are present in the opening scene of Goldoni's *Belisario* as well as at the end of the play, constitute a group of characters who stand apart and essentially perform themselves – an occurrence that was still unthinkable for Cicognini or his imitators. It is no coincidence that Goldoni's tragicomedy opens with a long monologue by Justinian that is directed to the "Popoli di Bisanzio"

("People of Byzantium"), with whom he makes plans to demonstrate publicly his esteem for Belisario. The general's promotion thus takes place with the approval of the entire population of Constantinople: "vieni, e vedrai dove inalzarti anela / Cesare, a questo suo popolo fedele" ("come, and you will see where Caesar longs to raise you, / to this, his faithful people"). As Narsete confirms, "[i]l popolo l'approva" ("the people approve it"), and the new appointment assures the "gaudio comun" ("common joy," I.2).

While Cicognini – in order to further draw in his audience – deftly humoured his public's desire to see actors playing the part of spectators, Goldoni surpassed his predecessor's technique by putting the public itself upon the stage. In his rewriting, spectators not only see themselves mirrored on stage (and thus identify themselves among the *dramatis personae*) but also actually become characters in the dramatic performance. In Goldoni, the people become subjects not objects and actors not instruments; they take on the role of protagonists. Like the chorus in ancient tragedy, this collective character of the people represents public opinion onstage. Aware and proud of his shining reputation among the people, Belisario emphasizes (in a monologue addressed to the spectators) that his most grievous loss was not that of his sight and his honour (as was the case in pseudo-Cicognini's play) but that of his renown according to public opinion: "Nelle pupille e più nell'alma offeso. / Dura pena mi sia l'esser senz'occhi, / Ma la fama perduta è un maggior danno" ("In the eyes and more in the soul [am I] offended. / It is a hard punishment to be without eyes, / but a spoiled reputation is a greater loss," V.4).

Another of Goldoni's innovations here is to make Belisario not just the sovereign's favourite subject but also the mouthpiece of the people. Indeed, Antonia recounts that all Belisario need do in order to calm the revolt whipped up by Filippo and Teodora is to show himself to the people:

> Ei non sì tosto
> Al popolo mostrossi, che s'udìo
> Passar di bocca in bocca il suo gran nome.
> [...]
>
> Io so che appena
> Udiro i detti suoi, le genti tutte
> S'armaro a un punto solo, e corser tosto
> Dove più di bisogno esser parea,
> Gridando: "Viva Belisario, e pera
> L'inimico crudel." (V.9)

> He does naught but
> Shows himself to the public, [and] one hears
> Moving from mouth to mouth his great name.
> [...]
>
> I know that as soon as
> They hear his words, all the people
> Will arm themselves with one single aim, and run at once
> To where it seems there is greatest need,
> Shouting: "Live Belisario, and perish
> The cruel enemy."

Justinian, aware that Belisario is the champion of and spokesman for the people, swears fealty to him and declares himself, in the dénouement, his general's servant: "Popoli, in questo dì non fia chi nieghi / Obbedienza a lui; depongo anch'io / Lo scettro, e come voi, suddito e servo / Mi rendo, e ad obbedir insegno altrui" ("People, on this day I wish that there be no one who refuses / to obey him; I also lay down / The sceptre and, like you, subject and servant / Make myself, and I teach others to obey," V, final scene). Goldoni's emperor is thus a more positive figure than was pseudo-Cicognini's sovereign: in the Venetian version, Justinian distances himself from the exercise of power not because he is unable to govern the people but because he recognizes them as the ultimate authority and judge – equal, in fact, to himself. By sharing power with his former subject, who represents the people, Justinian admits their importance in the social and political arena, and this recognition translates, meta-theatrically, as an acknowledgment of the spectator's centrality to the adjudication of theatrical performances.

These innovations demonstrate definitively that all of the modifications Goldoni makes in his rewriting of the Belisario tale – from changes in narrative structure and form to his reworking of characters – are driven by their hoped-for effect on the spectator and are intended to make the audience recognize its critical role (an intention shared, as we have seen, by Cicognini). They are also active in the creation of a public that is both literary critic and political subject:

> Goldoni era un uomo profondamente apolitico. [...] E tuttavia raramente qualcuno dei suoi contemporanei rappresentò con tanta evidenza l'ideologia politica contemporanea, formulata e non formulata. [...] Tutte le sue figure [...] disposte in un determinato ordine, formulavano, senza che egli

> stesso ne avesse coscienza, talvolta contro la sua volontà, un determinato programma sociale e politico.
>
> Goldoni was a profoundly apolitical man. [...] And yet rarely did one of his contemporaries so clearly represent contemporary political ideology, [whether] directly or indirectly. [...] All of his characters [...] set in a specific order, formulated – without even being aware of it and at times against their will – a specific social and political program.[56]

Even in this early work, Goldoni insisted upon the right of the public to be represented on stage – a right that he would defend more explicitly in the preface to his *Baruffe chiozzotte* (*Chioggia Scuffles*). Responding from Paris in 1762 to the criticisms aimed at him by Carlo Gozzi in the *Ragionamento ingenuo*, which critiqued the low, vulgar characters upon which Goldoni based his everyday, popular comedies, he again affirmed the right of the people, as paying spectators at the public theatre, to "vedersi rappresentato" ("see themselves represented"): "ed era ben giusto che, per piacere a quest'ordine di persone, che pagano come i Nobili e come i Ricchi, facessi delle Commedie, nelle quali riconoscessero i loro costumi e i loro difetti, e, mi sia permesso di dirlo, le loro virtù" ("and it was absolutely right that, to please this kind of person – who paid just like the nobles and the rich – I made comedies in which they could recognize their own customs, their own faults – and, if I may say so, their own virtues").[57] To confirm the importance assigned by Goldoni to the audiences of his plays, it is worth citing Goethe's review of the *Baruffe* (which he attended on 10 October 1786 in Venice), in which he emphasizes just how hard it is to disentangle the roles of the characters from those of the people; the actors from the public; and the fiction from the reality:

> Die Handelnde sind lauter Seeleute, Einwohner von Chiozza und ihre Weiber und Schwestern und Töchter. Das gewöhnliche Geschrey im Guten und Bösen dieser Leute, ihre Händel, Heftigkeit, Manieren, Gutmütigkeit, Plattheit, Witz, Humor pp sind gar brav nachgeahmt. [...] Aber auch so eine Lust hab ich nicht gesehen als das Volck hatte, sich und die seinigen so spielen zu sehen. [...] Vorzüglich ist aber der Verfasser zu loben, der aus nichts den angenehmsten Zeitvertreib seinem Volck verschafft hat, man sieht die unendlich geübte Hand durchaus.
>
> The characters are all natives of that town, fishermen and their wives, sisters and daughters. The habitual to-do made by these people, their quarrels, their outbursts of temper, their good nature, superficiality, wit, humour and

> natural behaviour – all these were excellently imitated. [...] I have never in my life witnessed such an ecstasy of joy as that shown by the audience when they saw themselves and their families so realistically portrayed on the stage. [...] but the highest praise is due to the playwright for creating such a delightful entertainment out of thin air. Only someone in intimate contact with this pleasure-loving people could have done it. It is written with an expert hand.[58]

This brief comparison with mature Goldonian theatre demonstrates not only how rapidly and efficiently his reformative interventions were adopted but also how his reflection on the public undertaken via *Belisario* signals an important milestone along the path of inquiry that his theatre traced with respect to the bond between dramaturgical practice and audience function.

From Cicognini to Goldoni

Two conclusions emerge from this comparison of the *Belisari* by pseudo-Cicognini and Goldoni. First, Goldoni learned, implemented, and improved upon various dramaturgical practices that were designed specifically to grant absolute power to the audience by Cicognini, his imitators, and his followers, all of whom sought to change and improve communication between spectator and stage. Second, these two versions of the Belisario tale illustrate specific phases of the process that brought about the formation of the new spectator, who comes in this period to be endowed with a critical spirit and is progressively more active and more involved in the construction of the performance itself. This process began with Cicognini's recognition of the audience's critical role in the dramatic efficaciousness of performance and ended with his followers' and then Goldoni's purposeful inclusion of the spectator in the theatrical event itself and also, importantly, in political and social events. These dramatic works, therefore, consciously created an attentive and sophisticated recipient; they required focused and immersive consumption by their spectators. The next chapter shows how the process of public-making and the shift in the dramaturgy of the spectator entered a new phase with Scipione Maffei's *Merope*, a play that sharpened the audience's critical awareness in a yet more rigorous attempt to transform spectators into increasingly astute members of a politically engaged public sphere.

3 The Politics of Spectatorship

Sovereigns on Trial in Scipione Maffei's *Merope*

Polemical from the very moment of its creation, Scipione Maffei's *Merope* (Modena, 11 June 1713) stirred up a hornets' nest of critical opinion – including no small amount of praise – both within Italy and across Europe.[1] If Maffei indeed intended to write a tragedy that would challenge the pre-eminence of French theatre, the popularity of melodrama, and the moral decadence of Italian theatre, he succeeded – at least to the extent that *Merope* became the subject of a heated intellectual debate on the function of theatre that involved, among others, Luigi Riccoboni, Apostolo Zeno, Gotthold Ephraim Lessing, Vittorio Alfieri, and Voltaire.[2] Because of the avid interest the play engendered among authors, actors, critics, and, above all, the European public, *Merope* can be said to have been an essential milestone in the formation of the modern or "authentic" public sphere that, Habermas argued, was born within the republic of letters, where it already enjoyed institutional support as well as ample discursive space.[3]

Through the intellectual *querelles* that it sparked, *Merope* participated actively in and had substantial influence upon the public sphere that was forming within larger literary debates at the time. As Franco Longoni writes, Maffei's play represents "a kind of treatise on dramaturgy in action" and is thus a fundamental text for studying the formation of public opinion both in Europe more generally and specifically in Italy.[4] The history of the play's conception indicates that Maffei paid special attention to the theatre-going public and to public opinion. His interpretation of the Merope tragedy emerged only after lengthy preparatory work – both theoretical and practical – conducted with an eye to the reform of

Italian tragic theatre. During a three-year period beginning in 1710, Maffei – in collaboration with the renowned theatre company directed by Luigi Riccoboni and Elena Balletti (who used the stage names Lelio and Flaminia) – sought to bring a new artistic energy to sixteenth- and seventeenth-century texts.[5] The extraordinary public success of *Merope* – first in Venice (where it was staged in 1714 at the Teatro San Luca),[6] the most important city for theatre in the eighteenth century ("l'arbitra più autorevole e il più sicuro giudice"; "the most authoritative arbiter and most reliable judge"),[7] and then throughout Europe[8] – that followed the play's 1713 premiere in Modena demonstrates that Maffei was keenly aware of his audiences' needs and desires.[9] In fact, in the preface to the 1745 edition (published in Verona), the playwright linked his choice of Merope as the tragedy's subject not to the *auctoritas* of Aristotle – who, in the *Poetics* (XIV, 19–20), offered Euripides' lost *Cresphontes* (also based on the tragedy of Merope) as the best example of a recognition scene in all of tragedy – but rather to Maffei's own reflections on the relationship between performance and the theatre-going public.[10] As Paolo Scotton argues, "il veronese [è] riuscito ad aggiungere in maniera assai suggestiva alla *Poetica* aristotelica quell''altro discorso' riguardo il rapporto tra rappresentazione e pubblico, che lo Stagirita lascia in sospeso nella sua riflessione che non sembra avere riscontro in altri luoghi dei suoi scritti" ("the Veronese [playwright] succeeded in adding to Aristotle's *Poetics*, in a rather appealing way, that 'other discourse' regarding the relationship between performance and public which the [philosopher] had left undiscussed in his reflections [and] which does not seem to be encountered in other places in his writings").[11]

This chapter investigates and answers questions that relate specifically to these initial observations on *Merope*'s importance for the emergence of the modern public sphere. First, which dramaturgical elements caused the tragedy to take on a decisive role in the formation of the public's collective identity? Second, which aspects of the text's subject matter enabled Maffei to create an audience capable of exerting a critical judgment about what was performed both on stage and in the social and political environments of early-eighteenth-century Italy? Answers to these questions about Maffei's dramaturgy help establish the impact of theatrical practice on the production of a new critical consciousness – precisely the aspect of the Enlightenment that was least explored by Habermas and that remains under-studied.

Merope and the Political

Since Euripides' lost original inspired a great number of interpretations of Meropean material over the centuries, we must begin with a brief summary of Maffei's version. Merope, widow of the Messenian king Cresphontes, is forced to live at the court of the usurper Polyphontes, who murdered her husband and children. What makes her dreadful situation somewhat bearable is the one faint hope that her third son, who had been sent far away, might return to avenge the wrongful deaths of his father and siblings. During his voyage back to Messenia, this young man (whose name is Aegistus) kills a man who attacked him. As a result of this act of violence – and even though it was carried out in legitimate self-defence – Aegistus is arrested and brought to Polyphontes' court. Through a series of misunderstandings, the queen is led to believe that this stranger (Aegistus) is in fact her son's killer; she therefore attempts – in vain – to kill him herself. When the elderly servant who accompanied Aegistus to Messenia reveals her son's true identity to Merope, she reluctantly agrees to marry Polyphontes, both to avert the usurper's retaliatory threats against her faithful subjects and to give Aegistus time to enact his own revenge: to kill the hated tyrant during his wedding ceremony.

The first narrative element of Maffei's tragedy to guarantee the public's "smisurato favore" ("immeasurable approval")[12] was identified by the playwright himself. *Merope*'s representation of motherly love – a universal passion capable of both producing and influencing the spectators' collective emotions – brought audiences to tears of anguish and to screams of anger, as well as emptying the theatres in which musical dramas (usually a far more popular genre) were performed.[13] By pinpointing a reason for his tragedy's success, Maffei established a critical reading of his work that was destined to endure over the long term: criticism of *Merope* has reflected in depth on the theme of motherly love, leading scholars to consider the work a tragedy of familial passions and a precursor to the psychological *drame larmoyant.*[14]

What commentators have ignored as a result is the political dimension of *Merope,* to which Maffei never alluded in the work's numerous paratexts. The frequent comparison of Maffei's *Merope* with its precursor (by Pomponio Torelli, 1589) and with Alfieri's treatment (1783), both of which are tragedies with real political substance, has given scholars yet another reason to consider Maffei's *Merope* lacking in political reflection. That said, the Torellian *Merope,* which Maffei studied attentively and republished in the collection of tragedies "per uso della scena" ("for the stage") that he edited between 1723 and 1725, can hardly be ignored as an influence.[15] Indeed, it must have had a decisive impact on his interpretation of the ancient myth, as early audiences clearly knew: the day after the premiere, Maffei was accused of plagiarizing Torelli.[16]

The political dimension of Maffei's play appears as early as its opening lines. These neglect to include the queen's heartfelt revelation to her confidante – the traditional mechanism by which, from Giangiorgio Trissino's *Sofonisba* to Torelli's *Merope*, the scene was set for the spectator/reader. Maffei, instead, begins his version with a fraught debate between two representatives of political power – Merope and Polyphontes – regarding the fate of the kingdom and the return of its legitimate heir. Interested in the Merope fable as a means of avoiding the theme of romantic love that had been so popular in sixteenth- and seventeenth-century drama,[17] Maffei offers yet more persuasive proof of the presence of political content in his *Merope* by characterizing Polyphontes' love for the queen as political strategy rather than an affair of the heart. In Torelli's *Merope* as well as in *Telefonte* (1582) by Antonio Cavallerino of Modena and *Cresfonte* (1588) by Giovanni Battista Liviera of Vicenza, the audience is confronted by the coexistence of the themes of love and politics.[18] In Torelli, Polyphontes is genuinely in love with Merope, who calls him a "cortese" and "degno amante" ("gracious" and "worthy beloved," vv. 2647, 2664) and confesses – in the dénouement – that she had been "sopra ad ogni altra amata" ("loved [by him] more than any other," v. 2657).[19] In contrast, the point upon which Maffei's plot turns is the divide between – not the coincidence of – the private sphere and the interests of the state. For Maffei's Polyphontes, his desire for political stability rather than love or passion drives his ambition for union with the queen. Indeed, upon receiving a false report of Aegistus's death, the tyrant sustains the brief hope that he would no longer have to wed the queen: "or vo pensando, / se il già prefisso *a me troppo noioso* / imeneo tralasciar si possa; il volgo / non ha più che sperar" ("and now I am wondering / whether the already prearranged, *to me far too irritating* / wedding might be possible to avoid; the common people / can do nothing more than hope," III.1, vv. 43–5, my italics).[20] This tidy separation between the private and the political signals the wedding's politicization more emphatically than had the approaches of earlier Merope tragedies. Maffei, after all, was as fascinated by the political dimension of human existence, as was Torelli, "il primo drammaturgo ad occuparsi intenzionalmente della Ragion di Stato" ("the first playwright to intentionally concern himself with *raison d'état*").[21] Approximately twenty years after his drafting of *Merope*, Maffei completed his *Consiglio politico al Governo Veneto* (*Political Advice to the Venetian Government*, written in 1737 but not published until 1797, the year of the fall of the Venetian Republic),[22] a work that "deve considerarsi un eccellente documento del pensiero politico italiano nella prima metà del Settecento" ("must be considered excellent documentary evidence regarding Italian political thought during the first half of the eighteenth century").[23]

Investigation into the political dimension of Maffei's tragedy provides us with a privileged viewpoint from which to analyse the impact of the play on the creation of public opinion. Given the close tie that exists between national and public interests, as well as the historical link between theatre and the public sphere, the tragedy's figures of sovereignty – Polyphontes, Merope, and Aegistus – demonstrate how images of sovereignty change when, in Maffei (as in Cicognini), the theatrical spectacle transforms itself from a royal ceremony to a modern performance for a vast and heterogeneous public. Considering *Merope* with an eye to these recurrent motifs provides a further opportunity to trace the evolutionary narrative of playwrights who turn theatre into a space in which theatre-goers come into contact with aesthetic and political ideas.

Re Machiavelliero[24]

Throughout Maffei's *Merope*, Polyphontes is called a usurper, tyrant, and monster – characterizations that reach their peak in Merope's words to the Messenians in the final act of the drama:

> è quel tiranno, è quel ladron, quell'empio
> ribelle, usurpator, che a tradimento
> del legittimo re, de' figli imbelli
> trafisse il sen, sparse le membra; è quegli,
> ch'ogni dritto violò, che prese a scherno
> le leggi, e i Dei; che non fu sazio mai
> né d'oro, né di sangue; che per vani
> sospetti trucidò tanti infelici,
> ed il cener ne sparse, e fin le mura
> arse, atterrò, distrusse. A qual di voi
> padre, o fratel, figlio, congiunto, o amico
> non avrà tolto? (V.7, vv. 359–70)

He is that tyrant; he is that thief; that wicked
rebel and usurper, who in betrayal
of the true king and his defenceless sons
pierced their breasts, scattered their limbs; it is he
who violated every right, who mocked
the laws as well as the Gods; he who could never be satiated
by gold or by blood; who as a result of baseless
suspicions slaughtered many unhappy souls,
and scattered their ashes, and even the very walls
he burned, levelled, destroyed. From which of you
father, or brother, son, kin, or friend
has he not taken?

Merope here paints a vivid picture of Polyphontes' cruel domination of his people, extreme moods, haughty ambition, and greed; she also depicts his unrepentant exercise of both *mala potestas* and legislative excess. Since the tragedy tells the tale of Merope as a mother, however, we might legitimately ask whether Polyphontes is really as evil as the queen of Messenia describes, or whether her words instead exploit a relatively conventional depiction of tyranny aimed at inciting the Messenians to take up her son's cause. To cast doubt upon Merope's impartiality is the tack taken by Gotthold Ephraim Lessing (1729–81), an attentive reader of Maffei's tragedy who judges Polyphontes to be not so very evil at all, stating that Maffei's tyrant disturbs as much as would a tyrant made of papier-mâché.[25] Even Alfieri, who cared little for Maffeian tragedy, found this character to be merely a "crudelotto tiranno" ("cruel-ish tyrant").[26]

The first suggestion in the play itself that Merope's assessment of her betrothed is not completely impartial comes from the fact that Maffei's Polyphontes does not display unrestrained passion. In Torelli, in contrast, the desire for power and lust appear as two sides of the same coin.[27] As noted above, neither love nor unwholesome desire urge Maffei's usurper of Messenia to seek marriage with the widowed queen. Instead, it is Polyphontes' driving need to consolidate his power before the impending return of the legitimate heir to the throne. In the tragedy's opening dialogue, Merope herself says as much, refusing the tyrant's marriage proposal with the retort that

I pochi,
ma accorti amici tuoi sperar ti fanno,
che se t'accoppi a me, se regnar teco

mi fai, scemando l'odio, in pace al fine
soffriranno i messeni il giogo. Questo
è l'amor, che per me t'infiamma; questo
è quel dolce pensier, che in te si desta. (I.1, vv. 146–52)

A few
but clever friends of yours give you hope,
that if you join with me, if you make me reign by your side,
the Messenians will swallow their hatred, and in peace
will suffer the yoke. This
is the love that inflames you for me; this
is the sweet thought that awakens in you.

In the same scene, Polyphontes reminds Merope (and informs the audience) that his revolt against Cresphontes had been supported by broad popular consensus: "Poi tu ben sai, che accetto egli non era; / e che non sol gli esterni aiuti, e l'armi, / ma in campo a mio favor vennero i primi, / ed i miglior del regno" ("You know well that he was not accepted / and that not only foreign help and arms / but, rallying to my side, came [also] the best / and greatest from the realm," I.1, vv. 39–42). In the years that followed, he continues, Polyphontes defended the kingdom of Messenia from foreign threats, maintaining peace and caring for the public good during his reign:

Sai, che appena fui re, ch'esterne guerre
infestar la Messenia; e l'una estinta,
altra s'accese, e senza aver riposo
or qua accorrendo, or là, sudar fu forza
un decennio fra l'armi. In pace poi
gli estranei mi lasciar, ma allor lo Stato
cominciò a perturbar questa malnata
plebe [...]. (I.1, vv. 124–31)

You know that I had only just become king when foreign wars
came to plague Messenia; and when one was extinguished,
another ignited, and without rest,
rushing here and there, toil it was to sweat
a decade in arms. In peace
my foreign foes finally left me, but then in the State
these ill-begotten peasants began to cause strife [...].

With regard to his foreign policy, Maffei's Polyphontes was a clear precedent for Voltaire's tyrant in his *Mérope* (composed in 1736 and premiered on 20 February 1743), who is an able warlord and an iconic example of a self-determined man who dedicated his life to the service of his country:

Un soldat tel que moi peut justement prétendre
A gouverner l'Etat, quand il l'a su défendre.
Le premier qui fut roi fut un soldat heureux.
Qui sert bien son pays n'a pas besoin d'aïeux.
Je n'ai plus rien du sang qui m'a donné la vie:
Ce sang s'est épuisé, versé pour la patrie:
Ce sang coula pour vous: et malgré vos refus,
Je crois valoir au moins les rois que j'ai vaincus.
[...]
Le droit de commander n'est plus un avantage,
Transmis par la nature, ainsi qu'un héritage;
C'est le fruit des travaux et du sang répandu;
C'est le prix du courage: et je crois qu'il m'est dû.[28]

(I.3, vv. 173–80 and 201–4)

That soldier has a right
To rule the kingdom which his arm defended.
What was the first that bore the name of king,
But a successful soldier? he who serves
His country well requires not ancestry
To make him noble: the inglorious blood,
Which I received from him who gave me life,
I shed already in my country's cause,
It flowed for thee; and, spite of thy proud scorn,
I must at least be equal to the kings
I have subdued:
[...]
the right of power supreme
Defends no more the gift of nature, here
From son to son; it is the price of toil,
Of labor, and of blood; 'tis virtue's meed,
Which I shall claim [.]

Polyphontes' behaviour in Maffei's version lacks the trait that has been considered fundamental to the definition of tyranny since Aristotle's *Politics*, namely disregard for the public interest: "tyranny [...] pays regard to no common interest unless for the sake of its private benefit; and the aim of tyranny is what is pleasant [...]" (*Politics*, V.VIII, 1311 a 2–4).[29]

Another tyrannical trait that Merope attributes to Messenia's usurper is cruelty. It is impossible to deny that Polyphontes acted brutally in assassinating the queen's husband and children. However, these acts are justified by the usurper's need to stabilize the state and to consolidate his power, and are perfectly in line with Machiavellian precepts.[30] In the *Discorsi sopra la prima deca di Tito Livio* (*Discourses on Livy*), Machiavelli states that "si può avvertire ogni principe che non viva mai sicuro del suo principato, fino che vivono coloro che ne sono stati spogliati" ("every prince can be warned that he never lives secure in his principality as long as those who have been despoiled of [their possessions] are living"), adding that "si può ricordare ad ogni potente che mai le ingiurie vechie furono cancellate da' beneficii nuovi; e tanto meno, quanto il beneficio nuovo è minore che non è stata la ingiuria" ("every power can be reminded that old injuries are never suppressed by new benefits, and so much the less as the new benefit is less than the injury was").[31] Polyphontes is therefore most definitely a "new" breed of prince, as he shows elsewhere by stating that "ciò che a regnar conduce, ognor si loda" ("whatever helps one to reign is always praiseworthy," I.1, v. 43), an affirmation equally in line with Machiavellian political thought. Similarly, in his later *Consiglio politico*, which lays out a "percorso da visibili nervature machiavelliane" ("path with visible Machiavellian veins"),[32] Maffei maintains that the "uffizio e scopo della Politica esser dee di rendere uno Stato non sol felice, ma forte" ("obligation and goal of Politics is to render a State not only happy, but strong").[33]

What makes Polyphontes tyrant-like, then, is the way he acts rather than his brutal and lustful character. That is, he behaves in accordance with the principles of *Realpolitik* that distinguish, on the one hand, between ethical and religious problems and, on the other, between strategies of domination that entirely split off the political from the moral sphere. As demonstrated above, however, Polyphontes operates in the name of the public good, and his political actions conform to Machiavellian precepts. How then can the model of sovereignty that he embodies be defined as tyranny?

The only tyrannical characteristic from Merope's description that finds purchase in Polyphontes' actual behaviour is the fact that he places himself above the law. Many times over the course of the tragedy, Maffei's tyrant (like Torelli's) claims the superiority of prince over law:

> Io fermo
> son nel mio soglio sì, che nulla curo
> d'altrui favor, e di chi freme in vano
> mi rido, e ognor mi riderò. (I.1, vv. 154–7)

> I am so secure
> on my throne, that I have no care for
> others' favour, and at whoever trembles in vain
> I laugh, and I will laugh every time.

Should Merope refuse to marry him, Polyphontes plans to apply the law however he wishes, which includes disregarding it at his own whim:

> Quando
> saran da poi sopiti alquanto, e queti
> gli animi, l'arte del regnar mi giovi.
> Per mute oblique vie n'andranno a Stige
> l'alme più audaci, e generose. A i vizi,
> per cui vigor si abbatte, ardir si toglie,
> il freno allargherò. Lunga clemenza
> con pompa di pietà farò, che splenda
> su i delinquenti; a i gran delitti invito,
> onde restino i buoni esposti, e paghi
> renda gl'iniqui la licenza; ed onde
> poi fra sé distruggendosi, in crudeli
> gare private il lor furor si stempri.
> Udrai sovente risonar gli editti,
> e raddoppiar le leggi, che al sovrano
> giovan servate, e trasgredite. Udrai
> correr minaccia ognor di guerra esterna;
> ond'io n'andrò su l'atterrita plebe
> sempre crescendo i pesi, e peregrine
> milizie introdurrò. Che più? Son giunto,
> dov'altro omai non fa mestier che tempo
> anche da sé ferma i domini il tempo. (III.1, vv. 68–89)

When
they will finally be somewhat soothed, and
their souls quieted, the art of ruling will please me.
For along silent, secret paths they will go to the river Styx,
these most brave and generous souls. On the vices,
which destroy vigour [and] remove desire,
I will loosen the reins. I will bestow mercy with largess
and make a spectacle of pity that will shine
on the delinquents; and I will bring the greatest evils
to where the good are exposed, and payments
to grant the iniquitous licence; and when
then they destroy themselves, in cruel
private wars their fury will be quenched.
You will often hear decrees resounding
and laws redoubled, which benefit a sovereign
to keep or transgress as he wishes. You will always hear
the threat of foreign war flying about;
where I will go, over the terrified peasants,
always increasing their burdens, and I will introduce
foreign forces. What more? I have arrived,
where naught else plies its trade but time
[and] even time itself halts dominions.

Polyphontes, therefore, embodies tyranny insofar as he performs royal excess at the peak of frenzy, exploding with irrational fury. Though very different from his Torellian precursor, Maffei's Polyphontes is a character who adheres to a political model that is still, in essence, Baroque.[34] As Walter Benjamin explains in his study of the *Trauerspiel*,[35] this model of sovereignty consists precisely in the tendency for political action to become detached from morality.[36]

The separation of moral and political orders is a characteristic Habermas attributes to the "repräsentative Öffentlichkeit," a public sphere based on performance – the visible reproduction of hierarchies of power that distribute roles such that there is a clear distinction between the public (individual) who interprets the role of authority and the public (spectator) who observes it.

The function of the performative public sphere, which is based on the spectacularization of political action, is most clearly illustrated in the third scene of the second act in Maffei's *Merope*. Here Polyphontes' adviser, Adrastus, attempts to hurry along the wedding of tyrant to queen, insisting on the vital importance of this *mise-en-scène* for calming the Messenian people:

ADRASTO: Affretta, o re, queste tue nozze, affretta
di soddisfar con quest'immagin vana
di giustizia, e di pace il popol pazzo. (II.3, vv. 199–201)

POLIFONTE: E credi tu, che sia per poter tanto
nel sentimento popolare il solo
veder del regio onor Merope cinta?
ADRASTO: Sol l'incerto romor, che di ciò corre
molti già ti concilia; e ci ha chi spera,
che di Cresfonte la consorte debba
risvegliar di Cresfonte in te i costumi. (II.3, vv. 206–12)

ADRASTO: conviensi allora
forza, e minacce usar; che a tutto prezzo
vuolsi ottener di coronar nel tempio
a gli occhi de i messeni, in fra la pompa
di festoso imeneo, costei [...] (II.3, vv. 233–7)

ADRASTUS: Hasten, o King, your nuptials, hasten
to satisfy the angry masses
with this empty image of justice and peace.

POLYPHONTES: And do you believe that such an effect
on popular sentiment can come only
from the sight of Merope encircled with royal honour?
ADRASTUS: Only the uncertain rumour, which stems from that,
many already concede to you; and there are those
who hope
that the consort of Cresphontes would
reawaken the habits of Cresphontes in you.

ADRASTUS: It would be best, then,
to use force and threat and at all costs
to ensure that her coronation in the temple
takes place before the eyes of the Messenians,
with all the pomp
of the festive wedding [...]

Like his adviser Adrastus, Polyphontes demonstrates that he is fully aware of the correspondence between the roles of monarch and actor. He knows, in other words, that kings – like actors – must always be on stage, and he makes this clear precisely in the moment of his greatest weakness and melancholic desperation. Tired of being continually assaulted by foreign and domestic intrigues, Polyphontes confides in his adviser that he would like to create a space – literally, a void – around himself rather than being constantly required to perform his royal persona before his people, who are at once his subjects, his public, and his audience:

POLIFONTE:	Meglio saria far di costor scempio.
ADRASTO:	Tu stesso a te torresti allora il regno.
POLIFONTE:	In voto regno almen sarei sicuro.
ADRASTO:	Ma ciò bramar, non già sperar ti lice. (II.3, vv. 202–5)

POLYPHONTES:	It would be better to slaughter them.
ADRASTUS:	Then you would take your own realm from yourself.
POLYPHONTES:	In an empty realm at least I would be safe.
ADRASTUS:	But to desire that, let alone to hope it, is not permitted you.

When Polyphontes orders Adrastus to lead Merope to the altar for the wedding ceremony, we see yet again that the usurper's marriage to the queen is nothing more than sophisticated scenery for the *mise-en-scène* of power:

POLIFONTE: Or Merope si chiami. Io di condurla
a te lascio il pensier. Precorrer voglio,
ed ostentarmi al volgo; esso schernendo,
che non ha mente, ed i suoi sordi Dei,
che non ebbero mai mente, né senso. (V.2, vv. 137–41)

POLYPHONTES: Now go to call Merope. How you bring her
I leave to you to think upon. I want to go before,
and show myself off to the commoners; mocking them all the while,
they have no minds, and their deaf gods,
who have never had minds, nor reason.

With these words, Polyphontes exposes the relationship between theatricality and absolutism, revealing the profoundly theatrical roots of sovereignty as identified, again, by Benjamin, who illuminated the ways in which the *Trauerspiel* monarch uses the spectacle of power with the goal of silencing moral law.

Habermas, for his part, maintains that in the performative public sphere, control is based less on laws than on symbols – and on the staged spectacle of the monarch before a people who are drawn in like the passive spectators of a theatrical performance. In this context, the roles of subject and public converge: the people (subjects) are necessary, and yet they are external to (and excluded from) the spectacle that unfolds in front of their eyes. They thus become a public without critical awareness – an abstract entity before which authority displays itself and upon which it exerts its power.

Ultimately, then, what makes Maffei's Polyphontes a tyrant is his conception of the *vulgo* (common masses) as a blind, brutal, and irrational organism. For him the mob is a fearsome entity ("imbelle / domestico nimico assai più temo, / che armato in capo"; "an unarmed / domestic enemy I fear more / than a soldier in the field," III.1, vv. 48–50) that must be disciplined, tightly controlled, and – ideally – deprived of a voice.

Public/Private, Mother/Queen

From Merope's accusations of tyranny (which, as we have seen, is the term she uses to collectively describe Polyphontes' offences), a very different understanding of government – one unique to the queen – emerges. In order to clarify the distinction between the queen's and the usurper's concepts of governance, it is again useful to compare Maffei's with Torelli's *Merope.* Torelli's dialogue between the queen and her adviser, Gabria, reveals that, during the fifteen years of Polyphontes' tyrannical reign, Merope is always managing her kingdom and protecting her people:

MEROPE: Hor ch'al popolo mio non ho mancato
di proveder, quanto per me si possa,
giusto è pur ch'a me stessa anco riguardi,
et a tante fatiche, a tanti guai
con morte assai tranquilla imponga fine.
GABRIA: Molt' hai fatto, Reina, e molt'ancora
per tua gloria vivendo a far ti resta:
che, se non puoi sottrarre a l'aspro giogo

con forestiere forze il popol fido,
puoi con le proprie tue, che largo il cielo
di grazie e di bellezza ha in te versato,
sollevar la lor grave servitute. (vv. 219–30)

MEROPE: Since I have not failed
to provide for my people, as much as I could,
it is right that I also still look to myself,
and that to many hardships, to many woes,
I put an end with my quiet death.
GABRIA: Queen, you have done much, and much more
remains for you to do for your honour if you live:
since, if you cannot take the harsh yoke
from your faithful people with foreign forces,
you will with your own, which, given the
graces and beauty granted you by heaven,
will relieve their difficult servitude.

This is not, however, the case in Maffei's version: where Torelli's queen is a complex character, both mother and sovereign, in Maffei we find no evidence of Merope's political responsibilities. Indeed, her public actions are reduced almost entirely to waiting for the return of her son; she tends actively to reject every civic aspect of her role. For this reason, she most often responds to Polyphontes' marriage proposals as follows: "[u]n regno / non varrebbe il dolor d'esser [sua] moglie" ("[a] kingdom / would not be worth the torment of being [his] wife," I.1, vv. 23–4).[37]

That said, Merope's distant attitude towards matters of state does not necessarily mean that the fate of the Messenian kingdom is of no interest to her. Instead, her engagement (or lack thereof) in civic affairs shows us how matters of state can become private affairs. When presenting Aegistus to the people, for example, the queen elucidates a fundamental characteristic of her interpretation of good governance – namely, that a good monarch is one who establishes a kind of familial rapport with the people. This comes as no surprise, as Merope's late husband was more of a father than a king to the Messenians ("[...] Cresfonte che non ben sapeste / se fosse padre, o re"; "[...] Cresphontes who did not know well / whether he was father, or king," V.6, vv. 354–5).[38] Nor is it by chance that Aegistus's first political move as the newly installed king relates to the private sphere. His show of gratitude to an old tutor was a personal act of which Merope wholeheartedly approved.

EGISTO: Reina, a questo vecchio io render mai
ciò che gli debbo, non potrei: permetti
che a tenerlo per padre io segua ognora.
MEROPE: Io più di te gli debbo; e assai mi piace
di scorgerti sì grato, e che il tuo primo
atto e pensier di re virtù governi. (V.7, vv. 424–9)

AEGISTUS: Queen, to this old man I have never repaid
what I owe him, nor could I: allow
me to hold him as my father from now on.
MEROPE: I owe him more than do you; it is pleasing to me
to find you so grateful, and to find that your first
act and thought as king is governed by virtue.

The fusion of political and private gestures with explicitly political ends in the behaviour of both Merope and Aegistus reflects one of the defining characteristics of Habermas's modern public sphere: unlike the performative public sphere that preceded it, the modern public sphere is constituted not as a public space in which to exercise authority but rather as a private space that has much to do with individual subjectivity.[39]

The function of this newly emerging public sphere in Maffei's *Merope* is illustrated by the description of the wedding ceremony, as recounted to Polydorus by his confidant Eurisus. His tale makes it clear that the queen of Messenia envisages the public ceremony as the opportunity for a *mise-en-scène* of her own sovereignty before a crowd of spectators; but her self-representation before her people has an objective quite different from that of Polyphontes. Merope's use of theatrical practices aims to make her people – her audience – reflect upon what politics is and upon how a civic space open to the common people – not only to political players – might function:

EURISO: Or sappi, ch'ella in core
già si fermò, dove a sì duro passo
costretta fosse, in mezzo al tempio, *a vista*
del popol tutto, trapassarsi il core.
Così sottrarsi elegge, e si lusinga

che a spettacol sì atroce alfin si scuota
il popol neghittoso, e sul tiranno
si scagli, e 'l faccia in pezzi. (V.5, vv. 242–9, my italics)

EURISUS: Now understand, that she in her heart
had already decided, if she was forced into such a
difficult position, that in the middle of the temple,
in sight
of all the people, she would stab herself in the heart.
Thus she would choose to remove herself, and she
dreams
that a spectacle so atrocious would finally manage to rouse
the indolent people, and upon the tyrant
they would fall and tear him to pieces.

What most clearly highlights the difference between the debased royal ethics of Polyphontes from the more positive ethics of Merope is each ruler's distinct attitude towards their subjects.[40] The tyrant views his people, as we saw above, as a frightening entity that must be silenced through the performance of power. Merope, in contrast, sees them as a community of individuals who can be incited to action through dialogue with power. *Merope* therefore illustrates, through these two characters' embodiment of sovereignty, the transition from what Habermas defined as the performative public sphere – in which, as we have seen, the monarch stages his unchallenged power before his submissive subjects – to the modern public sphere – in which private individuals come together to discuss power, thereby becoming actors on the political stage. In the new public sphere, it is the people who become the source of political legitimacy.

One could therefore conclude, as does Carlotta Sorba, that Maffei's Polyphontes and Merope illustrate how

> si attua dunque un passaggio epocale nella rappresentazione simbolica del potere: dalla metafora della scena – il palcoscenico al centro dei cui riti sta il corpo sacro del re – si passa a quella del pubblico, come depositario ultimo della sovranità; nella maggior parte dei casi esso è poco più che un'entità retorica con cui misurarsi, ma diventa in ogni caso elemento chiave del quadro simbolico in via di ricostituzione, oltre che soggetto da istruire, convincere e controllare.[41]

> an epochal passage within the symbolic performance of power comes about: from the metaphor of the set – the stage at the centre of whose rites rests the sacred body of the king – one passes to that of the public as the final depository of sovereignty. In most cases this public is little more than a rhetorical entity against which to measure oneself, but it becomes, in every instance, a key element of the symbolic canvas being restored, in addition to a subject to instruct, convince, and control.

I would further suggest that we might consider the figure of Merope to be a mouthpiece for Maffei's political ideas. In fact, the notion of popular sovereignty[42] – still *in nuce* here, but reaching its fullest expression in Alfieri's *Merope* and two *Bruti*, in which "il potere dovrà confrontarsi con un popolo che, su ammissione d'autore, ha acquistato ancor più voce e protagonismo" ("power must contend with a populace that, as the author admits, has become even more vocal and even more of a protagonist")[43] – finds validation in Maffei's *Consiglio politico*. This treatise was written in the context of the growing sense of economic, religious, and political unease, especially after the loss of the Morea (1715), that threatened the stability of the Republic's political order.[44] Its author's political ideal, which is posited as a warning to the Venetian Republic, consists of that "arte d'insignorirsi del mondo" ("art of making oneself powerful in the world") inherited from ancient Rome, and "di volere gli altri popoli amici e non servi e di farli con le lor vittorie non sudditi, ma compagni" ("of wanting other people as friends, not servants, and of making them, through their victories, not subjects but allies").[45] The *Consiglio*, which "manifesta un generoso proposito di riscatto nazionale" ("produces a generous proposal for national redemption"),[46] expresses the idea that people participate in government through its representative forms. Maffei contrasts the example of the inefficient Venetian government – in which "[l]e città ed i popoli vi sono tenuti in condizione di meri sudditi, sono esclusi da ogni comunicazione della Repubblica, da ogni apparenza di società, e da qualunque partecipazione di libertà" ("cities and people are treated as mere subjects and are excluded from any communication with the Republic, from any semblance of society, and from any participation in liberty whatsoever")[47] – with that of the ancient Romans, who created not "subject citizens" but "una Repubblica universale, [...] una società di tutti i popoli, vincolata insieme dal mutuo e comun benefizio" ("a universal Republic, [...] a society of all people, linked together by mutual and common benefit").[48] According to Giovanni Quintarelli, Maffei displays "un pensiero politico ardito e diverso, anzi opposto a quello dei contemporanei" ("an ardent and unique political thought, one that is even in direct opposition to that of his contemporaries").[49] Giuseppe Silvestri adds that the playwright,

> al principio per cui l'uomo di stato può disporre a suo placito dei popoli soggetti, oppone un criterio per cui solo dall'intima energia vitale della società possono scaturire le forze capaci di creare la grandezza di un popolo, dato che questa risulta essenzialmente dalla collaborazione di tutte le classi sociali, dalla loro partecipazione al governo, dall'interesse che loro prendono al suo buon andamento.[50]

> on the assumption that a statesman is able to maintain total authority over his subject peoples, opposes the notion that only from the intimate and vital energy of society can spring the forces capable of creating the greatness of a people, given that this essentially results from the collaboration of all social classes, from their participation in government, and from the interest they take in its smooth running.

Popular Sovereignty

But how does one make the idea of popular sovereignty a topic for public discussion? How does one encourage this process via the relationship between dramatic fiction and its audience? I would argue that in *Merope* this occurs through Maffei's construction of Aegistus, who is symbolically associated with the people and takes on the role of mediator between the fiction of the play and its real-world spectators.[51]

Aegistus, "giovane d'alti sensi in basso stato, / ed in vesti plebee di nobil volto" ("a young man of high conscience [but] low state, / and in common clothes [but] of noble face," I.1, vv. 200–1), is an unremarkable figure until the moment he becomes aware of his true identity. Elena Sannia Nowé affirms that "[i]n tal modo lo spettatore potrà identificarsi con lui, soffrendo per le sue disgrazie e contemporaneamente nutrendo una salutare paura per i rischi nei quali egli stesso potrebbe incorrere" ("in this way the spectator can identify with him, suffering along with his misfortunes and simultaneously developing a healthy fear of the risks of which he might fall foul").[52]

The identification of the spectator with the figure of Aegistus is reinforced via the mechanism of recognition. In *Merope,* there are moments of recognition: first, the recognition of the hero by his mother; second, the recognition of the hero by himself.[53] Maffei believed the latter was the work's greatest innovation; because of it, he could boast of having surpassed all those who had revisited the Merope myth before him.[54] In earlier rewritings of the tale from the sixteenth and seventeenth centuries (as well as in the libretto by Apostolo Zeno), Aegistus is already aware of his royal identity when he arrives in the realm of Polyphontes. Maffei, in contrast, keeps his hero ignorant of his own identity.

Gian Paolo Marchi suggests that "la vicenda di Egisto-Cresfonte, impegnato nel graduale conseguimento di una nuova identità (da pastore a re), potesse essere recepita dal pubblico (più o meno consapevolmente) come allegoria di un difficile riscatto personale e sociale" ("the Aegistus-Cresphontes event, engaged in the gradual pursuit of a new identity (from shepherd to king), could be construed by the more or less aware public as an allegory of difficult personal and social redemption").[55] Our discussion thus far proves Marchi's hypothesis; but the most convincing evidence for my interpretation of the role of the public in Maffei's *Merope* is the author's own words on the public theatre audience:

> Bisogna parimenti aver la bontà di credere, che né del vero modo di recitare, né del vero modo di compor Tragedie può comunemente aversi molta idea in quelle Città dove uso di Teatro non sia: né basta che da particolari vi si reciti; bisogna che siano Teatri publici e prezzolati, dove gran moltitudine di gente e d'ogni condizione concorra e dove niun rispetto, niuna convenienza, niuna prevenzione, niuna parzialità alteri il giudicio e trattenga, o spinga i moti naturali d'approvazione o disapprovazione: allora si riconosce ciò che veramente faccia forza su la natura o nol faccia; però senza questo addottrinamento grand'uomini abbiam visto darci Tragedie che, se ben piene d'ingegno e di sapere, son rimaste inutili ed all'universale son parute ridicole. Certa cosa è che molto caso è da fare in ciò anche del minuto popolo che, non guasto da pregiudici inseriti tal volta nelle menti dalle regole e da gli studi, ci scuopre il sentimento della natura e rettamente giudicar può, dove d'imitar la natura si tratta.[56]
>
> It is equally necessary to have the goodness to believe that one cannot normally have much idea either of genuine acting or of genuine composing of Tragedies in those Cities where there is no Theatre. Neither is it enough to perform in private settings; it is necessary that there be public, ticketed Theatres, where a great multitude of people from all walks of life come together, and where no deference, no advantage, no interdiction, no bias alter their judgment and hold back or push around their natural impulse to approve or disapprove. Then one can recognize what truly holds – or does not hold – power over nature. But without this instruction we have

> seen great men produce Tragedies that, though chock full of genius and knowledge, have ended up being worthless and have seemed ridiculous to everyone. It is certainly often the case that this can be done even by the common people who, not spoiled by the prejudices sometimes placed in the mind by rules, and by study, can find there natural sentiment and can thus judge things rightly, when it comes to imitating nature.

If it is true that a public is born the moment an author begins to speak for it and of it, we might well conclude that Maffei's greatest value as a playwright was this representation of his public, by which he rendered it an active agent and a herald of free thought. By staging the idea of the citizen-spectator's centrality, Maffei paved the way for the formation of public opinion and for the evolution of the public itself. Of course, we must acknowledge that the figure of the public was most important, for Maffei, from the perspective of theatre business and that he did not yet conceive of the public as an expert judge and critic of works of art. As Giuseppe Leonelli rightly observes, on close inspection Maffei did not in fact address "gran moltitudine di gente e d'ogni condizione" ("a great multitude of people from all walks of life"). Instead, he maintained that it was necessary to study the public of the "Teatri publici e prezzolati" ("public, ticketed Theatres") – the "popolo minuto" ("common people") – in order to understand "ciò che veramente faccia forza su la natura o nol faccia" ("what truly holds – or does not hold – power over nature").[57] Indeed, even in *Merope*'s dedication to the Duke of Modena, Rinaldo I, Maffei confirmed that he wished to suspend "per qualche anno, o almeno per qualche tempo" ("for a few years, or at least for some time") the publication of his work, instead presenting the unpublished manuscript to the duke "a fine di sentirne prima il parere, o l'esame de' Letterati, senza di che non ho ardito mai di por cosa del mio in pubblico" ("in order first to hear the opinion, or undergo the examination, of the educated, without which I would not dare put anything of mine in the public eye").[58]

Maffei's *Merope* demonstrates that the impact of theatrical practice on the creation of the public sphere was more profound than Habermas ever suspected. The tragedy explored here exemplifies how theatre, as a public art, is able to offer the spectator an opportunity for self-reflection. The theatre thus becomes a form of mediation between private and public, individual and collective. It is a place of discussion and debate in which socio-political thought can find free expression; it is an invaluable laboratory for political analysis and, also, for the creation of the public sphere. It is precisely to this vision of the relationship between theatrical practice and spectatorship that Abbot Jean-Baptiste Dubos gave voice in 1719 with the publication of his *Réflexions critiques sur la poésie et sur la peinture* (*Critical Reflections on Poetry and Painting*), a treatise that attributed absolute predominance to the judgment of the public. With the political nature of *Merope* more clearly revealed, we can now see that Maffei was a precocious interpreter and champion of change with regard to the eighteenth-century Italian public sphere.[59] The following chapters investigate how the playwrights after Maffei – building upon his innovation – demonstrated more forcibly to theatre-goers why public opinion mattered, encouraged the political participation of audiences, and taught spectators to employ increasingly sophisticated modes of political thinking.

4 Public Emotions and Emotional Publics

Carlo Gozzi's Theatrical Fables

L'amore delle tre melarance (*The Love of the Three Oranges*, 1761) is the first in a series of ten meta-theatrical fairy-tale plays by Carlo Gozzi (1720–1806). Calling the play a "favola fanciullesca" ("childish fable") entirely without serious parts ("ignuda affatto di parti serie"),[1] Gozzi also referred to it as "[il] racconto delle Nonne a' lor Nipotini, ridotta a scenica rappresentazione" ("[the] tale that grandmothers tell to their grandchildren, adapted to theatrical performance").[2] These statements suggest that the comedy was nothing more than the staging of an old folk tale; but the description of its avid and passionate public reception ("allegra rivoluzione strepitosa, e una diversione così grande nel Pubblico"; "resoundingly happy transformation [of the tale], and such an immense diversion for the Public")[3] suggests that *L'amore*'s admirers were not just victims of a collective hallucination caused by the *favola*'s overwhelming visual representations of marvellous and magical metamorphoses. Even its undisguised satire of contemporary theatrical polemics – specifically the on- and offstage controversies between Carlo Goldoni and Pietro Chiari (1712–85) on Italian comic theatre reform – can hardly explain the play's immense success with audiences both erudite and uncultured. All of this indicates that there was something more at stake in this fairy-tale comedy than its author would have us believe. Indeed, in his *Ragionamento ingenuo, e storia sincera dell'origine delle mie dieci fiabe teatrali* (*Ingenuous Disquisition, and Sincere History of My Ten Tales for the Theatre*, 1772) – and in blatant contradiction to his previous statements – Gozzi admitted that "la scelta de' titoli, e degli argomenti fanciulleschi non fu, che un'arte insidiosa" ("the choice of titles, and of childish topics, was nothing more than an insidious art"), thus implying that the play was layered with meaning beyond that which meets the eye.[4] Similarly, in his retrospective account of the play's genesis in *Le memorie inutili* (*The Useless Memoirs*, 1797), the playwright confessed that the comedy's novelty could not be reduced to its satirical subject matter.[5] *L'amore* was thus allegorical in the specifically eighteenth-century sense of allegory: the play was intended to have a second, non-literal significance.

The existence of this second layer of interpretation is stated outright in a review of *L'amore*'s première by the critic Gasparo Gozzi (1713–93), who observed that the playwright "ha avuta l'intenzione di coprire sotto il velo allegorico certi doppi sentimenti, e significati, che hanno una spiegazione diversa dalle cose, che vi sono espresse [...] Quelle novelluzze e bagatelle racchiudono non piccola dottrina" ("had the intention of covering, under an allegorical veil, certain double sentiments and meanings that have a different explanation from what is explicitly declared therein [...]. These novelties and frivolous matters contain no small amount of doctrine").[6] With his customary perspicacity Gasparo here raises a fundamental question: is this fairy-tale drama no more than a cocktail of narrative structures characteristic of folk tales, stock characters from *commedia dell'arte*, and topical allusions to Venetian theatrical warfare? It is significant that Gasparo, while emphasizing the novelty of his brother Carlo's work and seeing in it the rise of a new dramatic genre, shows no interest in the polemical aspect of the play. In any case, neither Gasparo's questioning of the comedy's presumed simplicity nor Carlo's claims (which occlude as much as they bring to light) seem to have attracted the critical attention of either eighteenth-century or more recent interpreters.[7] Drawn instead to the manifestly polemical form of the play,[8] the majority of its scholarly readers continue to insist that *L'amore* is little more than a satirical allegory of contemporary Venetian debates on the reform of comic theatre and an undistorted reflection of Gozzi's antagonistic and militant self-posturing.[9]

The polemic against Goldoni's and Chiari's psychologically realistic character comedies and their abandonment of *commedia dell'arte* undeniably occupies a central place in *L'amore delle tre melarance*. In fact, it was with this very play that Gozzi brought what had already been a vicious assault against his opponents to a new level of intensity and visibility by shifting his attack from pamphlet writings circulating mostly in manuscript form to the highly public stage of the playhouse.[10] But Gozzi's intentions went far beyond straightforwardly supporting a *commedia dell'arte* comeback at the expense of his antagonists: I would argue that the comedy is his artistic manifesto. As such, I assert in the following pages that *L'amore* aptly expresses not only Gozzi's ideas about theatre and spectatorship but also his socio-political and aesthetic concerns. Although it has been acknowledged by recent scholarship that the play's main sources lie in the fairy-tale and *commedia* traditions,[11] Gozzi's claim of having undertaken much "la fatica, e lo studio [...] in que' dieci sterilissimi argomenti, perché riuscissero opere non indegne d'un Pubblico" ("effort and study [...] on these ten most unproductive subjects, such that works not unworthy of an Audience [literally, "Public"] resulted")[12] hints at his relentless reflection on and appropriation of other philosophical, political, and aesthetic writings. What calls into question the presumed simplicity of the play – and explains its dense cross-references to texts not belonging to improvised comedy *canovacci* or to the fairy-tale tradition – is the fact that Gozzi casts the heated debates over Italian comic theatre reform in distinctively political terms. A reconstruction of the references in *L'amore* sheds new light on the genesis of Gozzi's theatrical tales and strengthens our grasp of his conception of entertainment. More broadly, such an approach highlights how traditions and ideas come into circulation and become accessible, revealing how the transmission of different forms of knowledge occurs. In addition, given the play's allegorical association of theatre-goers in the Venetian Republic with Gozzi's protagonist prince – who embodies the political antithesis of a republican citizenry – this chapter investigates the role of audiences and their responses in both eighteenth-century theatre practice and critical theory.

A Melancholy of My Own

In order to understand what is fundamentally at stake in Gozzi's project, we must begin by exploring the motif of the melancholic sovereign that catalyses the entire action of the comedy. Prince Tartaglia, the protagonist of the play – and an allegory of the Venetian public that audience members themselves would have recognized[13] – suffers from hypochondriac melancholy. This disease affects the mind and digestive organs of the King of Hearts' only son and heir; the illness was brought upon him, the audience is told, by two "melancholic poets" ("poeti [...] malinconic[i]"),[14] whom the author intended (and his audience understood) to be Carlo Goldoni and Pietro Chiari. At war with each other and disguised, respectively, as the magician Celio and the evil fairy Morgana, these two allegorical characters practise magic with political aims. Morgana promotes the cause of Tartaglia's antagonists (Princess Clarice and First Minister Leandro), who want to kill the prince and take his kingdom for themselves. Celio intends to defeat the plotters' plans by sending Truffaldino (who represents *commedia dell'arte*) to the court in order to heal the prince's malady by making him laugh. During feasts and spectacles set up to amuse Tartaglia, fountains of oil and wine are erected in front of the palace with the idea that seeing passers-by slipping and bumping into each other would cheer up the prince – and indeed this occurs: Tartaglia cannot control his laughter when he sees Morgana slip on the oil. Celio and Truffaldino's plan is thus successful, but their victory is short-lived. Infuriated by Truffaldino's insults and by Tartaglia's laughter, Morgana casts a spell that makes the prince fall in love with three magic oranges allegorically representing the three theatrical genres of comedy, tragedy, and improvised comedy. The quest for these oranges and their eventual acquisition fill the second and the third acts of the play. Predictably enough, *L'amore* ends with the cured prince's marriage to a maiden hidden inside one of the enchanted oranges – a figure who represents *commedia dell'arte.* In the overtly allegorical and self-reflexive dimension of the play, therefore, the melancholy prince represents the Venetian audience, which is increasingly bored with the reformed plays of Goldoni and Chiari – plays that consciously suppressed improvised comedy. I argue that the prince's quest for the enchanted oranges allegorizes not only Gozzi's resuscitation of the *commedia dell'arte* tradition in order to revitalize Italian comic theatre but also Tartaglia's evolution as a spectator from passive observer to critically productive audience member.

Every time Gozzi refers to the sources of his fairy-tale drama, he claims to be faithful to the folk tradition, and Angelo Fabrizi has compellingly demonstrated that *L'amore* corresponds directly to northern Italian folk tales in several places (including the archetype of the prince who no longer laughs).[15] At the same time, melancholy has its own distinct cultural history. Considered by ancient medical doctrine to be a disorder arising from an imbalance in the body's four humours, melancholy came to denote a psychological state and even to acquire a certain intellectual prestige, eventually becoming a subject of fascination that inspired numerous artistic works. As Jean Starobinski puts it, melancholy had a long career,[16] and by the time it arrived on the early modern stage and printed page it was at once understood as a symptom of sickness, a form of madness, a feeling of sadness, a marker of acute intelligence, a way of perceiving the world, a mode of self-fashioning, and a type of personality.[17] Jennifer Radden claims that melancholy was a central cultural idea that served to focus, explain, and organize the way people saw the world and one another.[18] To expose the reasons why this malady was a productive choice for Gozzi is therefore particularly illuminating for our understanding of both the complex artistic personality of this Venetian playwright and the genesis of his new genre of fairy-tale plays.

The first and the most obvious significance of Tartaglia's humoral disease is explained by Gozzi himself in his "reflexive analysis": the prince's "lethal hypochondriacal symptom" ("mortale effetto ipocondriaco")[19] is brought on by his ingestion and subsequent digestion of the Martellian verses employed by Goldoni and Chiari in their dramatic works. In the undisguised allegorical context of the play, the prince's melancholy can be read as a physical manifestation of the emotional frustration of the character himself – and, by extension, of the play's audience – with the forms of theatre promoted by Gozzi's rival playwrights. Chiari, disguised as the "Queen of Hypochondria" Morgana, is a particular target of Gozzi's parody, as is made plain by a comic scene in the first act in which Tartaglia complains about his symptoms to Truffaldino, and in which the audience would easily have recognized Chiari's hypochondriac *malade imaginaire* Trifone from *Le sorelle rivali* (*The Rival Sisters,* 1755).[20]

There is, however, a significant difference between Gozzi's melancholic prince and his counterpart in *Le sorelle rivali.* Chiari's Trifone is a comic figure, and no attempt is made to elicit other characters' sympathy for his sufferings, which are instead deemed dubious and are repeatedly called into question.[21] Although Gozzi's universe is undeniably comic, the initial situation in *L'amore* is potentially tragic: Tartaglia's condition is contagious and lethal; it is analogous to the diseased society to which it is, simultaneously, a response.[22] Indeed, Truffaldino is summoned to court in order "preservare il re, il figliolo, e tutti que' popoli dal morbo degli accennati brevi [in versi martelliani]" ("to preserve the king, his son, and all those people from the contagious disease of the aforementioned [Martellian verses]").[23] Thus, as Socrates hints in Plato's *Symposium* (223c–d), a comic catastrophe that makes us laugh may at any moment take a turn for the serious and have a real, felt impact on individuals and society. What further elicits audience sympathy for Tartaglia and inspires respect for his (almost) heroic stance is that melancholy in *L'amore* is both a political ploy and a weapon aimed at ruining the kingdom and killing the prince. This being the case, we might legitimately inquire whence positive connotations of the prince's melancholy come and why Gozzi incorporates political terminology in his description of physical disease. Indeed, why set a play about public theatre in republican Venice at an imaginary absolutist court characterized by conspiracy and treacherous intrigues?

A Fashionable Malady

By the eighteenth century, melancholy was not only identified as a physical and mental disorder; it also had a long-standing positive association with genius, which can be traced back to the (pseudo-)Aristotelian discussion of melancholy in the *Problemata physica*. Chapter 30.1 of the *Problemata* begins by posing a problem: "Why is it that all men who have become outstanding in philosophy, statesmanship, poetry or the arts are melancholic and some to such an extent that they are infected by the disease arising from black bile as the story of Heracles among the heroes tells?"[24] In answering this question, Aristotle departs from the Hippocratic and Galenic model, arguing that melancholy is the natural temperament of those in whom black bile "naturally" predominates, and seeing it as a sign of extraordinary brilliance. Aristotle thus reinterpreted the entire problem of the melancholic disposition in terms of a condition of greatness; his examples of outstanding men afflicted by melancholy – Lysander, Ajax, Bellerophontes, Plato, Socrates, and Empedocles – indeed established the archetype of the melancholy man, who was likely to be a philosopher, poet, artist, or politician.

The Renaissance revival of antiquity and Marsilio Ficino's pronouncement that all men of genius and learning were melancholic to some degree[25] brought about the early modern notion of melancholy as a mark of superior social and intellectual status.[26] Shakespeare's Hamlet is perhaps the most conspicuous example of the transformation of melancholy into a preferred malady for many aristocrats and kings.

The authority of the (pseudo-)Aristotelian account that established a positive correlation between melancholy and artistic genius proved irresistible over the centuries, and explains Gozzi's fascination with this elite malady. Indeed, the playwright frequently fashioned himself as a melancholy man both in his memoirs[27] and in his private correspondence (under the pen name *il Solitario*, "the Solitary") as a member of the Granelleschi Academy. Fabio Soldini has pointed out that Gozzi's letters abound with self-representations of a withdrawn intellectual prone to hypochondria – to the point that he actually titled his correspondence the "Gazzette ipocondriache."[28]

Although the (pseudo-)Aristotelian emphasis on melancholy's intellectual prestige clearly offered an attractive model for Gozzi's self-fashioning (as well as for the portrayal of some melancholic characters in his works),[29] this model should not be regarded as the direct source for the melancholy prince in *L'amore*. Indeed, Tartaglia's condition is not "natural" (since it is caused by external circumstances), nor can the (pseudo-)Aristotelian account (according to which melancholy is a distinctive sign of the select few) explain why the prince is an allegory for the entire Venetian public. Rather, in his staging of Tartaglia's malady Gozzi interwove seventeenth- and early-eighteenth-century references to melancholy – and, more specifically, drew upon Blaise Pascal's and Jean-Baptiste Dubos's reflections on *ennui* and *divertissement*. The next section will explore these sources and their implications for Gozzi and his audiences.

Un roi sans divertissement[30]

Aristotle's question continued to intrigue and trouble not only the Renaissance, "the golden age of melancholy," but also the Baroque, which was replete with literary, dramatic, and pictorial representations of the melancholic condition. In fact, in the *Ursprung des deutschen Trauerspiels* (*The Origin of German Tragic Drama*, 1928), Walter Benjamin detects in melancholy a characteristic feature of the Baroque *zeitgeist* and of the German mourning play in particular.[31] Benjamin invokes Pascal as a central witness who "gives voice to [this] feeling of his age,"[32] making reference to the *Pensées*'s fragment on "un roi sans divertissement."[33] It is worth quoting this passage at length, since the connection that Pascal establishes between melancholy and sovereignty constitutes an important precedent for Gozzi's portrayal of his melancholic prince.

> La dignité royale n'est-elle pas assez grande d'elle-même, pour celui qui la possède, pour le rendre heureux par la seule vue de ce qu'il est? Faudra-t-il le divertir de cette pensée come les gens du commun? Je vois bien que c'est rendre un homme heureux de le divertir de la vue de ses misères domestiques pour remplir toute sa pensée du soin de bien danser, mais en sera-t-il de même d'un roi, et sera-t-il plus heureux en s'attachant à ses vains amusements qu'à la vue de sa grandeur, et quel objet plus satisfaisant pourrait-on donner à son esprit? Ne serait-ce donc pas faire tort à sa joie d'occuper son âme à penser à ajuster ses pas à la cadence d'un air ou à place adroitement une barre, au lieu de le laisser jouir en repos de la contemplation de la gloire majestueuse qui l'environne? Qu'on en fasse l'épreuve. Qu'on laisse un roi tout seul sans aucune satisfaction des sens, sans aucun soin dans l'esprit, sans compagnies, penser à lui tout à loisir, et l'on verra qu'un

> roi sans divertissement est un homme plein de misère. Aussi on évite ce la soigneusement et il ne manque jamais d'y avoir auprès des personnes des rois un grand nombre de gens qui veillent à faire succéder le divertissement à leur affaires, et qui observent tout le temps de leur loisir pour leur fournir des plaisirs et des jeux, en sorte qu'il n'y ait point de vide. C'est-à-dire qu'ils sont environnés de personnes qui ont un soin merveilleux de prendre garde que le roi ne soit seul et en état de penser à soi, sachant bien qu'il sera misérable, tout roi qu'il est, s'il y pense. (Laf. 136)[34]
>
> Is not the royal dignity sufficiently great in itself to make its possessor happy by the mere sight of what he is? Must he be diverted from this thought like ordinary people? I quite see that it makes a man happy to be diverted from thinking about his domestic woes by filling his thoughts with the concern to dance well. But will it be the same with a king, and will he be happier in the pursuit of these idle amusements than in considering his greatness? And what more satisfactory object could be presented to his mind? Would it not spoil his delight to occupy his soul with the thought of how to adjust his steps to the rhythm of a tune, or how to place a bar skillfully, instead of leaving him to enjoy quietly the contemplation of the majestic glory surrounding him? Let us test this. Let us leave a king all alone to reflect on himself at his leisure, without anything to satisfy his senses, without any care in his mind, without company, and we will see that a king without diversion is a man full of miseries. So this is carefully avoided; there never fail to be a great number of people near the retinues of kings, people who see to it that diversion follows the kings' affairs of state, watching over their leisure to supply them with pleasures and games, so that they have no empty moments. In other words, they are surrounded by people who take wonderful care to insure that the king is not alone and able to think about himself, knowing well that he will be miserable, though he is king, if he does think about it.[35]

Pascal argues that the peaceful contemplation of royal glory cannot be a satisfying way for a prince to fill his time, nor it is enough to make him happy. Without his affairs of state and diversions, the prince will be miserable, since he will inevitably end up "penser à soi." As Pascal goes on to explain, self-contemplation brings the prince to realize that his mortal human nature prevails over his immortal body politic, and that he is thus no different from his subjects. It is as if his supreme position among men, instead of making him less human, makes him even more fragile and miserable: "un homme plein de misère." The prince's recognition that his greatness only underscores his "condition faible et mortelle" presents itself through what Benjamin calls melancholy and Pascal terms *ennui*. Thus, by implicitly providing yet another answer to the Aristotelian question as to why rulers are melancholic, Pascal – as Benjamin puts it – makes the sovereign "the paradigm of the melancholy man."[36]

What, however, differentiates the Pascalian discussion of melancholy from the (pseudo-)Aristotelian account – and what makes it relevant for our understanding of Gozzi's association of the prince with the theatre-going public – is that, for Pascal, melancholy is, rather than a rare and distinguishing feature of the chosen few, a common human condition. Indeed, his example of "un roi sans divertissement" highlights that man is born into the condition of *ennui*, and that no one can escape from it – not even a prince.[37] In the *Pensées*, Pascal in fact maintains that human existence is defined by the impossibility of complete rest: "tout le malheur des hommes vient d'une seule chose, qui est de ne savoir pas demeurer en repos dans une chambre" (Laf. 136; "man's unhappiness arises from one thing alone: that he cannot remain quietly in his room," Ari. 38). For Pascal, *ennui* thus represents the external manifestation of human nature's inner restlessness and lack of self-sufficiency. *Ennui*, moreover, is what renders the human condition intolerable and is the very root of man's *misère*:

> Rien n'est si insupportable à l'homme que d'être dans un plein repos, sans passions, sans affaires, sans divertissement, sans application. Il sent alors son néant, son abandon, son insuffisance, sa dépendance, son impuissance, son vide. Incontinent il sortira du fond de son âme l'ennui, la noirceur, la tristesse, le chagrin, le dépit, le désespoir. (Laf. 622)

> Nothing is so intolerable for man as to be in complete tranquillity, without passions, without dealings, without diversion, without effort. He then feels his nothingness, isolation, insufficiency, dependence, weakness, emptiness. Immediately there arises from the depth of his soul boredom, gloom, sadness, chagrin, resentment, despair. (Ari. 163)

Man therefore tries to escape the source of his unhappiness and disquiet through *divertissement*, which gives him momentary relief:

> La seule chose qui nous console de nos misère est le divertissement, et cependant c'est la plus grande des nos misères. Car c'est qui nous empêche principalement de songer à nous, et qui nous fait perdre insensiblement. Sans cela, nous serions dans l'ennui, et cet ennui nous pousserait à chercher un moyen plus solide d'en sortir. Mais le divertissement nous amuse, et nous fait arriver insensiblement à la mort. (Laf. 414)

> The only thing that consoles us for our miseries is diversion, and yet this is the greatest of our miseries. For it is mainly what prevents us from thinking about ourselves, leading us imperceptibly to our ruin. Without it we would be bored, and this boredom would drive us to seek a more solid means of escape. But diversion amuses us and guides us imperceptibly to death. (Ari. 6)

Pascalian *divertissement* is thus a mechanism by which man seeks to avoid both awareness of his unhappiness and meditation on his mortality. Entertainments – such as gambling, billiards, or sporting events – do not bring him happiness in themselves, but they can at least becloud the uneasiness of existence and alleviate its inherent *ennui*.

Two opposing attitudes towards *divertissement* are discernible throughout the fragments of the *Pensées*. On the one hand, its meaning is almost always negative ("la plus grande des nos misères"), for in the logic of Pascal's unfinished apology all human pleasures are essentially corrupt. Since diversions and pleasures are inseparable from man's fallen state, they only intensify his disquietude in his state of wretchedness without God: "Si l'homme était heureux, il le serait d'autant plus qu'il serait moins diverti, comme les saints et Dieu" (Laf. 132; "If man were happy, the less diverted the happier he would be, like the Saints and God," Ari. 38). At times, however, Pascal invests *divertissement* with positive meaning, since it is what allows men to forget their all-encompassing sense of *ennui* ("sans cela, nous serions dans l'ennui," Laf. 414). The Pascalian notion of diversion thus includes the more literal notion of turning away from one's concerns and of keeping one's mind off worrying topics: "Si notre condition était véritablement heureuse, il ne faudrait pas nous divertir d'y penser" (Laf. 70; "If our condition were truly happy, we would not need to divert ourselves from thinking about it," Ari. 22). As Nicholas Hammond has argued, Pascal "returns to the etymological sense of *divertir*, that of 'action de détourner, de se détourner,' a meaning that was hardly apparent in seventeenth-century usage of the term."[38]

What is also worth noting, before we return to Gozzi's play, is Pascal's choice of theatrical imagery to describe the human condition as well as the distinctively theatrical connotations of *divertissement*.[39] The end of human life is perceived by Pascal as both theatrical and tragic – "le dernier acte est sanglant, quelque belle que soit la comédie en tout le reste" (Laf. 165; "the final act is bloody, however lovely all the rest of the play is")[40] – and Pascal views life offstage more generally as equally theatrical in nature.

A reflection on melancholy and entertainment runs along strikingly similar lines in writings by Gozzi that reconstruct the genealogy of his dramatic works. A passage from *Le memorie inutili*, for instance, recalls his public reading of *L'amore* for the Accademia dei Granelleschi before submitting the "script" to Antonio Sacchi's comic troupe.[41] Describing his discussion with the Granelleschi members (who advised him against staging the play, predicting its instant failure and challenging his daring theatrical innovation), *il Solitario* recounts how he rejected their criticism by arguing that

> conveniva *assalire l'intero Pubblico sul Teatro per cagionare una scossa di diversione.* Ch'io donava, e non vendeva il mio tentativo di nobile vendetta all'Accademica vilipesa a torto, e che le loro Signorie intelligentissime di coltura, d'esattezza, e di buoni libri, *conoscevano molto male il genere umano, e i nostri simili.*

> It was worth *assaulting the entire Audience in the Theatre in order to cause a jolt of diversion.* Because I gave and did not wrongly sell my attempt at noble revenge against the despised Academics, and because their Signorias, [which are] most intelligent with regard to culture, precision, and good books, *very poorly comprehended humankind, and ours as well.*[42]

Two aspects are important to emphasize here. First, Gozzi's defence of his comedy is grounded neither on the efficacy of the allegorical fairy-tale formula for the purposes of anti-Goldoni and anti-Chiari revolt nor on the necessity of theatre reform. Rather, *il Solitario* refers to his knowledge of humankind, closely mirroring Pascalian reflections on the "condition de l'homme." Second, Gozzi invests the diversionary effect ("scossa di diversione") that he intends to trigger among the play's spectators with the Pascalian etymological force of a *divertissement* capable of turning the audience's attention away from its unpleasant concerns. This conception of theatrical entertainment as an activity designed to provide relief from the tediousness of life is intensified in his *Prefazione al "Fajel"*:

> L'umanità per lo più oppressa dalle amare circostanze, e dagli acerbi pensieri, concorre alla Commedia per trarne qualche sollievo. Nella Tragedia ella lo riceve insensibilmente dal vedere i Principi soggetti alle passioni, alle debolezze, alle afflizioni, ed a tutte quelle miserie che eguagliano la umanità.

> Humankind, burdened with sad circumstances and bitter thoughts, comes to the Comedy to get some relief. In Tragedy it gets [relief] from watching

> the princes be subjected to passions, weakness, afflictions, and all these miseries that are the same for all humankind.[43]

What puts the theatre-goers "on the trail of diversions" ("in traccia di divertimenti") and makes them "eager for new productions" ("bramos[i] di produzioni novelle"),[44] therefore, is less their hedonistic impulses or insatiable longing for novelty (which is understandable, considering the flooded Venetian theatre market) than the audience's need to be distracted from the many anxieties of daily life: "amare circostanze, e [...] acerbi pensieri" and "tutte quelle miserie che eguagliano la umanità."

Gozzi's tragic vision of the human condition, which lurks behind his ruminations on theatre, thus directly evokes Pascalian *divertissement* as a means by which man can distract himself from "a thousand mishaps, which cause inevitable distress" ("mille accidents, qui font les afflictions inévitables," Laf. 132). The playwright's assertion is even more remarkable, since it is anomalous in the context of seventeenth- and eighteenth-century dramatic criticism, "which tended to evoke the deterrent value of theatre as compared to other (dissolute) diversions, or its ethico-cognitive function."[45] The anomalous nature of Gozzi's arguments supports the notion that his position shared a deep affinity with Pascalian theories of *ennui* and *divertissement.* If, as Gasparo Gozzi observed, the play stemmed from the idea of a game ("Que' Re di Coppe, que' Maghi, quegli scompigli, quelle malinconie, quelle allegrezze dinotano le vicende del giuoco, e l'incantesimo or buono, ora contrario delle fortuna in esso"; "Those Kings of Cups, those Magicians, those confusing muddles, those melancholic and exhilarating moments express the moves of the game and the enchantment of fortune that is at times good, at times the contrary, in [the game]"),[46] it can be argued that the playwright's portrayal of the entire world in terms of mere card-playing represents a dramatization of the Pascalian concept of *divertissement.* Indeed, far from simply mirroring the Venetian obsession with gambling (as has been proposed by DiGaetani, among other scholars),[47] this idea is clearly traceable back to Pascal, who saw *divertissement* as encapsulating "not only the pursuit of particular pleasures such as gambling and hunting, but a whole way of life."[48]

Gozzi's affinities with Pascal are so suggestive that it does not seem unreasonable to argue that, although the playwright was employing the fairy tale as his mode of storytelling, in his reflections on the function of theatrical entertainment he was actually looking to Pascal for insight. Of course, parallels and points of resemblance between two authors, however significant, do not constitute proof of influence. Since Gozzi never explicitly referred to the French philosopher in any of his writings nor kept any volume of Pascal's works in his library,[49] the question remains as to whether Gozzi actually read the *Pensées.*[50] Nonetheless, it has recently been demonstrated that the playwright was familiar with (and influenced by) the 1719 *Réflexions critiques sur la poésie et sur la peinture* by Jean-Baptiste Dubos (1670–1742).[51] This treatise, authored by a learned diplomat, historian, and member of the Académie Française, was one of the most widely circulated works of the eighteenth century;[52] it marked a turning point in both theatre and art criticism by inaugurating proto-reception theory and modern aesthetics. What is crucial to emphasize here is that the underlying principle of Dubos's entire aesthetic theory in the *Réflexions critiques* is that of Pascalian *ennui* and the need to escape it.[53] Dubos, however, secularizes the Pascalian concept, moving the debate from knowledge of God to the role of literature and the visual arts in providing man with an escape from tedium.[54] In fact, Dubos begins his treatise by claiming that *ennui,* also envisaged here as a languid state of indolence or mental inactivity, is one of the most unpleasant aspects of the human condition:

> L'ame a ses besoins comme le corps; & l'un des plus grands besoins de l'homme, est celui d'avoir l'esprit occupé. L'ennui qui suit bientôt l'inaction de l'ame, est un mal si douloureux pour l'homme, qu'il entreprend souvent les travaux les plus pénibles, afin de s'épargner la peine d'en être tourmenté.[55]

> The soul hath its wants no less than the body; and one of the greatest wants of man is to have his mind incessantly occupied. The heaviness which quickly attends the inactivity of the mind, is a situation so very disagreeable to man, that he frequently chooses to expose himself to the most painful exercises, rather than be troubled with it.[56]

Dubos maintains that arousal of the passions is one of the most effective means of dispelling boredom. Arguing that any engaging spectacle – from gladiatorial combat and public executions to less frightful and bloody diversions, such as gambling or watching tragedies on stage – might prove pleasant to spectators to the extent that it diverts them from *ennui,* Dubos goes on to connect the importance of the arts with their capacity to provide pleasant relief from the tedium of everyday life: "ces phantômes de passions que la Poësie & la Peinture sçavent exciter, en nous émouvant par les imitations qu'elles nous présentent, satisfont au besoin où nous sommes d'être occupés" (I.3, 27; "those imaginary passions which poetry and painting raise artificially within us, by means of their imitations, satisfy that natural want we have of being employed," I.5, 22). According to the French aesthetician, the passions to which works of art give rise are able to keep men occupied – and do so without causing suffering – since they are only superficial "phantômes de passions" with meagre strength and of short duration.[57] Dubos consequently defines the excellence of an artwork in relation to its capacity to impact the beholder – and to the resulting effect, namely art's capacity to please and excite the passions, exposing viewers to virtuous models that might help them know themselves better and encourage them to emulate good behaviours.

When Gozzi represented the Venetian audience's disappointment with the dramatic works of Goldoni and Chiari through the allegory of Tartaglia's melancholy, he was articulating the inspiration he drew from Dubos's elaboration of the Pascalian themes of *ennui* and *divertissement*.[58] Like Dubos, Gozzi advocated for a form of theatre that enhances the spectator's sensory pleasure and satisfies a very human need to be diverted from melancholy:

> Collo sguardo sull'Italia, e spezialmente sopra a Venezia, di cui mi vanto buon Cittadino; ho ordite, e composte forse venti rappresentazioni teatrali di nuovo e bizzarro aspetto, ed ho avuto l'ardire di farle esporre sulle nostre scene *coll'unico desiderio di giovare, e di divertire.*
>
> Il vedere i grandi che reggono, i Cittadini colti, e il minuto popolo d'un Pubblico ch'io amo, *occupati, ed attenti in vari apparecchi d'innesti,* ch'io mi sono ingegnato a proccurare che sieno cangianti, e proporzionati a tutti quegl'intelletti differenti che compongono un Uditorio, fu il compenso non meritato de' miei spettacoli teatrali, quali si sieno.

> With my eye upon Italy, and especially upon Venice (of which I pride myself on being a good Citizen), I formulated and composed about twenty plays of a new and bizarre kind, and I had the courage to have them performed on our stages *with the sole desire to please and to entertain.*
>
> To see the great who rule, the cultured Citizens, and the small [lower-class] people of a Public that I love, *absorbed in, and attentive to various interpretive devices* that I designed to provoke in order that they be changeable and proportional to all those different minds of which an Audience is composed, was undeserved compensation for my theatrical spectacles, such as they are.[59]

The fact that Gozzi echoes Dubos's ruminations on the role of artwork-as-*divertissement* allows us to see more clearly the value that the playwright ascribes to theatrical entertainment. If theatre, according to Gozzi's own definition, is an "enclosure of diversion" ("recinto di divertimento"),[60] it is not because watching a play is a vain and mindless leisure activity. Instead, it is because the theatre allows its audience to be temporarily relieved of the tedium of humanity's earth-bound existence.

Una artifiziosa difficile illusione[61]

Gozzi's critical engagement with Pascal's and Dubos's ideas elucidates why, for the playwright, the most important aspect of theatre was the entertainment of the audience. Why, then, did Venetian cultural life – so vibrant and intense that it rendered the entire society "nauseata de' piaceri" ("sick of pleasures")[62] – and the various forms of theatre available – ranging from character comedies to translations of French *drames bourgeois* and *comédies larmoyantes* – remain incapable of diverting spectators from their *ennui*? Why, specifically, did Goldoni's and Chiari's realistic plays fail to create a dramatic illusion that would emotionally engage spectators – fail, indeed, to the extent that they became the target of Gozzi's parody in *L'amore*? These two queries raise yet another set of questions: How and why did Gozzi come to conceive his "nuovi generi di mirabile, e di forte passione" ("new, marvellous, and strongly passionate genres")[63] precisely when Italian dramatists were searching for a model that would revitalize Italian theatre in French dramatic practice, unable as this practice was to do justice to the onstage manifestation of magic and the marvellous? (Indeed, magic and the *merveilleux* were deemed inappropriate for onstage representation by French Enlightenment dramatists and critics in particular, who dismissed fantastic spectacles as disruptive of the illusion created by theatre.)[64] In other words, what – in enlightened eighteenth-century Venice, which was dominated by mistrust of the irrational and by abandonment of the world of illusions – made Gozzi convinced that "la passione del mirabile [...] sarà sempre la regina di tutte le umane passioni" ("the passion of the wondrous [...] will always be the queen of all human passions")?[65]

If Tartaglia's melancholy represents Gozzi's and the audience's discontent with Goldoni's and Chiari's plays, revisiting the fundamental points of disagreement between Gozzi and his adversaries would seem a logical next step in attempting to answer these queries. These more general considerations of Gozzi's poetics will also bring us closer to answering the question raised at the outset: Why is the (republican) audience's emotional response to art translated, in *L'amore*, into the sovereignty of a prince?

Since Gozzi considered Chiari to be merely the Plagiarist (*il Saccheggio*), a blind and talentless imitator of Goldoni, we will focus primarily on the aesthetic grounds of the quarrel between Gozzi and Goldoni. The latter notoriously claimed – in the preface to the Bettinelli edition of his works (1750), the most well-known exposition of his poetics of drama – that "[q]uanto si rappresenta sul Teatro […] non deve essere se non la copia di quanto accade nel Mondo" ("what is represented in Theatre […] should not be other than a copy of what happens in the world").[66] He also made it plain that "sopra del maraviglioso, la vince nel cuor dell'uomo il semplice, il naturale" ("over the marvellous, the simple and natural wins in the heart of man").[67] From Goldoni's standpoint, theatre is continuous with life, and its heroes have the capacity to reflect their times. In his *Teatro comico* (*Comic Theatre*, 1750) – a comedy that he defined as "poétique mise en action" ("poetics put into action") and designed as a model for Italian theatre reform – Goldoni claimed that comedy should have a "stile familiare, naturale e facile, per non distaccarci dal verisimile" ("familiar, natural, and easy style, in order not to depart from the verisimilar").[68] He therefore staged such an accurate representation of domestic life that the audience was convinced it was watching real events affecting real people during the performance. The aesthetic illusion he sought to produce required an error of perception: he hoped his spectators were deceived, if only for a moment, into mistaking art for reality.

It is this conception of the role of dramatic illusion that constitutes the fundamental point of disagreement between Gozzi and Goldoni. According to the former, the latter was oriented wrongly from the beginning because his plays were an onstage facsimile of real life:

> [Goldoni] espose sul Teatro tutte quelle verità che gli si pararono dinanzi, ricopiate materialmente, e trivialmente, e non imitate dalla natura, né coll'eleganza necessaria ad uno Scrittore.
>
> Non seppe, o non volle separare le verità che si devono, da quelle che non si devono porre in vista sopra un Teatro; ma si è regolato con quel solo principio che la verità piace sempre.

> [Goldoni] presented onstage all the truths that he saw in front of him, copied out in a rough and trivial manner and imitated neither from nature, nor with the elegance necessary for a Writer.
>
> He did not know [how], or did not want, to separate the truths that one must bring onto the stage from those that one must not, but [instead] ruled himself with the sole principle that the truth always pleases.[69]

Goldoni was convinced that only a dramatic work that holds a mirror up to life and nature can please its spectators; Gozzi, in contrast – drawing on Pascalian *divertissement* – believed instead that theatre should provide a type of illusion that allows theatre-goers to avoid seeing reality as it is. For Gozzi, therefore, it was important that playwrights represent their characters and their adventures on stage as overtly fictitious, and that the action take place in a world of pure fantasy. If the human condition is indeed miserable, a universe visibly distinct from the one actually inhabited by the play's spectators will seem to them more interesting, more believable, and more intoxicating than their own reality. From this perspective, the setting of an imaginary realm populated by princes and kings is not an expression of Gozzi's reactionary and aristocratic ideology. Rather, it is indicative of his perceived need to create an unambiguous dissimilarity between the action onstage and the world from which that action draws its inspiration.

Gozzi was not unconditionally opposed to Goldoni's imitation of the real world, however. Instead, he was reacting against the trivial, graceless, and thoughtless copying of nature ("ricopiate materialmente, e trivialmente, e non imitate dalla natura"):

> Moltissime delle sue Commedie non sono, che un ammasso di scene, le quali contengono delle verità, ma delle verità tanto vili, goffe, e fangose, che, quantunque abbiano divertito anche me medesimo animate dagli attori, non seppi giammai accomodare nella mia mente, che uno Scrittore dovesse umiliarsi a ricopiarle nelle più basse pozzanghere del volgo, né come potesse aver l'ardire d'innalzarle alla decorazione d'un Teatro, e sopratutto come potesse aver fronte di porre alle stampe per esemplari delle vere pidocchierie.

> Many of [Goldoni's] comedies are no more than an agglomeration of scenes that contain truths, but truths so base, clumsy, and sloppy, that, however much they might have entertained even me [when] brought to life by actors, I don't remotely know how to make space in my mind for the notion that a Writer must humiliate himself by copying truths from the lowest, most vulgar mud puddles, nor how he could dare raise them up to ornament a Theatre, and above all how he could have the courage to place them with publishers as specimens of real garbage.[70]

Gozzi thus advocates a theatre that can provide its audience with more than just a perfect facsimile of the mundane world. As follows from his synthetic description of what his theatrical tales present – namely "una forte passione, un seriofaceto, una chiara allegoria, una critica ragionata, la morale" ("a strong passion, a serious facetiousness, a clear allegory, a reasoned critique, morality")[71] – he argues for a dramatic form that offers the true and the fantastical in a combination that both pleases spectators (through its dramatic marvels) and shows them something true to nature (through its realism).

According to Gozzi, Goldoni's approach was also wrong because verisimilar drama could not emotionally engage the audience: "[la materia teatrale] ridotta questa al vero, e alla natura piacque, ma piacque sino al nascere di quella noia ch'è naturale negli uomini, spezialmente nelle cose di voluttà" ("[theatrical subject matter], reduced to truth and to nature, was pleasing, but it was pleasing [precisely] from the birth of that boredom that is natural in men, especially in matters of delight").[72] And, furthermore, "la noia ne' popoli fu una conseguenza di queste ristrette regole, e molti Scrittori teatrali, ostinatisi in queste, empierono le opere di maggiori assurdi che non le avrieno empiute, se se ne fossero dispensati" ("boredom among the people was a consequence of these restrictive rules, and many Playwrights, [who] persisted in [following] these rules, filled their works with great absurdities that [Writers for theatre] would not have filled [their works] with, if it had not been permitted").[73]

In Gozzi's quarrel with Goldoni's adherence to verisimilitude, the imprint of Dubos's aesthetic arguments (as presented in the *Réflexions critiques*) is clearly discernible. And in fact, in addition to its concern with the centrality of the emotional appeal of the arts, Dubos's treatise marked a turning point in debates on the problem of *vraisemblance*. Reacting against neoclassical doctrine, Dubos was the first to disconnect the pleasure produced by dramatic illusion from the imitation of reality, remaining convinced that the theatre's engendering of pleasure in the spectator was not triggered by the illusion of reality:

> Des personnes d'esprit ont cru que l'illusion était la première cause du plaisir que nous donnent les spectacles & les tableaux. Suivant leur sentiment, la représentation du *Cid* ne nous donne tant de plaisir que par l'illusion qu'elle nous fait. Les vers du grand Corneille, l'appareil de la Scène et la déclamation des Acteurs nous en imposent assez pour nous faire croire, qu'au lieu d'assister à la représentation de l'événement, nous assistons à l'événement même, & que nous voyons réellement l'action, & non pas une imitation. Cette opinion me paroît insoutenable. (I.43, 451)[74]

> 'Tis the opinion of several men of sense, that the pleasure we receive from spectacles and pictures is merely the effect of illusion. Pursuant to their way of thinking, the representation of the Cid affords us so much pleasure merely thro' the illusion that deceives us. The verses of the great Corneille, the apparatus of the scenes, and the declamation of the actors, impose upon us so as to make us believe, that instead of assisting at the representation of the event, we are present at the event itself, and that we really see the action, and not the imitation. But this opinion seems to me to be quite unwarrantable. (I.43, 349)

Dubos thus substituted the values of *vraisemblance* with those of sentiment and emotion, espousing a radically new approach to understanding our relationship to art. Rather than looking for beauty in a work's objective qualities or in its conformity with established aesthetic rules, he argued that the real measure of art's perfection lies instead in the reaction it elicits from its observer:

> Non seulement le public juge d'un ouvrage sans intérêt, mais il en juge encore ainsi qu'il en faut décider en général, c'est-à-dire, par la voie du sentiment, & suivant l'impression que le poëme ou le tableau font sur lui. Puisque le premier but de la Poësie & de la Peinture est de nous toucher, les poëmes & les tableaux ne son de bons ouvrages qu'à proportion qu'ils nous émeuvent & qu'ils nous attachent. Un ouvrage qui touche beaucoup, doit être excellent à tout prendre. Par la même raison l'ouvrage qui ne touche point & qui n'attache pas, ne vaut rien; & si la critique n'y trouve point à reprendre des fautes contre les règles c'est qu'un ouvrage peut être mauvais, sans qu'il y ait des fautes contre les règles, comme un ouvrage plein de fautes contre les règles, peut être un ouvrage excellent. (II.22, 339–40)

> The public gives not only a disinterested judgment of a work, but judges likewise what opinion we are to entertain of it in general, by means of the sense, and according to the impression made thereon by the poem or picture. Since the chief end of poetry and painting is to move us, the productions of these arts can be valuable only in proportion as they touch and engage us. A work that is exquisitely moving, must be an excellent piece, take it all together. For the same reason, a work which does not move and engage us, is good for nothing; and if it be not obnoxious to criticism for trespassing against rules, 'tis because it may be bad, without any violation of rules; as on the contrary one full of faults against rules, may be an excellent performance. (II.22, 237)

Dubos believed, moreover, that the audience forms its judgment by relying not on reason or on a code of fixed rules but on sentiment and taste; he was the first to point out that drama is effective only if it evokes strong emotions. Dubos thus initiated a new trend in critical thinking: before him, critical reviews had formulated their judgment of a given dramatic work in terms of its aesthetic merit, but from the mid-eighteenth century on, works of art started to be evaluated based instead on their effect upon spectators. Public response thus began to rival specialist judgment as the predominant arbiter of the quality of theatrical performances.

These ideas appear to have had a most profound effect on Gozzi, who maintained that "è bello sol tra noi quello che piace" ("only what pleases us is beautiful") and that "[il] Pubblico ha somma ragione di allettarsi di ciò che lo alletta, e di non voler cadere negli effetti ipocondriaci" ("the Public has the supreme right to be fascinated by what fascinates it and to wish not to be affected by hypochondria").[75] He was thus convinced that the audience relies upon the emotional appeal of theatre in making its judgments, and – much like Dubos, who argued that the opinions of the *doctes*, which were based upon rational reasoning, led to false conclusions – empowered the public with an ability to decide for itself: "senza distinzioni di teste, il Pubblico intero ha una ragione comperata, di trovar cosa che lo intrattenga, e lo diverta" ("without any distinction, the whole Public has bought the full right to expect entertainment and amusement").[76]

I suggest that acknowledging Gozzi's placement of public opinion at the forefront of the theatrical enterprise opens up new perspectives on his dramaturgy. His theatrical fables might appear to be nothing more than an antidote to (and an attack on) Goldoni's shallow, predictable, and impoverished constructions of reality, but this is only a superficial reading. Gozzi's plays also provided him with an excellent means to compete for the favour of the Venetian audience (which thrived on scandal and novelty); but even this was not his sole purpose. As Gasparo Gozzi observed in another review of his brother's plays, with a reference to the Aristotelian theory of catharsis, "le trasformazioni e la maraviglia servono a maneggiare la passione" ("the transformations and the marvellous serve to manage passion")[77] – an effect that is so important in the diversion of spectators from their boredom and melancholy. On careful reflection, therefore, the "nuovi generi di mirabile, e di forte passione" are, for Gozzi, genres that first and foremost allow for the creation of a new relationship between dramatic performance and the subjectivity of the spectator – a relationship in which audience responsiveness to art becomes of primary importance.

The Public and the Public Stage

The rise of an aesthetic attentive to the emotional response of the public – which had, as we have seen, emerged from Dubos's insights, and which began to dominate art and theatre criticism from 1750 onward – provides one explanation for Gozzi's allegorical equation of audience and prince in *L'amore*. Suggesting that the spectator can match the sovereign in greatness, however, is highly charged – even more so considering that theatre performance is a powerful form of symbolic action and a potent social force. Once again, then, we return to our initial question: Why, in a play so intimately related to the Venetian context, is the republican citizenry of *La Serenissima* allegorized by its exact opposite: a prince, the figure for and source of absolutist political authority? Why, in other words, does the audience's response in *L'amore* come to exercise an aesthetic and cultural authority previously reserved only for a monarch?

The theory of public opinion articulated by Habermas is once again useful in finding a multifaceted answer to these questions. Habermas argued that in the "bourgeois" or "authentic" public sphere, public opinion became the authoritative judgment of a collective consciousness, and by 1750 the public was becoming a sovereign tribunal to which even governing institutions were subjected. Building on this Habermasian account, recent scholarship on public opinion has underscored that theatre, along with print culture, was one of the principal media involved in shaping and constructing an increasingly influential and politically engaged public.[78] Going far beyond the government's less ambitious (and more self-protective) intention to keep the public pleased and entertained by spectacle, *a* public (which, of course, self-constitutes as an audience upon arrival at the theatre) translated itself into *the* public – a new and powerful socio-political and critical entity. In this respect, Johann Wolfgang von Goethe's description of the city of Venice is revealing. What made *La Serenissima* remarkable in the eyes of Goethe is that she was "ein groses, respecktables Werck versammelter Menschenkraft, ein herrliches Monument, nicht *Eines Befehlenden* sondern eines Volcks" ("a grand venerable work of combined human energies, a noble monument, not of a ruler, but of a people").[79] That Goethe's portrayal of 1786 Venice in his *Italienische Reise* is more than the routine praise of a foreign traveller and that the city really was a living exemplar of conscious citizenship and of the public's critical power are attested to by recent historical assessments.[80] Indeed, though Habermas argued his case on examples of the emergence of the public sphere in England and France, insisting on the geographical specificity of his analysis, I add the evidence of Venetian theatre to that of myriad literary scholars and historians of cultural and political communication who have dated this hypothetical "public sphere" to early modernity and have expanded the relevance of the Habermasian framework to encompass the Italian context.[81]

With this theoretical model in mind, Gozzi's transfer of agency from the aristocratic arena of government to republican public authority – allegorized in his equation of audience and prince – clearly demonstrates the extent to which his first fairy-tale drama both reflected and helped conjure into being a new and critically productive spectatorship. According to Habermas, the emergence of the public sphere mirrored an ongoing shift away from princely authority towards an authority rooted in the enlightened and rational processes of the *Publikum* itself. It is therefore significant that it is Gozzi, long considered a reactionary promoter of the aristocracy's elitism and the values of Venice's conservative oligarchy, who was witness to and instigator of the transfer of power from state to citizen. Furthermore, Gozzi's vision of the public, which comprises "a learned and unlearned Audience" ("un Uditorio dotto, ed indotto"),[82] is even broader than that of Dubos. Indeed, while conferring significant decision-making power upon the public, Dubos still narrowed it to a restricted circle of learned "men of taste."[83] The expansive and thus revolutionary nature of Gozzi's bestowal of critical power upon public opinion is also apparent in comparison with Pietro Chiari's scornful representation of theatre-goers. Comparing the reading public to theatre audiences, Chiari – in many respects a progressive intellectual likewise influenced by the tenets of the French Enlightenment, though a less talented dramatist than either Goldoni or Gozzi – suggested that the latter were too ill-informed, capricious, and uneducated to form an accurate opinion on aesthetic and artistic matters: "Questo Pubblico, che deve di essi decidere non è così mescolato di feccia plebea, ed ignorante, come lo è il più delle volte la platea d'un Teatro" ("This Public, which must itself decide, is not as mixed with plebeian and ignorant dregs as is, the majority of the time, the Theatre audience").[84]

The sources for Gozzi's fairy-tale drama and its reference to the philosophical, political, and aesthetic postulations individuated in Pascal's *Pensées* and Dubos's *Réflexions critiques* highlight that it is ultimately complex cultural encounters (both in terms of participants involved and information transmitted), as well as the circulation of knowledge across national borders, that bring about the creation of publics – and, in particular, Gozzi's innovations in dramaturgical practice. As Voltaire eloquently wrote:

> Ainsi presque tout est imitation. L'idée des *Lettres persanes* est prise de celle de *l'Espion turc*. Le Boiardo a imité le Pulci, l'Arioste a imité le Boiardo. Les esprits les plus originaux empruntent les uns des autres. [...] Il en est des livres comme du feu dans nos foyers; on va prendre ce feu chez son voisin, on l'allume chez soi, on le communique à d'autres et il appartient à tous.

> Thus nearly everything is imitation. The idea of *The Persian Letters* was taken from the idea of *The Turkish Spy*. Boiardo imitated Pulci, Ariosto imitated Boiardo. The most original writers borrowed from each other. [...] There are books that are like a fire in our hearths; we go to take fire from our neighbour, we light our own, we give it to others, and it belongs to everyone.[85]

As this chapter shows, Gozzi's *L'amore delle tre melarance* encodes meanings other than those that were played out in the form of dramatic performance and, I would argue, can in fact be considered his artistic manifesto – one that most fittingly expresses his ideas on both theatre and spectatorship. This reconstruction of Gozzi's intellectual sources thus challenges – if not overturns – the long-standing critical attitude according to which he is considered a conservative-minded and uncultivated playwright. Gozzi's engagement with Dubos's treatise (a work that exercised significant influence on numerous men of letters and philosophers of the Enlightenment)[86] reveals the Venetian playwright to be a progressive intellectual and a most original theorist of theatre. His placement of the public at the forefront of the theatrical enterprise and his concern with its emotional response further illuminates how the centrality of spectators in the socio-political sphere and their impact as art critics informs his dramatic writing and influences his relationship with his audiences. Each of the playwrights examined thus far – from Cicognini to Gozzi – offered their audiences the means to understand themselves as participants in a public sphere and ushered in their more active political participation. Looking ahead now to the last decades of the eighteenth century, I will consider how playwrights reacted to this rise of a new and critically impactful public and what innovations in theatrical practice occurred in response to audiences' changing horizons of expectation. The following chapters will explore the evolution of dramatists' techniques of communication in response to the public's increasing power as critics of theatrical production.

5 Playwrights Fight Back

Carlo Goldoni and Public-Fashioning

Previous chapters have shown how the gradual distancing of theatrical practice from its institutional frameworks of court, aristocratic salon, and academy – along with the emergence of a theatre market based on economic values – transformed the playhouse into a public venue open to a diverse audience for the first time in Italian history. While the figure of the citizen-spectator, broadly conceived, was becoming more and more central in the socio-political sphere, in the world of the theatre the spectator went yet further to take on the stature of a *dominus* – a master, so to speak – of dramatic production. Indeed, the concept of "the public" appears over and over in the treatises of theatre theorists, whose writings take seriously into consideration spectators' general inclinations and specific needs. To know one's audience and to know how to appeal to its tastes and attitudes became a top priority for playwrights in this period. To cite but two examples, Carlo Gozzi, for instance, confesses "di essere stato un diligentissimo esploratore per tutto il corso degli anni [suoi] sui talenti, sugli animi, e sulle inclinazioni della [sua] Nazione, e ch'[egli] non h[a] mai scelto argomento, o ideata una scenica rappresentazione senza prima bilanciarla col riflesso all'indole dei [suoi] ascoltatori" ("to having been, for all the years of [his] life, a most diligent explorer of the abilities, attitudes, and inclinations of [his] Nation, and that [he has] never chosen a topic nor devised a theatrical performance without first having weighed it in light of the temperament of [his] listeners").[1] Similarly, Carlo Goldoni asserts that the relationship between playwright and public is indispensable for "uno scrittore [...] che scrive per il Teatro, ch'è quanto a dire principalmente pel Popolo" ("a writer [...] who writes for the Theatre, which is to say principally for the People").[2]

Playwrights of the late eighteenth century were prepared, therefore, to give the spectator the right to judge their works and to return a final verdict on them. In his famed *Lettre à M. D'Alembert sur les spectacles* (*Letter to M. D'Alembert on the Theatre*, 1758), Jean-Jacques Rousseau observes that "[l]es spectacles sont fait pour le peuple, et ce n'est que par leurs effets sur lui, qu'on peut déterminer leurs qualités absolues" ("the theatre is made for the people, and it is only by its effects on the people that one can determine its absolute qualities").[3] Similarly, Gotthold Ephraim Lessing, in his *Hamburgische Dramaturgie* (*Hamburg Dramaturgy*, 1767–9), affirms that the public is a "severe master" and an omniscient and all-powerful judge.[4] During the height of the debates on theatre that saw Goldoni and Pietro Chiari on one side opposing Elisabetta Caminer Turra and Gozzi on the other, the latter – referring to 1740s to 1770s Venetian culture – claimed that "in una battaglia di poeti teatrali, la diversione del pubblico decide delle perdite e delle vittorie" ("in a battle among dramatists, the enjoyment of the public decides the losses and the victories").[5] Chiari, in his *Osservazioni critiche sopra* Le Sorelle rivali (*Critical Observations on* The Rival Sisters, 1755), similarly affirmed that "quando la Commedia piace, c'è sempre stile, e teatro; ma non c'è nè teatro nè stile, quando ella non piace, se fosse ancora composta dal più accreditato maestro dell'arte. Ecco l'unica, e più sicura regola per decidere sanamente in somiglianti materie" ("when the Play pleases there is always style, and theatre; but there is neither theatre nor style when it does not please, even should it be written by the most lauded master of the art. This is the single and surest rule for rationally judging amongst similar material").[6] Thus, as Hans Robert Jauss puts it, over the course of the second half of the eighteenth century, an aesthetic attentive to the response of the public emerged, born of a new interest in the experience of a receptive subject and in the imaginative power of the observer.[7]

Even contemporary critical reviews of performances and authors' prefaces shift attention from evaluating works based upon their intrinsic qualities towards their encounter with the public, revealing how the spectator of this later period was not only an active consumer but also a perceptive critic – one well-equipped with the cultural knowledge required to formulate an informed, individual, and personal judgment.

Whereas I have to this point depicted theatre as an important tool of public-making, it is the aim of this chapter to explore how this new kind of critically productive theatre-goer, who had become vital to dramatic practice and to aesthetic criticism, established power over the playwright. In particular, the following pages investigate how Venetian theatre of the late eighteenth century fashioned itself with respect to the emergence of this new public and reflect upon what kinds of innovations playwrights developed in response to spectators' changing horizons of expectation as well as upon how actor performance practices shifted. Also at stake here is whether the dramatic devices developed by Italian playwrights in response to (but also in order to shape and manipulate) the public's horizons of expectation entered fully into the flow of theatrical practices that circulated in Europe both within and beyond the confines of national cultures.

Compelling answers to these questions emerge from an analysis of another play by Carlo Goldoni: his Parisian period comedy *Il genio buono e il genio cattivo* (*The Good Genie and the Evil Genie*). In his *Mémoires*, the Venetian playwright recounts having written *Il genio* for the company of the Comédie Italienne in 1764. The play, however, was never performed in Paris. Some years later, Goldoni decided to send his script to Venice in an attempt to counteract the scant favour Venetians had bestowed upon his three-act play *Zelinda e Lindoro*.[8] *Il genio* was thus staged by Girolamo Medebach's company in February 1767 at the Teatro di San Giovanni Crisostomo, a prestigious opera house belonging to the Grimani family. With Antonio Sacchi in the role of Arlecchino and Maddalena Marliani, the celebrated Mirandolina in Goldoni's 1752 *La locandiera* (The Innkeeper Woman), the play met with considerable public and critical success.[9] In fact, during its debut season, *Il genio*'s run was twenty-seven consecutive nights long.[10] Though appearing in substantially altered and rearranged form, the comedy was published in volume thirty-four of the Zatta edition in 1793.[11]

This particular play by Goldoni is one in which modern criticism has rarely taken an interest,[12] and yet it is a particularly clear window through which to view the late-eighteenth-century transformation of the relationship between stage, playwright, and public. There are three primary reasons for this. First, this magical and comic fable for theatre better reflects the importance that the figure of the spectator acquires in this period than do other dramatic works by Goldoni. In fact, it is precisely his desire to regain the approval of the Venetians that prompts Goldoni to tackle, in the words of Antonio Piazza, "un genere sì contrario a suoi retti principi" ("a genre so contrary to his held values").[13] Second, *Il genio* is from Goldoni's French period, which produced meta-theatrical comedies containing reflections on his reform of comic theatre and thus on the relationship between author and public.[14] Furthermore, since it was written late in Goldoni's theatrical career, this comedy allows us to trace the evolution of the playwright's relationship to and strategies of communication with his audience. Third, Goldoni conceived of *Il genio* precisely in order that it be performed – though in different form – in both France and Italy. We do not have sufficient information to permit a comparison between the printed edition by Zatta, the Parisian manuscript, and the text performed in Venice (which, based upon the summary Goldoni provided in his *Mémoires*, had substantial differences with respect both to the Parisian script and to the printed version). Nevertheless, the play's mirrored aspect – that is, its being written almost simultaneously for audiences in two different countries – allows us to explore how it was possible for Goldoni to write a comedy that would both please the Parisians (whom he considered "[u]n popolo sì illuminato per natura, per educazione, e per genio, avvezzo alle più brillanti e alle più regolate rappresentazioni"; "[a] people so enlightened by nature, education, and inclination, accustomed to the most brilliant and erudite plays")[15] and regain the esteem of the Venetians.

This chapter demonstrates that, in order to achieve these objectives, Goldoni composed a play that is focused entirely on the audience and that is capable of engendering a theatrical experience of collective collaboration in which the spectator is involved in the onstage action as an active participant.

The Spectator's Theatre

We begin with an analysis of the compositional and theatrical techniques that Goldoni employed in order to offer the spectator the role of active participant. At the beginning of *Il genio*, the uneducated and naïve peasants Arlecchino and Corallina, newly married, live happily in the solitude and serenity of the open valleys near Bergamo. It is not long, however, before they encounter the *genio cattivo* (evil genie), who persuades them to undertake a journey to discover the outside world and to seek the prospect of a better life. He even freely offers them the items they will need on their voyage: money and two magic rings that permit the couple to transport themselves instantly from place to place. Just when Arlecchino and Corallina are on the point of departure, the *genio buono* (good genie) appears and, via a shadow puppet play, forecasts their future, warning them of mundane corruption and its dangers as well as of the futility of pursuing worldly pleasures. Nonetheless, the spouses' desire to see the world proves the stronger, and thus begins the voyage of initiation that takes them to Paris (act 2), to London (act 3), and to Venice (act 4, in the version performed in Venice – in the Zatta version they travel to Tripoli). Lacking any knowledge of the behavioural conventions of the countries they visit, the protagonists are forced to rely on the cultural mediation of others, which is offered to them by both local and foreign inhabitants.

Goldoni criticizes these models of urban sociability through the unknowing glance of the protagonists and their manipulation by the natives, who direct the attention of the two simple travellers wherever they see fit. In the act set in Paris, which unfolds in the Tuileries Gardens and the Bois de Boulogne, Goldoni takes aim at the attitudes and behaviours of the Parisians. The London act, though presenting the English in a favourable light (III.4), nonetheless makes evident how the city disorients, assaults, and lures the peasant couple away from upright action, putting their moral integrity at risk. It is in London, in fact, that we witness the destruction of the protagonists' marriage and their decision to continue the voyage apart. They reunite in Venice (Tripoli) in act IV, where Arlecchino, who was imprisoned for having entered a mosque dressed as a eunuch during women's prayer, is freed thanks to the intervention of Corallina and the help of Pantalone, a generous and locally respected Venetian merchant. At the conclusion of an accelerating sequence of events, the protagonists return home, compelled to admit that the cautions of the *genio buono* were far better than the poor advice they had heeded. The play concludes with a return to the rustic-pastoral mode for a fifth act that functions also as an epilogue.

On the level of macrostructural narration, then, we can immediately see that the entire play is permeated with imagery of the gaze and of observation. The first method by which Goldoni cultivates spectator involvement in the affairs of his characters is evident in an analogy between the audience's experience of and the protagonists' behaviour in the theatrical fiction. Like the theatre-goers attending the play, Arlecchino and Corallina are attentive and interested observers of a "novel spectacle" just as, simultaneously, they are the objects of autochthonous observation – inasmuch as "the traveller becomes, despite everything, an implicit ambassador of his native land."[16] What the spectator sees during the play is thus precisely a mirror image of the experience of being a spectator. Numerous *mises-en-abyme* reinforce this identification of audience with character: for instance, the scene in the first act (described above), in which Arlecchino and Corallina attend the shadow puppet play that predicts their future, and in which they see themselves as protagonists (I.4); the end of the second act, in which they participate in a public ball in the Bois de Boulogne (II.26); and the finale of the third act, in which Arlecchino, accompanied by a woman, and Corallina, arm in arm with two Englishmen, arrive separately at London's Vauxhall theatre (III.13). The protagonists are thus voyeurs just like the audience, and the play provides a rationale for its performance while vindicating the position of its watchers.

The model of the travel and adventure journal – a genre very much in vogue during the eighteenth century – offered Goldoni an opportunity to describe to his fellow citizens, via the play, his arrival at Paris in August 1762. If we compare the attempts of Arlecchino and Corallina to emulate Parisian behaviours and to adapt themselves to their new social environment with a passage from Goldoni's autobiography ("Je demandai quatre mois de tems pour examiner le goût du Public, pour m'instruire dans la maniere de plaire à Paris, et je ne fis pendant ce tems-là que voir, que courir, que me promener, que jouir"; "I demanded four months' time to examine the public taste, to ascertain the mode of pleasing at Paris; and during that time I did nothing but run about, pry into everything, and enjoy myself"),[17] we might well hypothesize that Goldoni was also positioning himself, metaphorically, onstage – costumed as a character who explores the cultural climate of the French capital. Goldoni, therefore, not only "staged" his audience, constructing a theatrical mirror that reflects the image of the Venetian spectators, but also dissolved the distance between playwright, spectator, and play. These dramaturgical devices convey how during the second half of the 1700s, to quote Habermas,

> [d]ie Beziehungen zwischen Autor, Opus und Publikum verändern sich: sie werden zu intimen Beziehungen der psychologisch am "Menschlichen," an Selbsterkenntnis ebenso wie an Einfühlung interessierten Privatleute untereinander. [...] Autor und Leser werden selbst zu den Akteuren, die "sich aussprechen."

> [t]he relations between author, work, and public changed. They became intimate mutual relationships between privatized individuals who were psychologically interested in what was "human," in self-knowledge, and in empathy. [...] Author and reader themselves became actors who "talked heart to heart."[18]

Poetics and Polemics

Despite Goldoni's attempt to erase from his *Mémoires* any hint that might encourage an allegorical reading of *Il genio*, scholars who have studied the play agree that it is a self-reflexive text.[19] Given that Goldoni substantially changed the plot he had outlined in France before sending it to Venice, critics have related its allegorical elements to activities that occurred before his departure for France and consider the play to be a commentary on his reform of comic theatre that had taken place years before in Italy. In particular, it is the presence of the character Anzoletto – an Italian emigrant to France – that has enabled scholars to "unmask" the self-reflexive nature of *Il genio.* Anzoletto, whom the protagonists encounter during their stay in Paris, recalls the homonymous character from Goldoni's earlier autobiographical play *Una delle ultime sere di carnovale* (*One of the Last Nights of Carnival,* 1762), with whom the playwright openly identified.[20] Thus, according to the "allegorical-theatrical" interpretation of Javier Gutiérrez Carou, if Anzoletto represents Goldoni in both plays, then Arlecchino (and to some extent Corallina) might be read as symbolic of the improvised theatre that was foundational to Gozzi's "counter-reform."[21] For Anzoletto, being identified with the two protagonists would be shameful because their coarseness cast a shabby light on his nation and its inhabitants ("Chi diavolo xe sto martuffo che vien qua a discreditar la nostra nazion?"; "Who the devil is this idiot who comes to discredit our nation?," II.3; and "I omeni della vostra sorta no i xe fatti per viazar, no se va per el mondo co sto boccon d'ignoranza a svergonar la so patria"; "Men of your kind are not made to travel, not if [they go] around the world with this mouthful of ignorance that shames their homeland," II.6). In Gutiérrez Carou's examination of the summary of the Venetian version that appears in the *Mémoires,* he asserts that "the good genie cannot be read as anything but the [Goldonian] reform of Italian comedy."[22] Specifically, he argues, the protagonists' marriage represents the survival and transformation of the old genre of *commedia dell'arte,* thanks to the changes brought about by Goldoni during the years of his reform.

This reading, which interprets the protagonists of the play as "the theatrical models that were at the core of Gozzi's counter-reform,"[23] seems not to account for a problem of context, however: at the time Goldoni wrote the French scenario (along with the portion of his *Mémoires* that contains the description of the Venetian performance), he was already in Paris and, most likely, was no longer interested in the theatrical career of his rival. It is even less likely that the Parisians were familiar with Gozzi's fairy-tale comedies, given that he became popular much later and via the reception of his plays in Germany. In addition, the figure of Arlecchino in *Il genio* shares many characteristics of the Arlequin *forain* and, especially, Pierre de Marivaux's Arlequin – the simple, naïve stock character who is kidnapped by a wizard or fairy and taken to a strange land (as occurs, for example, in *Arlequin poli par l'Amour*, 1720).[24] The allegorical meanings of *Il genio* might instead be more fruitfully interpreted as suggestive of highly complex cultural processes involving both the theatrical tastes of individual nations and the contemporary polemic on the use of *commedia dell'arte* stock characters. In any case, it is true that Goldoni substantially modified the text of his drama in order to send it to Venice, and it is precisely in this moment of rewriting that he engaged in the polemic against Gozzi's theatrical fables – full, as they are, of magic, wonders, and the *merveilleux* – and attempted to point out the errors inherent in his adversary's dramas. In sum, then, though in part agreeing with Gutiérrez Carou (who sees, as described above, Goldoni and his reform in the *genio buono*; Gozzi and his "counter-reform" in the *genio cattivo*), I would argue that Arlecchino and Corallina, far from straightforwardly representing Gozzi's reform, are a powerful metaphor for the theatre-going public.

In the print edition, when the evil genie first appears to the characters he introduces himself as "il Genio dominatore di queste selve" ("the Genie who is ruler of these woods") and as their "amico" ("friend," I.2) – just as Gozzi became the leading playwright on the Venetian scene after the departure of Goldoni and Chiari. This genie, moreover, declares that he wants to do good, and that he comes to "procurare la felicità" ("seek the happiness") of the protagonists. Analogously, as discussed in the previous chapter, Gozzi called theatres "recinti di divertimento" ("enclosures of diversion") and seduced the public with fables full of false marvels that were pure, hedonistic spectacles. In contrast, when the good genie first appears to the characters, he refers to his harmful counterpart as "mio nemico" ("my enemy") and "mio rivale [che] vi ha empita la testa delle bellezze del falso mondo" ("my rival [who] has filled your heads with the beauties of the false world," I.4). This declaration is of course an expression of Goldoni's contempt for the allure Gozzi's fantastical fables held for audiences. In this way, Arlecchino and Corallina find themselves implicated in the polemic between the two genies (*genii* as magical conjurors) and thus between the two theatre reformers (*genii* as genius playwrights).[25]

As we have seen, Goldoni constructs – at a structural level – a theatrical mirror that reflects an image of the Venetian public. The indecision of his protagonists regarding which genie to heed and their choice to accept the deceptive offer of the evil genie might therefore be interpreted as a metaphor for the unfaithfulness of the Venetian public to Goldoni and to his reformed plays, which he openly laments in his autobiography: "Je savois que depuis mon départ les troupes de Venise avoient souffert des changemens qui avoient altéré ce zele, cette méthode qu'on avoit suivi sous mes yeux, et que le succès d'une Piece de caractere ou à sentiment n'etoit plus aussi sûr qu'il étoit de mon tems" ("I was aware that, after my departure, the Venetian companies had undergone changes; that the zeal and the method of my time were no longer the same, and that the success of a piece of character or sentiment was less secure than at that period").[26] Arlecchino's hunger for and seeking out of new pleasures, which guides the two characters on their Grand Tour, might then symbolize the insatiable longing for surprises and for new theatrical genres of the Venetian audience, which disregarded moral reflection and was drawn to theatre primarily for its hedonistic impulses. Even Corallina's desire to see herself appreciated for her physical and intellectual qualities – the driving force behind her decision to set out on the voyage – can represent the desire of the public to see recognized its rightful role as critic and judge of works of art.

The unvoiced desires of the protagonists, which the evil genie (that is, Carlo Gozzi) makes magically visible at the beginning of the first act, reveal an image of the Venetian public as changeable, incoherent, and never satisfied – an image that even Gozzi, arch-rival and heir to Goldoni in Venetian theatre after his departure for Paris, described in these terms:

> [...] la verità è, che nell'Italia, un Poeta teatrale per quanto favore egli abbia avuto nell'animo, e nella opinione del Pubblico, non deve lusingarsi di perseverare con una lunga sussistenza sulle nostre scene [...]. Annoja il genere, annoja lo stile, annoja per sino il suono del nome dell'autore prima gradito, e un genere di nuovo aspetto non senza sali, e non senza ripieno, ch'abbia la fortuna di piacere, cagiona una tal diversione che lo fa quasi dimenticare.
>
> La non estesa, o poca, o superficiale, o mal ferma educazione, non lascia concepire alla generalità del popolo italiano una stima solida per gli scrittori de' nostri climi, specialmente teatrali, che sono soltanto guardati come sorgenti noncurabili d'un passeggero divertimento. Venezia supera ogn'altra Metropoli dell'Italia in questa maniera di pensare.

> [...] the truth is that, in Italy, a Dramatist – no matter how much favour he has obtained in the hearts and in the opinion of the Public – must not hope to persist in a long career on our stages [...]. [The Public becomes] bored by the genre, bored by the style, even bored by the very sound of the name of a playwright who had before been enjoyed, and a show with a new look – one not without interest and not without substance, that has the

[good] fortune to be pleasing – [well,] such a diversion would all but cause [the Public] to forget him.

Their limited, or modest, or superficial, or weak education does not permit the majority of Italian people to conceive a lasting esteem for the writers of our climes – [and] especially of our theatres, which are merely regarded as non-curative founts of fleeting enjoyment. Venice surpasses every other Italian Metropolis in this way of thinking.[27]

Only with great difficulty would Goldoni have been able to disagree with his rival on this particular point.[28] And in fact, writing from Paris to his friend Francesco Griselini, Goldoni bitterly observed that, after his departure, Italian theatres "sono ricaduti nell'antico genio mostruoso" ("again fell into their former monstrous tendencies"),[29] and that he felt betrayed by the Venetians. As Maddalena Agnelli has observed, theatre in Venice – atypically with respect to other Italian cities – was a social space accessible to all, and anyone could contribute to the debates on theatre that enlivened streets, shops, and piazzas.[30] If this is indeed the case, it seems likely that Goldoni intended the close association of audience members with characters within the frame of a dramatic fable to engage the public in the action of the play by placing spectators at the centre of the debates on theatre and making them an integral part of the polemic with his adversary.

The good genie's final victory confirms that the function of Goldoni's fairy-tale comedy was not limited to indulging a momentary taste for marvels and that his intention was not to pander to trends.[31] In the play's last act, the good genie tells Corallina, who by now has very much repented of having followed the advice of the evil genie, "io sono che l'ho [Arlecchino] salvato, io che malgrado i torti che fatti mi avete, non vi ho mai perduti di vista, non vi ho mai abandonati del tutto" ("I am the one who saved [Arlecchino] – it was me who, despite the wrongs you committed against me, never lost you from sight; never abandoned you completely," V.7). This affirmation also lends itself to an allegorical interpretation as a demand on the part of Goldoni, who never gave up despite the betrayal of the Venetian public that applauded Gozzi's fables with great enthusiasm.

For Goldoni, therefore, it was not enough to seduce spectators with magical transformations, quick set changes, and the kinds of spectacles that formed the basis of his rival's dramas. Indeed, critics agree that with this comedy Goldoni sought to confront Gozzi on his home turf – using, at least in part, his own fantastical weapons – in an attempt to highlight the error of Gozzi's "counter-reform" of Italian theatre.[32] Goldoni himself witnesses to this in his letter to Stefano Sciugliaga:

> Vorrei che faceste a S. E.za Vendramin ed ai comici una proposizione. Sapete, che ho quel soggetto indicatovi del *Genio buono, e del Genio cattivo.* Commedia piena di caratteri, di moralità e di critica. [...] Avrei piacere di far vedere in Venezia come si fanno le commedie di trasformazione, senza le fiabe, senza i diavoli, e senza le piazzate.
>
> I would like you to make a proposal to His Excellency Vendramin and to the actors. You know that I have told you about this subject of *The Good Genie and the Evil Genie.* A comedy full of characters, of morality, and of critique. [...] I would be pleased to demonstrate in Venice how one makes comedies of transformation without fables, without devils, and without buffoonery.[33]

The playwright's intention was thus to give the Venetians an example of a "reformed" fable – one that engaged their imagination without sacrificing realism and that provided them with the guidance of a moral message.[34] Goldoni achieved this objective by employing a different kind of theatricality that was aimed at establishing a new equilibrium between word and stage; between performance and spectator. While the evil genie (Gozzi) tempts Arlecchino and Corallina with magic, producing artificial *coups de théâtre* (the *genio cattivo* waves a magic wand at a fountain and it transforms into a boiling pot of macaroni; he strikes a tree with it and first cheese, then money, erupts forth, I.2), the good genie (Goldoni) tries to persuade the couple to take the right path by employing moments of less melodramatic pictorial vividness, as with, for example, the show-within-a-show of the shadow puppet theatre (I.4).

Tableaux: Theatre as Painting

Goldoni thus directs his audience's attention towards the visual dimension of his play, making its spectators active observers of all that is pictorial in its performance. Indeed, stage directions invade the pages of *Il genio* almost to the point of competing with the dialogue; they reveal the playwright's concern with the accurate representation of spaces and settings onstage. The beginning of each act is accompanied by numerous instructions regarding the set and the staging, including decorative details, the placement of objects and characters, and musical arrangements.[35] The abundance of such directions can be explained by the fact that they were addressing the players putting on the comedy in Venice – in the absence of its author. Their abundance might also be due to the fact that the version Goldoni sent to Zatta had not yet been fully revised. In any case, reading these many stage directions gives one the distinct impression that Goldoni modelled the text of his play on the art of painting. As his summary of the Venetian performance reveals, the set in fact included actual paintings during the first four acts:

> Le mauvais génie paroît à son tour [in the first act]; il trouve les deux [Arlecchino and Corallina] mariés malheureux, il les plaint, il leur trace le tableau des plaisirs du monde; il les gagne, il leur fournit de l'argent, il les engage à aller à Paris [...].
>
> Il y dans les actes deuxieme, troisieme et quatrieme [sic] assez de mouvement et d'intrigue, de petits tableaux et de légeres critiques.
>
> [When] the evil genie appears in his turn [in the first act], he finds the couple [Arlecchino and Corallina] unhappily married. Feeling sorry for them, he presents them with a *tableau* of worldly pleasures. He wins them over, provides them with money, and convinces them to go to Paris.
>
> In the second, third, and fourth acts, there is a lot of action and intrigue, as well as some small *tableaux* and slight critiques.[36]

The presence of the term "*tableau*" here is not coincidental. Indeed, if we examine the illustrations representing *Il genio* in the Zatta edition (1788–95), they confirm the specifically pictorial manner in which the play was staged (or, at least, in which Goldoni envisaged it as being staged). In the first of Goldoni's editions to be illustrated (Pasquali, 1761–77), the figures are often presented frontally and the scenes are arranged vertically. The Zatta edition engravings differ substantially in format: in outdoor scenes, the figures move in a broad horizontal space; in indoor scenes, the frame consists of all three of the room's walls. The four Zatta engravings, moreover, display the characters closely assembled together – practically immobilized by their proximity – and distributed on various levels so that they occupy the entire space. In other words, they constitute actual *tableaux*.

The term "*tableau*" (as employed in the passage from Goldoni's autobiography cited above), together with the Zatta engravings, suggests a key hypothesis. In his research into new forms of performance and into novel instruments of communication with the public (which had both to reform the model provided by Gozzi's theatrical fables and to intensify the emotional and imaginative involvement of the audience itself), Goldoni sought a model in the art of painting. In this, he was inspired by the writings of late-eighteenth-century French theorists of theatre. The *tableau*, after all, was one of the motifs of the new dramatic aesthetic that Denis Diderot came to assert against the classicism of the Académie française.

Among the various French Enlightenment figures who were concerned with the renewal of theatrical practice, Diderot was the first to realize that drama was a genre capable of pairing the verbal description of actions with the direct presentation of visual images. For Diderot, figurative painting represented an art that was closer to nature and more able to engage the spectator than was contemporary theatrical practice. To counter the artificial nature of theatre in general and the privileging of the word in French neoclassical theatre in particular – which Diderot criticized for its mannerisms, its unnatural acting, its unlikely dialogues, and its forced narratives – he offered a rather sophisticated theory of verisimilitude and theatrical illusion.[37] More specifically, he proposed a new formal conception of drama that underlined the important role played by non-verbal components of performance as carriers of meaning, and attempted to use the staging, the physical expressions, and the pantomimic actions of the actors to the utmost. His most important contribution to theatrical reform consisted, however, in "aver spostato la riflessione estetica dalla parola all'immagine" ("having shifted aesthetic reflection from word to image")[38] and in having theorized the notion of the *tableau*.[39]

Diderot hoped his first dramatic work would offer a new model for the morality play that called for the development of a new dramaturgy that would find in certain exemplary paintings the inspiration for a more convincing representation of action than any provided by the theatre of his time. In this play, the first of the *Entretiens sur le fils naturel* (*Conversations on The Natural Son*, 1757), he compares *tableaux* – visually satisfying, essentially silent, seemingly accidental groupings of figures – with *coups de théâtre* – surprising plot twists. As the protagonist of the *Entretiens*, Dorval, declares, "J'aimerais bien mieux des tableaux sur la scène où il y en a si peu, et où ils produiraient un effet si agréable et si sûr, que ces coups de théâtre qu'on amène d'une manière si forcée" ("I would prefer to see *tableaux* on the stage, where they are so rarely seen, and would produce such a pleasing effect, rather than *coups de théâtre*, which are introduced in such an artificial way").[40] His fictional interlocutor, Moi (Diderot himself), clarifies Dorval's argument, contrasting the *coup de théâtre* ("[u]n incident imprévu qui se passe en action, et qui change subitement l'état des personnages"; "an unforeseen incident that takes the form of action, and that suddenly changes the situation of the characters")[41] with dramatic painting – or, more accurately, the *tableau* – defining it as "[u]ne disposition de ces personnages sur la scène, si naturelle et si vraie, que, rendue fidèlement par un peintre, elle me plairait sur la toile" ("the placement of these characters on the stage, so natural and so true to life that it would please me as a painting").[42]

As follows from this definition, one function of dramatic painting is to produce a realistic effect[43] as well as a necessary illusion of reality whenever the narrative is unable to do so. Furthermore, insofar as the *tableau* substitutes for a *coup de théâtre,* it banishes "le merveilleux" ("the marvellous") from the stage so that "les dieux de la fable, les oracles, les héros invulnérables, les aventures romanesques, ne sont plus de saison" ("pagan gods, oracles, invulnerable heroes, fanciful adventures, are no longer in season"),[44] and simplicity and naturalism appear in their place. At the same time, according to Diderot, the capacity of *tableaux* to express emotional force and visual intensity – and to focus the attention of the observer on a specific situation – served to strengthen the mimetic identification of the spectators with the onstage characters. In this way, the public could easily glean the moral implications of the events represented onstage.[45]

We can detect, therefore, a certain affinity between the aesthetic of the *tableau* – as elaborated by the French encyclopaedist – and *Il genio,* in which magic and marvels come to be substituted by numerous pictorial images. By insisting on the noteworthy differences that separate his creation from Gozzi's fables (and from French productions that indulged the Parisian public's taste for *féeries*), Goldoni emphasized how the fantastical elements of his play were reduced to an absolute minimum: "Cette Comédie d'ailleurs ne donnoit pas dans les extravagances des anciennes Pieces à machines: il n'y avoit de merveilleux que les deux Génies qui faisoient passer les Acteurs en très-peu d'instans d'une région à l'autre; tout le reste étoit dans la nature" ("This Comedy in any case did not contain the extravagances of the ancient machine Plays: of marvellous [elements] it had but two Genies who made the Actors move almost instantly from one place to another; all the rest was in nature").[46]

There is no doubt that the *Entretiens sur le fils naturel* – a rapidly and widely disseminated text that was fundamental to the aesthetic of the *tableau* – was known to Goldoni. In fact, almost immediately upon his arrival at the French capital (and much to his dismay), the Venetian playwright found himself involved in the famous *querelle* that had exploded in Paris in response to Diderot's play.[47] The French theatre reformer had been accused by the gazetteer and sworn nemesis of the encyclopaedists, Élie Catherine Fréron, of having copied his play from Goldoni's *Il vero amico.* In a series of articles published in the journal *L'année littéraire* – which opened with insinuations of doubt regarding the originality of Diderot's *Fils naturel* and then offered a direct comparison of his and Goldoni's plots – Fréron eventually came to denounce it openly as plagiarism. Diderot defended himself against this accusation in his essay *Discours de la poésie dramatique* (*Discourse on Dramatic Poetry,* 1758), a theoretical manifesto concerning the new genre of the bourgeois drama that was published to accompany his second play, *Le père de famille* (*The Father of the Family*). In addition to defending its author, the essay made a serious attack on the guiltless Goldoni, whom Diderot decried as a modest "author of farces [...] an even more bitter description when one considers the Europe-wide distribution of [Diderot's] essay."[48]

At the time, Goldoni had not thought it wise to intervene in the polemic between those who were for or against the encyclopaedists. In any case, it appears that he was disposed to pardon Diderot for his dismissive statement and for the other claims he had made – assertions that discredited Goldoni's entire dramatic production and impeded his entrance into *théâtre français.*[49] Goldoni began speaking about Diderot's plagiarism only when he was already in Paris, in 1764. In the "Autore a chi legge" that prefaces *Il vero amico* (and appears in volume seven of the Pasquali edition), Goldoni summarizes this unpleasant event, but does so without any apparent resentment. He states that he has read Diderot's play and that it seems to him, as well, "specialmente nelle prime scene dell'atto primo, che sia seguitata la traccia del *Vero Amico*" ("especially in the first scenes of the first act, that the play followed the outline of *Il vero amico*").[50] He goes on to describe just how unfair and mortifying Diderot's judgment had been:

> Spiacemi amaramente, che senza alcuna mia colpa si è scaricato il suo sdegno contro di me. Egli ha creduto, per abbattere i suoi nemici, dover discreditare le opere mie, ed ha creato una nuova *Poetica,* niente per altro che per poter dire che io era un cattivo Comico; e per giustificarsi ch'egli non aveva niente preso da me, *sfidava il Pubblico a poter trovare in tutte le mie Commedie una scena, che fosse degna del Teatro Francese.* Non tocca a me a rispondere ad una simile proposizione.

> I was most bitterly saddened that, without any fault of my own, [Diderot] vented his disdain against me. He thought that, in order to combat his

> enemies, he had to discredit my works, and he created a new *Poetics*, for no other reason than to be able to say that I was an incompetent Comic [playwright]; and to acquit himself from having taken anything from me, *he challenged the Public to find in all of my Comedies a [single] scene that was worthy of French Theatre.* It is not for me to respond to such a provocation.[51]

Nevertheless – and demonstrating the high esteem in which he held the French dramatist – Goldoni expressed a desire to meet Diderot in order to clear up all the misunderstandings. Long awaited by the Venetian playwright, the encounter took place only towards the end of 1764 (or early the following year), thanks to the mediation of the composer Egidio Romualdo Duni, who was a friend of both parties.[52] Goldoni made no record of the meeting either in his letters to his Venetian friends or to his frequent correspondent from Bologna, the Marquis Francesco Albergati Capacelli, and spoke of it only many years later in his reconstruction of the event in the *Mémoires.* This may well suggest that the encounter did not go as Goldoni had hoped. The conversation between the two dramatists must have been rather formal, and Diderot may well have demonstrated an unjustified rancour towards the man who had been nothing more than a scapegoat in the polemic between the encyclopaedists and the conservatives.

Considering the timing of these events, I do not think it coincidental that the Parisian version of *Il genio* dates from 1764 – that is, precisely a year after the publication of Diderot's *Discours de la poésie dramatique* and at approximately the same time as the playwrights' face-to-face meeting. Moreover, it seems entirely possible that Goldoni's extensive use of *tableaux* in *Il genio* (and in pantomime dance, as we shall see) was inspired by Diderot's idea of theatre as a consequence of pictorial *tableaux.* In this way Goldoni established, publicly, the ability of such a modest "author of farces" to integrate himself into the Parisian theatre context and implicitly asserted his capacity to prove himself in all theatrical registers. Neither is it mere chance that the play was never staged in Paris. Although Goldoni recounted, in his *Mémoires,* that *Il genio* was refused by the Comédie Italienne for the cost of its set, the above evidence seems instead to indicate that the comedy was not staged in Paris for entirely other reasons: the play's references to Diderot's writings on theatrical aesthetics were likely too much in evidence for Parisian spectators (whom, we recall, Goldoni considered the most intelligent audience in the world)[53] and might thus reopen the polemic in which he had been involved only tangentially.

The Third Wheel

I have avoided describing the relationship between Goldoni and Diderot as one of direct competition because I would argue instead that what is (and was) commonly alleged to be plagiarism among competing playwrights was in fact simply one aspect of a much broader and more complex process of the circulation of ideas, theories, and dramatic inventions – one within which is it difficult to establish clear lines of influence of one playwright or one national theatrical culture on another. To demonstrate the complexity of this process, I will introduce a third historical figure as a complicating factor into the so-called *querelle* between these two theatre reformers. In his article on production methods in eighteenth-century comic theatre, Piermario Vescovo hypothesizes that Goldoni's dramatic techniques – the continuous succession of stage directions defining space and character, the arrangement of onstage movement, and mimetic acting, all of which come together to great effect in performance – emerge from his experience in theatre before his arrival at Paris and, in particular, from his relationship with Neapolitan theatre culture.[54] Vescovo observes a certain affinity between Goldoni's staging and that of Domenico Luigi Barone, knight of Liveri (1685–1757), official playwright of the Neapolitan court of Charles III of Spain, as well as impresario and director *par excellence.*[55] Barone's success as the author of thirteen comedies was due in large part to the extreme care with which he rehearsed his actors; to his perfectionism as a director; and to his introduction, well before Diderot, of simultaneous scenes and lifelike pictorial scenes.[56] It was Benedetto Croce who (though he considered Barone's comedies to be essentially illegible, crowded as they were with "an unbelievable number of characters, with an incredibly complicated plot that was simultaneously of no interest whatsoever") explained a likely reason for the Neapolitan director's success, taking inspiration, in part, from what had already been observed on the topic by Pietro Napoli Signorelli:

> Nondimeno [le commedie di Barone] piacevano infinitamente, e re Carlo si sorbiva con grande letizia le sette ore di recita. Il che proveniva dall'abilità grande del Liveri come dispositore di commedie e maestro di attori: egli ordinava la scena in modo [...] che vi si potevano "indicare a un tempo diverse azioni e più colloqui," e presentava "l'immagine parlante di una gran parte della città o di una gran casa." Gli attori erano da lui esercitati per ogni commedia un anno intero e per più ore al giorno; e soprattutto

curava la mimica, volendo che il sembiante parlasse "più delle parole," perché nei punti in cui la passione giunge al colmo "l'anima a far mostra di quel che sente s'affaccia nel volto."

Nevertheless, [Barone's plays] were infinitely pleasing, and King Charles happily endured the seven-hour performance. This was due to Liveri's great ability as a writer of plays and master of actors: he arranged the stage [...] so as to be able to "display several actions and more conversations at once," and presented "a speaking image of a large part of the city or of a large house." For every comedy, he rehearsed his actors for an entire year and for many hours every day; and above all he attended to gesture, striving for appearance to speak "more than words," because during moments when passion reaches its peak "the soul must show what it feels on the face."[57]

Barone was famous beyond the Kingdom of Naples for his "multiple scenes" above all – his ability to represent simultaneously more than one place or dialogue in a single scene – famous to the extent that he was imitated by Goldoni in the *Filosofo inglese* (*The English Philosopher*, 1754).[58] Barone's dramatic production was also known to the French encyclopaedist: Diderot mentions him in his *Paradoxe sur le comédien* (*Paradox of the Actor*, penned in 1770, but not published during the eighteenth century). In support of the work's central thesis – on the alienation of the actor from the fictional character he is representing as the necessary condition for creating persuasive theatrical illusion – Diderot recounts the unsurpassed mastery of Barone specifically in terms of the rehearsal practices he required of his actors without, however, naming him explicitly:

[...] c'est qu'à Naples [...], il y a un poète dramatique dont le soin principal n'est pas de composer sa pièce. [...]

On en a donné quatre représentations de suite devant le roi, contre l'étiquette de la cour qui prescrit autant de pièces différentes que de jours de spectacle, et le peuple en fut transporté. Mais le souci du poète napolitain est de trouver dans la société des personnages d'âge, de figure, de voix, de caractère propres à remplir ses rôles. On n'ose le refuser, parce qu'il s'agit de l'amusement du souverain. Il exerce ses acteurs pendant six mois, ensemble et séparément. Et quand imaginez-vous que la troupe commence à jouer, à s'entendre, à s'acheminer vers le point de perfection qu'il exige? C'est lorsque les acteurs sont épuisés de la fatigue de ces répétitions multipliées, ce que nous appelons blasés. De cet instant, les progrès sont surprenants, chacun s'identifie avec son personnage; et c'est à la suite de ce pénible exercice que des représentations commencent et se continuent pendent six autres mois des suite, et que le souverain et ses sujets jouissent du plus grand plaisir qu'on puisse recevoir de l'illusion théâtrale.

[...] at Naples, [...] there is a dramatic poet whose chief care is not given to composing his piece.

Four representations running were given before the King. This was contrary to court etiquette, which lays down that there shall be as many plays as days of performance. The people were delighted. However, the Neapolitan poet's care is to find in society persons of the age, face, voice, and character fitted to fill his parts. People dare not refuse him, because the Sovereign's amusement is concerned. And when, think you, do the company begin really to act, to understand each other, to advance towards, the point of perfection he demands? It is when the actors are worn out with constant rehearsals, are what we call "used up." From this moment their progress is surprising; each identifies himself with his part; and it is at the end of this hard work that the performances begin and go on for six months on end, while the Sovereign and his subjects enjoy the highest pleasure that can be obtained from a stage illusion.[59]

Diderot explains that he became aware of Barone's methods through his Neapolitan friend Abbé Ferdinando Galiani (1728–87), who was secretary to the Neapolitan embassy in Paris during the years 1759–69 (Domenico Caraccioli, ambassador to the Kingdom of Naples in Paris in 1753, also spoke of Barone).[60] This is precisely the period during which Diderot was developing his theoretical writings on French theatre reform.[61] It is thus no coincidence that, in the midst of his account of Barone's stage-management skills, the first speaker in the *Paradoxe* (Diderot himself) tells the second speaker about the unparalleled success of *Le père de famille* in Naples in 1773 – the play in which he put into practice the techniques of simultaneous scenes (which he called *scènes composées*) and of *tableaux*.[62]

It is in this way that Barone (who had experimented with new approaches to stage design and management before either of the late-eighteenth-century theatre reformers under discussion here) appears as a kind of "third wheel" to Diderot and Goldoni, and redirects the emphasis on what, until now, has been considered by scholars a straightforward polemic between them. Via this triangulation of Barone-Diderot-Goldoni, we espy evidence of a non-linear process in which texts, actors' work practices, and theories of drama circulate and assume transnational characteristics and dimensions. If the origins of this process are traceable to the dramatic practice of Barone, it is difficult to establish – at least in unidirectional terms – the resulting sequence of influences. Was it admiration for Diderot that made Goldoni experiment with the use of *tableaux* in *Il genio*? Or was it the different work conditions of the Comédie Italienne in Paris that permitted him to employ Barone's method? What effect, within this complex narrative, did the application of Barone's techniques – born within and for a court theatre context – have on the radically new dimensions of the public bourgeois theatre? None of these hypotheses, of course, excludes the others.

Given that *Il genio*'s draft script and Diderot's writings on the aesthetics of theatre are contemporary, I might argue that Goldoni did want to pay a kind of homage to the French philosopher (who was the first to theorize the notions of *tableaux* and of *scènes composées*) but that he was, at the same time, entirely aware that Diderot was not the first to comprehend and harness the dramatic effectiveness of these methods. In any case, it is interesting to note that, while it is possible to establish the precise starting point of this circulation of ideas, by the second half of the eighteenth century Barone's name was already lost and forgotten. In fact, Diderot makes no mention of his predecessor's name in the *Paradoxe*, and Charles-Simon Favart (1710–92), one of the creators of comic opera in France and the director of the Comédie Italienne after its merger with the Opéra Comique in 1762, attributes the invention of simultaneous scenes to Goldoni. Favart makes plain his complete ignorance of Barone's existence and of his theatrical innovations in a letter from 1762 (one that is interesting also for what its author says regarding the Venetian public) to Count Giacomo Durazzo. Sending news about Parisian theatrical life to Durazzo (who was, from 1754 to 1764 the superintendent of the court theatres in Vienna), Favart wrote:

> J'ai reçu de Venise les quatre derniers volumes du *Nouveau Théâtre de Goldoni*; nous n'avons pas, selon moi, d'auteurs dramatiques modernes qui entendent mieux la scène, qui développent mieux les caractères, et qui ayent mieux saisi le ton de la vérité. Le seul reproche qu'on peut lui faire, est de s'écarter des autres règles du théâtre. Ce n'est point qu'il ne les connoisse et ne l'ait très-bien prouvé dans sa *Sposa Persiana*, et quelques autres ouvrages; mais un auteur dramatique n'est pas toujours ce qu'il devroit et ce qu'il pourroit être; il est souvent obligé de sacrifier au goût de son siècle et de son pays, et selon toute apparence, les Vénitiens ne s'accommoderoient pas toujours d'une comédie conduite à la Française. Il leur faut plus de mouvemens, d'incidens et de variété. Ils veulent que les yeux soient amusés

par les changements de décoration; ils aiment les sujets compliqués: je ne déciderai point s'ils ont tort de s'amuser de ce qui leur plaît, le goût est une chose arbitraire, et ce qui est beauté dans un pays, peut être défaut dans un autre. Quoi qu'il en soit, Goldoni, malgré ses irrégularités, sert aujourd'hui de modèle à nos auteurs comiques français, c'est lui qui est l'auteur des *Scènes simultanées*, dont M. Diderot s'est fait honneur mal à propos dans sa nouvelle poétique.[63]

I received from Venice the last four volumes of *The New Theatre of Goldoni*. We do not have, in my opinion, modern dramatists who better understand the stage, who better develop characters, and who have better captured the tone of reality. The only criticism one can make of him is that he strayed from the other rules of theatre. It is not that he did not know them and that he did not demonstrate them very well in his *Persian Bride*, and in a few other works, but a dramatist is not always what he should and could be: he is often required to sacrifice [this] to the taste of his era and of his country, and by all appearances, the Venetians would not always put up with comedies in the French style. They needed more action, mishaps, and variety. They wanted their eyes to be entertained by set changes; they loved complex plots. I shan't decide whether they were wrong to be amused by what pleased them, [as] taste is an arbitrary matter, and what is beauty in one country might be a flaw in another. Whatever the case, Goldoni, despite his idiosyncracies, is today a model for our French comedy authors; it is he who is the creator of *Simultaneous scenes*, an honour that M. Diderot dishonestly claims for himself in his new poetics.

This letter by Favart, who was Goldoni's admirer and affectionate friend but also even more a man of the theatre than was Diderot, shows how, throughout this process of the circulation of ideas and dramatic practices, Barone was destined to remain an entirely secondary if not forgotten figure in the history of theatre. Though in Paris *Il genio* was never staged, in Italy, where references to Diderot's theories would have been understood only with difficulty (or more likely not at all) by a Venetian audience, the substitution of marvels with *tableaux* within the framework of the fairy-tale genre had a different significance: it corrected the errors Goldoni viewed in his rival Carlo Gozzi's theatrical fables. The theatre reform that Goldoni achieved, however, was not only occupied with eliminating the magic and plot twists so typical of Gozzi; it was also, and above all, concerned with capitalizing on *tableaux* as a resource for constructing a new and different relationship between spectator and stage.

Absorptive Theatre and the Hidden Spectator

Two terms from art historian Michael Fried's widely read *Absorption and Theatricality: Painting and Beholder in the Age of Diderot* will help us even better understand Goldoni's dramatic techniques.[64] Fried introduces the notions of "absorption" and "theatricality" to distinguish the different approaches of a beholder to a work of art. He posits that a painting is "theatrical"[65] precisely when its subject matter directly addresses an external beholder. When the figures in a painting reveal their awareness of being observed, the painting exists only for the spectator. If, instead, the painted subject appears enclosed within his own internal frame of reference and entirely focused on his own activity, the image maintains its internal coherence, intentionally ignoring the presence of the observer. In this case, when the painting treats the beholder as if she were not there, the relationship between observer and work of art is defined by Fried (following Diderot's criticism of French theatre) as "*anti*-theatrical," or "absorptive." The beholder's sense of being ignored by the painting produces an unexpected – and in some ways paradoxical – effect. That is, although the very existence of paintings presupposes viewers, the images must appear to be "unconscious" – oblivious of the presence of the spectator – for it is this effect that draws beholders into the represented world before them. In other words, viewers are able to experience the sensations of entering into the painted scene and identifying with the painted figures precisely because they remain unaware of their role as external observers.[66] In absorption, Fried argues, a work of art maintains a genuine and authentic relationship with the observer precisely because she is all the more attracted to it the more it, in turn, denies or ignores her existence.[67]

Returning to the engravings of *Il genio* in the Zatta edition, we might note that the viewer's eye stays within the engraved scenes because – in contrast with the Pasquali edition illustrations – they do not represent objects that recall stage scenery, such as curtains, proscenium arches, or double frames that "on the one hand draw the eye of the observer to the outside and, on the other, are easily interpreted as the edges of the stage."[68] The figures in the Zatta engravings, therefore, appear to be engaged in "absorptive" activities: for instance in the first engraving (which references the first act), we see Arlecchino and Corallina entirely involved in collecting money. Their activity is observed by the evil genie, but there is no reference to an external spectator. The Zatta engravings unconsciously document the contemporary mode in which theatre was perceived, presenting us with theatre that is not particularly theatrical. The relationship here between image and observer could therefore be defined, using Fried's term, as "absorptive."[69]

Given that only eight years passed between the publication of the last volume of the Pasquali edition in 1780 and the first volume of the Zatta edition in 1788, and that the design of both editions was done by the same artist – Pietro Antonio Novelli – and executed by the same team of Novelli's collaborators,[70] the profound differences between the two editions in terms of iconographic choice and manner of execution can only be explained, I would argue, by changing intentions towards the public. The Zatta engravings confirm Goldoni's deep awareness that the role of the public – which was becoming an "active interlocutor in a discourse oriented towards the future"[71] – had changed, and that new communicative techniques were needed in order to establish a relationship with this new audience. I suggest that Goldoni responded to the demands of this new public with *Il genio* – a play focused entirely on the experience and reception of the spectator – and that this focus was obtained via pictorial images that were made specifically to produce the dramatic illusion of absorption in their spectators. As Gerardo Guccini notes pointedly in his fine study on Goldoni's pictorial imagination,

> Lo spettatore, in questo teatro, cessava di essere destinatario puramente passivo d'un meraviglioso effimero e scenograficamente progettato, per farsi soggetto d'una illusione più tenace e pervasiva, che esso stesso alimentava addentrandosi, per via empatica e di interpretazione critica, nella comprensione d'una realtà, in sé, drammatica, ma percepita "come se" fosse vera. Il realismo goldoniano sostituiva l'esplicita alterità fenomenologica delle maschere e del meraviglioso visivo con ambigui simulacri del vero, che raffinavano, di fatto, le tecniche dell'inganno teatrale, non più affidato, in questa particolare declinazione, a ciò che è manifestamente fittizio, artificioso o artistico, ma ad una virtuosistica sovrapposizione di "Mondo" e "Teatro" – anzi, per dirla con Goldoni, del "libro del Mondo" e del "libro del Teatro."[72]

> The spectator, in this [Goldoni's] theatre, ceased to be a purely passive receptacle for an ephemeral, staged marvel, in order to become subjected to a stronger and more pervasive illusion, which he fed even as he entered it, by means of empathy and critical interpretation, in understanding a reality that was, in itself, dramatic, but that was perceived "as though" it were real. Goldoni's realism substituted the explicit phenomenological alterity of the masks and of visual marvels with ambiguous simulacra of the truth

that actually refined the techniques of the theatrical trick, no more entrusted, in this specific form, to what is obviously fictional, artificial, or artistic, but to a virtuosic overlapping of "World" and "Theatre" – indeed, to say it with Goldoni, of the "book of the World" and of the "book of the Theatre."

The Eloquence of Pantomime and Dance

Writing about the figures represented in the Zatta illustrations, Cesare Molinari observes that, "rispetto a quelli della Pasquali, i personaggi delle ilustrazioni Zatta parlano di meno e dicono di più: perfino nelle scene di conversazione si può talvolta trovare un quasi complete silenzio gestuale" ("with respect to those in the Pasquali [edition], the characters [portrayed] in the Zatta edition speak less but say more: indeed, even in conversational scenes one can at times find an almost complete gestural silence").[73] Along with the strong presence of the visual in *Il genio*, we see an extensive use of silence on the stage that brings us into the territory of pantomime performance. In fact, every act of the comedy ends with a pantomime that functions as an *intermezzo*: the pantomime dance at the end of the first act accompanies the departure of the protagonists for Paris; the second pantomime occurs during their departure for England. Pantomime movements, which fill the entire third act, intensify the physical and verbal violence of the encounter between Arlecchino and four Englishmen and anticipate the rift between Arlecchino and Corallina. The exotic dimension of the fourth act is the pretext for pantomime dances of battles and for the joyous pantomime dance (with liberated slaves and both Turkish and Venetian soldiers) that accompanies the departure of the protagonists from Venice (Tripoli).

The inclusion of a large number of pantomimes in *Il genio* can be explained by Goldoni's original intent to write a comedy for the Parisian public. Pantomime – a genre very much of the *forain* theatres (but also in use at the Comédie Italienne and the Opéra Comique) that is characterized by stylized, extravagant gesture and mime as its primary means of communication – developed between 1729 and 1745 under the influence of the *commedia dell'arte* and the theatrical dances of Italian Baroque opera. This historical continuity between *divertissement forain* and seventeenth-century court dances, on the one hand, and the Italian opera *intermezzo*, on the other, allowed Goldoni to construct a comedy that could function well in both Paris and in Venice.

During the years 1740 to 1765 in France and Italy, pantomime dances – performed as the *entr'actes* in *opera seria* and in comic plays – came to occupy an ever more central place in theatrical performances and were enthusiastically received by a vast audience. But it was in France, above all, that pantomime attracted the attention not only of spectators but also of theatre theorists, who were interested in the renewal of an acting style that would permit actors to communicate various emotions via facial expression.

It was Diderot, again, who attributed great importance to the gesture – which he felt was better able than speech to elicit emotion – and who argued that silent acting could at times be more eloquent than words. Recalling Dubos's recommendation in his *Réflexions* that the pantomime of the ancients must be revived as an element of theatrical performances,[74] Diderot was the first theorist to grant gesture an almost autonomous significance, rather than viewing it as a simple explication or mirroring of the dialogue:

> Il faut écrire la pantomime toutes les fois qu'elle fait tableau; qu'elle donne de l'énergie ou de la clarté au discours; qu'elle lie le dialogue; qu'elle caractérise; qu'elle consiste dans un jeu délicat qui ne se devine pas; qu'elle tient lieu de réponse, et presque toujours au commencement des scènes.
>
> [It is necessary to write pantomime] every time it constitutes a tableau, whenever it intensifies or clarifies the dialogue, whenever it reveals character, when it is some subtle form of byplay that cannot be guessed at, whenever it represents an answer, and almost always at the beginning of scenes.[75]

In the *Entretiens sur le fils naturel*, Diderot declares that a playwright is a genius if he knows how to combine pantomime with words and to alternate dialogue with silent scenes containing pantomime action. As Graham Ley states, "the essence of Diderot's modernity"[76] is in having grasped how pantomime can express a sense of the unsaid and, therefore, how it represents the sublime form of the art of drama.

As in the case of Goldoni's use of *tableaux*, his inclusion of pantomime dances participates in his ongoing search for new means of communication between playwright and spectator. The function of pantomime dances in *Il genio* is to make spectators perceive onstage action as though it were a living painting and to thereby reinforce the illusion of unity between audience and stage.

In closing this chapter, I would like to stress the extent to which this minor comedy by Goldoni exemplifies the radical transformation of the relationship between playwright and public that occurs in the second half of the eighteenth century. In this period, the public became extraordinarily influential and thus an inescapable respondent – one that playwrights could both impact and exploit in their competition for a front-and-centre position within the Parnassus of European theatre. From this point of view, *Il genio* reveals Goldoni's keen awareness of the spectator's centrality in the socio-cultural sphere and, by extension, the necessity of finding new dramatic forms that were adapted to the new audience's demands, tastes, and inclinations.

In order to indulge this new public, but also to influence and educate it, Goldoni employed the stage techniques of *tableaux* (with the function of creating a dramatic illusion of "absorption" in the viewer); of pantomime; of visual effects; and of choral-like staging. His use of these techniques demonstrates his ability to adapt and to integrate himself, as an Italian, into a European context; it calls attention to his lively curiosity; and it confirms the quality of his experience as a man of the theatre. As reconstructed here, Goldoni put into practice many of the practical directions and dramatic suggestions formulated by Diderot in his writings on theatrical aesthetics, writings that were, themselves, a critical intervention in late-eighteenth-century debates on theatre. In applying, furthermore, the theoretical suggestions of his brilliant predecessor, Domenico Barone, Goldoni constructed plausible and coherent narratives even within the narrow confines of the fable; he avoided artificial and unnatural plot twists in favour of more believable and moving "paintings"; and he gave ample space to gesture and other modes of silent expression.

What did Goldoni wish to demonstrate by following so faithfully the directorial guidelines suggested by Diderot – who did, after all, call his Venetian colleague a modest "author of farces"? I would argue that he wished to demonstrate that he was never less than avant-garde with respect to the renewal of theatrical practice, which is precisely what he was doing in *Il genio,* a theatrical fable and deliberate farce with its mixing of diverse theatrical genres and contamination of dramatic languages. While Goldoni may not have owed a direct debt to Diderot or to Barone, all three were engaged in a common search for new forms of performance aimed at revolutionizing contemporary theatrical practices in order to respond to the demands of a new public. In sum, therefore, this chapter recounts an exemplary instance of the circulation and triangulation of artefacts, ideas, and theories of theatre in Europe; further, it points to a question regarding how intensely one European theatrical culture affected another, a question that has yet to be examined deeply.

Il genio is also exemplary in that it furthers the argument put forward in the previous chapter: that the construction of both theatre audiences and dramatists was a complex and fraught process. Through the playwright's efforts to cultivate the competency of theatre-goers in matters of drama and aesthetics – and to engage them as direct participants in the onstage action (and in the public sphere), encouraging them away from their less explicitly critical (and political, as the previous chapters have shown) stance – theatre audiences, or publics, became more actively and productively critical. At the same time, the recognition of the playwright as an "author" happened via his response to the demands of his public. Just as the playwright created the active, critical, eighteenth-century audience, this new public constituted the eighteenth-century figure of the dramatist.

6 Liberty and the Audience

Vittorio Alfieri's Theatre of the Dead

The plays of Vittorio Alfieri (1749–1803) were written and performed precisely during the transformative era during which court theatre became public, civic, and political theatre; his theoretical reflections on theatre further usher in the phenomenon of spectator formation that results, by the end of the eighteenth century, in the development of the audience into a critical force – the process that has been explored in its earlier stages over the course of the preceding chapters. Considering that Alfieri himself felt a political and dramaturgical duty to create and shape the next generation of "the public," an investigation into his theatrical production provides unique insights into the audiences of Romantic Risorgimento theatre. An initial brief glance at Alfieri's self-representation reveals clearly why his writings illuminate spectatorship in this period.

Though born a nobleman, Alfieri refused to adopt the burdensome position of the aristocrat because, he observed, the existence of the nobility unfolds under the prince's eye. A nobleman does not and cannot live in the private sphere: "in ogni più privata cosa in quel benedetto paese sempre c'entra il Re" ("the King [always] interferes in all domestic concerns of his subjects").[1] In his autobiography, which he wrote in 1790 at the age of fifty-one, Alfieri represents himself as a free poet, uncontaminated by life at court, intentionally contrasting his situation with that of Voltaire, "Gentiluomo ordinario del Re" ("Gentleman in ordinary to the King").[2] In the treatise *Del principe e delle lettere* (*Concerning the Prince and Letters,* 1778–86), Alfieri affirmed the moral value of literature – which he saw as adversely affected by any sort of patronage – declaring that "lo scrittore, eletto all'arte sua da sè stesso, non serve a nessuno, altro che al vero; e non solo per la patria sua, ma per gli uomini tutti e presenti e futuri ei lavora" ("the writer, self-appointed to his profession, serves no one but the truth, and works not only for his country but for all men present and future").[3] According to Alfieri, men of letters must distance themselves from princely protection rather than collaborate with power so as to earn the patronage "del pubblico illuminato, quando perverrà ad esserlo; protezione, la sola, che onoratamente si possa e bramare e ricevere" ("of the enlightened public, when such a public is established. This patronage alone can honourably be desired and accepted").[4]

Alfieri, therefore, presents himself as a rebellious, counter-culture figure – and as a radically unrooted and solitary author. He claimed that the theatre was responsible for his public presence and that it forced him out of the isolation that had him "essere sepolto prima di morire" ("being buried before death").[5] The aim of his theatre was, above all, to spread a message of liberty: "Il teatro, la storia, i poemi, l'eloquenza oratoria, le lettere tutte in somma, e sotto gli aspetti tutti, una vivissima scuola divengono di virtù, e di libertà" ("Drama, history, poetry, the art of oratory, all forms of literature in short, become a living school of virtue and liberty in every aspect").[6] His works for theatre thus seek to create, in citizens who are both spectators and readers, an impetus towards increased critical freedom – to construct, in short, an enlightened public. While Alfieri felt that literature had an undeniable obligation to promote liberty, in his *Risposta al Calzabigi* (*Reply to Calzabigi*, 1783) – a well-known librettist and a reformer of the operatic genre who lauded the first edition of Alfieri's tragedies – he also argued that "il miglior protettore del teatro, come d'ogni nobile arte e virtù, sarebbe pur sempre un popolo libero" ("the best protector of theatre, as well as of any other noble art and virtue, would always be a free people").[7] Alfieri's theatre, then, is not so much a school of virtue, in which actors educate spectators who are expected to reproduce the deeds of freedom-loving tragic heroes, as it is a theatre in which the public has a crucial and active role.

It is for this reason that Alfieri made the character of *il popolo* – the people – not only the protagonist of his dramas but also a "personaggio parlante e operante, in un tempo dove egli era affatto muto e sepolto" ("speaking and active character at a time when [the people] were entirely mute and buried").[8] The importance of this collective character is immediately evident from its constant presence in his tragedies. As Denise Alexandre has shown, the people appear in the list of *dramatis personae* in all eight of his tragedies; in five of these (*Virginia*, *Merope*, *Agide*, *Bruto primo*, and *Bruto secondo*) the people have lines to speak and are active participants in the onstage narrative.[9] In the "Greek" tragedies[10] that belong to Alfieri's first creative period – *Oreste* (sketched out in 1776 and put into verse in 1782) and *Agide* (first conceived in 1784 and completed in 1785) – the people are given the function of judge. His *Merope* (conceived of and composed six years after *Oreste,* in 1782) confers an even greater importance on the people: a comparison with Alfieri's models (the homonymous tragedies by Maffei and Voltaire) reveals that his innovation was to make the people participate directly in the death of the tyrant and in the reinstatement of the legitimate king on the throne. The first instance of a choral character called "the people" is to be found in Alfieri's *Virginia,* which was first conceived in 1777 and printed at Siena in 1783. This tragedy is closely tied to the playwright's reading of Machiavelli,[11] whose *Prince* promoted a new kind of ruler: a model for republican reform who, rather than support the nobility, gives military and economic power to the people.[12] The chorus was also to be an indispensable character in all of Alfieri's "Roman" works, peaking in substance and status when exalted as the "principalissimo personaggio in ambedue i Bruti" ("most important character in both *Bruti*"), which were written between 1786 and 1787.[13] Referring to *Bruto primo,* Mario Fubini observes that "il dramma di Bruto o il dramma dei suoi figli [non] stette a cuore al poeta, bensì la possibilità che gli fu offerta di far muovere sulle scene un popolo libero, guidato da un grande capo e degno di lui" ("the drama of Brutus or the drama of his sons is [not] close to the poet's heart, but rather [it is] the possibility that was offered him to bring to life onstage a free people, guided by a great leader and worthy of him").[14]

Despite the fact that the character of the people has increasing importance and appears with growing frequency in his tragedies, Alfieri presents himself as an author without a public who writes, instead, "per popolo morto" ("for the dead people").[15] He explains what this means in his *Reply to Calzabigi,* which suggests that an informed and engaged public doesn't (yet) exist in provincial and ignorant late-eighteenth-century Italy, and that audiences still need to be taught how to be active interlocutors:

> Il pubblico italiano non è ancora educato a sentir recitare: ci vuol tempo, e col tempo si otterrà; ma intanto non per questo lo scrittore deve essere lasso o triviale. Se le cose sue meritano, non è egli meglio, e più giovevole, che il volgo faccia un passo verso il sapere, imparando, che non l'autore un passo verso l'ignoranza, facendo in sue mani scapitar l'arte che tratta e la lingua che scrive?[16]

> The Italian public has not yet been educated to attend performances: this will require time, and with time it will be obtained; but meanwhile the playwright should not for this reason be lax or trivial. If his things have merit, is it not better for him and more beneficial so that the vulgar masses take a step towards knowledge [and] learning, rather than the author take a step towards ignorance, causing, by his own hand, a loss of the art which he practises and the language that he writes?

Condemning "la cecità degli spettatori, la bestialità e barbarie degli attori" ("the blindness of spectators; the beastliness and barbarities of actors")[17] and denouncing the absence of rich and stable theatrical activity in Italy, Alfieri turns instead to the audience of the future: "Io scrivo con la sola lusinga, che forse, rinascendo degli Italiani, si reciteranno un giorno queste mie tragedie: non ci sarò allora; sicché egli è un mero piacere ideale per parte mia" ("I write with the sole hope that perhaps, with the Italians reborn, they will one day perform these my tragedies: I will not be there then; therefore this is merely an ideal pleasure on my part").[18]

In his *Parere sull'arte comica in Italia* (*Opinion on Comic Art in Italy*, 1785), Alfieri, "attore di se stesso e capocomico" ("an actor [playing] himself and a director"),[19] proves highly aware of the fact that in order for the playwright to create the new modern spectator it is necessary for the relationship among audience, author, and actors to be not only theatrical but also social:

> Per far nascere teatro in Italia vorrebbero esser prima autori tragici e comici, poi attori, poi spettatori.
>
> [...]
>
> Gli spettatori pure si formeranno a poco a poco il gusto, e la loro critica diventerà acuta in proporzione che l'arte degli attori diventerà sottile ed esatta: e gli attori diventeranno sottili ed esatti, a misura che saranno educati, inciviliti, agiati, considerati, liberi, e d'alto animo; questo vuol dire, per prima base, non nati pezzenti, né della feccia della plebe.
>
> Gli autori in fine si perfezioneranno assai, quando, recitati, da simili attori, potranno veder in teatro l'effetto per l'appunto d'ogni loro più menoma avvertenza, e giudicare dall'effetto dove s'abbia a mutare, dove a togliere, dove ad aggiungere. E fra autori, attori, e spettatori, che tutti tre sanno e fanno il dover loro, presto si cammina d'accordo; e non solo ogni sillaba e punto, ma ogni più sottile intenzione dell'autore ha e dimostra, per mezzo dell'attore, il suo effetto presso gli spettatori. Questi tre si danno

la mano, e sono ad un tempo stesso tutti tre a vicenda cagione e effetto della perfezione dell'arte.[20]

For theatre to be born in Italy there must first be writers of tragedy and comedy, then actors, then spectators.

[...]

The spectators, furthermore, will develop their taste bit by bit, and their critique will become more acute in proportion to the subtleness and exactitude of the actors' art: and the actors will become subtle and exact to the degree that they are educated, civilized, well-off, respected, free, and of elevated spirit; this means, at a most basic [level], born neither as beggars nor of the dregs of the commoners.

Finally, authors will perfect themselves significantly when, performed by such actors, they can see in the theatre the precise effect of even their most minimal directions, and judge from this effect where to modify, where to cut, where to add. And authors, actors, and spectators, who all three know and do their duty, will soon come to agree; and not only every syllable and period, but every subtlest author's intention [will] have and reveal, via the actors, its effect upon the spectators. These three will join hands to be simultaneously, all three [and] each other, the reason for and the effect of the perfection of the art.

This denunciation of the absence of competent authors, of actors capable of interpreting someone else's text, and of a cultured and perceptive audience is of course not new – all eras lament precisely the same thing. Indeed, Alfieri repeats almost exactly the opinion of Scipione Maffei who, in his treatise *De' teatri antichi e moderni* (1753), writes of the necessity to provide a new foundation for theatrical communication that can only be constructed by first raising the cultural and moral level of authors, actors, and audience. Alfieri's position is thus neither unique nor innovative; it inscribes him into the intense theoretical reflection on theatre that was blossoming in Italy (and in the rest of Europe) during the 1700s. In line with what has been observed in earlier chapters, Marco Ariani suggests that the tendency visible in these theoretical writings is to see the spectator emerge "come primario 'luogo' ricettivo, e spazio privilegiato di azione del messaggio tragico" ("as a primary receptive 'place' and as a privileged space for making active the tragic message").[21] What makes Alfieri, a tragic author long awaited by educated eighteenth-century Italians, a representative playwright – from the point of view of the process by which both theatrical writing and the dramaturgy of the spectator were transformed – is his conception of theatre, which rests upon the collaborative complicity of its practitioners. It is due to his shrewd perception of theatrical performance (which unites participants on- and offstage via the recounting of a story, of a thought, and of an entire community) that Alfieri, even from the early 1800s, was seen as a national author like Goldoni, "capace di suscitare un senso di appartenenza" ("able to elicit a sense of belonging").[22]

This chapter analyses the complex relationship of Alfieri to the recipients of his theatre – those contemporary and past figures, both real and fictional, to whom the playwright entrusted his tragedies. Alfieri's reflections on the characteristics of the ideal spectator permit us to explore how he created collaboration among author, actors, and audiences as well as how he realized his goals of educating and refining the taste of the spectator, and of creating and shaping a critical public.

Ancient People and the New Public

The tragedy *Bruto primo*[23] is an apt choice for the first stage of this exploration because, as Angelo Fabrizi has noted,

> [i]n nessuna altra tragedia, l'Alfieri sentì e rappresentò più fortemente come personaggio il popolo [...] e si può pur dire, cautamente, che la volontà di assumere il popolo come personaggio equivaleva a voler spostare l'antitirannismo eroico delle precedenti tragedie di libertà verso una dimensione meno staccata dal momento storico e più determinata nella sua ansia di patria e di nazione.[24]

> In no other tragedy does Alfieri more strongly feel and represent the people as a character [...] and one can even say, with caution, that the desire to adopt the people as a character was equivalent to wanting to shift the heroic anti-tyranny of earlier tragedies on freedom towards a dimension less removed from the historical moment and more definite in its stress on homeland and nation.

In order to begin our investigation into the role of the public in Alfieri's theatre, we must first ask why this playwright, who sought to offer his contemporaries a tragedy that was "meno staccata dal momento storico," chose a classical subject? What, exactly, was happening during the historical moment when *Bruto primo* was composed?

An answer to the first question is provided by Alfieri himself in his *Della tirannide* (*Of Tyranny*, 1777–89). This treatise states that republican Rome "in cui ogni Romano nascea cittadino e riputavasi libero" ("where every Roman was born a citizen and considered himself free") is the model "della più splendida politica libertà che siasi mai vista sul globo" ("of the most glorious political liberty which has ever existed on this earth").[25] Alfieri then proceeds to attribute various foreshadowings and much significance to the events of Roman history. As Mariasilvia Tatti argues, "per Alfieri la storia romana [...] è la storia per eccellenza (e il popolo romano nel *Parere alla Virginia* è 'il più sublime popolo che si sia mai mostrato nel mondo'), è portatrice di verità, come la storia sacra per i credenti, ed è la massima manifestazione di virtù, libertà, gloria, le 'tre sacre faville'" ("for Alfieri Roman history [...] is history *par excellence* (and the Roman people, in his *Parere alla Virginia*, are 'the most superb people who have ever shown themselves in this world') and is the bearer of truth, like sacred history to the believers, and is the greatest manifestation of virtue, freedom, glory, the 'three sacred flames'").[26] In addition, as Alessandro Pellegrini notes, Alfieri "non poteva pronunciare il giudizio di condanna contro l'aristocrazia in nome di un popolo, che sembrava inesistente, bensì in nome dell'idea del popolo libero, quale un tempo era esistito" ("could not pronounce a guilty verdict against the aristocracy in the name of a people that seemed not to exist, but [he could do so] rather in the name of the idea of a free people that had existed at one time").[27] In Alfieri's search for a theatre of civic truth, therefore, the conflicts of Roman history became essential. The events represented in *Bruto primo* that induced the birth of the Roman Republic must have been seen by Alfieri as a perfect *exemplum* for the "popolo italiano futuro" ("future Italian people") to whom the famous dedication of 17 January 1789 from *Bruto secondo* was addressed.[28]

We have still to clarify, however, why the people came to have a fundamental role for Alfieri between 1786 and 1789 – and, more precisely, around the end of 1786, when the tragedy was drafted; in 1787, when it was put to verse in a version where the people were assigned an even broader role that included longer lines and more of them – "battute più numerose e anche più ampie";[29] and 1789, when the tragedy was printed in the fifth volume of the *Tragedie* by Didot's Parisian press.

The observations of Michel Foucault prove useful here. In his course at the Collège de France, the French philosopher spoke of the birth of a political sensibility that brought the notion of population to the forefront and discussed his preoccupations both with this notion and with the mechanisms that might secure its regulation. Before the eighteenth century, he writes,

> *raison d'État* really did define an art of government in which there was an implicit reference to the population, but precisely population had not yet entered into the reflexive prism. From the beginning of the seventeenth to the middle of the eighteenth century there is a series of transformations thanks to which and through which this notion of population, which will be a kind of central element in all political life, political reflection, and political science from the eighteenth century, is elaborated.[30]

It is worth placing Foucault's observations concerning the importance that the concept of the public came to acquire during the first half of the 1700s side by side with the reflections of Habermas. In his essay *Naturrecht und Revolution* (*Natural Law and Revolution*), which was published around the same time as *The Structural Transformation of the Public Sphere*, the German sociologist pinpoints 1789 as the year of political triumph for public opinion. Habermas states, borrowing Emmanuel Joseph Sièyes's definition, that this year represents the moment in which "die öffentliche Meinung schließlich sogar den Gesetzgebern Gesetze diktiert[e]" ("public opinion even dictates the laws for the lawgivers").[31]

These later sociological and historiographical observations resonate strongly when brought into direct conversation with Alfieri, whose treatise *Del principe e delle lettere* was composed around the same time as *Bruto primo*. In this treatise, which is where his political passions are most clearly expressed, he writes that:

> L'opinione è la innegabile signora del mondo. L'opinione è sempre figlia in origine di una tal qual persuasione, e non mai della forza. Ora, chi negarmi ardirà, che gli eccellenti scrittori non siano stati sempre assai più fabri e padroni dell'opinione a lungo andare, che i principi? Ragionano quelli, e sforano questi: ma la verità, allorchè vien presentata sotto forme intelligibili da ogni classe di uomini, può penetrare in ogni uomo, e diventa ella quindi propria di tutti: all'incontro la forza del principe, che per via del timore penetra pur anche nel cuore di tutti, e l'abborrimento e la rabbia vi genera, in chi sta ella riposta questa sì temuta forza, fuorchè nel volere di tutti, o dei più? [...] La ragione dunque e la verità, per via di scrittori penetrando infino al più infimo di noi, tosto verremo a riguardare i re tutti per quello appunto ch'ei sono. E in una moltitudine d'uomini, dal veramente conoscere i proprij diritti al ripigliarseli e difenderli, egli è brevissimo il passo.

> Public opinion is the undeniable mistress of the world; public opinion is always born of some kind of persuasion, never of force. Now, who will dare deny that great writers have always eventually been more effective than princes as creators and masters of public opinion? The former uses reason, the latter, force; but truth, when it is presented in forms intelligible to every class of men, can penetrate every mind and so becomes the common property of all; on the contrary, the power of the prince penetrates the hearts of all through fear, and generates hatred and rage. Yet where does this dreaded power reside but in the will of all or of the majority: [...] If reason and truth were to penetrate the humblest man through the efforts of our writers, we should soon come to appreciate all kings for exactly what they are. And in most men there is only a step between fully recognizing one's own rights and regaining and defending them.[32]

By considering Foucault's, Habermas's, and Alfieri's words on this historical moment, we can see how *Bruto primo*'s date of composition, its theme, and its versification correspond precisely to the mode of political and ideological thought that is characteristic of 1780s Europe more generally and as evidenced by this specific play. The tragedy is thus a dramatization of the history of public opinion, and an analysis of *Bruto primo* can help us trace the primary ways in which public opinion came into its own – as well as confirm the importance of its role, upon which Alfieri insisted. These observations on the complex meaning of Alfieri's drama, furthermore, permit us to specify the boundaries of our study. The following pages show which historical figures brought about the emergence of public opinion, investigate its function, and examine how it operated in practice. Keeping in mind that Alfieri, according to Saverio Bettinelli, was "un politico, che vuol fare il poeta" ("a politician who wishes to be a poet")[33] and that these are therefore not "just" plays, we will also ask what political and civic role the people were assigned in his Roman tragedy.

Koselleck and the Origins of Public Opinion

The story of *Bruto primo* is well known: it recounts the overthrow and exile of the last king of Rome, Tarquinio il Superbo (Lucius Tarquinius Superbus or Tarquin the Proud) for his abuses of monarchical power and the resulting reallocation of power between the two consuls.[34] In Alfieri's version, the curtain opens on the immediate aftermath of Lucretia's suicide. The consul Brutus (who had secretly been preparing – for twenty years – to be the instrument of a long-awaited civic renewal) enters the stage, grasping the weapon with which the violated Lucretia ended her life. He invites her husband, Collatinus, and the Roman people to join him in an act of revenge. Collatinus declares himself ready to follow Brutus, to avenge Lucretia, and to spill his own blood for his nation; the people join together in their promise to the consuls to free themselves from Tarquin. In the second act, Mamilius, the tyrant's ambassador, comes to Rome – officially to beg pardon for his sovereign but in reality to reinstate the old order by conspiring against Brutus with the support of Brutus's own sons, Titus and Tiberius (who were drawn into the plot against their father by this deceitful ambassador).[35] Deeply shocked by his own sons' participation in the conspiracy, Brutus pardons them as their father but, as the public magistrate, finds them guilty of treason. Both sons, as a result, are sentenced to beheading. Thus, in acts IV and V, a tragedy about liberty and public action becomes a private, personal drama about paternal love.

The play, it should be evident, thus revolves around the tension between the moral and political spheres. This philosophical problem (and *Bruto primo*'s representation of a series of contrasting forces and opposing concepts – like freedom and despotism) recalls contemporary themes identified by Reinhart Koselleck's *Kritik und Krise. Ein Beitrag zur Pathogenese der bürgerlichen Welt* (*Critique and Crisis: Enlightenment and the Pathogenesis of Modern Society*, 1959). This work, which focuses on an analysis of the origins of the European Enlightenment, identifies the delicate balance between public governance and private conscience as the genesis of modern malaise. Given that *Bruto primo* is centred on the history of Habermasian public opinion, we might productively bring Habermas to bear on Koselleck's interpretation of the Enlightenment – especially given that one of *Kritik und Krise*'s more prominent themes is the birth and function of public opinion.[36] This comparison is particularly useful because, while Habermas describes the functioning of modern society in what we might call "normal" situations, Koselleck focuses on politically dysfunctional or revolutionary moments – precisely like the one represented by Alfieri's tragedy.[37]

In the first part of his study, Koselleck describes the emergence of absolutism as the political solution to violent religious wars via the concentration of physical force in the hands of the state. The function of the absolutist state, then, was to keep the peace among parties who were in conflict. Koselleck's thesis on the origins of absolutism takes its impetus from *Leviathan* (1651); he in fact observes that Thomas Hobbes was the first to formulate the principle of the separation of politics from moral conscience. The English philosopher had explained that, because of the weakness of human nature, men's innate wickedness, and people's continual aspiration to power, human beings would always be in a state of conflict that would result in civil and religious wars.[38] As a response to this situation, Hobbes claimed, politics came to be contained by the power of the state, and morality was relegated to the private sphere of citizen-subjects. (Indeed, the reading of Maffei's *Merope* undertaken in chapter 3 demonstrates how Baroque rulers – like Maffei's Polyphontes – adhered to the concept of pure politics, which removed the concerns of moral order from the mechanisms of governance.) Though it asked for the obedience of its subjects in exchange for safeguarding its integrity and for keeping peace, the state permitted them to conserve a certain freedom in their authority over moral questions. This separation and reassignment of moral and political codes meant that subjects were deprived of political power and of the right to criticize rulers but retained the freedom to make moral judgments and decisions regarding the private sphere.

The private sphere could not, however, be prevented from slowly invading the public sphere. Excluded from the political sphere, citizens began actively directing their personal freedom towards the emerging public sphere, within whose multifaceted discursive space they applied their moral values to controversial questions, including those having to do with state politics. The opinions of citizens, therefore, did not remain within the bounds of private opinion but rather started to take on the character of laws. Koselleck notes that, while Hobbes subordinated human conscience to the laws and authority of the state, John Locke attributed a political role to individual conscience. In the political theory he elaborated in the *Essay Concerning Human Understanding* (1699), "[c]ivic morality becomes a public power, one that works only intellectually but which has political effects, forcing the citizen to adapt his actions not just to State law but simultaneously, and principally, to the law of public opinion."[39]

In the second part of *Kritik und Krise*, Koselleck describes the radical revision of the relationship between morality and politics that occurred during the Enlightenment. The emergence of the bourgeoisie brought with it a new moral and political awareness. The bourgeois classes saw moral authority as superior to political authority and began to criticize the absolute state. What united the members of the bourgeoisie, who were economically powerful but socially disenfranchised (and who formed one part of the tripartite division of Enlightenment society along with the nobility, which had always had exclusive jurisdiction with regard to political authority but was deprived of political power, and the philosophers, who were intellectually powerful but deprived of executive authority), was their contestation of a political order based not on moral law but on *raison d'état* – a concept that, according to Foucault, describes the relationship of the state to itself.[40] As noted briefly above, Koselleck argues that the new Enlightenment society had a fundamentally dual vision of the world based upon a series of paired opposites that contrasted politics with moral law and ethics; the world of wrongdoing with the world of equality and humanity. This dualistic society had begun calling into question the legitimacy of the absolutist state by developing a new system of moral values. In an unanticipated turn, it was precisely the separation of morality from politics – which had seemed the strongest rationale for absolutist power in the first place – that became the weakness the Enlightenment could attack in order to destroy the *ancien régime.*

If we return to *Bruto primo,* we can now see how, despite its setting in ancient Roman times, its plot mirrors this more recent historical period as described by Koselleck and, in particular, reflects the moment when moral critique – understood here as subjects' assessments of and verdicts on power and authority – prevails over the laws of the state. The very beginning of Alfieri's drama explicitly shows us that the fall of tyranny and the proclamation of the republic are caused not by a political but by a private event: the offence and the violence to which Lucretia is subjected by Sextus, son of Tarquin the Proud. It is significant that Lucretia's vendetta does not take place on a more familial level – as might more normally occur, for example, in Elizabethan revenge tragedy. Here, instead, it takes place on an entirely public level. Brutus even asks Collatinus not to hide away his own private pain but rather to expose it before all of Rome:

BRUTO: – Agli occhi intanto
Di Roma intera, in questo foro, è d'uopo
Che intero scoppi e il tuo dolore immenso,
Ed il furor mio giusto. (I.1, vv. 6–9, p 27)

BRUTUS: – Meanwhile,
'Tis indispensable, that in this forum
Thy boundless sorrow, and my just revenge,
Burst unreservedly before the eyes
Of universal Rome. (p. 267)

As a result, the vengeance for Lucretia's dishonour becomes "ampia" (v 13, p 27; "complete," p 268) and "universal[e]" (v 18, p 28; "universal," p 268). The people's dismay with the Tarquin regime and the eventual expulsion of the tyrant also sheds light on how the actions of the sovereign come to be judged, fundamentally, by moral – not state – laws. The events that set the tragedy's plot in motion illustrate how society's moral critique expands into public affairs, while the private space of human conscience simultaneously takes on a political role. This affirmation of the individual as morally responsible for public and political life is exemplified by Consul Collatinus, who declares that he is disposed to put his duty as a citizen ahead of his private sorrow:

> Sol per la patria vera, alla svenata
> Moglie mia sopravvivere potrei. (I.1, vv. 31–2, p. 28)

> I, for a genuine country's sake alone,
> Could now survive my immolated wife. (p. 268)

This diffusion of moral critique across the private/public spectrum – to the point that morality becomes genuinely public – causes moral laws to appear alongside the laws of the state. Swearing to the people that he will free them from the tyrant – a promise that embodies Alfieri's own political convictions and that expresses his concept of liberty – Brutus states,

> BRUTO: – Io giuro inoltre,
> Di far liberi, uguali, e cittadini,
> Quanti son or gli abitatori in Roma;
> Io cittadino, e nulla più: le leggi
> Sole avran regno, e obbedirolle io primo.
> POPOLO: Le leggi, sì; le sole leggi: ad una
> Voce noi tutti anco il giuriamo. (I.2, vv. 182–8, p. 34)

> BRUTUS: – I further swear,
> Many as Rome's inhabitants may be,
> To make them equal, free, and citizens;
> Myself a citizen, and nothing more:
> The laws alone shall have authority,
> And I will be the first to yield them homage.

PEOPLE: The laws, the laws alone: we with one voice
To thine our oaths unite. (pp. 272–3)

The laws to which Brutus refers here are clearly not the laws of the state. Instead, they are the laws of public opinion that have taken on the characteristics of state laws – laws, therefore, that have behind them the force of justice and that recognize the principle of equality.[41] This is confirmed in *Della tirannide*, where Alfieri argues that no king, however legitimate, should have more right than the people to create and enforce laws: "le leggi, cioè gli scambievoli e solenni patti sociali, non debbono essere che il semplice prodotto della volontà dei più; la quale si viene a raccogliere per via di legittimi eletti del popolo" ("laws, that is, mutually accepted solemn social contracts, must be only the simple product of the will of the majority, expressed through the duly elected representatives of the people").[42] Here Alfieri illustrates Koselleck's observation that "it is no longer the sovereign who decides; it is the citizens who constitute the moral laws by their judgement, just as merchants determine a trade value. [...] Their private views rise to the level of laws purely on the strength of the inherent censure."[43] The reflections of Koselleck, who proposes a genetic theory of the modern world, and of Habermas on the birth of the public sphere describe from two distinct but complementary perspectives the same phenomenon of the transition from political regimes of the early modern age to those of modernity. Indeed, Habermas's representative public sphere was based on the *mise-en-scène* of sovereign power with the aim of silencing moral law – the very dynamic that distinguishes modernity from the period preceding the Enlightenment as theorized by Koselleck. The Habermasian modern public sphere, then, has to do with individual subjectivity and, in Koselleck's terms, with how moral judgment comes to have the upper hand over state laws.

The setting of Alfieri's tragedy thus illuminates how, with the advent of the Enlightenment, the relationship between morality and politics comes to be substantially revised and how, in this same period, public opinion comes to attain the status of state law. Since, again, *Bruto primo* is a tragedy about the history of public opinion, we can now explain that (at least according to Alfieri) it emerges in an attempt by civic society to offer a solution to the dialectical tension between the moral and political spheres. We can also now define the function of public opinion, which is to challenge absolute power. Indeed, in the final chapter of *Della tirannide*, Alfieri sees in "universal volontà e opinione" the final remedy for despotism and tyranny (which for him meant any form of monarchical government): "[...] conchiudo con questo capitolo il libro, col dire; che non vi essendo alla tirannide altro definitivo rimedio che la universal volontà e opinione" ("[...] I will close my book with this chapter, and will say: that there is no definitive remedy for tyranny but universal will and opinion").[44]

If public opinion is instrumental in political reform and in the instituting of liberty and equality, the theatre, as a public space for citizens, is the most effective vehicle for the development and dissemination of the will of the people. Indeed, in his *Risposta al Calzabigi*, Alfieri declares that his duty is to create a theatre capable of producing a palingenesis that is both social and political:

> Io credo fermamente, che gli uomini debbano imparare in teatro ad essere liberi, forti, generosi, trasportati per la vera virtù, insofferenti d'ogni violenza, amanti della patria, veri conoscitori dei proprj diritti, e in tutte le passioni loro ardenti, retti, e magnanimi. Tale era il teatro in Atene; e tale non può esser mai un teatro cresciuto all'ombra di un principe qualsivoglia.
>
> I firmly believe that men must learn in the theatre to be free, strong, generous, inspired by true virtue, intolerant of all violence, lovers of their country, fully conscious of their proper rights, and in all their passions, ardent, honest, and magnanimous. Such was the theatre in Athens: and such a theatre can never be if it grows in the shadow of a prince.[45]

With this declaration, the tragedy of *Bruto primo* shows its audience and readers how – and employing what model of governance – a renewal of the political system can be effected.

Un popol re[46]

As suggested above, the political model that is challenged by Alfieri's tragedy is characterized in part by the twin separations of politics and morality, and of the public and private spheres.[47] This form of governance is represented by the figure of Tarquin, in whom the two halves – private and public – of the ruling individual are in fact explicitly opposed to each other. Hoping to convince the Romans to bestow favour once again upon their deposed king, Ambassador Mamilius explains that Tarquin's son, Sextus, was punished for the rape of Lucretia and that, in following through with the punishment of his offspring, the tyrant had had to act not as a father but as a king:

MAMILIO: ma Tarquinio stesso,
Più re che padre, il suo figliuol traea,
Per sottoporlo alla dovuta pena. (II.6, vv. 257–9, p. 49)

MAMILIUS: But Tarquin, *more a monarch than a father,*
Thither enticed his son, to subject him
To a retributory punishment. (p. 282, my italics)

Tarquin's character illustrates how, in an absolutist system, the public and the private exclude each other and how, in fact, there is no private sphere beyond the public sphere: to act in a manner consistent with his public role as king, the tyrant must renounce his private role as father. Like the other tyrants studied here (Cicognini's Don Pedro d'Aragona and Maffei's Polyphontes), Tarquin incarnates a model of sovereignty that is based upon representative *Öffentlichkeit.* Among his tyrannical behaviours, it is this one in particular that the Romans, who had by then adopted an entirely different value system, find contemptible. The people's disdain is a response to that which had long been considered a privilege reserved for the sovereign – that is, the power of life and death; the power held by the father as head of the household. Their disapproval is expressed by Brutus, the "vero interprete" of the people (II.6, p. 232; "our true interpreter, the only one / worthy to be the organ of our thoughts," p. 281), in his response to Mamilius:

BRUTO: Menzogna è questa, e temeraria, e vile;
E me pur, mal mio grado, a furor tragge.
Se, per serbarsi il seggio, il padre iniquo
Svenar lasciasse anco il suo proprio figlio,
Forse il vorremmo noi? (II.6, vv. 260–4, p. 49)

BRUTUS: This is an impudent unmanly lie;
And robs me utterly of self-control.
If, to preserve his throne, the guilty father
Offer'd to sacrifice his guilty son,
Should we consent to it? (p. 282; my italics)

Brutus demonstrates that what makes his model of governance different from Tarquin's is his attempt to align moral actions with the interests of the state – and the public with the private – in a single figure who both governs the republic and represents the people. Indeed, the collective character *il popolo,* addressing Brutus and Collatinus, expresses its faith that the two consuls could become simultaneously rulers and fathers of the Romans: "Ma intanto, voi / *Consoli e padri* ne sarete a un tempo" (I.2, vv. 196–7, p. 34; "But ye meanwhile / Will be to us *our consuls and our fathers,*" p. 273, my italics). This title is repeated once again in an exchange between Brutus and the people of Rome:

POPOLO: Il dignitoso e forte
Tuo aspetto, o Bruto, e il favellar tuo franco,
Tutto, sí, *tutto in te ci annunzia il padre*
Dei Romani, e di Roma. (II.5, vv. 129–32, p. 43)

PEOPLE: Thy dignified
And manly looks, O Brutus, thy frank speech,
All, all announce in thee to us the father
Of Rome and of the Romans. (p. 278; my italics)

In his response to the people, Brutus demonstrates his readiness to take on this paternal role and emphasizes that being called and then actually becoming father of the Romans is for him an honourable burden:

BRUTO: *O figli, dunque;*
Veri miei figli, (poiché a voi pur piace
Onorar me di un tanto nome) io spero
Mostrarvi in breve, ed a non dubbie prove,
Ch'oltre ogni cosa, oltre a me stesso, io v'amo. (II.5, vv. 132–6, p. 43)

BRUTUS: *O my sons,*
My genuine sons, (since with the name of father
Ye have been pleased to honor me,) I hope
Shortly to show you, by no doubtful proofs,
That beyond all, beyond myself, I love you. – (p. 278; my italics)

Brutus's great affection for and attachment to his people make it clear that the kind of paternity he embodies neither seeks to exercise the right of *patria potestas* – that is, the authority of a parent over his subject-children – nor to benefit from the *vitae necisque potestas* of which Tarquin availed himself. For Brutus (as for the good ruler Cresphontes in

Maffei's *Merope*) this relationship is instead intimate and reciprocal; it exists between equal members of the community.

Brutus is a positive figure precisely because he represents the union of the qualities of father and ruler; his character thus invites comparison with another of Alfieri's kings: Ciniro from *Mirra* (*Myrrha*, written between October 1784 and September 1786). Ciniro is a model human being because (and in contrast to the representations of tyrants in earlier tragedies by Alfieri) the two figures of father and king co-exist in him. For this reason, Mirra's love for his father is, simultaneously and inevitably, his love for his king.[48] As Niccolò Mineo observes, the two figures – father and son – are inseparable in Alfieri's theatre.[49]

In this way, Brutus embodies the transition away from the "Stato come famiglia" ("State as family") model – that is, away from thinking of the state as a family (the metonymic offshoots of this analogy are evident, for example, in the dynastic transmission of sovereignty) towards considering the family to be like the state.[50] In other words, political power and the family – the public and the private – end up being inextricably intertwined. This is the form of government that, according to Alfieri, permits the sovereign to rule in the name of individual morality and the community to command in the name of the king, becoming the "popol re" (I.2, v. 200, p. 35; "people king"). Only characters like Brutus, Collatinus, and, in smaller measure, Ciniro – all of whom bring together private and public virtue in a single personage – are able to teach the people to be free. Indeed, in his treatise *Del principe e delle lettere* (which is indispensable for understanding his two *Bruti*), Alfieri writes:

> La libertà dunque nasce, e vien promulgata conservata e difesa da quegli uomini principalmente, che insegnando ai popoli i loro diritti, somministrano loro gli opportuni mezzi al difenderli. La libertà in oltre, è la sola e vera esistenza di un popolo; poiché di tutte le cose grandi operate dagli uomini la ritroviamo sempre esser fonte. In Roma dunque ed in Londra erano e sono necessariamente illuminati e sovrani oratori quegli uomini, cui con sì bel privilegio la libertà destinava e destina a stabilire conservare ed accrescere le più sacre e legittime prerogative di tutti. Ma fra noi popoli servi, che non abbiamo tribuni, chi altri mai ci potrà insegnare a conoscere i nostri diritti, a ripigliarcegli, e a difenderli, se ciò gli scrittori non fanno?

> So liberty is born and promulgated, preserved, and defended, principally by those men who, by teaching peoples their rights, provide them with the

necessary means of defending them. Moreover, liberty represents the only true life of a people; for we find it to be the source of all great things accomplished by men. In Rome, then, and London, the enlightened and supreme orators were and are by necessity those men on whom liberty conferred and still confers the great privilege of establishing, preserving, and expanding the most sacred legitimate prerogatives of all men. But among us enslaved peoples, without tribunes, who else can teach us to know our own rights, to recapture them and defend them, if writers do not?[51]

By seeking to reconcile, in himself, the private and public dimension as well as political action and individual morality – thereby uniting, in his one figure, the roles of father, consul, and citizen – our protagonist illustrates Koselleck's observation that

> [t]he private and public domains are not mutually exclusive; as a matter of fact, the public realm arises from the private one. The self-assurance of the moral inner space lies in its ability to "go public." The private domain can expand on its own into a public one, and it is only in the public sphere that personal opinions prove to have the force of law. [...] The citizens' verdict legitimises itself as just and true; their censure; their critique – these become the executive of the new society.[52]

The solution proposed by the new civic (bourgeois) society to the dialectical tension between politics and individual morality thus consists in the fusion of the public and private spheres. Brutus shows that public and private are not binary entities that exclude each other; rather, these two spheres complete each other. On a more theoretical level, the structure of these father-king characters illustrates Habermas's argument that

> [t]he sphere of the public arose in the broader strata of the bourgeoisie as an expansion and at the same time completion of the intimate sphere of the conjugal family. Living room and *salon* were under the same roof; and just as the privacy of the one was oriented toward the public nature of the other, and as the subjectivity of the privatized individual was related from the very start to publicity, so both were conjoined in literature that had become "fiction."[53]

The tragedy of *Bruto primo* thus spurs on the politicization of the private, a development that begins with Maffei's *Merope* and is exemplified by the figure of Cresphontes-Aegistus's mother-queen. This process demonstrates that, while in absolutist states the public and the private exclude each other, in the political space of modernity the public and the private lose their distinctiveness and merge together.

Agamben and the Genealogy of Power

Given that Alfieri situates the origins of public opinion in the Enlightenment attempt to bridge the politics/morality binary and that he casts it in the role of promoting his ideology of freedom, we might now inquire as to how he was able to realize his lofty political project and how public opinion actually functioned in practical terms.

In *Della tirannide*, Alfieri explains that recourse to violence and force is necessary in order to convince people who had long suffered tyranny of the advantages of the republic. To prove his point, he employs the example of Brutus's sacrifice of his own sons:

> Ma, la nascente libertà, combattuta ferocissimamente da quei tanti che s'impinguavano della tirannide, freddamente spalleggiata dal popolo, che, oltre alla sua propria lieve natura, per non averla egli ancora gustata, poco l'apprezza e mal la conosce; [...] ov'essa per qualche beata circostanza perviene a pigliare alcun corpo, non dovendo trascurar l'occasione di mettere, se può, profonde e salde radici, si trova pur troppo costretta ad abbattere quei tanti rei che cittadini ridivenir più non possono, e che pur possono tanti altri impedirne, o guastarne. Deplorabile necessità, a cui Roma, felice maestra in ogni sublime esempio, ebbe pur anche la ventura di non andar quasi punto soggetta; poichè dal lagrimevole straordinario spettacolo dei figli di Bruto fatti uccider dal padre, ella ricevea fortemente quel lungo e generoso impulso di libertà, che per ben tre secoli poi la fece sì grande e beata.

> But the nascent liberty, fiercely opposed by all those who have battened on tyranny, and coldly supported by the people who, naturally frivolous and still unacquainted with its sweetness, hold it in small esteem and do not understand it; [...] nascent liberty, I say, if it does succeed by some happy chance in making its appearance in some society, since it must not neglect the opportunity of striking deep and tenacious roots there if it can, is often unfortunately constrained to strike down many wretches who can never again become citizens, and who yet can impede or corrupt many others. A lamentable necessity, to which Rome, however, our happy mistress in every sublime example, was fortunate enough almost never to be subjected; for from the deplorable and amazing spectacle of Brutus's sons put to death by their own father's

> order she received so powerful and generous a final incitement to liberty that it made her great and blessed for the next three centuries at least.[54]

Bruto primo thus dramatizes the impossibility of peaceful change and the political necessity of history drenched in blood. Just like Tarquin the Proud (who should have chosen to act either as a father or as a public figure), now Brutus finds himself having to decide whether he should prefer the ties of blood to liberty. When the consul spots the names of his own sons on the list of conspirators against the republican regime, he declares that private interest – even when it is as sacrosanct as the act of saving one's own sons – cannot overpower the superior interests of the state:

> – Misero Bruto! …
> *Padre omai più non sei* … – Ma, ancor di Roma
> *Consol non men che cittadin, tu sei.* – (IV.2, vv. 110–12, p. 72)

> – Unhappy Brutus! …
> *Thou art no more a father* … – But, thou'rt yet
> *Consul, no less than citizen, of Rome.* – (my italics, p. 296)

Brutus's renunciation of family ties in favour of serving society as a whole is reaffirmed in his speech to his sons:

> Voi, traditori della patria dunque
> Siete, non più di Bruto figli omai;
> Figli voi de' tiranni infami siete. (IV.3, vv. 158–60, p. 75)

> Ye to your country, then, are traitors, now
> No more the sons of Brutus; but the sons
> Of infamous expatriated tyrants. (p. 297)

Before sacrificing them on the altar of the state, Brutus, first consul of Rome, makes explicit the insuperable rift between the role of public official and of father, revealing an "I" no less torn than that of Tarquin before him:

> – Può il padre
> Piangerne in core; ma secura debbe
> Far la cittade il vero consol pria: … (V.2, vv. 235–7, p. 92)

The father in his heart may weep for this;
But in the first place should the genuine consul
Secure the safety of his native city: ... (p. 309)

Thus the character of Brutus, who aspired but failed to be "padre, console e cittadino" ("father, consul, and citizen"), embodies the impossibility of a definitive reconciliation of individual morality and *raison d'état*, and incarnates the missing solution to the problem of moral dualism. This idea is proposed again by Alfieri in the final chapter of *Della tirannide*:

> [...] si consideri che le importantissime mutazioni non possono mai succedere fra gli uomini [...] senza importanti pericoli e danni; e che a costo di molto pianto e di moltissimo sangue (e non altramente giammai) passano i popoli dal servire all'essere liberi, più ancora, che dall'esser liberi al servire. Un ottimo cittadino può dunque, senza cessar di esser tale, ardentemente desiderare questo mal passeggero; [...]. E giunge avventuratamente pure quel giorno, in cui un popolo, già oppresso e avvilito, fattosi libero felice e potente, benedice poi quelle stragi, quelle violenze, e quel sangue, per cui da molte obbrobriose generazioni di servi e corrotti individui se n'è venuta a procrear finalmente una illustre ed egregia, di liberi e virtuosi uomini.

> [...] let it be considered that changes of great importance can never take place in human affairs [...] without serious danger and losses; and it is at the cost of many tears and much blood (never otherwise) that people pass from slavery to freedom, much more so than from freedom to slavery. An excellent citizen, then, without ceasing to be so, may ardently desire this passing evil, because it puts an end at one blow to many other evils no less serious and much more durable, and at the same time the good which is necessarily born of it is much greater and more permanent. [...] And perhaps the day is fortunately dawning when a people, formerly oppressed and debased, now free, happy, and powerful, will bless that slaughter, that violence, that blood, by means of which there has at last been created out of many generations of enslaved, corrupted individuals, an illustrious distinguished generation of free and virtuous men.[55]

It seems, therefore, that *Bruto primo* along with the political theory Alfieri developed in his *Della tirannide* were influenced by Machiavelli's *Discorsi*: "E chi piglia una tirannide e non amaza Bruto, e chi fa uno stato libero e non amaza i figliuoli di Bruto, si mantiene poco tempo" ("whoever takes up a tyranny and does not kill Brutus, and whoever makes a free state and does not kill the sons of Brutus, maintains himself for little time").[56]

The tragedy of *Bruto primo* lends itself to being interpreted as an awareness on the part of its author that fully realizing his project for reform was impossible and, more generally, as the Enlightenment's failure to fuse politics and morality. We can further deepen our understanding of the tragedy, however, by bringing together Koselleck's theory of the political origins of public opinion with the philosophical and political reflections of Giorgio Agamben. His *Homo sacer. Il potere sovrano e la nuda vita* (1995) explores the implications of Western political history for human life, in particular demonstrating the unique relationship that exists between sovereign and subject. According to Agamben, the sovereign defines and legitimizes himself because he acts with respect to *homo sacer*, an exemplary figure from Roman law and an archetypal figure who has the power of life and death over his citizens. Agamben writes that the "sovrano è colui rispetto al quale tutti gli uomini sono potenzialmente *homines sacri* e *homo sacer* è colui rispetto al quale tutti gli uomini agiscono come sovrani" ("sovereign is the one with respect to whom all men are potentially *homines sacri*, and *homo sacer* is the one with respect to whom all men act as sovereigns").[57] In other words, sovereignty is exercised via its capacity of controlling "[la] vita nuda" ("[the] naked life" – a key concept for Agamben), which is a life from which political significance is withheld. To better explain this concept, the philosopher looked to Aristotle's distinction between *zoē* – natural life, or simple biological existence – and *bios*, living as an individual and in community, or political life. The "vita nuda" is the result of the violence of sovereignty – it is what remains of individual political *bios*, life that has been damaged by politics and stripped of political influence. The human being is thus replaced by a merely "living" being, transformed into a simple biological body:

> Dietro il lungo processo antagonistico che porta al riconoscimento dei diritti e delle libertà formali, sta ancora una volta, il corpo dell'uomo sacro col suo doppio sovrano, la sua vita insacrificabile e, però, uccidibile. Prendere coscienza di questa aporia non significa svalutare le conquiste e i travagli della democrazia, ma provarsi una volta per tutte a comprendere perché, nel momento stesso in cui sembrava aver definitivamente trionfato dei suoi avversari e raggiunto il suo apogeo, essa si è rivelata inaspettata-

> mente incapace di salvare da una rovina senza precedenti quella *zoē* alla cui liberazione e alla cui felicità aveva dedicato tutti i suoi sforzi. [...] La decadenza della democrazia moderna e il suo progressivo convergere con gli stati totalitari nelle società postdemocratiche spettacolari [...] hanno, forse, la loro radice in questa aporia che segna l'inizio e la stringe in segreta complicità con il suo più accanito nemico.

> Behind the long, strife-ridden process that leads to the recognition of rights and formal liberties stands once again the body of the sacred man with his double sovereign, his life that cannot be sacrificed yet may, nevertheless, be killed. To become conscious of this aporia is not to belittle the conquests and accomplishments of democracy. It is, rather, to try to understand once and for all why democracy, at the very moment in which it seemed to have finally triumphed over its adversaries and reached its greatest height, proved itself incapable of saving *zoē*, to whose happiness it had dedicated all its efforts, from unprecedented ruin. Modern democracy's decadence and gradual convergence with totalitarian states in post-democratic spectacular societies [...] may well be rooted in this aporia, which marks the beginning of modern democracy and forces it into complicity with its most implacable enemy.[58]

In Agamben's view, then, the schism between *zoē* and *bios* represents normative political action. With this suggestion in mind, we might see Alfieri's tragedy as presenting a genealogical myth that exposes the secret bond linking power and human life. In other words, *Bruto primo* shows how the power of Western government (whether monarchical or republican) is directly practised upon the lives of individuals. Indeed, by putting to death his own sons (sons who are stained with the sin of treason), Brutus himself ends up exercising the same power over life and death upon which Tarquin's rule was based. The tragedy thus reveals how, in the age of the political success of the modern state (an era that the play mirrors allegorically), the ways in which human life finds itself inscribed into politics do not change substantially. This conclusion is all the more dramatic when at the end of the eighteenth century, as we have seen, the public and private spheres are increasingly intertwined and family life is increasingly politicized.

To recapitulate, we might say that the point at which these two critical perspectives – the historical and philosophical notions of Koselleck (who describes the insuperable schism between private morality and politics) and Agamben's biopolitics (which instead delineates the schism between *zoē* and *bios*) – intersect is their clear demonstration of how mechanisms of power are founded upon the exclusion of the individual from political life – or, at the very least, upon the reduction of the individual's political role.

But if his tragedy permits us to glimpse Alfieri's awareness of the difficulties inherent in translating his mythology of freedom into a project of reform because of the ways in which power relationships have historically been constructed, at the same time the play makes evident how his convictions remained firm regarding the ability of theatre to make, "a poco a poco dei nuovi popoli" ("bit by bit a new people")[59] through his will to create "una sana opinione" ("a reasoned opinion"):

> E si noti per cosa certissima, che la influenza degli scritti, allorchè tendono a rinnovare o confermare una sana opinione, riesce molto superiore al poter delle leggi; appunto perché il libro cortesemente soggioga col solo convincere, e la legge duramente fa forza coll'assolutamente costringere. Io perciò mi riprometterei piuttosto di pervenire più brevemente e efficacemente a innestare nel cuore di una moltitudine una qualunque verità, porgendogliela replicatamente per via di diletto in una teatrale rappresentazione da tutti intesa e gustata, che non per via di una diretta concione, e molto meno per via di una costringente ancora che giusta e legittima legge.

> And let it be accepted as fact that the influence of the written word, when it tends to revive or confirm healthy public opinion, is far superior to the power of the laws; because a book sways by gentle persuasion alone, while the law harshly constrains by stern coercion. So I should hope to succeed in instilling some truth more quickly and effectively into the hearts of a multitude by presenting it as entertainment in a play which everyone understands and enjoys rather than by a public speech; and even less by a coercive law, though just and legitimate.[60]

That the tragedy in fact succeeded in educating new and active political subjects is confirmed by Alfieri himself in the dedication to *Bruto secondo*, where he claims that the play gave "e lingua, e mano, e intelletto, a chi (per essere interamente scordato d'aver avuto questi tre doni dalla natura) credeva impossibile quasi, che altri fosse per riacquistarli giammai" ("language, strength, and intellect to those who – since they had completely forgotten they had these three gifts from nature – thought it was almost impossible that others should ever reacquire them").[61] The reception of *Bruto primo* also suggests that it was a powerful and creative ideological force for social and political palingenesis, as Francesco De Sanctis indicates:

> Gli effetti della tragedia alfieriana furono corrispondenti alle sue intenzioni. Essa infiammò il sentimento politico e patriotico, accelerò la formazione di una coscienza nazionale, ristabilì la serietà di un mondo interiore nella vita e nell'arte. [...] [N]elle nuove generazioni, travagliate da' disinganni e impedite nella loro espansione, quegl'ideali tragici così vaghi e insieme così appassionati rispondevano allo stato della coscienza, e quei versi aguzzi e vibrati come un pugnale, quei motti condensati come un catechismo, ebbero non poca parte a formare la mente ed il carattere.[62]

> The effects of Alfieri's tragedy corresponded to his intentions. The play inflamed political and patriotic sentiment, accelerated the formation of a national consciousness, re-established the seriousness of an interior world in both life and art. [...] [I]n the new generations, which were afflicted by disillusionment and were impeded in their expansion, these tragic ideals – so ambiguous and yet so impassioned – responded to the state of the conscience; and those verses, honed to a dagger-fine point, those words, as concise as a catechism, had no small part in shaping their mind and their character.

Public Opinion Reigns

At this point we must ask what strategies Alfieri used to transform his Settecento public into critical Enlightenment spectators who were aware of his political message and were competent judges of dramatic works. To respond to this question, it will be useful to turn once more to *Bruto primo* with Koselleck's theory of modernity in mind – and, in particular, his notion of the Enlightenment as a moral process and as a force that pressed everyone to critique everything. As the title of his book *Kritik und Krise* suggests, the German historian explains that social critique became the most crucial component of the Enlightenment posture and of the intellectual practice that catalysed the crisis of absolutism.[63]

As we have seen so far, Alfieri's tragedy reflects, in allegorical form, a historical reality. It is therefore not difficult to find, in the play, a substantial number of scenes in which the collective character *il popolo* is placed in situations where it has to discern the contradictions inherent in a discourse or where it is called upon to make decisions on various questions regarding the republic. Significant from this point of view is the reaction of the people to Mamilius's speech, which attempts to absolve the tyrant of the crimes committed by Sextus, his son:

MAMILIO: Io tremo.
– Tarquinio re …
POPOLO: Di Roma no.
MAMILIO: – Di Roma
Tarquinio amico, e padre …
POPOLO: Egli è di Sesto
L'infame padre, e non di noi …
[…]
MAMILIO: Qual è il delitto, onde appo voi sì reo,
A perder abbia oggi ei di Roma il trono
A lui da voi concesso …
POPOLO: Oh rabbia! Oh ardire!
Spenta è Lucrezia, e del delitto ei chiede? …
MAMILIO: Fu Sesto il reo, non egli …
TIBERIO: E Sesto, al fianco
Del padre, anch'ei veniva or dianzi in Roma:
E se con lui volto non era in fuga,
Voi qui il vedreste.
POPOLO: Ah! perché in Roma il passo
Lor si vietò? già in mille brani e in mille
Fatti entrambi gli avremmo (II.6, vv. 235–56, pp. 47–8)

MAMILIUS: I tremble. – Tarquin, king …
PEOPLE: Not king
Of Rome.
MAMILIUS: – Of Rome, the friend and father, Tarquin …
PEOPLE: He is the wicked father of that Sextus,
And not of us …
BRUTUS: Whate'er his words may be,
May ye be pleased to hear him in complete
Dignified silence.
MAMILIUS: – To yourselves erewhile
Came Tarquin, at the earliest news that Rome
Rebell'd; almost defenceless and alone,
Fully relying on his innocence,
And on his people's loyalty, he came:
But armed men repell'd him. Hence he sent me,

	A messenger of peace; and by my means
	Enquires, what is the crime, whence in your sight
	So guilty, that to-day he's doom'd to lose
	The throne of Rome, once his by your consent ...
PEOPLE:	O rage! Incredible audacity!
	Slain is Lucretia, and he asks the crime? ...
MAMILIUS:	That was the guilt of Sextus, not his own ...
TIBERIUS:	And Sextus also at his father's side
	Erewhile repair'd Rome: and had they not
	Both been compell'd to save their lives by flight,
	Here had ye seen him now.
PEOPLE:	Ah, why did ye
	Frustrate their wish to gain access to Rome?
	Already had we torn their scatter'd limbs
	In thousand thousand pieces. (pp. 281–2)

This scene describes a process of collective decision making in which all participants in the discussion reveal an awareness sufficient to the task of forming their own opinions. This excerpt, in which the people are required to practise hermeneutics and are called upon to exercise their own critical judgment, is not unique: in act IV, scene 1 (where Collatinus and the patrician Valerius update the Romans on the status of the conspiracy), the people are invited to judge the traitors and to make a difficult decision about the destiny of Brutus's sons, who are both guilty (as conspirators against the state) and not guilty (as sons seeking to protect their father).

It is worth remembering that Maffei positioned *il popolo* such that his citizen characters became participants in the execution of a tyrant. *Merope* thus illustrates Habermas's thesis that the birth of the public sphere emerged within the republic of letters and from debates among private citizens on questions that had nothing to do with politics.[64] The fact that Maffei's tragedy did not contain a direct objection to the *ancien régime* reveals how criticism at this earlier time was disinterested and apolitical. Alfieri's tragedy instead shows the advent of a criticism with political force – to quote Koselleck: "[c]riticism assumed the role Locke had at one time assigned to moral censorship; it became the spokesman of public opinion."[65]

By making available to the people/public the information upon which they must reflect critically and take a firm position, Alfieri's tragedy requires the spectator not just to act as the bearer of a critical contribution but also to take on a new role as an actor/interpreter. Considering the increasing political significance of criticism as the primary instrument of morality, Alfieri's education of the spectator as critic can be seen not only as aesthetic but also – and above all – as political. For Alfieri, "tragediografo di profondo pensiero teorico" ("a tragedian of profound theoretical thought"),[66] tragedy was the highest form of politics and a concrete metaphor for the national political scene. His work thus sought to create a politically engaged spectator-judge – a public capable of determining the truths at the heart of social and political questions.

The Visual Order of Things

According to his *Parere sull'arte comica*, Alfieri wanted to reform theatrical practice by creating a collaboration among authors, actors, and spectators; he employed specific dramaturgical strategies to create solidarity among the diverse participants in his plays. Marzia Pieri argues that "la drammaturgia alfieriana è intimamente performativa nei suoi processi genetici" ("Alfieri's dramaturgy is intimately performative in its genetic processes").[67] How then did he manage to forge an indissoluble bond between spectator and stage, and how were his receptive publics rendered active subjects capable of bringing their own critical contributions to both theatrical and political life?

I hypothesize that, in order to make the real people in the audience identify with the tragic fictional *popolo* onstage (who make their decisions about power based on moral criteria), Alfieri turned to, emulated, and then perfected the dramaturgical tools that were put into practice by his predecessors: Cicognini, his imitators, and Goldoni. As we have seen, these tools, techniques, and strategies often have to do with the gaze. Mario Fubini observes that it is "[s]ignificativa [...] l'insistenza con la quale quei personaggi [Bruto e Collatino] invitano il popolo a contemplare gli spettacoli che gli sono offerti e a trarre da quella vista un incitamento e un monito. [...] Tutto in questa tragedia si converte in spettacolo" ("significant [...], the insistence with which those characters [Brutus and Collatinus] invite the people to contemplate the spectacles that are offered to them and to take from that sight a spur and a warning. [...] Everything in this tragedy becomes performance").[68]

The first spectacle that is offered for the Romans to see is Collatinus's public expression of pain and sorrow:

BRUTO: Voi tutti,
Carchi di pianto e di stupor *le ciglia,*
Su l'infelice sposo *immoti io veggo*!

Romani, *sí miratelo*; scolpita
Mirate in lui, padri, e fratelli, e sposi,
La infamia vostra. (I.2, vv. 97–100, p. 31)

BRUTUS: I *see*
That all of you *regard* the hapless spouse
With weeping eyes, by stupor petrified.
Yes, Romans, look at him; ah, see in him,
Ye brothers, fathers, and ye husbands, *see*
Your infamy *reflected.* (p. 270, my italics)

Brutus intends this spectacle to function as a kind of anticipatory preparation for the appearance of Lucretia's body, which, he feels, will reinforce the effect of his oath of freedom on the Romans: "Sarà nei cor l'effetto, in veder morta / Di propria man la giovin bella e casta" (I.1, vv. 56–7, p. 29; "More the effect will be upon their hearts / When they behold the chaste and beauteous lady," p. 269). Brutus first requires the people's gazes to converge upon him:

– *In me,* Romani,
Volgete in me pien di ferocia il guardo:
Dagli occhi miei di libertade ardenti
Favilla alcuna, che di lei v'infiammi,
Forse (o ch'io spero) scintillar farovvi. (I.2, vv. 105–9, p. 31)

– O Romans, *tow'rds me,*
Turn tow'rds me, Romans, your ferocious looks:
P'rhaps from my eyes, with liberty all-burning,
Ye may collect some animating spark,
Which may inflame you with its fost'ring heat.
I Junius Brutus am; (p. 270; my italics)

before offering the Romans the spectacle of Lucretia's body, which is brought to the Forum:

COLLATINO: Ma, qual *spettacol veggio!* ...
POPOLO: *Oh vista atroce!*
Della svenata donna, ecco nel foro ...
BRUTO: Sì, Romani; *affissate,* (ove pur forza
Sia tanta in voi) nella svenata donna

Gli occhi affissate. Il muto egregio corpo,
La generosa orribil piaga, il puro
Sacro suo sangue, ah! tutto grida a noi:
"Oggi, o tornarvi in libertade, o morti
Cader dovrete. Altro non resta."
POPOLO: Ah!
Tutti Liberi, sì, sarem noi tutti, o morti. (I.2, vv. 161–70, p. 33)

COLLATINUS: But ah!
What spectacle is this! ...
PEOPLE: Atrocious sight!
Behold the murder'd lady in the forum ...
BRUTUS: Yes, Romans; fix, (if ye have pow'r to do it,)
Fix on that immolated form your eyes.
That mute fair form, that dreadful gen'rous wound,
That pure and sacred blood, ah! All exclaim:
"To-day resolve on liberty, or ye
"Are doom'd to death. Nought else remains."
PEOPLE: All, all,
Yes, free we all of us will, or dead. (p. 272)

A superb *metteur-en-scène* of spectacles of cruelty – and thus clearly aware of their extraordinary efficacy in moving the people emotionally – Brutus might be read not only as an alter-ego of the author – a character who expresses Alfieri's political position – but also as a spokesman for the playwright's reflections on dramaturgy. As Vincenzo Gioberti has suggested, "[n]ei drammi dell'Alfieri non vi ha, propriamente parlando, che un solo personaggio, cioè l'autore medesimo; e il suo Teatro è un'autobiografia come la sua *Vita*" ("in Alfieri's dramas there is only, properly speaking, a single character, that is the author himself; and his Theatre is an autobiography like his *Vita*").[69] In a passage from *Della tirannide*, Alfieri – like Brutus – discerns, in performances that are "terribili e sanguinosi" ("terrible and bloody"), successful mechanisms for engrossing spectators and stirring their souls to the point that the audience is deeply moved:

> Il popolo di Roma si sollevò contro ai tiranni, congiurò felicemente contr'essi, e la tirannide al tutto distrusse, allorchè finalmente si mosse, dopo tante altre battiture, colpito dal compassionevole *atroce spettacolo di Lucrezia contaminata dal tiranno, e di propria mano svenata.* Ma,

> se Lucrezia non avesse in sè stessa generosamente compiuta la prima vendetta, egli è da credersi che Collatino, o Bruto, inutilmente forse, e con grave dubbio e pericolo, avrebbero congiurato contro ai tiranni: perché il popolo, e il più degli uomini, non son mai commossi, nè per metà pure, dalle più convincenti ragioni, quanto lo sono da una giusta e compiuta vendetta; massimamente allorchè *ad essa si aggiunge un qualche spettacolo terribile e sanguinoso, che ai loro occhi apprestatosi, i loro cuori fortemente riscuota.*

> The people of Rome rose up against the tyrants, conspired successfully against them, and completely destroyed tyranny when they finally roused themselves, after so many other blows, deeply moved by the pitiful shocking spectacle of Lucretia, polluted by the tyrant, and killed by her own hand. But if Lucretia had not nobly carried out the act of vengeance, it is credible that Collatinus or Brutus would have perhaps conspired uselessly against the tyrants, with doubtful success and peril to themselves, because the people and the majority of men are never moved even half as much by the most convincing reasons as by a just, complete vengeance; especially when to it is added some terrible and bloody spectacle, which takes place before their very eyes and strangely moves their hearts.[70]

Indeed, Brutus orders the Romans to consider the agony of the father even as they fix their gaze upon his sons' torture:

> L'orrido stato
> Mirate or voi, del padre … Ma già in alto
> Stan le taglienti scuri … Oh ciel! partirmi
> Già sento il cor … *Farmi del manto è forza*
> *Agli occhi un velo … Ah! ciò si doni al padre*
> *Ma voi, fissate in lor lo sguardo:* eterna,
> Libera sorge or da quel sangue Roma. (V.2, vv. 252–8, p. 93)

> Now,
> Think of the pangs of the distracted father …
> Each cleaving axe already gleams on high …
> O Heav'ns! my very heart is rent in twain …
> I needs must in my mantle veil my eyes …
> Ah! This may to the father granted be …
> But ye, fix ye on them your eyes: now Rome
> Free and eternal rises from that blood. (p. 310)

What would the effect of these scenes have been on the contemporary spectator? First, if Alfieri's poetics, as he himself writes, is a poetics of "forte sentire" ("strong feeling"),[71] the objective of their focus on the gaze is to coax empathy from the spectator. Second, as Fubini has noted, "il popolo romano 'principalissimo personaggio' del *Bruto primo* e gli altri personaggi tutti, non possiamo idealmente disgiungerli da un altro popolo, da quel 'popolo vero ascoltante in platea,' di cui parla l'autore nel *Parere*, da un popolo, che veda sulla scena un'immagine idealizzata di sè medesimo" ("the Roman people, 'the most protagonist character' in *Bruto primo* and of all his other characters cannot ideally be distinguished from another people – from that 'true people listening in the audience' of whom the author speaks in his *Parere*, of a people who see onstage an idealized image of themselves").[72] Within scenes of the gaze that are orchestrated by Brutus-Alfieri we espy a strategy of communication that exalts the active role of spectators, stimulating them to see over and over again, simultaneously making evident the aesthetic function of the play. Scenes of the gaze also establish a reciprocal rapport among the actors, who direct their eyes towards spectators even as audience members watch those onstage from the house. In this mirroring of spectator and actor – a relationship that is more precisely triangular (with the playwright at the vertex and the actor-characters, models for the public, and the audience at the two bases) – the watcher and the watched continuously reflect each other. The character-actors look out at the audience, before whose eyes the people onstage are offered as a scene for contemplation; the onstage figures behold a scene for which they are, in turn, a scene.

If the public (*popolo*) onstage and the public (audience) in the theatre mirror each other, the internal logic of their mutual gaze (by means of which actors look at spectators and vice versa) would seem to have a focus outside of itself, in a space that is not represented onstage but that orders everything that appears in the play. The scenes in which Brutus and Collatinus offer themselves as spectacles to the people, encouraging them to gaze at the performances of cruelty they represent are thus brilliantly constructed scenes aimed at making present an absence: the absence of the spectator, the very subject that is essential to theatre. (As the previous chapter has pointed out, the alienation of the actors from the audience, thus treated as invisible, is a cornerstone of the naturalistic effect of dramatic fiction and a condition for persuasive theatrical illusion). If the people onstage function as a mirror, then the tragedy thematizes the invisibility of the spectator as well as the invisibility of the gaze that is the ordering force of the entire performance. *Bruto primo*, in other words, was conceived so as to make apparent – visible – to spectators the fact that they are invisible precisely so as to emphasize to them their importance. By bringing together character and spectator so that they essentially become a single *popolo*/people/public, Alfieri perfects the strategies first deployed, in more rudimentary form, by Cicognini, his imitators, and Goldoni, all of whom sought to reduce the distance between spectator and character in order to encourage maximum involvement of the public and to make it an active subject in the performance.

Political and Spectacular Palingenesis

The interpretive framework proposed here suggests that *Bruto primo* is not only a key text – an occasion for "taking stock," given that Alfieri intended it to end his career as a tragedian – that signals an important stop along the dramatist's ideological path. The play is also a profoundly significant work from the point of view of the transformation both of performance practice and the theatre spectator. *Bruto primo* is a quintessentially eighteenth-century drama that is representative of eighteenth-century theatre more generally for three primary reasons. First, Alfieri's tragedy illustrates the factors that contributed to the birth of public opinion, situating them in the context of the Enlightenment attempt by civic society to resolve the binary dividing private morality and state politics.

Second, the representation of power dynamics is, to varying extents, the *leitmotif* of the theatrical works we have considered here. Alfieri's play is a tragedy about power in a double sense of the word: *Bruto primo*, of course, has as its subject a political legend, but it is above all a work that, more than any other play discussed here, reveals the internal functioning of power structures and can be read as a history of biopolitical practices and genealogies of power. What makes the play a *tragedia di potere* is its bringing to light of the affinities between monarchical and republican regimes, both of which are founded on authorities' exercising of control over human beings to their exclusion from political life. By exposing the Enlightenment crisis caused by the insuperable tension between politics and morality and by the similarly oppressive operation of different forms of government, *Bruto primo* reveals theatre's vital role in furnishing a response to the crisis and in being a vehicle for reform and renewal. Thanks to its capacity for creating public opinion, theatre becomes the most important tool for Alfieri in his quest to oppose the official politics of the state and to render citizen-spectators politically active.

Third – and this last is the reason why *Bruto primo* is a crucial turning point along a path that is centuries long – is the play's positioning of the education of the spectator and the shaping of audience tastes and ideals as the end goal of the theatrical experience. As we have seen, the audience increased in relevance and importance beginning with the plays of Cicognini and his imitators through those of Maffei, Gozzi, and Goldoni – all authors who made the spectator the subject of and an active participant in their plays. This process culminates in Alfieri's tragedy, which was consciously constructed to call attention to the problem of representation and to complicate the passive act of reception, producing an audience that was a shrewd and informed critic not only of theatre but also of socio-political reality. *Bruto primo* is thus an example *par excellence* of a tragedy that illustrates the circular process by which theatrical practice responds to the expectations and habits of spectators while simultaneously contributing to their reshaping and reconfiguration.

Alfieri's dramatic production is often seen as disconnected from the environment and events of Enlightenment Italy; as detached from the present and oriented towards abstract ancient models or to the future; and as a theatre that evades historicization. Read anew, however – alongside Koselleck's philosophical history and the reflections of Foucault, Habermas, and Agamben – Alfieri's theatre reveals an essence no less rooted in late-eighteenth-century theatre than that of Goldoni. It is a theatre that intrudes into life itself and that actively refashions the conduct of the people – both onstage and off – in a new image.

Epilogue

Public Dramas and Dramatic Publics, a Dialectic

My primary aim in writing this book was to investigate the role played by Italian theatre in shaping the emergence of a critically productive spectatorship and of the public sphere from the middle of the seventeenth to the end of the eighteenth centuries. As we have seen, this period was the heyday not only of intense theoretical reflection on drama, and of major theatrical innovation, but also of the spectator, who ultimately brought about the political triumph of public opinion.

The preceding chapters reconstruct the ways in which the process of Italian and European public-making occurred, tracing the gradual movement away from the perception of the audience as a heterogeneous, conflicted mass of pleasure-seeking individuals towards its perception as an enlightened public, capable of discussing issues of public concern in a critical fashion. I have also described the shift during this period towards an increasingly spectator-centred conception of the dramatic arts. The evidence presented here suggests that the process by which the spectator moved from the marginalized position of a passive subject sitting in detached contemplation of a theatrical performance to centre stage of the contemporary critical discourse on theatre and of actual performance practice began with the transition of theatre from court to public playhouse as well as with the emergence of a theatrical market based on economic values and open to a diverse public. Chapters 1 and 2 locate the advent of an aesthetic attentive to public response in the dramatic production of Giacinto Andrea Cicognini and his imitators, who compelled the audience to recognize its own centrality in theatrical as well as social and political domains. Chapter 3 reveals how the notion of the citizen-spectator's paramount importance was transmitted to Scipione Maffei, who further rendered the audience a herald of critical social thought and an agent capable of informed political analysis. The analysis in chapters 4 and 5 of works by rival Venetian playwrights Carlo Gozzi and Carlo Goldoni shows how dramatists and critics bestowed the power of critique upon the audience and evinces the fact that, by the middle of the eighteenth century, public opinion had begun to rival specialist judgment and to take its place as the predominant arbiter of the quality of dramatic performances. The final chapter demonstrates how, in the plays of Vittorio Alfieri, the spectator becomes not only an active consumer and judge of dramatic works but also a competent critic of larger socio-political issues in late-eighteenth-century Italy.

Alongside the major social and political changes that this transformation from audience to public implies, the present volume has explored some of the stage devices and dramatic techniques that were developed by playwrights as a means of responding to the evolving audiences' demands, tastes, and expectations. These devices include the conscious creation of a close association between audience members and onstage characters; the establishment of an absorptive relationship of spectator to dramatic fiction; the involvement of spectators as active participants in (rather than passive observers of) plays; the placement of the audience at the centre of debates on theatre and politics; the bridging of the gap between author, audience, and stage; and the actual staging of spectators themselves. All of these techniques were aimed at creating a performance focused entirely on the audience and at calling into being a fully engaged, committed, and educated spectator. As we saw in chapters 2 and 6, playwrights learned from one another how to heighten spectators' emotional involvement in the theatrical performances they witnessed and how better to refine their means of communication with their audiences. Goldoni, for instance, enhanced the visual dimension of his plays, employing elements such as images of the gaze, pantomime dances, and *tableaux* gleaned from Cicognini and his followers as well as from Denis Diderot and Domenico Barone. Alfieri, too, perfected the techniques he had learned from his predecessors, composing a tragedy that not only emphasized the centrality of the spectator but also established a collaboration among authors, actors, and audience members. What the sustained close readings of all six chapters thus bring to light is that public-making in Italy was a long-term process requiring complex and intensive cultural encounters and the continuous circulation of knowledge, artefacts, ideas, and theories, both within and across national borders. As Michael Warner neatly puts it:

> No single text can create a public. Nor can a single voice, a single genre, or even a single medium. All are insufficient to create the kind of reflexivity that we call a public, since a public is understood to be an on-going space of encounter for discourse. It is not texts themselves that create publics, but the concatenation of texts through time.[1]

It is through this same kind of lengthy, tangled, and nuanced process that spectatorship in Italy shifted bit by bit from little more than an abstract rhetorical entity to a new and powerful critical association of individuals built on shared views and concerns. Taken together, the chapters of this book paint a picture of the evolution of a radically new kind of theatre-goer who was, by the end of the eighteenth century, an informed and engaged critic of theatre, an inescapable interlocutor with playwrights, and a genuinely impactful political actor.

In the introduction, I suggested that, by revealing the dialectical – rather than unidirectional – relationship that existed between dramatists and their audiences, this book would seek to overturn the long-held notion that playwrights influenced and manipulated passive spectators. Indeed, this study has demonstrated the consistent reciprocal constitution of theatre audiences – what we might call "dramatic publics" – and dramatists, suggesting that the emergence of modern spectatorship did not feed off the decline of the author or entirely oppress authorial self-assertion and expression. On the contrary, it was only through the rise of the dramatic public that playwrights discovered that they too had a voice. In other words, the theatre-going public did not destroy playwrights; instead, it helped create them. Gozzi's placement of public opinion at the forefront of the theatrical enterprise opened up new perspectives into his dramaturgical research. The evolution of Goldoni's strategies of communication and innovations in theatrical practice occurred in response to his desire to indulge his audience and to fashion works with an eye to the emergence of the new dramatic public. It is thus by responding to the demands of their critical publics and by developing new techniques catering to spectators that playwrights and audience fashioned each other anew.

By shedding light on the public-making capacity of dramatic works and by providing a historical account of the experience of theatre-going in Italy, this book substantially revises our understanding of the relationship of theatre to the emergent public sphere and to the workings of public opinion. The case studies undertaken herein expand Habermasian insights about later northern Europe into a Sei- and Settecento Italian context, demonstrating the profound impact of theatrical practice on the creation of a new critical consciousness and an "authentic" public sphere. My analyses of how sovereignty and symbolic representations of power are depicted in the plays employed as case studies here – works that represent important stages of the transition from court to commercial playhouse – demonstrate that theatre during this period both heralded and reflected the simultaneous transition from representative publicity to the modern public sphere. Thus, theatre emerges – from the mid-1600s to the late 1700s – as the most prominent cultural institution in Italy, one that became a crucial site for the articulation and contestation of aesthetic, social, and political matters as well as a battleground for the most heated debates of the time. All of the theatrical texts considered here mirror, in different ways, the rise of public opinion. In fact, by making theatre-goers pay attention to the affairs of state; by offering audiences the means to understand modern political culture; by revealing the extent to which early modern sovereigns depended on a popular opinion that could subject their rule to informed and critical scrutiny; by allegorically translating the centrality of audience responsiveness to art into the sovereignty of the prince; and, ultimately, by reshaping spectators from passive receivers of rules and regulations to direct interlocutors with authority, playwrights of this transformative era catalysed and then fostered the formation and evolution of public opinion in Italy. In the mid-seventeenth century, the theatre was a place one could go for useful political information and practical political language. It was also a key site where theatregoers could gain, through a kind of simulation, experience that would help them critique an increasingly public political sphere. By the end of the eighteenth century, the boundaries between the world of the stage and the daily world had become fluid, and the symbolism of the stage and that of socio-political reality intermingled and were not easily disentangled. All of the plays examined here reveal more about the period during which they were written than about the events they recount. Read from the perspective of public-making, they make a compelling case for theatre as a medium for the circulation of information concerning political institutions and events, and as a vital site for the formation of public opinion in seventeenth- and eighteenth-century Italy.

I conclude by reaching beyond the specific historical parameters of my study to point out what this mid-seventeenth- and eighteenth-century project of creating a critical and politically engaged spectatorship bequeathed to the following period. Who were "the future Italian people" to whom Alfieri famously dedicated his *Bruto secondo*, and when did they fully emerge?

At the end of the eighteenth century, the French Revolution and Napoleonic wars upset the order not only of absolutist political regimes but also of Enlightenment reform projects throughout Europe, accelerating the birth of democratic republics and the transformation of society on the Italian peninsula. The Jacobins – who were politically active during the revolutionary triennium that began with the French invasion of 1796 and ended in 1799 when the French were driven out by the Austrian armies – addressed the problem of the Risorgimento (Resurgence) and the people's participation in the renewal of Italy. Jacobin politics and propaganda accorded a new centrality to theatre, which became the principal institution entrusted with representing the new order and shaping the process of the country's emerging identity. Thus the Enlightenment idea of theatre as an instrument that mediated the passage of individual to collective opinion – and that was therefore able to construct public opinion – was translated into a focused and militant ambition to educate an entire national *popolo*. To achieve this end, the Jacobins set in motion a complete reorganization of the theatre industry and embarked upon yet another project of theatre reform. Inspired by Johann Schlegel's idea of *Nationaltheater*, understood as an educational institution for the nation, their central concern was the abolition of the impresario circuit in favour of the creation of a theatre administered by the public authorities that was both accessible to the largest possible public and devoted to its education. This republican period, though short-lived, set an important precedent for the granting of access to a sector of the population that was normally excluded from theatre-going, namely members of the lower and lower-middle classes.[2] Indeed, it is telling that Alfieri's *Bruto primo* was performed free of charge in 1796 at the Teatro La Scala in Milan before a huge audience.

The influence of Jacobin theatre reforms and the patriotic impulse to create a militant theatre for all was visible on the stage itself, which continued to encourage spectators to recognize themselves in dramatic heroes and consciously addressed an audience of "citizen-spectators." Brutus, Caius Gracchus, William Tell, and other popular stage heroes became relevant metaphors for the republican struggle against foreign domination.[3] Vincenzo Monti's *Caio Gracco* (*Caius Gracchus*, 1788) gave important space to the representation of crowds onstage, and the main character of Alessandro Manzoni's *Adelchi* (*Adelchis*, 1822) promoted the egalitarian principle as a foundation of the nation. In the works of Giovanni Pindemonte (*I coloni di Candia*, 1785), Vincenzo Monti (*Aristodemo*, 1787), Antonio Simone Sografi (*Il matrimonio democratico*, 1798), and Francesco Saverio Saffi (*Il General Colli in Roma*, 1797) the people became protagonists of a dramaturgy that privileged choral structure, thus anticipating nineteenth-century Italian opera choruses, which were a focal point for nationalistic sentiment.

In light of these turn-of-the-nineteenth-century innovations, which for the most part continue the trends this volume has tracked through the seventeenth and eighteenth centuries, Alfieri's profoundly pessimistic vision of his generation as on its knees, as fully conquered, and as populated by the "subject" – by which he meant people in the psychological condition of submission – may seem paradoxical. Even in the face of some progress towards educating the theatre-going public, there remains an important reason for Alfieri's despair. The picture, even around 1800 and somewhat beyond, was not entirely rosy: the absence of a political centre and the diversity of local political circumstances made effective mobilization and collective action impossible in Italy and in Europe more generally. The moderate Jacobin movement, which claimed to have been acting for the benefit of the public but which consisted of intellectuals and representatives of the bourgeoisie, hindered the active participation of people from the urban and agrarian classes. These latter populations saw the political changes in the last years of the 1700s as a bourgeois revolution that did not improve their situation and failed to alter the structures of political authority. The revolution in Italy in particular had an elite character and neither fostered public education nor garnered broadly unifying national sentiments across classes. The reception of Alfieri's tragedies during this period proved that the supporters of the republic themselves were not on the side of the lower classes. His *Virginia*, which was chosen to inaugurate the 1798 season of the Jacobin theatre in Rome and criticized the nobility for its abuses of power (thus perfectly aptly sustaining the Jacobin's egalitarian ideology), met with little public acclaim. The 1799 performance of *La congiura de' Pazzi* in Rome provoked a serious polemic related to its subject matter (the unsuccessful attempt to overthrow the Medici tyranny in Renaissance Florence) – in short, the opposite of the reaction one would expect to a patriotic historical tragedy.[4]

Despite this failure of militant Jacobin theatre to shape a shared, cross-class Italian national identity in the midst of foreign conquest, late-eighteenth-century reflections on spectatorship left an indelible mark on the performance history of the post-1815 (Restoration) period and influenced dramatic forms such as opera, which became the nation's principal art form for self-representation – and, indeed, eventually came to be synonymous with being Italian. What encouraged and supported the unification movement in Italy were thus neither Alfieri's tragedies nor those of his successors (such as Pindemonte). Instead, it was the nineteenth-century melodrama, deliberately infused either with anti-tyrannical and anti-Austrian ideas or with political significance attributed to this newly reimagined form of theatre by audiences even when operas had not been conceived by composers, librettists, and directors as political works. The scope of opera repertoire – its patriotic choruses, which performed the role of "the people" (the most famous example of which being, perhaps, the chorus of Hebrew slaves, "Va' pensiero," from Verdi's 1842 *Nabucco*), and its large-scale *tableaux*, which provided opportunities for the development of nationalist sentiment – appealed to a broader and more diverse public than did the more narrow form of tragedy. The latter had audiences that were, traditionally, highly cultivated; the former was able, instead, to establish a far closer and more affective relationship with its more socio-economically (and otherwise) diverse publics. It is in nineteenth-century musical drama, therefore, that Italian audiences came finally to articulate fully their political status and to display completely their affiliation with the ideological and political statements dramatized on the stage. Alfieri's imagined and hoped-for future – an era of critical spectatorship in which audiences came to be politically engaged in the public sphere – therefore arrived only long after his death, when theatre finally became a focal point for the long-awaited formation of nationalistic sentiment and national identity on the Italian peninsula.

Notes

Introduction

1 Goldoni, *Mémoires* (1787), part II, chap. 15 (hereafter *Mémoires*, followed by part in roman numerals and chapter in arabic numerals), in *Tutte le opere*, 1: 308 (hereafter *TO*, followed by volume and page number(s), both in arabic numerals).
2 Dedication to Francesco Albergati Capacelli, in Goldoni, *La serva amorosa*, 65.
3 Goldoni, *La bella verità*, in *TO*, 12: 117.
4 On the Italian theatre-going public (and its social composition) during the first half of the eighteenth century in tourist travel diaries, see Guccini, "Introduzione," in *Il teatro italiano del Settecento*, 18–32, and Zorzi, *Il teatro e la città*, 240–2.
5 Habermas, *Strukturwandel der Öffentlichkeit.* English translations are from Habermas, *The Structural Transformation of the Public Sphere.*
6 Ibid., 27.
7 Feldman, *Opera and Sovereignty*, 34–5.
8 Recent studies that discuss, critique, and examine Habermas's theory of the public sphere include Calhoun, ed., *Habermas and the Public Sphere*; Warner, "Publics and Counterpublics"; Gvozdeva, Korneeva, and Ospovat, eds, *Dramatic Experience*; the project "Making Publics: Media, Markets and Association in Early Modern Europe, 1500–1700" (MaPs), which produced several essay collections that develop a post-Habermasian understanding of the early modern public sphere. See note 10.
9 On the role of literature and drama in the formation of public opinion, see Bloemendal and van Dixhoorn, "Literary Cultures and Public Opinion in the Early Modern Low Countries."

10 Mullaney and Vanhaelen, "Introduction: Making Space Public in Early Modern Europe – Performance, Geography, Privacy," 3–8. This discussion of Habermas was adapted from the introductory essay to Gvozdeva, Korneeva, and Ospovat, eds, *Dramatic Experience.*

11 On the emergence of early modern conceptions of the public in seventeenth-century France, see Merlin-Kajman, *Public et littérature en France au XVII*[e] *siècle.* On the conflation of the terms "audience" and "public" during the *Querelle du Cid,* see DeJean, *Ancients against Moderns.*

12 Darnton, *The Forbidden Best-Sellers of Pre-Revolutionary France,* 236.

13 See, for instance, Doty, *Shakespeare, Popularity, and the Public Sphere,* for a discussion of how Shakespeare's plays, by addressing theatre-goers as a critical public, made them aware of themselves as members of a public and sharpened their political literacy.

14 On the uses of the character "Popolo" in eighteenth-century tragedy, see Zucchi, "Suddito or giudice? Il contributo della tragedia italiana del Settecento alla definizione del concetto 'popolo.'"

15 Habermas, "Naturrecht und Revolution," in *Theorie und Praxis,* 95. English translations are from Habermas, "Natural Law and Revolution," in *Theory and Practice,* 89.

1 How Theatre Invents the Public Sphere

1 Giacinto Andrea's father, Jacopo Cicognini (1577–1633), was a poet, playwright, and member of the Intronati, Instancabili, and Incostanti academies. He may have been a correspondent of Lope de Vega, who wrote a letter to convince his Italian fellow dramatist that blind obedience to the rules laid down by Aristotle's *Poetics* was nothing short of foolish. Although Jacopo refers to Lope's advice in the preface to his play *Il trionfo di David* (composed 1628, printed 1633), their direct acquaintance has been questioned by Maria Grazia Profeti in "Jacopo Cicognini e Lope de Vega: 'Attinenze strettissime'?" Legend has it that Jacopo entrusted his son's education to a prominent actor of the day, Pietro Maria Cecchini. The most recent account of Cicognini's life and dramatic production is Cancedda and Castelli, *Per una bibliografia di Giacinto Andrea Cicognini: Successo teatrale e fortuna editoriale di un drammaturgo del Seicento,* 25–74.

2 Castelli, "Il teatro e la sua memoria," 86; Maranini, "Il comico nel tragico: I drammi per musica di Giacinto Andrea Cicognini," 185.

3 Cicognini's departure from Florence has been attributed to his serious falling-out with some of the Medici *protegés,* whom he accused of being

panderers. See Crinò, "Documenti inediti sulla vita e l'opera di Jacopo e Giacinto Andrea Cicognini," 258–82.

4 Rosand, *Opera in Seventeenth-Century Venice*, 37. The membership of this academy, which was founded in 1630 by the patrician Giovan Francesco Loredano, consisted almost entirely of important upper-class Venetian intellectuals, along with a few non-Venetians. The Incogniti were distinguished from other learned academies by their involvement in most aspects of *La Serenissima*'s cultural, social, and political life. They were also remarkable for their openness to unorthodox thinking: they opposed cultural conformism and had a distinct predilection for licentious living. Prolific writers of prose, moral and religious tracts, and opera librettos, members of this powerful academy found their models in the allegorical and satirical literature inspired by Traiano Boccalini's socio-political compendium *Ragguagli di Parnasso* (*Advice from Parnassus*, 1612–14) and expressed their anti-conformist views in covert and highly allusive ways. On the Incogniti, see Miato, *L'Accademia degli Incogniti di Giovan Francesco Loredan (1630–1661)*; Spera, *Due biografie per il principe degli Incogniti*; Spini, *Ricerca dei libertini*; and Lattarico, *Venise incognita*. Cicognini was not considered an official member of the academy, and evidence of his relationship to various of its members is somewhat speculative. For the connections he may have had after he settled in Venice, see Melcarne, "Giacinto Andrea Cicognini."

5 There is a growing literature on Cicognini's role in disseminating Spanish theatre in Italy and on the notable bravura with which he transformed his Spanish sources. See, for example, Antonucci and Bianconi, "Plotting the Myth of *Giasone*"; Gobbi, "Le fonti spagnole del teatro drammatico di G.A. Cicognini"; Michelassi and Vuelta García, "La fortuna del teatro spagnolo a Firenze"; Michelassi and Vuelta García, "Il teatro spagnolo sulla scena fiorentina del Seicento"; and Símini, "Alcune opere 'spagnole' di Giacinto Andrea Cicognini fra traduzione, adattamento e creazione." Whereas scholars have focused either on his role in the diffusion of Spanish Golden Age theatre in Italy or on his opera librettos, little if any attention has been paid thus far to the political dimension of Cicognini's dramatic works.

6 The bibliography on the *raison d'état* (*ragion di stato*) is vast. See, for instance, Baldini and Battista, "Il dibattito politico nell'Italia della controriforma"; Stolleis, *Stato e ragion di stato nella prima età moderna*, 31–68.

7 It is difficult to establish definitively the parameters of Cicognini's political thought: as was the case with many of the Incogniti with whom he likely associated, he was too enigmatic a playwright to express openly his stance on political and ideological matters. Nevertheless, certain discernible

patterns emerge in his dramatic output. In particular, his interest in politics and in a variety of forms of government suggests that these were central concerns of his writing career and were not exclusively imposed by a need to please either patrons or spectators.

8 Cf Mamone, *Il teatro nella Firenze medicea.*

9 Carter and Goldthwaite, *Orpheus in the Marketplace,* 105–6; Treadwell, *Music and Wonder at the Medici Court.*

10 On Venetian opera's political purposes and social agendas, see Feldman, *Opera and Sovereignty.*

11 Carter and Goldthwaite, *Orpheus in the Marketplace,* 111–21.

12 For the broader political, historical, and economic context related to the openings of the first public theatres in Venice, see Zorzi, "Venezia: La Repubblica a teatro," in *Il teatro e la città,* 235–83; Mangini, "Alle origini del teatro moderno."

13 Doglio, "La tragedia barocca," CV.

14 Cicognini famously claimed in the preface ("A i Lettori, & Spettatori del Drama") to *Giasone* that he composed the play on a whim and with no aim other than to delight: "Io compongo per mero Capriccio; Il mio capriccio non hà altra fine che dilettare; L'apportar diletto appresso di me, non è altro che l'incontrare il genio, & il gusto di chi ascolta, ò legge." *Giasone. Dramma musicale del D. Giacinto Andrea Cicognini,* 13. The importance of pleasing a wide audience was also a leitmotif of the Incogniti's literary production.

15 For example, on the performance of Cicognini's plays in Russia under Peter the Great (and, in particular, of his *Tradimento per l'onore,* which was adapted for Russian audiences from a German translation), see Tikhonravov, *Russkie dramaticheskie proizvedenia 1672–1725 godov,* 1: 40–1, 48, and 2: 80.

16 All citations of the play are from *Il Don Gastone di Moncada* (Bologna: Per Gioseffo Longhi, 1682). Translations of the plays and of other sources, here and throughout the volume, are mine unless otherwise noted.

17 On the Florentine theatre of the Dogana, see Zorzi, *Il teatro e la città,* 124–8; Evangelista, "Le compagnie dei Comici dell'Arte nel teatrino di Baldracca a Firenze"; and Alberti, "Il teatrino detto della Dogana o di Baldracca."

18 The direct involvement of the grand ducal administration in the management of the theatre in comparison to the handling of other European theatres has been explored in detail by Ferrone, in *Attori mercanti corsari,* 67–74.

19 On the socio-economic diversity of the spectators at the Teatro della Dogana, see Michelassi, "La 'Finta pazza' a Firenze," 315: "Baldracca non appare dunque uno stanzone malfamato condannato alla sterile ripetizione

dei lazzi dell'Arte, ma un luogo di irradiamento culturale, pacificamente condiviso da tutte le fasce sociali (compresa l'aristocrazia nobiliare e i principi medicei, che vi si recavano regolarmente), dove si potevano apprezzare novità spettacolari di portata determinante."

20 The success of this performance is mentioned in a letter from Leopoldo de' Medici to Mattias de' Medici: "Mi son trattenuto la sera a giocare a dadi nella mia stanza e alla commedia, e stasera con gran concorso e di dame ancora si è recitata per la terza volta una commedia nominata Don Gastone di Moncada, opera veramente bella e recitata bene, e dall'esserci più gente questa terza volta che la prima Vostra Altezza si può immaginare che sia riuscita bene. Il passatempo della commedia finisce presto perché sabato vanno via i commedianti. Di Vostra Altezza. Di Firenze 10 decembre 1641." Cf Leopoldo de' Medici to Mattias de' Medici, Archivio di Stato di Firenze, MdP 4560, c.40r; cited in Michelassi, "La 'Finta pazza' a Firenze," 318. See also Castelli, "Il teatro e la sua memoria," 92–4; Michelassi and Vuelta García, *Il teatro spagnolo a Firenze nel Seicento*, 29–30.

21 *Il Celio*, Cicognini's first *dramma per musica*, was performed in 1646 by a travelling Venetian company at the Teatro della Dogana with music by Niccolò Sapiti and Baccio Baglioni. It had as its protagonist Don Gastone's son Celio. See Michelassi and Vuelta García, *Il teatro spagnolo a Firenze*, 105.

22 Cicognini, *Celio*, 10: "Insomma, ti prego a gradire *Celio* mio se no per altro, almeno perché è figlio del mio *Don Gastone*, che è stato all'universale così gradito." The preface is dedicated to Leopoldo de' Medici, who commissioned and promoted the production of Florentine librettos that imitated Venetian ones. Cf Michelassi, "La 'Finta pazza' a Firenze," 335.

23 Michelassi and Vuelta García, *Il teatro spagnolo a Firenze*, 105. On the confraternity of the Arcangelo Raffaello to which the elder and the younger Cicognini belonged, see Eisenbichler, *The Boys of the Archangel Raphael*, 225–6 and 231–3.

24 Michelassi and Vuelta García, *Il teatro spagnolo a Firenze*, 117.

25 Michelassi and Vuelta García, "La fortuna del teatro spagnolo," 22.

26 Ibid., 31.

27 Antonucci, "Spunti tematici e rielaborazione di modelli spagnoli nel *Don Gastone di Moncada* di Giacinto Andrea Cicognini."

28 Ibid., 80–1. On Cicognini's relationship to his Spanish sources and on his compositional technique, see also Antonucci and Bianconi, "Miti, tramiti e trame," in Cicognini et al., *Il novello Giasone*, XXXIII–XXXIV: "Cicognini non si proponeva di 'imitare' o 'riscrivere' un testo singolo del teatro spagnolo coevo; piuttosto, componeva opere originali nell'assetto complessivo della trama, intessute di situazioni e sequenze che rimandano,

in modo ora più ora meno puntuale, al vastissimo patrimonio di temi e motivi messo in scena dal teatro aureo spagnolo. Per questo credo, Cicognini tacque le 'fonti' di tante sue opere, anche di quelle che pure i contemporanei, come Bartolommei, qualificarono come derivate dal teatro spagnolo coevo: perché il rapporto di intertestualità che esse intrattengono con la drammaturgia ispanica è assai più complesso di un semplice rapporto di 'derivazione' o 'adattamento,' trattandosi piuttosto di una vera e propria riscrittura che si appropria degli eventuali ipotesi per costruire un assetto, testuale e ideologico, del tutto nuovo e originale."

29 The play was defined as an *opera spagnola* in the Laurenziano manuscript and as an *opera tragicomica* in the 1658 editions of Rome (published by Angelo Bernabò dal Verme with the title *Il D. Gastone, overo la più costante tra le maritate. Opera tragicomica*) and Perugia (published by Sebastiano Zecchini with the title *Il gran tradimento contra la più costante delle maritate, overo L'amico traditor fedele. Opera tragicomica*); and as an *opera scenica e morale* in the 1658 Venetian edition (published by Nicolò Pezzana with the title *Il Don Gastone di Moncada, Opera scenica e morale*). On the complex textual tradition and printing history of the play, see Antonucci, "Spunti tematici," 67–8.

30 I owe this point to the discussion of political messaging in Italian tragicomedies in Yoch, "The Renaissance Dramatization of Temperance." See also Herrick's still valuable *Tragicomedy. Its Origin and Development in Italy, France, and England.*

31 Guarini, *Il pastor fido e il Compendio della poesia tragicomica*, 229. The English translation is from Guarini, "*The Compendium of Tragicomic Poetry*," 511. On Giraldi's and Guarini's theorizations of the tragicomic form, see the excellent essay by Zilli, "Fonti italiane della teoria tragicomica." On seventeenth-century tragedy and tragicomedy, see also Zanlonghi, "La tragedia fra *ludus* e *festa*."

32 Giraldi Cinzio, "*Discorso intorno al comporre delle commedie e delle tragedie* (*Discourse on the Composition of Comedies and Tragedies*, 1543)," 184: "E ancora che Seneca tra i Latini non abbia mai posta mano alle tragedie di fin felice, ma solo si sia dato alle meste con tanta eccellenza che quasi in tutte le tragedie egli avanzò (per quanto a me ne paia) nella prudenza, nella gravità, nel decoro, nella maestà, nelle sentenze, tutti i Greci che scrissero mai [...]. Nondimeno noi, n'abbiamo composta alcuna a questa immagine, come l'Altile, la Selene, gli Antivalomeni e le altre, solo per servire agli spettatori, e farle riuscire più grate in iscena, e conformarmi più con l'uso dei nostri tempi."

33 Ibid., 184.

34 Cicognini's dramatic works and opera librettos (as well as seventeenth-century Venetian librettos more generally) are replete with comic, clownish, Spanish *gracioso*-like characters of low estate or rank. Their function is to play the role of sidekick to highborn characters, to support lead characters in helper roles, and (as is the case with Scappino) to predict the deeds of the hero. See Antonucci and Bianconi, "Plotting the Myth," 202.

35 Elias, *Über den Prozess der Zivilisation*. English translations of this text are from Elias, *The Civilizing Process*.

36 In Elias's scenario, the civilizing process was most pronounced in the French absolutist court (*The Civilizing Process*, 190–1, 205). On the applicability of Elias's model to the Italian Baroque court, see Fantoni, *La corte del granduca*, 131: "Quanto è rilevato per Firenze contraddice l'ipotesi che il Re Sole sia stato il primo sovrano a fare del cerimoniale uno strumento di potere. Nonostante che dalla fine del XVII secolo Versailles assurga a modello europeo, quello descritto da Elias non può quindi definirsi un fenomeno storicamente originale: i codici comportamentali che improntano la società di corte si elaborano altrove, ed in un periodo precedente." See also Snyder, *Dissimulation and the Culture of Secrecy in Early Modern Europe*, 69: "The courts of Europe, which grew in power and number during the early modern period with the weakening of feudalism and rise of absolutism, drew extensively on the Italian model at first, only subsequently to surpass it, a process culminating at Versailles under Louis XIV." On the functioning of the Italian courts, see also Bertelli, Cardini, and Garbero Zorzi, eds, *Le corti italiane del Rinascimento*.

37 According to Elias's paradigm, it is with the arrival of the absolutist court, which took on the "monopoly organization of physical violence," that "individuals learn to control themselves more steadily; they are now less a prisoner of their passions than before. But [...] they are much more restricted in their conduct, in their chances of directly satisfying their drives and passions. Life becomes in a sense less dangerous, but also less emotional or pleasurable, at least as far as the direct release of pleasure is concerned [...]. Physical clashes, wars and feuds diminish. [...] But at the same time the battlefield is, in a sense, moved within. Part of the tensions and passions that were earlier directly released in the struggle of man and man, must now be worked out within the human being. [...] [A]n individualized pattern of near-automatic habits is established and consolidated, a specific 'super-ego,' which endeavours to control, transform or suppress his or her feelings in keeping with the social structure." Elias, *The Civilizing Process*, 374–5.

38 Ibid., 70.

39 Gracián, *Oráculo manual y arte de prudencia,* 26; the English translation is quoted in Snyder, *Dissimulation and the Culture of Secrecy,* 43.
40 Gracián, *Oráculo manual,* 117; Snyder, *Dissimulation and the Culture of Secrecy,* 43.
41 Elias elaborates on this argument in *Die höfische Gesellschaft.* English translations of this text are from *The Court Society.*
42 van Krieken, *Norbert Elias,* 87.
43 Basile, *Lo cunto de li cunti, overo Lo trattenemiento de' peccerille,* 1: 200–1. The English translation is from Basile's *The Tale of Tales, or Entertainment for Little Ones,* 117.
44 From this point of view, the queen's accusation of her husband is also revealing: "I tuoi gusti hanno hauuto sempre per fine il tuo sfrenato piacere, il tormento della moglie, la vergogna d'altrui" (III.17).
45 Although *The Court Society* was published after *The Civilizing Process* (1969, in German; 1983, in English), Elias wrote it in 1933, and it thus anticipates the subsequent development of his ideas in *The Civilizing Process.*
46 See Elias, *The Court Society,* esp. chap. IV, "Characteristics of the Court-Aristocratic Figuration," 66–77.
47 van Krieken, *Norbert Elias,* 88.
48 Castiglione, *Il libro del cortegiano,* 71, and chap. II.26. The issue of appearances in Castiglione is explored in depth by Ferroni, "'Sprezzatura' e simulazione."
49 As Peter Burke suggests in *The European Reception of Castiglione's* Cortegiano, 31: "[C]ourtier is itself such a role, and one which was becoming institutionalized into what Castiglione himself calls a 'profession' (II.10), in other words an art or discipline (*arte e disciplina*)." See also Stephen J. Greenblatt's discussion of Castiglione's *The Courtier* in his *Sir Walter Ralegh,* 38: "Castiglione offers not a paradigm of man's freedom, but a model for the formation of an artificial identity; his courtier is an actor completely wedded to his role."
50 Rossi, *Il convito morale per gli etici, economici e politici,* 1: chap. "Secolo corrotto," 428. For more information on Rossi, see Biondi, "Il *Convito* di Don Pio Rossi."
51 Duindam, *Myths of Power,* 166.
52 See the astute analysis of friendship at the court of Versailles in Saint-Évremond, "Sur l'amitié" [1689], in *Oeuvres en prose,* 3: 308–9: "The usual relationship of kings and their courtiers is a relationship of interest. Courtiers seek fortunes of kings; kings require services from their courtiers."
53 Orgel, *The Illusion of Power*; Strong, *Art and Power.*
54 Apostolidès, *Le roi-machine,* 8. See also his *Le prince sacrifié.*

55 Greenblatt, *Renaissance Self-Fashioning.*
56 Greenblatt, "Invisible Bullets: Renaissance Authority and Its Subversion, *Henry IV* and *Henry V*," 44.
57 Marin, *Le portrait du roi.*
58 Habermas, *Strukturwandel der Öffentlichkeit,* 61; *The Structural Transformation,* 8.
59 See, for example, Elliott, "Power and Propaganda in the Spain of Philip IV," which explores how symbols were manipulated to enhance the power and majesty of Philip IV. On the Italian context, see Casini, *I gesti del principe.*
60 See Snyder, *Dissimulation and the Culture of Secrecy,* 5. See also Villari, *Elogio della dissimulazione*; Zagorin, *Ways of Lying.*
61 Zagorin, *Ways of Lying,* 3: "Although the term *dissimulation* occurs somewhat more commonly in the literature than *simulation,* the two are simply different sides of the same coin. [...] *Dissimulatio* signified dissembling, feigning, concealing, or keeping secret. *Simulatio* also meant feigning or a falsely assumed appearance, deceit, hypocrisy, pretence, or insincerity. The two words might therefore be used interchangeably, each denoting deception with the further possible connotation of lying."
62 Machiavelli, *Il principe,* 1: chap. 18, 166.
63 Ibid.
64 Castiglione's *regula universalissima* for court behaviour consists in avoiding "quanto più si po, e come un asperissimo e pericoloso scoglio, la affettazione; e per dire forse una nova parola, usar in ogni caso una certa sprezzatura, che nasconda l'arte, e dimostri, ciò che si fa e dice, venir fatto senza fatica e quasi senza pensarvi." Cf Castiglione, *Cortegiano,* I.26, 81.
65 Snyder, *Dissimulation and the Culture of Secrecy,* 6.
66 Ibid., 75.
67 *Cortegiano* I.26 is an important chapter for the praise of apparent effortlessness ("certa sprezzatura," or "sprezzata disinvoltura"). For further discussion, see Whigham, *Ambition and Privilege,* 93–5.
68 Sarpi, Letter to Jacques Gillot, 12 May 1609, quoted in Wootton, *Paolo Sarpi,* 119. For more detailed information on Sarpi, see De Vivo, "Paolo Sarpi and the Uses of Information in Seventeenth-Century Venice."
69 Castiglione, *Cortegiano,* II.7, 122–3: "Voglio adunque che 'l nostro cortegiano in ciò che egli faccia o dice usi alcune regole universali, le quali io estimo che brevemente contengano tutto quello che a me s'appartien di dire; e per la prima e più importante fugga [...] sopra tutto l'affettazione. Appresso consideri ben che cosa è quella, che egli fa o dice, e 'l loco dove la fa, in presenzia di cui, a che tempo, la causa perché la fa, la età sua, la professione, il fine dove tende, e i mezzi che a quello condur lo possono."

70 On the flourishing of the *theatrum mundi* topos in early modern writing and the Baroque fascination with the theatricality of the world, see Curtius's foundational *European Literature and the Latin Middle Ages*, 138–44. See also the excellent surveys by Christian, *Theatrum mundi*, 150–92; Yates, *Theatre of the World*; and Forestier, *Le théâtre dans le théâtre sur la scène française du XVIIe siècle*, 341.

71 Castiglione, *Cortegiano*, II.29, 236. On the performance of emotions and their political uses in a courtly context, see Kolesch, *Theater der Emotionen*.

72 Rossi, *Convito*, 2: chap. "Grandezza regale," 175.

73 Kastan, "Proud Majesty Made a Subject," 466.

74 Hénaff, Morhange, and Allen, "The Stage of Power," 22.

75 Habermas's contention is confirmed by a brilliant aphorism of Pio Rossi, who compared the great to the actors who fill the stage, leaving commoners to watch them from the dark of the parterre: "Vn gran torchio leua il lume à i piccioli: E le picciole candele non vagliono gran fatto à rischiarar le tenebre, se i maggiori non s'ecclissano." *Convito*, 1: chap. "Grande Primate," 214.

76 One example of the declining taste for tragic plots in the mid-sixteenth century is the influential statement by dramatist and theatre theorist Angelo Ingegneri, who claimed that "le tragedie, lasciando da canto che così poche se ne leggono che non abbiano importantissimi, e inescusabili mancamenti, onde talora divengono anco irrappresentabili, sono spettacoli malinconici, alla cui vista malamente si accomoda l'occhio disioso di dilettazione." *Della poesia rappresentativa e del modo di rappresentare le favole sceniche*, 7. On Cinquecento tragedy see the excellent essay by Calzavara, "L''amor soverchio' e lo 'sfrenato sdegno.'"

77 Theories that stressed the necessity of providing satisfaction to the audience were postulated in an Italian context by Giambattista Guarini, Giovan Battista Giraldi Cinzio, Angelo Ingegneri, and Leone de' Sommi in particular. Anna Tedesco has recently linked Cicognini's dramatic aesthetics (which emphasizes keeping the public pleased and entertained) to the shaping influence of Lope de Vega's treatise *El arte nuevo de facer comedias en este tiempo* (*The New Art of Writing Plays in This Age*, 1609, first printed in Italy in 1611), which oriented Italian playwrights towards a new kind of dramaturgy that recommended against the Aristotelian rules in favour of a more public-oriented paradigm. See her "'Capriccio,' 'Comando,' 'Gusto del pubblico' e 'Genio del luogo' nelle premesse ai libretti per musica a metà del Seicento."

78 Crescimbeni, *La bellezza della volgar poesia*, Dialogo VI, 142.

2 The Privileged Visibility of the Viewer

1 On pre-Goldonian theatre and the corpus of authors and texts it includes, see Gutiérrez Carou, "Pregoldoniano," and Vescovo "La biblioteca di Carletto Goldoni."

2 Goldoni, *Mémoires*, I.1, in *TO*, 1: 13. The English translation is from Goldoni, *Memoirs of Goldoni, Written by Himself*, trans. John Black, I.1, 5 (hereafter *Memoirs*, followed by part in roman numerals, chapter, and then page number(s), both in arabic numerals). Note that the division into chapters in Black's translation does not correspond to the French original.

3 Goldoni, "Prefazione dell'autore alla prima raccolta delle commedie," in *TO*, 1: 762.

4 Goldoni, "L'autore a chi legge," preface to the first volume of the Pasquali edition, in *Memorie italiane*, vol. 3 of *Prefazioni e polemiche*, ed. Turchi, 96.

5 Epifanio Ajello, "Introduzione," in Goldoni, *Memorie italiane*, ed. Ajello, 22. On the Pasquali frontispieces, which mark several important Goldonian milestones, see Turchi, "'Un'edizione colta e magnifica.'"

6 Goldoni, "L'autore a chi legge," preface to volume eleven of the Pasquali edition, in *Memorie italiane*, vol. 3 of *Prefazioni e polemiche*, 189.

7 Goldoni, "L'autore a chi legge," preface to volume eight of the Pasquali edition, in *Memorie italiane*, vol. 3 of *Prefazioni e polemiche*, 134.

8 Goldoni, "L'autore a chi legge," in *TO*, 9: 215.

9 Ortolani, ed., *Nota storica* to *Enrico*, in *TO*, 9: 1320–1.

10 Fido, "'I portentosi effetti.'"

11 Goldoni, *Le inquietudini di Zelinda*, in *TO*, 8: 601.

12 Agnelli, "Il pubblico veneziano di Carlo Goldoni," 184.

13 See Sìmini, *Il corpus teatrale di Giacinto Andrea Cicognini.*

14 Sìmini, *Il corpus teatrale*; Cancedda and Castelli, *Per una bibliografia.*

15 See Michelassi, "La 'Finta pazza,'" 324, n35.

16 Cf Allacci, *Drammaturgia Diuisa in Sette Indici*, 727–8, and Stramboli's preface to his *Il finto paggio, overo Amare e non sapere chi.* See also Sanesi, *La commedia*, 2: 702.

17 Bottacchiari, "Recensione a R. Verde"; Sanesi, *La commedia*, 2: 702; Grashey, *Giacinto Andrea Cicogninis Leben und Werke*, 104–7.

18 I am inclined to side either with Sìmini and Franchi, according to whom *Belisario* is decidedly apocryphal, or with Scaramuzza Vidoni, who prefers to treat the tragedy as though it were anonymously written by a pseudo-Cicognini. See Sìmini, *Il corpus teatrale di Giacinto*, 46; Franchi, *Le impressioni sceniche*, 565; Franchi, *Drammaturgia romana*; and Scaramuzza Vidoni, *Relazioni letterarie italo-ispaniche: Il "Belisario,"* 8 passim and 33.

19 Goldoni, *Mémoires*, I.29, in *TO*, 1: 134; *Memoirs*, I.10, 193. See also Herry, *Carlo Goldoni*, 156–8. On Gaetano Casali, "le promoteur et le propriétaire de mon *Bélisaire*" (Goldoni, *Mémoires*, I.33, in *TO*, 1: 156), see Mangini, *I teatri di Venezia*, 125–46.
20 On the sources for *Belisario*, see Ortolani, *Nota storica*, in *TO*, 9: 1281–3.
21 Rieger, "Tra Mira de Amescua / Rotrou e Marmontel," 235.
22 Mamczarz, "Esperienze e innovazioni di Carlo Goldoni prima della riforma del 1748," 17–19.
23 Goldoni's claim appears in the preface to volume eleven of the Pasquali edition: "Vedrete il mio *Bellisario* finito, e mi vedrete, fra le armi e fra le disgrazie, giungere al desiderato impiego di Compositor di Commedie" ("L'autore a chi legge," in *Memorie italiane*, vol. 3 of *Prefazioni e polemiche*, 208).
24 Goldoni, *Mémoires*, I.36, in *TO*, 1: 163; *Memoirs*, I.13, 239.
25 Scaramuzza Vidoni, *Relazioni letterarie italo-ispaniche*, 9–10, 33–45.
26 Among various adaptations of Belisario subject matter are: Nicolas Desfontaines, *Bélisaire* (1641), Jean Rotrou, *Bélisaire* (1643), François Chantonnière de Grenaille, *Bélisaire ou le conquérant* (1678), and Jean-François Marmontel, *Bélisaire* (1767).
27 The edition consulted here is *La caduta del gran capitan Belissario sotto la condanna di Giustiniano Imperatore* (Bologna: Antonio Pisarri, 1661). This copy is held at the Biblioteca Estense di Modena, raccolta "Drammatica," LXXXIII. A. 31, G.A. Cicognini.
28 The study that has most impacted my thinking about the gaze, visuality, and the sovereign-as-spectator in pseudo-Cicognini's play is Ferrone, "Attori: L'archivio di Molière."
29 On the relationship between drama and penal reform in eighteenth-century France, see Bryson, *The Chastised Stage*.
30 Hénaff, Morhange, and Allen, "The Stage of Power," 18–19.
31 In Renaissance and Baroque culture, the physical body carried full responsibility for the actions and thoughts of the individual. For how punishments during this period were designed to symbolically fit the crime in ways that often literally inscribed the misdeed on the body, see Maza, "The Theatre of Punishment," 193: "And just as power was vested in and displayed through the body of the king, punishments that spelled out the hideous nature of the crime were performed on the body of the criminal – a branded letter for theft, a severed tongue for blasphemy, a body reduced to ashes for crimes such as parricide that defiled society."
32 Foucault, *Discipline and Punish*, 47.
33 On this theatre venue, see Guccini, "Dall'innamorato all'autore."

34 Luciani, "Esordi tragici," 11–12.
35 Mamczarz, "Esperienze e innovazioni," 16–17.
36 Ibid., 15.
37 Agnelli, "Il pubblico veneziano di Carlo Goldoni," 189.
38 Herry, *Carlo Goldoni. Biografia ragionata,* 171–94.
39 Goldoni, *Mémoires,* I.33, in *TO,* 1: 152; *Memoirs,* I.12, 221–2.
40 Goldoni, *Mémoires,* I.36, in *TO,* 1: 163; *Memoirs,* I.13, 239.
41 This unauthorized edition, which was made from a stolen copy ("sopra un originale rubato," Bologna: Pisarri, 1738, repr. in 1740) is reproduced in *TO,* 9: 1284–310. *Belisario* appears in volume eleven of the third volume (*Commedie e tragedie in versi di vario metro*) of Goldoni's *Opere teatrali,* Zatta edition. See also Luciani, "Esordi tragici," 13–15.
42 The *primo amoroso* Antonio Vitalba (d. 1758) played Belisario; the *prime amorose* Adriana Sambucetti, called "La Bastona," performed Teodora, and Cecilia Rutti, "La Romana," was cast in the role of Antonia. Among others were the *seconda amorosa* Zanetta Casanova ("La Buranella," 1708–76); the *primo zanni* Pietro Gandini (Brighella); Antonio Costantini; and Tommaso Monti. The actors employed by the Imer company are described in detail in "L'autore a chi legge," Goldoni's preface to the thirteenth volume of the Pasquali edition. Cf Goldoni, *Memorie italiane,* ed. Ajello, 270–5. See also Angelini, *Vita di Goldoni,* 84–92; Ferrante, *I comici goldoniani (1721–1960),* 42–6.
43 See, for example, Justinian's words in act I, scene 1: "In me, fidi, scorgete il signor vostro, / Ma in Belisario ravvisar dovete / Il nume tutelar di questo impero. / Che s'io detto le leggi, ei le difende; / E se impugno lo scettro, ei lo sostiene" (I.1).
44 Goldoni, *Mémoires,* I.36, in *TO,* 1: 163; *Memoirs,* I.13, 240.
45 The presence of inappropriately vulgar characters is what most bothered Goldoni about the *commedia dell'arte* version he attended in Milan: "Justinien étoit un imbécile, Théodore une courtisanne, Bélisaire un prédicateur. Il paroissoit les yeux crevés sur la scene. Arlequin étoit le conducteur de l'aveugle, et lui donnoit des coups de batte pour le faire aller; tout le monde en étoit révolté, et moi plus que tout autre [...]" (*Mémoires,* I.29, in *TO,* 1: 134).
46 Goldoni, "L'autore a chi legge," preface to volume thirteen of the Pasquali edition, in *Memorie italiane,* vol. 3 of *Prefazioni e polemiche,* 236.
47 Ibid.
48 Ibid.
49 Even in this early tragicomedy, we see a tendency towards the later concept of the bourgeois drama. In fact, according to Beaumarchais,

if the characters of classical tragedy move us, "c'est moins parce qu'il sont héros ou rois que parce qu'ils sont hommes et malheureux […]. Le véritable intérêt du cœur, sa vraie relation, est donc toujours d'un homme à un homme, et non d'un homme à un roi." Beaumarchais, *Essai sur le genre dramatique sérieux* [1767], 124. See also the point of view provided by Sébastien Mercier, who stated that tragic kings "m'intéressent comme hommes, mais non comme rois: en mettant bas sceptre et couronne, ils ne m'en deviendront que plus chers." *Du théâtre, ou Nouvel essai sur l'art dramatique* [1773], quoted in Delmas, *La tragédie de l'âge classique (1553–1770)*, 102.

50 I cite *Belisario* from *TO*, 9: 1–73.

51 Luciani, "Esordi tragici," 11.

52 On Crescimbeni's role in the Arcadian Academy, see Tcharos, *Opera's Orbit*, 29–30.

53 Crescimbeni, *La bellezza della volgar poesia*, 140–2.

54 Antonucci and Bianconi, "Plotting the Myth of *Giasone*," 202. Square brackets surround my annotations; braces indicate my translations.

55 Pompejano Natoli, "La seduzione in tragicommedia," 204.

56 Aleksei Karpovich Dzhivelegov, "Carlo Goldoni e le sue commedie," quoted in Goldoni, *Scelta e introduzione di Renzo Rosso*, 31.

57 Goldoni, "L'autore a chi legge," in *Le baruffe chiozzotte*, 77. See also Vescovo, "L'esperienza del quotidiano nel teatro veneziano tra Goldoni e Gallina," 296–7.

58 Goethe, "*Tagebuch der italienischen Reise für Frau von Stein*," 714. The English translation is from Goethe, *Italian Journey: 1786–1788*, 100–1.

3 The Politics of Spectatorship

1 On the literary polemic that Maffei hoped to occasion with the performance of his *Merope*, see Placella, "La polemica settecentesca della *Merope*"; and Leonelli, "La regina ha la febbre," 4.

2 "Credo d'avere in gran parte gettato a terra i Francesi con un colpo solo" ("I believe I have, for the most part, thrown the French to the ground with a single blow"), wrote Maffei, the day after the first performance of *Merope*. See his letter of 13 June 1713 to Bertoldo Pellegrini, Modena, in Maffei, *Epistolario: 1700–1755*, 1: 110. Cf also Tcharos, *Opera's Orbit*, 39–40; and Marchi, "Voltaire, Lessing e Alfieri di fronte alla *Merope* di Scipione Maffei."

3 On the relationship between the theatre and public debate, and on the importance and impact of literary and dramatic works for understanding

public opinion, see Bloemendal, Eversmann, and Strietman, "Drama, Performance, Debate."

4 Longoni, "'Ecco il tiranno,'" 115. On the quality of dramatic writing in Maffei's theatre, see also La Torre, "Scrittura drammatica e fascinazione del teatro: La Merope."

5 On Luigi Riccoboni, see Cappelletti, *Luigi Riccoboni e la riforma del teatro*; and Courville, *Un artisan de la rénovation théâtrale avant Goldoni.* On the actress Elena Balletti and her husband Riccoboni's relationship with Maffei, see Zaccaria, "Elena Balletti attrice e letterata."

6 See Guccini, "Il teatro San Luca," 309–13. On the relationships among theatre buildings, their geographical locations, and the social and political significance of performances, see Kruger, *The National Stage,* 12–13.

7 Maffei, *Istoria del Teatro italiano e difesa di esso* (1723), preface to *Teatro italiano o sia scelta di Tragedie per uso della scena,* 27.

8 On the success of *Merope* in Italy and Europe, see Placella, "La polemica settecentesca della *Merope,*" 320–1; Longoni, "*Merope*"; Marchi, *Un italiano in Europa,* 84.

9 See Senardi, "Alle origini del dramma borghese," 90: "L'essenza dell'esperienza drammatica di Maffei è nel rapporto pubblico-spettacolo, mentre la sua intuizione che la realtà del gusto non si risolve unicamente sul piano razionale contribuisce a spostare l'attenzione dalle caratteristiche compositive e strutturali ai processi di formazione del giudizio e di identificazione dello spettatore."

10 Maffei, *Proemio alla* Merope (1745), in *De' teatri antichi e moderni e altri scritti teatrali,* 77.

11 Scotton, "La poetica della *Merope* nella *Drammaturgia amburghese* di Lessing," 155. See also Sannia Nowé, who notes that the playwright, "nell'introduzione al *Teatro italiano,* riconosce un più alto valore poetico a quelle tragedie che sanno 'mettere un popolo a sussurro e destar furori d'applauso di tanto in tanto e far disfare ogni persona di buon senso in affetti.' Ciò significa che il Maffei privilegia, almeno al livello intuitivo, il metro soggettivo di valutazione che traspare dall'incontrollata manifestazione vocale o gestuale degli spettatori." Sannia Nowé, "Introduzione. Il Marchese Scipione Maffei," XXIV.

12 The "smisurato favore" with which the tragedy was met at Venice during the 1714 Carnival was recalled by Giulio Cesare Becelli in the note to the reader (*Al lettore*) in the 1730 Verona edition of Maffei's theatre. See Maffei, *Teatro del sig. marchese Scipione Maffei cioè la tragedia la comedia e il drama non più stampato,* X.

13 Maffei wrote to Abbot Antonio Conti two months after *Merope*'s first performance: "Una mia Tragedia recitata il passato Carnevale in Venezia ha incontrato tanta fortuna, che non s'è veduta mai più tal cosa. I Teatri di Musica sono rimasti abbandonati, si è fatta replicare 12 volte e il Teatro risuonava più di 20 volte d'acclamazioni [...]." Maffei, *Epistolario*, 1: 166.

14 See Sannia Nowé, "Il 'Tiranno' e la 'Madre' nella 'Merope' alfieriana," 210–14; Ringger, "La *Merope* e il 'furor d'affetto'"; Senardi, "Alle origini del dramma borghese"; Luciani, "Passioni tragiche e affetti domestici: La *Merope* di Scipione Maffei," in *Le passioni e gli affetti. Studi sul teatro tragico del Settecento*, 92.

15 Maffei, *Teatro italiano o sia scelta di Tragedie per uso della scena.*

16 On the relationship between the two interpretations of Merope's tale, see Trivero, "La ricezione settecentesca della *Merope.*"

17 Maffei, *Proemio alla* Merope (1745), in *De' teatri antichi e moderni*, 84: "L'esser poi il fatto di Merope lontanissimo per sé dal contenere amori, fece in oltre avvertire che si sarebbe con esso potuto tentare, se fosse possibile di rendere anche a nostri giorni accetta e gradita una Tragedia senza amoreggiamenti; mentre l'uso già da gran tempo introdotto di non rappresentar quasi altro, [...] disperdere avea quasi fatto la vera Tragedia e svanire."

18 On Torelli's *Merope*, see Montorfani, *Uno specchio per i principi*, 43. On precedents for Maffei's *Merope*, which were based on the Meropean myth and were composed by French and Italian authors during the fifteenth, sixteenth, and seventeenth centuries, see Selmi, "Alla ricerca di una tradizione moderna."

19 Torelli, *La Merope*, 257.

20 I cite the modern edition of Maffei's *Merope* edited by Stefano Locatelli (Pisa: ETS, 2008).

21 Montorfani, *Uno specchio per i principi*, 14. For the first scholarly account of the political aspect of Torelli's tragedies, including *Merope*, see Croce, *Poesia popolare e poesia d'arte*, 329–37, and his "La *Merope* di Pomponio Torelli e l'*Andromaque* di Racine." For an engaging (and more recent) political reading of Torelli's *Merope*, see Bertini, "*Hor con la legge in man giudicheranno*," 185–225.

22 Maffei, *Consiglio politico.* The modern edition from which I cite was edited by Paolo Ulvioni and appears in his "*Riformar il mondo*," 353–420.

23 Silvestri, *Scipione Maffei europeo del Settecento*, 156.

24 "Machiavellian King." Alfieri, Satira VIII "I Pedanti" (1797), in *Scritti politici e morali*, 3: 126 (v. 105).

25 Lessing, "*Hamburgische Dramaturgie*," in *Werke und Briefe in zwölf Bänden*, 4: 409–18 (chapters XLVI–XLVII). See also Senardi, "Alle origini del dramma borghese," 105.

26 Alfieri, Satira VIII "I Pedanti," 3: 126 (v. 104). In Alfieri's satire, the character of Don Buratto (who appears ridiculous in part because of his name, "imperatore dei pedanti" or "emperor of pedants") condemns Alfieri's tragedies – above all his *Merope* – by comparing them unfavourably to the undisputed model tragedies of the eighteenth century, namely those by Metastasio and Maffei. Alfieri pretends to accept Don Buratto's chastisements, which critique Alfieri's characters for failing to achieve the simple, natural quality of Maffei's, but in fact finds the latter's characterizations to be both banal and overly conventional. Alfieri promises to better reproduce Maffei's style in the future, thus mocking his Arcadian poetics. Of course, the resulting effect is to discount traditional tragedy by making it seem ridiculous and to rank Alfieri's style above all others. For an analysis of this *Satira*, see the excellent essay by Sterpos, "La 'nuov'arte del dir molto in poco.'"

27 Denarosi, *L'Accademia degli Innominati di Parma*, 306.

28 Voltaire, "*Mérope*," 254–6. The English translation is from *The Works of Voltaire*, 36–7.

29 Aristotle, *Politics*, 441.

30 The moment of Cresphontes' assassination by Torelli's Poliphontes is, however, described quite differently: "ch'io tolsi al padre suo non già per odio, / né lo spogliai per crudeltà di vita: / ma il desio de la gloria e del regnare, / che ne i più generosi più s'indonna, / mi rapì ne la guerra, e quell'impresa / died'a me la vittoria, a lui la morte" (vv. 901–6, p. 197).

31 Machiavelli, *Discorsi sopra la prima deca di Tito Livio (libro III)*, bk III, ch. IV, 968. The translation is from *Discourses on Livy*, 216.

32 Marchi, "La vocazione teatrale di Scipione Maffei," 92. For an accurate analysis of Maffei's political thought, see Pii, "Il pensiero politico di Scipione Maffei," 96.

33 Maffei, *Consiglio politico*, in Ulvioni, "*Riformar il mondo*," 357.

34 Here there is actually some continuity between the tyrants in Maffei and Torelli. In the latter, Polyphontes, addressing the Captain of the Guard (his most trusted confidant), states outright his understanding of politics: "Le leggi e 'l giusto, di che tanto parli, / e per parlarne assai poco n'intendi, / non hanno sopra 'Principi potere, / che mal si converria, s'essi le fanno, / ch'essi a l'opera lor fosser soggetti" (vv. 953–7, p. 199).

35 Benjamin, *Ursprung des deutschen Trauerspiels*, 52.

36 See Koepnick, "The Spectacle, the 'Trauerspiel,' and the Politics of Resolution," 279–80: "Moving history into the center of its scenes and focusing on realpolitik rather than divine authority, the *Trauerspiel* engages with secularized forms of political domination only to expose the baroque's final hesitation to embrace them resolutely. In the midst of a world devoid of transcendental values, a cosmos emptied of metaphysical security, the *Trauerspiel* shows political rulers who subscribe to unprecedented models of political sovereignty, concepts of pure politics that remove religious, moral, or aesthetic concerns from the mechanics of domination and, therefore, explicitly endorse the differentiation of an autonomous sphere of politics. Baroque drama represents the emergence of the political as a nonmetaphysical arena of human interaction in which leaders and subjects negotiate social targets, institutions, and legal norms and contest competing ambitions."

37 We should note that the mother character in Maffei is very different from the one written by Alfieri, who described the former as a "mother-queen": "Merope mi pare esser madre dal primo all'ultimo verso; e madre sempre; e nulla mai altro, che madre: ma, madre regina in tragedia, non mamma donnicciuola." Alfieri, "*Parere sulla Merope*," in *Parere sulle tragedie e altre prose critiche*, 119.

38 It is somewhat odd, given Alfieri's harsh critique of Maffei's *Merope*, to note just how similar the Polyphontes character is in their respective versions. According to Alfieri's queen, Polyphontes is a tyrant precisely because he was never a father to his people: "[Merope]: Ben veggo; / Padre non fosti mai: tutto tiranno / Tu sei; nè vedi altro che regno [...]" (I.2, vv. 116–18). Cf Alfieri, *Merope*, 9.

39 Cf Calhoun, "Introduction: Habermas and the Public Sphere," in *Habermas and the Public Sphere*, 7: "unlike the Greek conception, individuals are here [in the modern public sphere] understood to be formed primarily in the private realm, including the family. Moreover, the private realm is understood as one of freedom that has to be defended against the domination of the state."

40 The influential role of the people and their centrality to the concerns of Maffei's Polyphontes and Merope contrast markedly with their role in Torelli's tragedy, where the Nurse expresses a rather conservative vision of a populace that, upon the death of its king, is "fiume senz'acqua e senza gemma anello" (v. 1965, p. 233). Similarly, Gabria ("consigliere di due padroni" because he advises both monarchs) supports the marriage

of queen and usurper, seeing it as the only way Merope's subjects would tolerate the tyrant (vv. 170–9, p. 171):

> mira il popolo tuo, che lagrimoso
> sol da le nozze tue spera conforto,
> ché per te sol placar si può il tiranno.
> Tu puoi la fiera tigre far clemente;
> se intrepida sei tu, temi per noi,
> ché non sol per se stessi i Re son nati,
> ma per la greggia ch'a lor data è in sorte:
> per cui, s'espor la vita a te conviensi,
> perché non dèi tu, per salute nostra,
> serbar te stessa a più felici giorni?

41 Sorba, "Teatro, politica e compassione," 430. See also Maza, *Private Lives and Public Affairs*, 314.
42 For a historical reconstruction of the concept of popular sovereignty, see the collaborative volume edited by Bourke and Skinner, *Popular Sovereignty in Historical Perspective*.
43 Costa, "Merope," 582.
44 Barricelli, "Imperial Mythologies," 264–5. See also Del Negro, "La fine della Repubblica aristocratica."
45 Maffei, *Il consiglio*, in Ulvioni, "*Riformar il mondo*," 378–9.
46 Marchi, "La vocazione teatrale di S. Maffei," 92.
47 Maffei, *Il consiglio*, in Ulvioni, "*Riformar il mondo*," 375.
48 Ibid., 379.
49 Giovanni Quintarelli, *Il pensiero politico di Scipione Maffei*, in *Studi Maffeiani* (Turin: Bocca, 1909), 429–74, quoted in Silvestri, *Scipione Maffei europeo*, 153.
50 Silvestri, *Scipione Maffei europeo*, 153–4.
51 On *Merope*'s questioning of the Aristotelian precept that required the presence of a protagonist displaying perfection with respect to virtue and on the gradual development of the "sympathetic" theory that instead insisted on a more moderate character as a device that would more strongly bind the hero onstage with the spectator in the house, see Mattioda, *Teoria della tragedia nel Settecento*, 107–21.
52 Sannia Nowé, "Introduzione. Il Marchese Scipione Maffei," in Maffei, *De' teatri antichi e moderni e altri scritti teatrali*, XXII.
53 Maffei, *Proemio alla* Merope (1745), in *De' teatri antichi e moderni e altri scritti teatrali*, 82: "Ora parea però […] che restasse luogo, tenendo via diversa da tutti, a tentar nel nodo qualche cosa di più d'Euripide; perché facendo il

giovane ignoto a se stesso [...] si veniva a introdurre un nuovo genere di riconoscimento, di cui non parlò Aristotele, ma atto con tutto ciò a far sul Teatro niente minor effetto d'ogn'altro. Dove si tratta nella *Poetica* delle agnizioni, si assegnano per l'ottime e più atte a generar maraviglia, quelle di fratello o sorella, di madre e figliuolo; ma c'è qualche cosa di più intimo ancora, cioè quando altri riconosca se stesso; il che tanto maggiormente dilettar potrà, quando tal notizia debba in un subito far cangiar sentimenti e pensieri, e tramutare in Eroe."

54 In the note to the reader (*Al lettore*) prefacing the 1730 Verona edition of Maffei's theatrical works, Giulio Cesare Becelli (though it is not difficult to imagine that Maffei provided every word) suggested that the real reason for the success of the tragedy was the recognition of Cresphontes (Aegistus): "il nuovo grado di Riconoscimento dall'Autore qui introdotto, cioè di riconoscer se stesso, è superiore a tutti gli altri, e più intimo, ed è di sua invenzione." Maffei, *Teatro del sig. marchese Scipione Maffei cioè la tragedia la comedia e il drama non più stampato,* XIII.

55 Marchi, "La vocazione teatrale di S. Maffei," 96.

56 Maffei, *Istoria del teatro italiano e difesa di esso* (1723), in *De' teatri antichi e moderni e altri scritti teatrali,* 33–4.

57 Leonelli, "La regina ha la febbre," 17.

58 Maffei, *Merope. Tragedia del marchese Scipione Maffei dedicata all'Altezza Serenissima di Rinaldo I duca di Modena, Reggio, Mirandola, etc. e illustrata. Colla Giunta d'essa Dedicatoria e d'una Prefazione, in Modena MDCCXIV, per Antonio Capponi Stampator Vescovale,* V and VII. I cite from Placella, "La polemica settecentesca della *Merope,*" 332.

59 On Maffei's elaboration of an aesthetics of reception that anticipated the ideas of Dubos, see Sannia Nowé, "Introduzione. Il Marchese Scipione Maffei," XXIV and XXXI; La Torre, "Scrittura drammatica," 138. A deeper consideration of Dubos's *Réflexions* follows in chapter 4.

4 Public Emotions and Emotional Publics

1 All quotations from the play are from Carlo Gozzi, *L'amore delle tre melarance,* in *Fiabe teatrali,* ed. Alberto Beniscelli (Milan: Garzanti, 2004); this quotation from p. 6.

2 Carlo Gozzi, *Memorie inutili,* 1: part I, chap. 34, 402.

3 Ibid., 403.

4 Carlo Gozzi, *Ragionamento ingenuo. Dai "preamboli" all' "Appendice." Scritti di teoria teatrale,* ed. Anna Scannapieco (Venice: Marsilio, 2013), 408. Subsequent quotations from the *Ragionamento ingenuo,* as well as from the

Appendice al "Ragionamento ingenuo" and the *Prefazione al "Fajel,"* refer to page numbers from this edition.

5 Cf Carlo Gozzi, *Memorie inutili*, 1: part I, chap. 34, 403: "la novità d'una tal Fola, ridotta ad azione teatrale, che non lasciava d'essere una parodia arditissima sull'opere del Goldoni, e del Chiari, nè vuota di senso allegorico [...]."

6 Gasparo Gozzi, *Gazzetta Veneta*, np. On Gasparo Gozzi's activity as a theatre reporter, see Beniscelli, "I due Gozzi tra critica e pratica teatrale"; and Mangini, "Gasparo Gozzi, cronista teatrale."

7 See Bordin and Scannapieco, eds, *Antologia della critica goldoniana e gozziana*, 249 passim. Two exceptions are Beniscelli's lucid study of the play's structure in his *La finzione del fiabesco*, 61–73, and Vescovo's fine "Lo specchio e la lente."

8 It is useful to recall that *L'amore delle tre melarance* is the only one of Gozzi's plays that was published (both in the Colombani *editio princeps* of 1772–4 and in the subsequent Zanardi edition of 1801–4) not as a fully scripted dramatic text, as was the case for his other nine fairy-tale dramas, but in the unusual form of a "reflexive analysis" (a term taken from the complete title of the play, *Analisi riflessiva della fiaba "L'Amore delle tre melarance," Rappresentazione divisa in tre atti*): a dramatic outline with extensive authorial commentary on the comedy's content.

9 The recent discovery of a family archive that sheds new light on Gozzi's compositional process for theatrical and theoretical writings (and the subsequent acquisition of this archive by the Biblioteca Nazionale Marciana in 2003) has led to a revival of scholarly interest in Gozzi and to the appearance of a number of valuable studies that have highlighted various aspects of the playwright's production. For instance, Gutiérrez Carou, *Metamorfosi drammaturgiche settecentesche*, which explores Gozzi's adaptations of Spanish drama from the *Siglo de Oro*.

10 By the time *L'amore* premièred on the stage of the Teatro San Samuele on 25 January 1761, the battle between Gozzi, Goldoni, and Chiari, which had begun in the late 1750s, was at its height. Gozzi's pamphlet writings – such as *Il teatro comico all'osteria del pellegrino*, *La tartana degl'influssi per l'anno bisestile 1756* (1757), and *La scrittura contestativa al taglio della tartana* (1758) – however, could not give the playwright his desired level of public visibility in this polemic affair. In particular, the publication of *Il teatro comico* was not authorized by the censors, and it therefore remained unpublished until 1805. On these issues, see Soldini's introduction to Carlo Gozzi, *Commedie in commedia*, 9–107, esp. 44–51; and Scannapieco, "Noterelle gozziane."

11 On folk tales as a principal source of Gozzi's inspiration, see Fabrizi, "Carlo Gozzi e la tradizione popolare." Fabrizi's analysis of the six Italian versions

of *L'amore* underscores the divergence of Gozzi's play from the literary tradition of fairy tales stemming from Giambattista Basile's collection *Lo cunto de li cunti*, highlighting instead *L'amore*'s affinity to northern Italian folk tales. Vescovo, "Lo specchio e la lente," and Scannapieco, "Noterelle gozziane," esp. 112–16, emphasize, on the other hand, Gozzi's heavy reliance on the *commedia* tradition. Both Vescovo and Scannapieco quote from the letters of Abbot Gennaro Patriarchi, a member of the Granelleschi Academy who – in an update to his friend on the novelties of the Venetian stage – wrote on 31 January 1761: "L'Amore delle tre melarancie è l'antica fiaba, ma tutta allusione come rileverete dalla Gazzetta n° 103. I Comici di S. Samuelo ne sono autori, ma vi so dire che alquanti accidenti o episodj le furono appiccati dal C. Carlo Gozzi per orticheggiare il Goldoni ed il Chiari." With Patriarchi's account in mind, Vescovo claims that, although the actors were authors of an improvised dialogue ("a soggetto") in the play, the real creator and director of the performance was the playwright. In contrast, according to Scannapieco (who, interestingly, does not mention Vescovo's 1989 analysis of Patriarchi's letter in her article), Gozzi's tacit renouncing of authorship (the play was indeed staged anonymously) reveals that the actors' contribution to the creative process was more decisive than we have yet acknowledged. None of these three scholars' reconstructions of the play's sources contradict each other, nor do scholars dispute the density of the play's cross-references to other writings, as I will argue in the ensuing pages.

12 Gozzi, "*Ragionamento ingenuo*," 409.

13 See note 8 on *L'amore* as an unusual "reflexive analysis": a sketch of the comedy's content with extensive authorial commentary. Also striking is a fact not yet sufficiently addressed by Gozzi scholarship: though the play was published ten years after its first performance, it gives the impression of having been written down immediately after its première because it describes the public's reaction so vividly.

14 Gozzi, *L'amore delle tre melarance*, 14.

15 Fabrizi, "Carlo Gozzi e la tradizione popolare," 339–42.

16 Starobinski, *Histoire du traitement de la mélancolie des origines à 1900.*

17 This mixture of meanings and styles of melancholic performance is brilliantly summarized by Shakespeare's Jaques in *As You Like It*: "I have neither the scholar's melancholy, which is emulation, nor the musician's, which is fantastical, nor the courtier's, which is proud, nor the soldier's, which is ambitious, nor the lawyer's, which is politic, nor the lady's, which is nice, nor the lover's, which is all these; but it is a melancholy of mine own, compounded of many simples, extracted from many objects, and indeed

the sundry contemplation of my travels, in which my often rumination wraps me in a most humorous sadness" (IV.1. 10–18). As Drew Daniel points out, the melancholy Jaques recognizes in himself "an assemblage": a hybrid constellation of disparate "objects" and a bewildering array of postures out of which he has formed a "melancholy of [his] own." Cf Daniel, *The Melancholy Assemblage*, 7.

18 Radden, *The Nature of Melancholy*, vii.

19 Carlo Gozzi, *L'amore delle tre melarance*, 11.

20 Ibid., 15–16.

21 Gozzi's melancholic prince differs from Chiari's Trifone, but Tartaglia's has significant similarities to earlier prototypes, namely Molière's Alceste (*Le misanthrope*) and Argan (*Le malade imaginaire*). Just as Tartaglia's melancholy represents Gozzi's and the Venetian spectators' discontent with Goldoni's and Chiari's dramas, so too does the condition of Molière's characters symbolize their refusal to accept social norms.

22 As Adam Kitzes argues, the introduction of melancholy into early modern discourse in the late 1500s took place in the context of a renewed interest in the classical theory of the "body-politic," which "had posited an analogy between the individual human body and the collective 'body' that political organizations consisted of." Cf Kitzes, *The Politics of Melancholy from Spencer to Milton*, 5.

23 Carlo Gozzi, *L'amore delle tre melarance*, 14.

24 Aristotle, *Problems*, 2: 155. Recent scholarship has attributed the discussion of melancholy in Aristotle's chapter to Theophrastus. For a thorough discussion of Aristotle's account, see Eijk, *Medicine and Philosophy in Classical Antiquity*, esp. chap. 5, "Aristotle on Melancholy," 139–68; and Klibansky, Panofsky, and Saxl, *Saturn and Melancholy*.

25 In *De vita triplici*, the Florentine philosopher Marsilio Ficino combined the Aristotelian theory of natural and genial melancholy with Platonic ideas about divine frenzy, and placed all melancholics under the astrological influence of Saturn, as is famously illustrated in Albrecht Dürer's iconic 1514 *Melencolia I*.

26 Babb, *The Elizabethan Malady*, 74.

27 Cf Carlo Gozzi, *Memorie inutili*, 1: part I, chap. 31, 356.

28 Cf Gozzi's letter to his friend Innocenzo Massimo from 18 April 1785, in Carlo Gozzi, *Lettere*, 153. See also the 12 February 1785 letter to the same correspondent, in which the playwright wrote: "Sarà vero che il mio male non sia che un'affezione ipocondriaca" (ibid., 147). Soldini argues that "raramente il Gozzi trattiene stati d'animo o giudizi e in prevalenza – s'è visto – è l'ipocondria il sentimento dominante." Cf "Introduzione," in

ibid., 8. Gozzi's melancholy, as it emerges in his epistolary exchange with Innocenzo Massimo, is also elegantly analysed in Ortolani, "Carlo Gozzi ipocondriaco."

29 Examples are many; it is sufficient here to recall the consumptive king ("re tisico") from "*I due fratelli nimici*," in Gozzi, *Opere del Co: Carlo Gozzi*, 5: 281–388.

30 "A king without diversion."

31 Benjamin, *The Origin of German Tragic Drama*, 142.

32 Christopher Braider claims that despite the apparent "absence" of the Baroque during the "classical" century in France, between the founding of the Académie Française (1635) and the Revocation of the Edict of Nantes (1685), "Pascal's vaunted 'classical' austerity incorporates a deeply baroque perspectivism." Cf Braider, *Baroque Self-Invention and Historical Truth*, 145.

33 For an excellent discussion of the function of this reference to Pascal in Benjamin's argument, see Bjørnstad, "'Giving Voice to the Feeling of His Age.'"

34 Pascal, *Pensées* (1670), in *Œuvres complètes* (L'intégrale), ed. Louis Lafuma (Paris: Seuil, 1963). The numbering of fragments from the *Pensées* follows this edition and is given in the text with the abbreviation 'Laf.'

35 Pascal, *Pensées*, ed. and trans. Roger Ariew, 42. Unless otherwise noted, English quotations of Pascal are from this edition. Since Ariew's translation follows Philippe Sellier's ordering of the fragments, I give page references to this edition that hereafter appear in the text with the abbreviation "Ari."

36 Benjamin, *The Origin*, 142.

37 Nicholas Hammond, in "The Theme of Ennui in Pascal's *Pensées*," 1, has pointed out that Pascal most likely derived his definition of man's *ennui* from Michel de Montaigne's "humeur mélancolique […] produit par le chagrin et la solitude." Cf Montaigne, *Essais*, 2: 370.

38 Hammond, *Playing with Truth*, 109.

39 On theatrical undertones in the Pascalian description of the human condition, see Hammond, "'Levez le rideaux,'" 280; and Philips, *The Theatre and Its Critics in Seventeenth-Century France*, 152.

40 I follow W.F. Trotter's translation here – *Thoughts*, 79 – whereas Ariew translates the famous fragment quite literally as "the final act is bloody" (Ari. 52).

41 On the playwright's relationship with Sacchi's comic troupe, see Bazoli, *L'orditura e la truppa*.

42 Carlo Gozzi, *Memorie inutili*, 1: part I, chap. 34, 403; my italics.

43 Carlo Gozzi, *Prefazione al "Fajel,"* 182.

44 Ibid., 178.

45 Scannapieco, commentary on *Prefazione al "Fajel,"* in Carlo Gozzi, *Ragionamento ingenuo*, 191–242: 228.
46 Gasparo Gozzi, *Gazzetta Veneta*, np.
47 DiGaetani, *Carlo Gozzi*, 110.
48 D.C. Potts, "Pascal's Contemporaries and 'Le Divertissement,'" 31.
49 Cf the inventory of Gozzi's library, which is conserved in the State Archive of Venice (ASVE, Notarile, Atti, busta 13191, notaio Raffaele Todeschini (25 aprile 1792–30 aprile 1806), cc 1925v–1934r). I wish to thank Giulietta Bazoli for making available to me a digital reproduction of this document, which was found by Marta Vanore. The absence of Pascal's works in Gozzi's library does not constitute a decisive proof that Pascal had no influence on the Venetian playwright: Gozzi did not possess any of Goldoni's plays and yet quoted extensively from them, often indicating the page of reference. The inventory is from the last years of the dramatist's life, and it would be worth investigating the possibility that his complete library had been dispersed or moved to his country house or to the libraries of his parents at an earlier date.
50 Another issue is what edition of Pascal was known to eighteenth-century readers. As Mara Vamos argues, confusion reigned in the first Port-Royal edition of the *Pensées*, and Pascal's original work was not restored by modern scholarship until well into the nineteenth century: cf Vamos, "The Forgotten Book of Pascal's *Pensées*." If Gozzi was as familiar with the *Pensées* as he appears to have been, he must have read it in the Port-Royal version, as this was the only edition available to readers in Europe. (It was reprinted about thirty times before the 1844 Faugère edition.) As Vamos notes, the Port-Royal *Pensées* was an incomplete and distorted version of what we read under the same name today, since it suppressed many fragments, altered the author's style and the ordering of the material, and even contradicted Pascal's original text (265). The *pensées* dealing with *divertissement* and *ennui* discussed above, however, were present and unaltered in the Port-Royal edition.
51 Dubos (sometimes spelled Du Bos), *Réflexions critiques sur la poésie et sur la peinture*. For a discussion of the relationships between Dubos's aesthetic arguments and Gozzi's theoretical writings on theatre, see Scannapieco's introduction to Gozzi, *Ragionamento ingenuo*, 9–92, esp. 44. On the circulation of Dubos's treatise in Venice, see Jonard, "L'abbé Du Bos en Italie."
52 Cf Charlton, "Jean-Baptiste Du Bos and Eighteenth-Century Sensibility," 152: "The publication of seven editions in French in its first half-century down to 1770, plus three reprinted editions, and translations into Dutch, English and German, serve to illustrate Lombard's claim that the

author was ‘un initiateur de la pensée modern’ who exercised significant influence on numerous readers, both French and foreign.” On Lombard, see the next note.

53 On the sources of the *Réflexions critiques* and the relationship between Dubos’s and Pascal’s concepts of *ennui*, see Lombard, *L’Abbé Du Bos*; and Tedesco, “Du Bos fra retorica e antropologia,” 45–6.

54 On Dubos’s secularization of the epistemological and critical tradition that preceded him, see Delehanty, “Dubos and the Faculty of Sentiment.” Cf also Saisselin, *The Rule of Reason and the Ruses of the Heart*, 20–1: “Du Bos’s theory of art resolves the problem posed by Pascal [...]. The hedonistic theory of art turns into a therapeutic of the distressed soul of man in his fallen state, and Du Bos and others formulate, in effect, the classical solution to man’s condition. An ideal solution to the problem of the human condition is reached when the passions and the imagination, that source of error, are kept occupied without harm. [...] The Abbé Du Bos’s solution may not be the Christian solution to the problem of man’s estate, but it may be significant that the greater degree of secularisation of his time also corresponded to a greater interest in the arts.”

55 Dubos, *Réflexions critiques*, I.1, 6. All references to Dubos’s text are by volume, chapter, and page number in the seventh edition (Paris, 1770; Reprint, Geneva: Slatkine, 1967). Dubos’s orthography and punctuation have been retained.

56 Dubos, *Critical Reflections on Poetry, Painting and Music*, 1: 5.

57 Dubos, *Réflexions critiques*, I.3, 28: “Cette impression superficielle faite par une imitation, disparoît sans avoir des suites durables, comme en auroit une impression faite par l’objet même que le Peintre ou le Poëte a imité.”

58 If Gozzi did not in fact read Dubos directly, he was at the very least reusing ideas in circulation in Venice that originated with Dubos and his followers.

59 Carlo Gozzi, *Prefazione al “Fajel,”* 186–7. My italics.

60 For Gozzi’s definition of theatre as a “recinto di divertimento” or “recinto di passatempo,” see esp. the *Prefazione al “Fajel,”* 184: “Lunge dal credere i Teatri una catedra, io non ho mai potuto giudicarli più che recinti, ne’ quali delle adunanze vanno in traccia di spassarsi per il corso di tre ore circa; e senza paragonare le colte colle incolte opere di Teatro, anzi separandone il genere; ho creduto a proposito quelle che hanno intrattenuto un Pubblico senza pregiudicarlo nel buon costume, recando dell’utilità a’ Comici.”

61 “An artificial and difficult illusion.” Carlo Gozzi, *Processo a difesa, ad offesa della Commedia*, in *Amore assottiglia il cervello, Opere edite ed inedite*, 13: 154.

62 Ibid.

63 Carlo Gozzi, *Appendice al "Ragionamento ingenuo,"* 531.
64 For this generation of French critics, as Marian Hobson observes, "theatrical reality must not obtrude. [...] Nothing must refer away from the subject, from what is seen: there must be no awareness that what is seen is appearance, no flickering between the reality of the theatre and the subject which is represented." Cf Hobson, *The Object of Art*, 144.
65 Carlo Gozzi, Preface to "*Zeim, Re de' genj*," in *Opere del Conte Carlo Gozzi*, 3: 131.
66 Goldoni, "L'autore a chi legge," in *Polemiche editoriali*, vol. 1 of Turchi, ed, *Prefazioni e polemiche*, 100. Goldoni's famous description of his poetics paraphrases René Rapin's *Réflexions sur la Poétique d'Aristote et sur les ouvrages des Poètes anciens et moderns*. See Accorsi, "La prefazione di Goldoni all'edizione Bettinelli e il razionalismo arcadico," on how Rapin's and D'Aubignac's treatises served as the principal points of reference for Goldoni's formulation of dramatic principles. According to Accorsi, Goldoni continues to refer to the terms of neoclassical poetics (*bienséance*, *vraisemblance*, order, nature) in all his later statements about the poetics of theatre, clearly positioning himself in the context of French rationalist aesthetic thought.
67 Goldoni, "L'autore a chi legge," 95.
68 Goldoni, *Il teatro comico* (II.2), in *TO*, 2: 1068.
69 Carlo Gozzi, "*Ragionamento ingenuo*," 398. Gozzi also criticized Goldoni on ideological grounds, claiming that his plays constituted a moral threat to Venetian society and undermined traditional values.
70 Ibid., 399.
71 Carlo Gozzi, *Prefazione al "Fajel,"* 189.
72 Carlo Gozzi, *Appendice al "Ragionamento ingenuo,"* 531.
73 Carlo Gozzi, "*Ragionamento ingenuo*," 391–2. In the passage immediately preceding, Gozzi claimed: "Le regole lasciateci da' rigidi maestri antichi sull'opere di Teatro, particolarmente nell'unità della scena, e nel giro di ventiquattr'ore di tempo, non furono che per vincolare i talenti a comporre un'opera, che la probabilità, e l'unione delle parti facesse comparire un idoletto di perfetta armonia, proporzione, e interezza" (391).
74 Dubos argues that complete illusion in the mind of the spectator cannot take place because he or she, unlike Pridamant in Corneille's *L'illusion comique*, does not arrive at the theatre predisposed to believe that what s/he sees is real. Anticipating the central concern of Ernst H. Gombrich's *Art and Illusion* about the role of convention in our response to art, Dubos goes on to explain that the spectator knows that s/he is going to see a play because the playbill says so: "L'affiche ne nous a promis qu'une imitation ou des

copies de Chimène & de Phèdre. Nous arrrivons au théâtre, préparés a voir ce que nous y voyons; & nous y avons perpétuellement cent choses sous les yeux, lesquelles d'instant en instant nous font souvenir du lieu où nous sommes, & de ce que nous sommes" (I.43, 452). This leads Dubos to question whether illusion and its intensity are the source of the spectator's pleasure. Arguing that the better one knows a work the more one enjoys it, Dubos demonstrates that pleasure and illusion do not occur in proportion to each other: "Le plaisir que les tableaux & les poëmes dramatiques excellents nous peuvent faire, est même plus grand, lorsque nous les voyons pour la seconde fois, & quand il n'y a plus lieu à l'illusion" (ibid., 456). On Dubos's differentiation between the beholder's reaction to art on the one hand and to external reality on the other, see Hogsett, "Jean-Baptiste Dubos on Art as Illusion."

75 Carlo Gozzi, *Prefazione al "Fajel,"* 190. Cf also: "Il pubblico genio non va soggetto alle leggi delle Poetiche nella pubblica materia teatrale, e queste leggi non devono avere nè la facoltà, ne la sopraffazione di scemare d'un atomo il Pubblico ne' sui teatrali piaceri, se questi piaceri sono innocenti, e non feriscono le leggi de' Principati." Gozzi, *Processo a difesa*, 157.

76 Carlo Gozzi, "*La più lunga lettera di risposta*," in *Opere edite ed inedite*, 14: 10.

77 Gasparo Gozzi, *Osservatore Veneto*, quoted in Vescovo, "Lo specchio e la lente," 411.

78 On the role played by the press and print culture in the evolution of public opinion, see Darnton and Roche, eds, *Revolution in Print*; Chartier, *The Cultural Origins of the French Revolution*; and Ozouf, "'Public Opinion' at the End of the Old Regime." On the importance of theatre in crafting the public sphere, cf recent studies including Gvozdeva, Korneeva, and Ospovat, eds, *Dramatic Experience*; Connors, *Dramatic Battles;* and Ravel, *The Contested Parterre.*

79 Goethe, *Tagebuch der italienischen Reise*, 682. The English translation is from Goethe, *Letters from Italy*, in *The Auto-Biography of Goethe*, 2: 294. I prefer Oxenford's translation to Auden and Mayer's, which reads: "Everything around me is a worthy, stupendous monument, not to one ruler, but to a whole people" (Goethe, *Italian Journey: 1786–1788*, trans. Auden and Mayer, 78).

80 See Serra, "Piazze d'Italia," 632 and 634: "Le città dell'Italia settecentesca si presentavano ai viaggiatori come un rosario di città-teatro, dove non si entrava senza prima varcare le soglie di quel formidabile compendio urbano che era l'edificio teatrale. Senza prima trasformarsi in spettatori: secondo uno dei fenomeni di maggiore importanza del secolo, promosso dal nuovo

mezzo, trionfante e nomade, dei giornali, che alla figura dello spettatore innalzò una sorta di moderno altare."

81 On the extension of the Habermasian model to Italy and its relevance to seventeenth-century Venice in particular, see the excellent volume by De Vivo, *Information and Communication in Venice.* See also Rospocher, "Beyond the Public Sphere."

82 Carlo Gozzi, "*Ragionamento ingenuo,*" 409. See also the revealing observation of Paolo Farina, who points out that "[t]rent'anni più tardi, nella sua conclusiva riflessione critica sul teatro e sulla propria attività teatrale, svolta nella *Più lunga lettera,* rivendicando la coerenza di una vita, Carlo mette a fuoco ancora una volta la sua idea di teatro 'per tutti' con parole non dissimili da quelle usate un tempo: 'Io guardai sempre, e guardo tutt'ora la moltitudine de' nostri Teatri aperti all'universale con occhio poetico è vero, ma altresì con occhio morale, non meno che con occhio politico.'" Cf Farina, "Carlo Gozzi 'conservatore rivoluzionario'?," 75.

83 Dubos, *Réflexions critiques,* II.22, 316: "C'est que je ne comprends pas le bas peuple dans le public capable de prononcer sur les poëmes ou sur les tableaux, comme de decider à quel degré ils sont excellents. Le mot de Public ne renferme icy que personnes qui ont acquis des lumieres, soit par la lecture soit par le commerce du monde. Elles sont les seules qui puissent marquer le rang des poëmes & des tableaux, quoiqu'il se rencontre dans les ouvrages excellents des beautés capables de se faire sentir au peuple du plus bas étage & de l'obliger à se recrier. […] Le public dont il s'agit icy est donc borné aux personnes qui lisent, qui connoissent les spectacles, qui voient & qui entendent parler de tableaux, ou qui ont acquis de quelque maniere que ce soit, ce discernement qu'on apelle *goût de comparaison,* & dont je parlerai tantôt plus au long." Cf also "Jean Baptiste Du Bos," in Russo, ed., *Il gusto,* 239, n. 15.

84 Chiari, "Autore a' Leggitori," preface to *Commedie rappresentate ne' Teatri Grimani di Venezia,* 1: x. For a valuable discussion of Chiari's distinction between readership and spectatorship, see Hallamore Caesar, "Theatre and the Rise of the Italian Novel," 40–1.

85 Voltaire, "Lettre XXII: Sur M. Pope et quelques autres poètes fameux," *Lettres philosophiques,* 1342.

86 On Dubos's wide-ranging impact on European Enlightenment thought regarding artistic matters and on the importance of his *Réflexions critiques* for the history of aesthetics, see Charlton, "Jean-Baptiste Du Bos and Eighteenth-Century Sensibility," 151–62; Migliorini, "Note alle *Réflexions critiques* di Jean-Baptiste Du Bos"; Jones, "Du Bos and Rousseau"; Kavanaugh, *Enlightened Pleasures*; and Harris, *Inventing the Spectator,* 139–63.

5 Playwrights Fight Back

1 Carlo Gozzi, Preface to *Zeim, Re de' genj*, in *Opere del Co. Carlo Gozzi*, 3: 133.

2 See Goldoni, "L'autore a chi legge" in *Due gemelli veneziani, TO*, 2: 155.

3 Rousseau, "*Lettre à D'Alembert sur les spectacles*," 498. The English translation is from Rousseau, *Politics and the Arts*, 17.

4 "Denn Sie glauben nicht, wie streng der Herr ist, dem wir zu gefallen suchen müssen; ich meine unser Publikum." Lessing, *Hamburgische Dramaturgie*, 387.

5 Carlo Gozzi, Preface to *La donna serpente*, 157.

6 Chiari, *Commedie in versi*, 3: 185.

7 Jauss, "La teoria della ricezione," 13–14.

8 Goldoni, *Mémoires*, III.9, in *TO*, 1: 487.

9 Antonio Sacchi's artistic career is outlined in Bazoli, *L'orditura e la truppa*, 197–288. On Maddalena Raffi Marliani (1720–84), see Mamone, "Introduzione," in Goldoni, *La locandiera*, 17–35, and Ferrone, *La vita e il teatro di Carlo Goldoni*, 80–6.

10 See the review in *Il burbero benefico* by Domenico Caminer, which was published in *Europa letteraria* on 1 January 1772. Quoted in Berengo, ed, *Giornali veneziani del Settecento*, 357.

11 Goldoni, *Commedie buffe in prosa del sig. Carlo Goldoni.*

12 For the only close reading of the text, see the recent "allegorical-theatrical" interpretation by Javier Gutiérrez Carou ("Goldoni fra riforma e controriforma"). See also Andrea Fabiano's introduction ("Introduzione. Il genio cattivo e il genio buono: Un percorso a ritroso dalla vecchiaia alla giovinezza") and critical apparatus to his edition of Goldoni's *Il genio buono e il genio cattivo.* All citations of the play are from Fabiano's edition. For a biblical reading and an analysis of the tale's philosophical implications, see Joly, "*Il genio buono e il genio cattivo.*" To date the note to the text by Giuseppe Ortolani in *TO*, 8: 1350–2 has been most influential.

13 *Gazzetta Urbana Veneta*, n 6, Wednesday, 21 January 1789, heading *Teatri.*

14 Roberta Turchi's outstanding analysis of Goldoni's three plays – *Il teatro comico* (*The Comic Theatre*), Goldoni's theatrical manifesto; *Il Moliere*, which prioritizes the relationship between author and public; and *Il festino* (*The Dancing Party*), in which the characters are themselves spectators – demonstrates that the playwright, at decisive moments during his theatrical career, felt a real necessity to directly dialogue with and confront his audience. Cf Turchi, "Spettatori in commedia (1750–1754)," 347.

15 Goldoni, *Lettera del Signor Goldoni al Signor Meslé*, from 2 November 1762, in *TO*, 8: 1264.

16 Fabiano, "Introduzione. Il genio cattivo," 22.

17 Goldoni, *Mémoires*, III.2, in *TO*, 1: 449; *Memoirs*, 2 (1828), III.11, 106. On the relationship between travel literature and theatre, see Cicali, "La lady, il drammaturgo e i marinai."

18 Habermas, *Strukturwandel der Öffentlichkeit*, 114; *The Structural Transformation*, 50.

19 See, in particular, Fabiano, "Introduzione. Il genio cattivo," 21; Gutiérrez Carou, "Goldoni fra riforma e controriforma," 57; Joly, "*Il genio buono*," 245–6; Ranzini, "I canovacci goldoniani," 22; and Ortolani, *Note* to the text of *Il Genio*, in *TO*, 8: 1352.

20 Ranzini ("I canovacci goldoniani," 22) observes that this "self-quotation" was introduced by Goldoni only in the version of the comedy that was destined for the Venetian public.

21 Gutiérrez Carou, "Goldoni fra riforma e controriforma," 64–5.

22 Ibid., 65. In this version the genies appear in a different order than they do in the Zatta edition – first the good genie, who supports the protagonists' marriage; then the evil genie, who afterwards finds them unhappy.

23 Ibid., 65.

24 For Goldoni's and Marivaux's different treatments of the Arlequin/ Arlecchino *commedia dell'arte* mask, see Capaci, "Le marivaudage de Arlequin."

25 Goldoni's allegory departs from meanings of "genio" (genie/genius) that refer to a protective divinity who presides over the arts or who is himself a personification of the arts. See Battaglia, *Grande dizionario della lingua italiana, ad vocem.*

26 Goldoni, *Mémoires*, III.11, in *TO*, 1: 488; *Memoirs*, III.15, 149.

27 Carlo Gozzi, *Memorie inutili*, 2: part II, chap. 4, 435.

28 Already in his *Moliere* of 1751 (another meta-theatrical comedy that was dedicated to Scipione Maffei), the homonymous character and alter-ego of the playwright himself complained about the bad habits of the audience and how difficult it was to eradicate them, claiming that "Del pubblico m'affligge la facile incostanza" (I.6, v. 56), in Goldoni, *Il Moliere*, 111.

29 Goldoni, Letter to Francesco Griselini from January 1766, in *TO*, 14: 358.

30 Agnelli, "Il pubblico veneziano di Carlo Goldoni," 201, n36.

31 Despite the fact that Goldoni insisted on the significant difference between *Il genio* and the theatrical fables of his rival Carlo Gozzi (*Mémoires*, III.11, in *TO*, 1: 489), his comedy was misunderstood in Venice. Indeed, Gozzi saw in it an imitation of (and recognition of the importance of) his own plays and thus extrapolated his final victory over his rival playwright. See the preface to *Zeim, Re de' genj*, 131. Domenico Caminer, though considering Goldoni's *pièce* to surpass earlier magical comedies, located it in the same

genre as Gozzi's fables: "Avvisato però il Goldoni che, per la sua partenza decaduta la buona commedia, piacevano vieppiú le *Favole*, ridotte a teatrale rappresentazione, scrisse il *Genio buono*, e il *Genio cattivo*, che superò tutte le altre [...]." Berengo, *Giornali veneziani*, 358.

32 See Gutiérrez Carou, "Goldoni fra riforma e controriforma," 59; Joly, "*Il genio buono*," 238; Momo, *La carriera delle maschere nel teatro di Goldoni, Chiari, Gozzi*, 82–4.

33 Goldoni, Letter to Stefano Sciugliaga from 10 November 1764, in *TO*, 14: 326.

34 Alonge, *Goldoni*, 34, demonstrates that the main thrust of Goldoni's theatrical research and reform is the *libro del mondo* and realistic (bourgeois) comedy: "Goldoni è inizialmente al servizio della commedia dell'arte, ma il suo punto d'arrivo è una indagine sulle classi sociali."

35 See, for example: "Piazza in Tripoli di Barbaria con veduta in prospetto della moschea con porta chiusa nel mezzo, che poi si apre. Due GUARDIE turche, una di qua, una di là della porta della moschea" (IV.1); "Al suono di tamburini e trombette turche ed altri strumenti, vengono le DONNE turche coperte dai loro veli, scortate dagli EUNICHI neri che precedono e chiudono la marcia. Si aprono le porte della moschea. Fanno il giro del teatro ed entrano per ordine nella moschea. Nel tempo che fanno il giro, verso la fine, comparisce ARLECCHINO in abito di eunuco nero con un tamburino. Seguita anch'egli la marcia ed entra con gli altri nella moschea" (IV.2); and, immediately after the beginning of IV.3: "Entrati tutti, si chiudono le porte e cambia subito la sinfonia della marcia in un'altra più dolce, al suono della quale discende una nuvola a terra, sparisce e vedesi CORALLINA seduta ed addormentata sopra un sedile laterale di pietra."

36 Goldoni, *Mémoires*, III.11, in *TO*, 1: 489–90. My translation (the passage is omitted in Black's edition).

37 See Worvill, *"Seeing" Speech*; and Castelvecchi, *Sentimental Opera*, 63–86.

38 Fazio, "Il rinnovamento del Settecento fra attori e autori," 164.

39 Essential readings on Diderot's theory and practice of *tableaux* include Frantz, *L'esthétique du tableau dans le théâtre du XVIIIe siècle*, 9–12; Worvill, "From Prose to *peinture* to Dramatic *tableau*," 152–4; and Goodden, "'Un peinture parlante.'"

40 Diderot, *Entretiens sur Le fils naturel*, in *Esthétique-théâtre*, in *Œuvres*, 4: 1136. The English translation is from a partial translation of Diderot's work: Diderot, "*Conversations on 'The Natural Son,'*" in Sidnell, ed., *Sources of Dramatic Theory*, 2: 39.

41 Ibid., *Conversations*, 40.

42 Ibid.
43 Diderot, *Entretiens*, 1174: "Quoi! vous ne concevez pas l'effet que produiraient sur vous une scène réelle, des habits vrais, des discours proportionnés aux actions, des actions, des actions simples, des dangers dont il est impossible que vous n'ayez tremblé pour vos parents, vos amis, pour vous-mêmes?"
44 Ibid., 1179.
45 Guerlag, "The *tableau* and Authority in Diderot's Aesthetics," 184.
46 Goldoni, *Mémoires*, III.9, in *TO*, 1: 489.
47 Critical readings of the polemic between Goldoni and Diderot are vast in number; most relevant here are Toldo, "Se Diderot abbia imitato il Goldoni"; Chouillet, "Dossier du *Fils naturel* et du *Père de famille*"; Frantz, "Un hôte mal attendu"; and Mangini, "La polemica Goldoni-Diderot."
48 Paola Luciani, introduction to Goldoni, *Le bourru bienfaisant / Il burbero di buon cuore*, 18; Diderot, *De la poésie dramatique*, in *Esthétique-théâtre*, vol. 4 of *Œuvres*, 1302: "Charles Goldoni a écrit en italien une comédie, ou plutôt une farce en trois acres, qu'il a intitulée *L'ami sincère*."
49 Luciani, introduction, 19.
50 Goldoni, "L'autore a chi legge," in *TO*, 3: 573.
51 Ibid., 573–4.
52 Mangini, "La polemica Goldoni-Diderot," 267.
53 See Goldoni's letter to Francesco Griselini from January 1766, in *TO*, 14: 358–60.
54 Vescovo, "'J'avois grande envie d'aller à Naples.'"
55 On the life and work of Domenico Barone, see Vescovo, "'J'avois grande envie d'aller à Naples'" and "Dei drammaturghi-concertatori"; Greco, "Ideologia e pratica della scena nel primo Settecento napoletano," and "Dal Belvedere al Liveri," 223–41; Napoli Signorelli, *Storia critica de' teatri antichi e moderni*, 6: 227–30; Croce, *I teatri di Napoli*, 194–8; Ruffini, "'Gens de letteres' e 'gens de theatre'"; Cotticelli, "Il teatro recitato," 472–8, and Ianniciello, *Marchese Domenico Luigi Barone*.
56 See Salfi, *Saggio storico critico della commedia italiana*, 48, who pointed out the importance of Barone for the introduction of scenery games and of simultaneous dialogues, dramatic innovations that had previously been attributed to Diderot. See also Busnelli, *Diderot et l'Italie*, 46, n1.
57 Croce, *I teatri di Napoli*, 195–6.
58 As Vescovo has pointed out ("'J'avois grande envie d'aller à Naples,'" 68–73), Goldoni defended himself against the accusation of plagiarism by stressing the difference between the working conditions and thus the

performance of the comedies: Barone was writing for the court theatre, whereas Goldoni was writing for the Venetian commercial playhouses. While the latter admitted that he had read Barone's works, he also insisted that the high-pressure context of the professional public theatre did not allow him long periods of time to dedicate to rehearsals and to meticulous preparation of the actors.

59 Diderot, *Paradoxe sur le comédien*, in *Esthétique-théâtre*, vol. 4 of *Œuvres*, 1415–16. The English translation is from *The Paradox of Acting*, trans. Pollock, 82–3.

60 On the relationship between Diderot and Galiani, see Davison, *Diderot et Galiani*, 9–25.

61 Despite the fact that the *Paradox* was published posthumously in 1830, it was first drafted at the end of the 1770s – that is, exactly during the time of Galiani's and Caraccioli's stays in Paris.

62 Diderot came to know of the great success of his comedy from Madame d'Epinay, correspondent of Abbé Ferdinando Galiani, following his return to Naples. In 1773, Galiani assisted with the staging of Diderot's play by the French troupe of actor d'Aufresne, which imported a number of recently composed French plays into Italy, including Diderot's *Père de famille*, Beaumarchais's *Eugénie*, and Voltaire's *Nanine*. See Galiani, letter of 16 January 1773 to Madame d'Epinay, in Galiani and d'Epinay, *Correspondance*, 3 (1994): 188.

63 See Favart's letter to Count Durazzo from 1762, in Favart, *Mémoires et correspondance littéraires, dramatiques et anecdotiques*, 2: 47–8.

64 Fried, *Absorption and Theatricality*.

65 For the definition of "theatrical" in reference to the painting, Fried draws on Diderot, for whom the terms "theatre" and "theatrical" have a pejorative connotation and are synonyms of falseness and the mannered. Consequently, Fried uses the concept "theatrical" in the negative sense to describe paintings that are not autonomous but depend upon the beholder who observes them, identifying the artificial relationship between painting and observer precisely in paintings by French artists that were criticized by Diderot because they fail to express true sentiment. See Fried, *Absorption and Theatricality*, 100.

66 Fried, *Absorption and Theatricality*, 103.

67 Some years later, Diderot departs from a similar consideration in his influential *Paradoxe*, where he claims that the actor should ignore the existence of the spectator, imagining instead a wall dividing performance from audience.

68 Molinari, "Un teatro immaginario per Goldoni," XVII.

69 The exemplary paintings to which Fried refers and which represent figures engaged in "absorptive" activity, action, or state of mind are: Jean-Baptiste Greuze, *Un père de famille qui lit la Bible à ses enfants* (1755), and *Le tendre ressouvenir* (Salon 1763); Jean-Baptiste Siméon Chardin, *Un philosophe occupé de sa lecture* (1753), *Un dessinateur d'après le Mercure de M. Pigalle* (Salon 1753), and *Le château de cartes* (1736–7); Carl Van Loo, *La lecture espagnole* (Salon 1761), and *St Grégoire dictant ses homélies* (Salon 1765); and Joseph-Marie Vien, *Ermite endormi* (Salon 1753). The paintings by Chardin, Greuze, and Van Loo were known in Venice through the foreign artists who travelled there; the ideas behind these works were quickly adopted by Venetian painters and designers. See Bassi, "Le illustrazioni italiane e francesi delle commedie goldoniane." Bassi also points out the close relationship between the paintings of Chardin and Pietro Longhi, whose artistic production had a close link to Goldoni's theatre.
70 On the illustrated edition of Goldoni's works, see Molinari, "Un teatro immaginario per Goldoni"; and Bassi, "Le illustrazioni italiane e francesi delle commedie goldoniane." On the editor Antonio Zatta and the illustrator Pietro Antonio Novelli, see De Grassi, *Il libro illustrato veneziano nel Settecento*, 45–8; and Zaniol, "Per una rilettura storico-filologica delle ultime edizioni goldoniane del Settecento."
71 Michelis, *Letterati e lettori nel Settecento veneziano*, 22.
72 Guccini, "Goldoni scenografo," 29.
73 Molinari, "Un teatro immaginario," XXXV.
74 Goodden, "'Un peinture parlante,'" 400.
75 Diderot, *De la poésie dramatique*, 1338. The English translation is adapted from Diderot, *Discourse on Dramatic Poetry*, in Sidnell, ed., *Sources of Dramatic Theory*, 68.
76 Ley, "The Significance of Diderot," 344.

6 Liberty and the Audience

1 Alfieri, *Vita scritta da esso*, 1: bk IV, chap. 6, p. 212. Hereafter *Vita*, followed by book in roman numerals, chapter in arabic numerals, and page numbers. English translation from Alfieri, *Memoirs of the Life and Writings of Victor Alfieri*, 2: bk IV, chap. 6, p. 71. Hereafter *Memoirs*, followed by book in roman numerals, chapter in arabic numerals, and page numbers.
2 Alfieri, *Vita*, IV.16, 267; *Memoirs*, IV.16, 186. On the complex relationship between Alfieri and Voltaire, see Santato, *Alfieri e Voltaire*.
3 Alfieri, "*Del principe e delle lettere*," bk II, chap. 11, pp. 190–1. Hereafter *Del principe*, followed by book in roman numerals, chapter in arabic numerals,

and page numbers. English translations are from Alfieri, *The Prince and Letters*, bk II, chap. 11, p. 91. Hereafter *The Prince and Letters*, followed by book in roman numerals, chapter in arabic numerals, and page numbers.

4 Alfieri, *Del principe*, II.1, 140; *The Prince and Letters*, II.1, 38.

5 Alfieri, *Vita*, IV.17, 274.

6 Alfieri, *Del principe*, III.10, 246–7; *The Prince and Letters*, III.10, 151.

7 Alfieri, "*Risposta dell'Alfieri al Calzabigi*," 228. Subsequent references are to the pages of this critical edition.

8 See the draft of *Bruto primo* in MS Laurenziano 26[2] "Alfieri," c. 159v. I quote from the note by Angelo Fabrizi to his critical edition of the tragedy: Alfieri, *Bruto primo*, 11–21: 15. The English translation is from Alfieri, "The First Brutus," in *The Tragedies of Vittorio Alfieri*, 2: 263–4. Subsequent page references to Bowring's revised text of C. Lloyd's 1815 translation will appear in parentheses in the text.

9 Alexandre, "Le peuple dans les tragédies d'Alfieri."

10 On Alfieri's choice of Greek and Roman subjects for his tragedies, see Mattioda, *Teorie della tragedia*, 236–7.

11 Zucchi, "La figura corale nelle tragedie alfieriane," 549–50. On readings of Machiavelli in Alfieri's writings, see Di Benedetto, "*Il nostro gran Machiavelli*," 119–40; and Mattioda, "Machiavelli nei trattati politici."

12 McCormick, "Machiavelli's Greek Tyrant as Republican Reformer," 339.

13 Alfieri, "*Il parere* sul *Bruto primo*," in *Parere sulle tragedie e altre prose critiche*, ed. Pagliai,137. My translation.

14 Fubini, *Vittorio Alfieri (Il pensiero-la tragedia)*, 319.

15 Alfieri, *Vita*, IV.17, 274; *Memoirs*.

16 Alfieri, *Risposta dell'Alfieri al Calzabigi*, 233–4.

17 Alfieri, *Lettera a Arduino Tana* del 26 aprile 1780, in *Epistolario*, 1: 106–7.

18 Alfieri, *Risposta dell'Alfieri al Calzabigi*, 227. There is a vast bibliography on performances of Alfieri's tragedy in Italy through the second half of the nineteenth century if not beyond. See, for example, the essays by Frattali in *Alfieri, lo spettacolo e le arti*; Ferrone, "Fortuna di Alfieri nell'Ottocento"; Cambiaghi, "*Rapida … semplice … tetra e feroce*"; and Geraci, *Destini e retrobotteghe*.

19 Barsotti, *Alfieri e la scena*, 48.

20 Alfieri, "*Parere dell'Autore sull'arte comica in Italia*," in *Parere sulle tragedie e altre prose critiche*, ed. Pagliai, 241–2. For an analysis of this piece by Alfieri, see Raimondi, "Le ombre sull'abisso," 72; Bragaglia, "Il parere dell'Alfieri"; and Decroisette, "'Un desiderio ignoto di qualcosa di più': Alfieri et ses spectateurs."

21 Ariani, "L'ossessione delle 'regole' e il disordine degli 'affetti,'"237.

22 Regarding the astounding fame that Alfieri, not to mention his legendary theatre as well as his dramas themselves, enjoyed through the nineteenth century, see Pieri, "Recitare/recitarsi fra Firenze Pisa e Siena," 21 and 28.

23 On the conception of the tragedies *Bruto primo* and *Bruto secondo*, and on Alfieri's positioning of himself as the anti-Voltaire, see the oft-cited passage from his *Vita*, IV.16, 266–7: "mi accade che in una delle tante e sempre graditissime lettere della mia donna, essa coma a caso mi accennava di aver assistito in teatro ad una recita del *Bruto* di Voltaire, e che codesta tragedia le era sommamente piaciuta. Io, che l'aveva veduta recitare forse dieci anni prima, e che non me ne ricordava punto, riempiutomi istantaneamente di una rabida e disdegnosa emulazione sì il cuore che la mente, dissi fra me: 'Che Bruti, che Bruti di Voltaire? io ne farò dei *Bruti*, e li farò tutt'a due: il tempo dimostrerà poi, se tali soggetti di tragedia si addicessero meglio a me, o ad un francese nato plebeo, e sottoscrittosi nelle sue firme per lo spazio di settanta e più anni: Voltaire *Gentiluomo ordinario del Re*.' Né altri dissi, né di amente d'questo toccai pur parola nel rispondere alla mia donna; ma subitamente d'un lampo ideai ad un parto i due *Bruti*, quali poi li ho eseguiti."

24 Fabrizi, "Sul *Bruto Primo* alfieriano," 187.

25 Alfieri, "*Della tirannide*," 1: bk II, chap. 6, pp. 96–7. Hereafter *Della tirannide*, followed by book in roman numerals, chapter in arabic numerals, and page numbers. For the English translation, see Alfieri, *Of Tyranny*, bk II, chap. 6, p. 91. Hereafter *Of Tyranny*, followed by book in roman numerals, chapter in arabic numerals, and page numbers.

26 Tatti, "Bruto secondo," 753.

27 Pellegrini, "Alfieri e la tragedia senza coro," 112.

28 Alfieri, *Bruto secondo*, 29. Despite the fact that *Bruto primo* and *Bruto secondo* feature two different historical figures named Brutus (Lucius Junius Brutus in *Bruto primo* and Marcus Junius Brutus in *Bruto secondo*), Alfieri seems to have wanted to suggest a continuity and complementarity between these two protagonists and their two tragedies.

29 Fabrizi, "Sul *Bruto Primo* alfieriano," 186.

30 Foucault, *Security, Territory, Population*, 278.

31 Habermas, "Naturrecht und Revolution," 95; "Natural Law and Revolution," 89. See also Popkin, "The Concept of Public Opinion in the Historiography of the French Revolution," 80–1.

32 Alfieri, *Del principe*, III.10, 247–8; *The Prince and Letters*, III.10, 152.

33 Bettinelli, "*Lettera diretta al signor canonico De Giovanni del Collegio delle Arti Liberali in Torino sulla nuova edizione delle Tragedie del c. Alfieri*," 20: 236. See

also Biondi, *Temi e stile del discorso politico alfieriano,* 1: 246: “La politica soffia ovunque nell’opera [di Alfieri], tanto da suggerire a Bettinelli e a Manzoni l’impressione di un politico intestarditosi a far versi, o di un oratore bravo a sfogarsi in dialoghi.” On eighteenth-century tragedy’s use of the ancient myths, see Mattioda, *Teorie della tragedia,* 225–31.

34 By the end of the 1700s, Brutus had become one of the most common subjects of political tragedy. For an analysis of Antonio Conti’s *Giunio Bruto* (1751) and its conflicted relationship with its source, Voltaire’s *Brutus* (1730) – as well as the political and ideological distance between the latter and Alfieri’s *Bruto primo* – see Luciani, “Riscritture di ‘Brutus,’” in *Le passioni e gli affetti,* 157–70; and Camerino, “Libertà e tirannide.” See also Alfonzetti, *Il corpo di Cesare.*

35 The most obvious narrative change imposed by Alfieri is the elimination of the romantic intrigue – the love story between Tito, Bruto’s son, and Tullia, Tarquinio’s daughter – upon which Voltaire and Antonio Conti had insisted. With Tito’s love-related motivation removed, this version finds reasons for his actions in misplaced filial affection and in the inexperience of youth.

36 Many scholars have compared Habermas and Koselleck; some have seen Koselleck’s *Critique and Crisis* as the primary source for Habermas’s *Structural Transformation.* See, for example, Hohendahl, “Recasting the Public Sphere”; and Hess, *Reconstituting the Body Politic.*

37 On the differences between Habermas and Koselleck, see Wetters, *The Opinion System Impasses of the Public Sphere from Hobbes to Habermas,* 89: “Koselleck’s *Critique and Crisis* (1959) and Habermas’s *Structural Transformation* (1962) are often read as if they were compatible, but the political implications of the two theories could not be more different.” See also Popkin, “The Concept of Public Opinion,” 83: “*Kritik und Krise* presents a concise dialectical argument to explain the triumph of public opinion as the basis of political authority. Unlike Habermas, Koselleck makes no reference to economic or social factors. For him, the private realm from which public opinion develops has purely political roots: it grows out of the structure of seventeenth-century absolutism.”

38 Koselleck, *Critique and Crisis,* 25.

39 Ibid., 59–60.

40 Foucault, *Security, Territory, Population,* 277.

41 On the contradictions inherent in the combination of Alfieri’s aristocratic status with his participation in the system of bourgeois values that accompanied the lifestyle of an independent man of letters, see Cantagrel; “Un autore in cerca di legittimità,” 69–73.

42 Alfieri, *Della tirannide*, I.2, 12; *Of Tyranny*, I.2, 11. Cf also Rando, *Alfieri europeo*, 19–76.
43 Koselleck, *Critique and Crisis*, 56.
44 Alfieri, *Della tirannide*, II.8, 106; *Of Tyranny*, II.8, 100.
45 Alfieri, *Risposta dell'Alfieri al Calzabigi*, 227.
46 "A People's King."
47 On the public/private distinction and the theoretical discussions that informed it, see Weintraub, "The Theory and Politics of the Public/Private Distinction."
48 Ciniro, from this perspective, represents the playwright himself: "Ciniro, è un perfetto padre, e un perfettissimo re. L'autore vi si è compiaciuto a dipingere in lui, o a provar di dipingere, un re buono ideale, ma verisimile; quale vi potrebbe pur essere, quale non v'è pur quasi mai." Alfieri, *Parere sulle tragedie*, 133.
49 Mineo, "Vittorio Alfieri nella crisi dell'antico regime," 425.
50 Jordan, "The Household and the State."
51 Alfieri, *Del principe*, III.10, 245–6; *The Prince and Letters*, 150.
52 Koselleck, *Critique and Crisis*, 56 and 58.
53 Habermas, *The Structural Transformation*, 50. See also Weintraub, "The Theory and Politics of the Public/Private Distinction," 11–13.
54 Alfieri, *Della tirannide*, II.8, 106; *Of Tyranny*, II.8, 100.
55 Ibid., II.8, 106–7; *Of Tyranny*, II.8, 100–1.
56 Machiavelli, *Discorsi sopra la prima deca di Tito Livio*, bk III, chap. III, 963–4; *Discourses on Livy*, 214.
57 Agamben, *Homo Sacer*, 93–4; *Sovereign Power*, 53.
58 Agamben, *Homo Sacer*, 13; *Sovereign Power*, 13.
59 Alfieri, *Del principe*, III.10, 244; *The Prince and Letters*, III.10, 149.
60 Alfieri, *Del principe*, III.10, 249; *The Prince and Letters*, III.10, 153.
61 Alfieri, *Bruto secondo*, 29. The English translation is from Alfieri, "The Second Brutus," 2: 369.
62 De Sanctis, *Storia della letteratura italiana*, 2: 822. On theatre as a space in which to assemble people as an audience and to reinforce a sense of national identity (as well as on the role of the audience itself in nation-building projects), see Kruger, *The National Stage*.
63 See Koselleck, *Critique and Crisis*, esp. chap. 8, "The Process of Criticism," 98–123.
64 According to Habermas, the modern public sphere emerged from critical discourse centred on cultural products that reflected new and growing forms of subjectivity as well as new literary genres such as memoirs and the sentimental novel. For Habermas, the content of these new genres became simultaneously more intimate and more explicitly political.

65 Koselleck, *Critique and Crisis,* 115.

66 Lukács, *Il romanzo storico,* 143.

67 Pieri, "Recitare/recitarsi fra Firenze Pisa e Siena," 23–4.

68 Fubini, *Vittorio Alfieri,* 320.

69 Gioberti, *Il gesuita moderno,* 1: LXIV n2.

70 Alfieri, *Della tirannide,* II.5, 94; *Of Tyranny,* II.5, 89.

71 See Alfieri, *Vita,* IV.2, 192: "sendomi ben convinto che al far tragedie il primo sapere richiesto, si è il forte sentire; il qual non s'impara. Restavami da imparare (e non era certo poco) l'arte di fare agli altri sentire quello che mi parea di sentir io."

72 Fubini, *Vittorio Alfieri,* 321.

Epilogue

1 Warner, "Publics and Counterpublics," 62.

2 Sorba, "National Theater and the Age of Revolution in Italy"; see also Kruger, *The National Stage.*

3 Azzaroni, *La rivoluzione a teatro,* 46; Barricelli, "'Making a People What It Once Was.'"

4 Mariti, "La pubblica utilità del teatro," 18.

Bibliography

Primary Works

Alfieri, Vittorio. *Memoirs of the Life and Writings of Victor Alfieri; Written by Himself.* Translated from the Italian. 2 vols. London: Henry Colburn, 1810.

– *The Tragedies of Vittorio Alfieri: Complete, Including His Posthumous Works.* Edited by Edgar Alfred Bowring. 2 vols. London: George Bell, 1876.

– "The First Brutus." In *The Tragedies of Vittorio Alfieri*, 261–310.

– "The Second Brutus." In *The Tragedies of Vittorio Alfieri*, 365–417.

– *Scritti politici e morali.* 3 vols. Vols 1 and 2 edited by Pietro Cazzani. Vol. 3 edited by Clemente Mazzotta. Asti: Casa d'Alfieri, 1951–84.

– "*Del principe e delle lettere.*" In *Scritti politici e morali.* Vol. 1 (1951), 111–254.

– "*Della tirannide.*" In *Scritti politici e morali.* Vol. 1 (1951), 1–109.

– *Vita scritta da esso.* Edited by Luigi Fassò. 2 vols. Asti: Casa d'Alfieri, 1951.

– *Of Tyranny.* Translated, edited, and with an Introduction by Julius A. Molinaro and Beatrice Corrigan. Toronto: University of Toronto Press, 1961.

– *Epistolario (1767–1788).* Edited by Lanfranco Caretti. Asti: Casa d'Alfieri, 1963.

– *Merope.* Edited by Angelo Fabrizi. Asti: Casa d'Alfieri, 1968.

– *The Prince and Letters.* Translated by Beatrice Corrigan and Julius A. Molinaro. Toronto: University of Toronto Press, 1972.

– *Bruto primo.* Edited by Angelo Fabrizi. Asti: Casa d'Alfieri, 1975.

– *Bruto secondo.* Edited by Angelo Fabrizi. Asti: Casa d'Alfieri, 1976.

– *Parere sulle tragedie e altre prose critiche.* Edited by Morena Pagliai. Asti: Casa d'Alfieri, 1978.

– "*Parere sull'arte comica in Italia.*" In *Parere sulle tragedie e altre prose critiche*, 239–45.

– "*Parere sulle tragedie.*" In *Parere sulle tragedie e altre prose critiche*, 79–167.

– "*Risposta dell'Alfieri al Calzabigi.*" In *Parere sulle tragedie e altre prose critiche*, 216–38.

– "*Satire.*" In *Scritti politici e morali.* Vol. 3 (1984), 63–190.

Allacci, Leone. *Drammaturgia diuisa in sette indici.* Rome: Mascardi, 1666.

Aristotle. *Problems.* Translated by W.S. Hett. 2 vols. Cambridge, MA: Harvard University Press; London: Heinemann, 1953–7.

– *Politics.* Translated by H. Rackham. London: W. Heinemann; Cambridge, MA: Harvard University Press, 1967.

Basile, Giambattista. *The Tale of Tales, or Entertainment for Little Ones.* Translated by Nancy L. Canepa. Foreword by Jack Zipes. Detroit, MI: Wayne State University Press, 2007.

– *Lo cunto de li cunti, overo Lo trattenemiento de' peccerille.* Edited by Carolina Stromboli. 2 vols. Rome: Salerno, 2013.

Beaumarchais, Pierre-Augustin Caron de. "*Essai sur le genre dramatique sérieux.*" In *Œuvres*, edited by Pierre Larthomas, 119–40. Paris: Gallimard, 1988.

Becelli, Giulio Cesare. "*Al lettore.*" In Maffei, *Teatro del sig. marchese Scipione Maffei cioè la tragedia la comedia e il drama non più stampato, aggiunta la spiegazione d'alcune antichità pertinenti al teatro, all'Altezza Serenissima di Rinaldo I duca di Modena &c. &c. &c.* Verona: Giovanni Alberto Tumermani, 1730, VII–XXX.

Bettinelli, Saverio. "*Lettera diretta al signor canonico De Giovanni del Collegio delle Arti Liberali in Torino sulla nuova edizione delle Tragedie del c. Alfieri.*" In *Opere edite ed inedite in prosa ed in versi.* 24 vols. Venice: Adolfo Cesare, 1801.

Castiglione, Baldassarre. *Il libro del cortegiano.* Edited by Giulio Carnazzi. Milan: Rizzoli, 2010.

Chiari, Pietro. *Commedie rappresentate ne' Teatri Grimani di Venezia, cominciando dall'anno 1749, d'Egerindo Critptonide, pastor arcade della Colonia Parmense.* 4 vols. Venice: Pasinelli, 1752–8.

– *Commedie in versi dell'abate Pietro Chiari bresciano, Poeta di S.A. Serenissima il Sig. Duca di Modana.* 10 vols. Venice: Bettinelli, 1756–62.

– "*Le osservazioni critiche sopra* Le sorelle rivali." In *Commedie in versi.* Vol. 3 (1758), 183–5.

– "*Le sorelle rivali.*" In *Commedie in versi.* Vol. 3 (1758), 181–268.

Cicognini, Giacinto Andrea. *Celio.* Florence: Per Luca Francesc & Alessandro Logi, 1649.

– *Giasone. Dramma musicale del D. Giacinto Andrea Cicognini.* Venice: Per il Giuliani, 1649.

– *Il Don Gastone di Moncada.* Bologna: Per Gioseffo Longhi, 1682.

[Cicognini]. *La caduta del gran capitan Belissario sotto la condanna di Giustiniano Imperatore.* Bologna: Antonio Pisarri, 1661.

Crescimbeni, Giovanni Maria. *La bellezza della volgar poesia.* Rome: Buagni, 1700.
Diderot, Denis. *The Paradox of Acting.* Translated by Walter Herries Pollock. London: Chatto & Windus, 1883.
– "*Conversations on 'The Natural Son.*" In *Sources of Dramatic Theory, 2: Voltaire to Hugo,* edited by Michael J. Sidnell, 36–57. Cambridge: Cambridge University Press, 1994.
– "*Esthétique-théâtre.*" In Vol. 4 of Diderot, *Œuvres,* edited by Laurent Versini. Paris: Robert Laffont, 1996.
– "*Entretiens sur Le fils naturel.*" In *Esthétique-théâtre,* 1131–90.
– "*De la poésie dramatique.*" In *Esthétique-théâtre,* 1278–350.
– "*Paradoxe sur le comédien.*" In *Esthétique-théâtre,* 1367–426.
Dubos, Jean-Baptiste. *Réflexions critiques sur la poésie et sur la peinture.* 2 vols. Paris: Jean Mariette, 1719. Reprint: Geneva: Slatkine, 1967.
– *Critical Reflections on Poetry, Painting and Music.* Translated into English by Thomas Nugent. 2 vols. London: John Nourse, 1748.
Favart, Charles-Simon. *Mémoires et correspondance littéraires, dramatiques et anecdotiques de C.S. Favart.* Edited by A.P.C. Favart. 3 vols. Paris: Léopold Collin, 1808.
Ficinus, Marsilius. *De vita.* Edited by Albano Biondi and Giuliano Pisani. Pordenone: Biblioteca dell'immagine, 1991.
Galiani, Ferdinando, and Louise d'Epinay, *Correspondance.* Edited by Georges Dulac and Daniel Maggetti. 5 vols. Paris: Desjonquères, 1992–7.
Giraldi Cinzio, Giovan Battista. "*Discorso intorno al comporre delle commedie e delle tragedie.*" In *Scritti critici,* edited by Camillo Guerrieri Crocetti, 169–224. Milan: Marzorati, 1973.
Goethe, Johann Wolfgang von. *Italian Journey: 1786–1788.* Translated by W.H. Auden and Elizabeth Mayer. Harmondsworth: Penguin Books, 1970.
– "*Tagebuch der italienischen Reise für Frau von Stein.*" In *Sämtliche Werke, Briefe, Tagebücher und Gespräche,* edited by Hendrick Birus et al. 40 vols. Frankfurt am Main: Deutscher Klassiker, 1985–99, Vol. 15.1 (1993), edited by Christoph Michel and Hans-Georg Dewitz, 599–745.
– *The Auto-biography of Goethe: Truth and Poetry: From My Own Life.* Translated by John Oxenford. 2 vols. Cambridge: Cambridge University Press, 2013.
Goldoni, Carlo. *Commedie buffe in prosa del sig. Carlo Goldoni.* Venice: Antonio Zatta, 1793.
– *Memoirs of Goldoni, Written by Himself.* Translated by John Black. 2 vols. London: Henry Colburn-Hunt and Clarke, 1814–28.
– *Tutte le opere.* Edited by Giuseppe Ortolani. 14 vols. Milan: Mondadori, 1935–56.
– *Mémoires.* In *Tutte le opere.* Vol. 1 (1935), 1–619.

– *I due gemelli veneziani.* In *Tutte le opere.* Vol. 2 (1936), 147–238.
– *Il teatro comico.* In *Tutte le opere.* Vol. 2 (1936), 1039–105.
– *Il Belisario.* In *Tutte le opere.* Vol. 9 (1950), 1–73.
– *La bella verità.* In *Tutte le opere.* Vol. 12 (1952), 109–59.
– *Le baruffe chiozzotte.* Edited by Piermario Vescovo. Introduction by Giorgio Strehler. Venice: Marsilio, 1993.
– *Il teatro illustrato nelle edizioni del Settecento.* Introduction by Cesare Molinari. Venice: Marsilio, 1993.
– *Scelta e introduzione di Renzo Rosso.* Rome: Istituto Poligrafico e Zecca dello Stato, 1995.
– *Le bourru bienfaisant / Il burbero di buon cuore.* Edited by Paola Luciani. Venice: Marsilio, 2003.
– *Il Moliere.* Edited by Bodo Guthmüller, Venice: Marsilio, 2004.
– *Il genio buono e il genio cattivo.* Edited by Andrea Fabiano. Venice: Marsilio, 2006.
– *La locandiera.* Edited by Sara Mamone and Teresa Megale. Venice: Marsilio, 2007.
– *La serva amorosa.* Edited by Paola Giovanelli and Clemente Mazzotta. Venice: Marsilio, 2007.
– *Prefazioni e polemiche.* Edited by Roberta Turchi. 3 vols. Venice: Marsilio, 2008–11.
– *Memorie italiane.* In Vol. 3 of *Prefazioni e polemiche,* edited by Roberta Turchi. Venice: Marsilio, 2008.
– *Polemiche editoriali.* In Vol. 1 of *Prefazioni e polemiche,* edited by Roberta Turchi. Venice: Marsilio, 2009.
– *Memorie italiane.* Edited by Epifanio Ajello. Naples: Liguori, 2012.
Gozzi, Carlo. *Opere del Co: Carlo Gozzi.* 8 vols. Venice: Colombani, 1772–4.
– "*Zeim, Re de' genj.*" In *Opere del Co: Carlo Gozzi.* Vol. 3 (1772), 123–231.
– "*I due fratelli nimici.*" In *Opere del Co: Carlo Gozzi.* Vol. 5 (1773), 281–388.
– *Opere edite ed inedite del Co: Carlo Gozzi.* 14 vols. Venice: Zanardi, 1801–4.
– "*Amore assottiglia il cervello. Commedia in verso sciolto del Co: Carlo Gozzi con due ragionamenti preliminari.*" In *Opere edite ed inedite.* Vol. 13 (1802), 141–336.
– "*La più lunga lettera di risposta che sia stata scritta inviata da Carlo Gozzi a un poeta teatrale italiano de' nostri giorni.*" In *Opere edite ed inedite.* Vol. 14 (1804), 3–168.
– *Fiabe teatrali.* Edited by Alberto Beniscelli. Milan: Garzanti, 2004.
– *Lettere.* Edited by Fabio Soldini. Venice: Marsilio, 2004.
– *Memorie inutili.* Edited by Paolo Bosisio with Valentina Garavaglia. 2 vols. Milan: LED, 2006.
– *Commedie in commedia. Le gare teatrali. Le convulsioni. La cena mal apparecchiata.* Edited by Fabio Soldini and Piermario Vescovo. Venice: Marsilio, 2011.

– *La donna serpente.* Edited by Giulietta Bazoli. Venice: Marsilio, 2012.
– *Ragionamento ingenuo. Dai "preamboli" all' "Appendice." Scritti di teoria teatrale.* Edited by Anna Scannapieco. Venice: Marsilio, 2013.
– "*La prefazione al 'Fajel.*" In Gozzi, *Ragionamento ingenuo. Dai "preamboli" all' "Appendice,"* 165–354.
– "*Ragionamento ingenuo, e storia sincera dell'origine delle mie dieci fiabe teatrali.*" In Gozzi, *Ragionamento ingenuo. Dai "preamboli" all' "Appendice,"* 357–523.
– "*Appendice al Ragionamento ingenuo.*" In Gozzi, *Ragionamento ingenuo. Dai "preamboli" all' "Appendice,"* 525–722.

Gozzi, Gasparo. *Osservatore Veneto,* 98, 9 January 1761.
– *Gazzetta Veneta,* 103, 27 January 1761.

Gracián, Baltasar. *Oráculo manual y arte de prudencia.* Edited by Miguel Romera-Navarro. Madrid: Consejo Superior de Investigaciones Científicas, 2003.

Guarini, Giambattista. *Il pastor fido e il compendio della poesia tragicomica.* Edited by Gioachino Brognoligo. Bari: Laterza, 1914.
– "*The Compendium of Tragicomic Poetry.*" In *Literary Criticism: Plato to Dryden,* edited and translated by Allan H. Gilbert, 504–33. Detroit, MI: Wayne State University Press, 1967.

Ingegnieri, Angelo. *Della poesia rappresentativa e del modo di rappresentare le favole sceniche.* Edited by Maria Luisa Doglio. Modena: Panini, 1989.

Lessing, Gotthold Ephraim. "*Hamburgische Dramaturgie.*" In *Werke und Briefe in zwölf Bänden.* Vol. 6, edited by Klaus Bohnen, 181–694. Frankfurt am Main: Deutscher Klassiker Verlag, 1985.

Machiavelli, Niccolò. *Discourses on Livy.* Translated by Harvey Clarlin Mansfield and Nathan Tarcov. Chicago and London: University of Chicago Press, 1996.
– "*Il principe.*" In *Opere,* edited by Corrado Vivanti. 2 vols. Turin: Einaudi-Gallimard, 1997.
– *Discorsi sopra la prima deca di Tito Livio (libro III).* Edited by Rinaldo Rinaldi, Vol. 1, Part 2. Turin: UTET, 1999.

Maffei, Scipione. *Teatro italiano o sia scelta di tragedie per uso della scena.* Verona: Vallarsi, 1723–5.
– *Teatro del sig. marchese Scipione Maffei cioè la tragedia la comedia e il drama non più stampato, aggiunta la spiegazione d'alcune antichità pertinenti al teatro, all'Altezza Serenissima di Rinaldo I duca di Modena &c. &c. &c.* Verona: Tumermani, 1730.
– *Epistolario: 1700–1755.* Edited by Celestino Garibotto. 2 vols. Milan: Giuffrè, 1955.
– "*Istoria del teatro e difesa di esso.*" In *De' teatri antichi e moderni e altri scritti teatrali,* edited by Laura Sannia Nowé, 15–49. Modena: Mucchi, 1988.
– "Proemio to *Merope.*" In *De' teatri antichi e moderni e altri scritti teatrali,* 76–86.

– "*Consiglio politico.*" In *"Riformar il mondo." Il pensiero civile di Scipione Maffei. Con una nuova edizione del Consiglio politico*, edited by Paolo Ulivioni, 353–420. Alessandria: Edizioni dell'Orso, 2008.

– *Merope.* Edited by Stefano Locatelli. Pisa: ETS, 2008.

Montaigne, Michel de. "*Essais.*" In *Œuvres complètes.* 2 vols. Paris: Gallimard, 1962.

Pascal, Blaise. *Thoughts.* Translated by W.F. Trotter. New York: F. Collier & Son, 1910.

– "*Pensées.*" In *Œuvres complètes* (L'intégrale), edited by Louis Lafuma. Paris: Seuil, 1963.

– *Pensées.* Edited and translated by Roger Ariew. Indianapolis: Hackett, 2005.

Rossi, Pio. *Il convito morale per gli etici, economici e politici.* 2 vols. Venice: Appresso i Guerigli, 1639) (first part)–1657 (second part).

Rousseau, Jean-Jacques. *Politics and the Arts: Letter to M. D'Alembert on the Theatre.* Translated from the French by Allan Bloom. Ithaca, NY: Cornell University Press, 1989.

– "*Lettre à D'Alembert sur les spectacles.*" In *Théâtre. Écrits sur le théâtre*, Vol. 16 of *Œuvres complètes*, edited by Alain Cernuschi. Geneva: Slatkin, 2012.

Saint-Évremond, Charles de Marguetel de Saint Denis, seigneur de. *Œuvres en prose.* Edited by René Ternois. 4 vols. Paris: Marcel Didier, 1966–9.

Torelli, Pomponio. *La Merope.* Edited by Vincenzo Guercio. Rome: Bulzoni, 1999.

Voltaire. "*Mérope.*" In *The Works of Voltaire: A Contemporary Version*, translated by William F. Fleming, 3–99. New York: E.R. Du Mont, 1901.

– "*Lettres philosophiques.*" In *Mélanges*, edited by Jacques van den Heuvel. Paris: Gallimard, 1961.

– "*Mérope.*" In *The Complete Works.* Vol. 17, edited by Jack R. Vrooman and Janet Godden, 244–344. Oxford: The Voltaire Foundation-Taylor Institution, 1991.

Secondary Works

Accorsi, Maria Grazia. "La prefazione di Goldoni all'edizione Bettinelli e il razionalismo arcadico: Rapin, D'Aubignac, Muratori." In *Scena e lettura: Problemi di scrittura e recitazione dei testi teatrali*, 141–200. Modena: Mucchi, 2002.

Agamben, Giorgio. *Homo Sacer. Il potere sovrano e la vita nuda.* Turin: Einaudi: 1995.

– *Homo Sacer: Sovereign Power and Bare Life.* Translated by Daniel Heller-Roazen. Stanford, CA: Stanford University Press, 1998.

Agnelli, Maddalena. "Il pubblico veneziano di Carlo Goldoni." *Problemi di critica goldoniana* 2 (1995): 183–230. http://digital.casalini.it/18267149.

Alberti, Maria. "Il teatrino detto della Dogana o di Baldracca." In *Teatro e spettacolo nella Firenze dei Medici. Modelli dei luoghi teatrali*, edited by Elvira Garbero Zorzi and Mario Sperenzi, 161–5. Florence: Olschki, 2001.

Alexandre, Denise. "Le peuple dans les tragédies d'Alfieri." *Italies* 6, no. 2 (2002): 503–22. http://doi.org/10.4000/italies.1744.

Alfonzetti, Beatrice. *Il corpo di Cesare. Percorsi di una catastrofe nella tragedia del Settecento.* Modena: Mucchi, 1989.

Alonge, Roberto. *Goldoni. Dalla commedia dell'arte al dramma borghese.* Milan: Garzanti, 2004.

Angelini, Franca. *Vita di Goldoni.* Bari: Laterza, 1993.

Antonucci, Fausta. "Spunti tematici e rielaborazione di modelli spagnoli nel *Don Gastone di Moncada* di Giacinto Andrea Cicognini." In *Tradurre, riscrivere, mettere in scena*, edited by Maria Grazia Profeti, 65–84. Florence: Alinea, 1996.

Antonucci, Fausta, and Lorenzo Bianconi. "Miti, tramiti e trame: Cicognini, Cavalli e l'augonauta." In Giacinto Andrea Cicognini, Giovanni Filippo Apolloni, Francesco Cavalli, Alessandro Stradella, *Il novello Giasone.* Partitura in facsimile ed edizione dei libretti, edited by Nicola Usula, saggi introduttivi di Fausta Antonucci, Lorenzo Bianconi, and Nicola Usula, IX–XL. Milan: Ricordi, 2013.

– "Plotting the Myth of *Giasone*." In *Readying Cavalli's Operas for the Stage. Manuscript, Edition, Production*, edited by Ellen Rosand, 201–27. Farnham, Surrey: Ashgate, 2013.

Apostolidès, Jean-Marie. *Le roi-machine: Spectacle et politique au temps de Louis XIV.* Paris: Minuit, 1981.

– *Le prince sacrifié: Théâtre et politique au temps de Louis XIV.* Paris: Minuit, 1985.

Ariani, Marco. "L'ossessione delle 'regole' e il disordine degli 'affetti': Lineamenti di una teoria illuministica del teatro tragico." *Quaderni di teatro* 11 (1981): 233–58.

Azzaroni, Giovanni. *La rivoluzione a teatro. Antinomie del teatro giacobino in Italia (1796–1805).* Rome: Bulzoni, 1985.

Babb, Lawrence. *The Elizabethan Malady: A Study of Melancholia in English Literature from 1580 to 1642.* East Lansing, MI: Michigan State University Press, 1951.

Baldini, Artemio Enzo, and Anna Maria Battista. "Il dibattito politico nell'Italia della controriforma: Ragion di Stato, tacitismo, machiavellismo, utopia." *Il pensiero politico* 30, no. 3 (1997): 394–439. http://digital.casalini.it/2517106.

Barricelli, Franca R. "'Making a People What It Once Was': Regenerating Civic Identity in the Revolutionary Theatre of Venice." *Eighteenth-Century Life* 23 (1999): 38–57. Project MUSE, muse.jhu.edu/article/10498.

– "Imperial Mythologies: Ethnicity and Rebellion on the Eighteenth-Century Venetian Stage." *Studies in Eighteenth-Century Culture* 32 (2003): 245–76. http://doi.org/10.1353/sec.2010.0201.

Barsotti, Anna. *Alfieri e la scena. Dai fantasmi di personaggi a fantasmi di spettatori.* Rome: Bulzoni, 2001.

Bassi, Elena. "Le illustrazioni italiane e francesi delle commedie goldoniane." In *Atti del colloquio sul tema: Goldoni in Francia,* 77–85 (Roma, 29–30 maggio 1970). Rome: Accademia Nazionale dei Lincei, 1972.

Battaglia, Salvatore. *Grande dizionario della lingua italiana.* Turin: UTET, 1961–2002.

Bazoli, Giulietta. *L'orditura e la truppa: Le Fiabe di Carlo Gozzi tra scrittoio e palcoscenico.* Padua: Il Poligrafo, 2012.

Beniscelli, Alberto. *La finzione del fiabesco: Studi sul teatro di Carlo Gozzi.* Casale Monferrato: Marietti, 1986.

– "I due Gozzi tra critica e pratica teatrale." In Crotti and Ricorda, eds, *Gasparo Gozzi: Il lavoro di un intellettuale nel Settecento veneziano,* 263–79.

Benjamin, Walter. *Ursprung des deutschen Trauerspiels.* Frankfurt am Main: Suhrkamp Verlag, 1978.

– *The Origin of German Tragic Drama.* Translated by John Osborne. London: Verso, 1998.

Berengo, Marino, ed. *Giornali veneziani del Settecento.* Milan: Feltrinelli, 1962.

Bertelli, Sergio, Franco Cardini, and Elvira Garbero Zorzi, eds. *Le corti italiane del Rinascimento.* Milan: Mondadori, 1985.

Bertini, Fabio. *"Hor con la legge in man giudicheranno": Moventi giuridici nella drammaturgia tragica del Cinquecento italiano.* Florence: Società Editrice Fiorentina, 2010.

Biondi, Albano. "Il *Convito* di Don Pio Rossi: Società chiusa e corte ambigua." In *Un modello europeo,* Vol. 2 of *La corte e il "Cortegiano,"* edited by Adriano Prosperi, 93–112. Rome: Bulzoni, 1989.

Biondi, Marino. *Temi e stile del discorso politico alfieriano.* In *Alfieri in Toscana.* Atti del Convegno internazionale di studi (Firenze 19–20–21 ottobre 2000). Vol. 1, edited by Roberta Turchi and Gino Tellini, 239–61. Florence: Olschki, 2002.

Bjørnstad, Hall. "'Giving Voice to the Feeling of His Age': Benjamin, Pascal, and the Trauerspiel of the King without Diversion." *Yale French Studies* 124 (2013): 23–35. https://www.jstor.org/stable/23646038.

Bloemendal, Jan, and Arjan Van Dixhoorn, "Early Modern Literary Cultures and Public Opinion: An Epilogue in the Form of Discussion." In *Literary Cultures and Public Opinion in the Low Countries, 1450–1650,* edited by Jan Bloemendal, Arjan Van Dixhoorn, and Elsa Strietman, 267–91. Leiden-Boston: Brill, 2011.

– "Literary Cultures and Public Opinion in the Early Modern Low Countries." In *Literary Cultures and Public Opinion in the Low Countries, 1450–1650*, edited by Jan Bloemendal, Arjan Van Dixhoorn, and Elsa Strietman, 1–35. Leiden: Brill, 2011.

Bloemendal, Jan, Peter G.F. Eversmann, and Elsa Strietman, "Drama, Performance, Debate. Theatre and Public Opinion in the Early Modern Period: An Introduction." In *Drama, Performance and Debate. Theatre and Public Opinion in the Early Modern Period*, edited by Jan Bloemendal, Peter G.F. Eversmann, and Elsa Strietman, 1–18. Leiden-Boston: Brill, 2012.

Bordin, Michele, and Anna Scannapieco, eds. *Antologia della critica goldoniana e gozziana.* Venice: Marsilio, 2009.

Bottacchiari, Rodolfo. "Recensione a R. Verde. Studi sull'imitazione spagnuola nel teatro italiano del Seicento. G.A. Cicognini." *La nuova cultura* 1, no. 5 (May 1913): 344–61.

Bourke, Richard, and Quentin Skinner. *Popular Sovereignty in Historical Perspective.* Cambridge: Cambridge University Press, 2016.

Bragaglia, Anton Giulio. "Il parere dell'Alfieri sull'arte comica in Italia." *Convivium* 3–4 (1949): 571–87.

Braider, Christopher. *Baroque Self-Invention and Historical Truth: Hercules at the Crossroads.* Burlington, VT: Ashgate, 2004.

Bryson, Scott. *The Chastised Stage: Bourgeois Drama and the Exercise of Power.* Stanford, CA: Anima Libri, 1991.

Burke, Peter. *The European Reception of Castiglione's Cortegiano.* Cambridge: Polity Press, 1995.

Busnelli, Manlio. *Diderot et l'Italie. Reflets de vie et de culture italiennes dans la pensée de Diderot. Avec des documents inédits et un essai bibliographique sur la fortune du grand encyclopédiste en Italie.* Paris: Champion, 1925.

Calhoun, Craig, ed. *Habermas and the Public Sphere.* Cambridge, MA: MIT Press, 1992.

Calzavara, Antonella. "L''amor soverchio' e lo 'sfrenato sdegno.' Rassegna di testi e studi sulla tragedia italiana del Cinquecento (con un'appendice secentesca) (1970–1993)." *Lettere italiane* 46, no. 4 (1994): 642–76. http://www.jstor.org/stable/26265247.

Cambiaghi, Mariagabriella. *"Rapida ... semplice ... tetra e feroce": La tragedia alfieriana in scena tra Otto e Novecento.* Rome: Bulzoni, 2004.

Camerino, Giuseppe Antonio. "Libertà e tirannide. Il 'Brutus' del Voltaire e il 'Bruto Primo' dell'Alfieri." *Italianistica* 12, no. 2–3 (May–December 1983): 265–75. https://www.jstor.org/stable/23928212.

Cancedda, Flavia, and Silvia Castelli. *Per una bibliografia di Giacinto Andrea Cicognini: Successo teatrale e fortuna editoriale di un drammaturgo del Seicento.* Florence: Alinea, 2001.

Cantagrel, Laurent. "Un autore in cerca di legittimità. Una lettura della *Vita scritta da esso.*" In *Vittorio Alfieri: Solitudine – potere – libertà.* Atti del Convegno di Berlino (Humboldt-Universität zu Berlin, 12–13 novembre 2003), edited by Roberto Ubbidiente, 63–78. Frankfurt am Main: Peter Lang, 2006.

Capaci, Bruno. "Le marivaudage de Arlequin." In Gutiérrez Carou, ed, *Goldoni "avant la lettre,"* 455–64.

Cappelletti, Salvatore. *Luigi Riccoboni e la riforma del teatro. Dalla commedia dell'arte alla commedia borghese.* Ravenna: Longo, 1986.

Carter, Tim, and Richard A. Goldthwaite. *Orpheus in the Marketplace. Jacopo Peri and the Economy of Late Renaissance Florence.* Cambridge, MA, and London: Harvard University Press, 2013.

Casini, Matteo. *I gesti del principe: La festa politica a Firenze e Venezia in età rinascimentale.* Venice: Marsilio, 1996.

Castelli, Silvia. "Il teatro e la sua memoria: La compagnia dell'Arcangelo Raffaello e il *Don Gastone di Moncada* di Giacinto Andrea Cicognini." In *Tradurre, riscrivere, mettere in scena,* edited by Maria Grazia Profeti, 85–94. Florence: Alinea, 1996.

Castelvecchi, Stefano. *Sentimental Opera. Questions of Genre in the Age of Bourgeois Drama.* Cambridge: Cambridge University Press, 2013.

Chartier, Roger. *The Cultural Origins of the French Revolution.* Durham, NC: Duke University Press, 1991.

Charlton, Donald Geoffrey. "Jean-Baptiste Du Bos and Eighteenth-Century Sensibility." *Studies on Voltaire and the Eighteenth Century* 266 (1989): 151–62.

Chouillet, Anne-Marie. "Dossier du *Fils naturel* et du *Père de famille.*" *Studies on Voltaire and the Eighteenth Century* 208 (1982): 73–166.

Christian, Lynda G. *Theatrum mundi: The History of an Idea.* New York: Garland, 1987.

Ciavolella, Massimo. *La 'malattia d'amore' dall'Antichità al Medioevo.* Rome: Bulzoni, 1976.

Cicali, Gianni. "La lady, il drammaturgo e i marinai. 'Drammaturgia turistica' italiana del XVIII secolo." *Drammaturgia* 5, n.s (2018). http://www.drammaturgia.fupress.net/saggi/saggio.php?id=7277.

Connors, Logan J. *Dramatic Battles in Eighteenth-Century France: Philosophes, Anti-Philosophes, and Polemical Theatre.* Oxford: Voltaire Foundation, 2012.

Costa, Simona. "Merope." *La Rassegna della letteratura italiana* 9, no. 2 (2003): 564–83.

Cotticelli, Francesco. "Il teatro recitato." In *Storia della musica e dello spettacolo a Napoli. Il Settecento,* edited by Francesco Cotticelli and Paologiovanni Maione, 455–510. Naples: Turchini, 2009.

Courville, Xavier de. *Un artisan de la rénovation théâtrale avant Goldoni. Luigi Riccoboni dit Lélio chef de troupe en Italie (1676–1715).* Paris: L'Arche, 1967.

Crinò, Anna Maria. "Documenti inediti sulla vita e l'opera di Jacopo e Giacinto Andrea Cicognini." *Studi secenteschi* 2 (1961): 255–86.

Croce, Benedetto. *Poesia popolare e poesia d'arte: Studi sulla poesia italiana dal Tre al Cinquecento.* Bari: Laterza, 1933.

– "La *Merope* di Pomponio Torelli e l'*Andromaque* di Racine." In *Aneddoti di varia letteratura.* 4 vols. 2: 33–6. Bari: Laterza, 1953

– *I teatri di Napoli dal Rinascimento alla fine del secolo decimottavo.* Edited by Giuseppe Calasso. Milan: Adelphi, 1992.

Crotti, Ilaria, and Ricciarda Ricorda, eds. *Gasparo Gozzi: Il lavoro di un intellettuale nel Settecento veneziano.* Atti del convegno (Venezia-Pordenone 4–6 dicembre 1986). Padua: Antenore, 1989.

Curtius, Ernst Robert. *European Literature and the Latin Middle Ages.* Princeton, NJ: Princeton University Press, 1990.

Daniel, Drew. *The Melancholy Assemblage: Affect and Epistemology in the English Renaissance.* New York: Fordham University Press, 2013.

Darnton, Robert. *The Forbidden Best-Sellers of Pre-Revolutionary France.* New York: W.W. Norton, 1995.

Darnton, Robert, and Paul Roche, eds. *Revolution in Print: The Press in France, 1775–1800.* Berkeley: University of California Press, 1989.

Davison, Rosena. *Diderot et Galiani: Étude d'une amitié philosophique.* Oxford: The Voltaire Foundation, 1985.

Decroisette, Françoise. "'Un desiderio ignoto di qualcosa di più': Alfieri et ses spectateurs." In *Vittorio Alfieri. Drammaturgia e autobiografia.* Atti della giornata di studi (4 febbraio 2005), edited by Pérette-Cécile Buffaria and Paolo Grossi, 39–54. Paris: Istituto Italiano di cultura, 2005.

Dzhivelegov, Aleksei Karpovich. "Carlo Goldoni e le sue commedie." *Rassegna sovietica* 4, no. 9 (September 1953): 9–32.

De Grassi, Marino, ed. *Il libro illustrato veneziano nel Settecento.* Catalogo della mostra. Monfalcone: Edizioni della Laguna, 1990.

DeJean, Joan. *Ancients against Moderns: Culture Wars and the Making of a Fin de Siècle.* Chicago: University of Chicago Press, 1997.

Delehanty, Ann T. "Dubos and the Faculty of Sentiment." In *Literary Knowing in Neoclassical France: From Poetics to Aesthetics,* 145–168. Lewisburg, PA: Bucknell University Press, 2013.

Del Negro, Pietro. "La fine della Repubblica aristocratica." In *Storia di Venezia,* edited by Pietro del Negro and Paolo Preto, Vol. 8: *L'ultima fase della Serenissima,* 191–262. Rome: Istituto della Enciclopedia Italiana, 1999.

Delmas, Christian. *La tragédie de l'âge classique (1553–1770)*. Paris: Seuil, 1994.

De Michelis, Cesare. *Letterati e lettori nel Settecento veneziano*. Florence: Olschki, 1979.

Denarosi, Lucia. *L'Accademia degli Innominati di Parma: Teorie letterarie e progetti di scrittura (1574–1608)*. Florence: Società Editrice Fiorentina, 2003.

De Sanctis, Francesco. *Storia della letteratura italiana*. 2 vols. Milan: Feltrinelli, 1978.

De Vivo, Filippo. *Information and Communication in Venice: Rethinking Early Modern Politics*. Oxford: Oxford University Press, 2003.

– "Paolo Sarpi and the Uses of Information in Seventeenth-Century Venice." *Media History* 11, no. 1–2 (2005): 37–51. https://doi.org/10.1080/1368880052000342406.

Di Benedetto, Arnaldo. "*Il nostro gran Machiavelli: Alfieri e Machiavelli*." In *Dal tramonto dei Lumi al Romanticismo*. Modena: Mucchi, 2000.

DiGaetani, John Louis. *Carlo Gozzi: A Life in the 18th Century Venetian Theatre, an Afterlife in Opera*. Jefferson, NC: McFarland & Company, 2000.

Doglio, Federico. "La tragedia barocca." In *Il teatro tragico italiano. Storia e testi del teatro tragico in Italia*, edited by Federico Doglio, LXXIX–CLXIV. Parma: Guanda, 1958.

Doty, Jeffrey S. *Shakespeare, Popularity and the Public Sphere*. Cambridge: Cambridge University Press, 2017.

Duindam, Jeroen. *Myths of Power: Norbert Elias and the Early European Court*. Amsterdam: Amsterdam University Press, 1995.

Eijk, Philip van der. *Medicine and Philosophy in Classical Antiquity*. Cambridge: Cambridge University Press, 2005.

Eisenbichler, Konrad. *The Boys of the Archangel Raphael: A Youth Confraternity in Florence, 1411–1785*. Toronto-Buffalo-London: University of Toronto Press, 1998.

Elias, Norbert. *Über den Prozess der Zivilisation: Soziogenetische und psychogenetische Untersuchungen*. 2 vols. Basel: Haus zum Falken, 1939.

– *Die höfische Gesellschaft. Untersuchungen zur Soziologie des Königtums und der höfischen Aristokratie. Mit einer Einleitung: Soziologie und Geschichtswissenschaft*. Berlin: Luchterhand, 1969.

– *The Court Society*. Translated by Edmund Jephcott. New York: Pantheon, 1983.

– *The Civilizing Process: Sociogenetic and Psychogenetic Investigations*. Edited by Eric Dunning, Johan Goudsblom, and Stephen Mennel. Translated by Edmund Jephcott. Oxford: Blackwell, 2000.

Elliott, John Huxtable. "Power and Propaganda in the Spain of Philip IV." In *Spain and Its World, 1500–1700. Selected Essays*, 162–88. New Haven, CT, and London: Yale University Press, 1989.

Evangelista, Annamaria. "Le compagnie dei Comici dell'Arte nel teatrino di Baldracca a Firenze: Notizie dagli epistolari (1576–1653)." *Quaderni di teatro* 24 (1984): 50–72.

Fabiano, Andrea. "Introduzione. Il genio cattivo e il genio buono: Un percorso a ritroso dalla vecchiaia alla giovinezza." In Goldoni, *Il genio buono e il genio cattivo*, 11–59.

Fabrizi, Angelo. "Sul *Bruto Primo* alfieriano." *Studi e problemi di critica testuale* 9 (1974): 170–92.

– "Carlo Gozzi e la tradizione popolare (a proposito de *L'amore delle tre melarance*)." *Italianistica* 7, no. 2 (May–August 1978): 336–45.

Fantoni, Marcello. *La corte del granduca. Forma e simboli del potere mediceo fra Cinque e Seicento.* Rome: Bulzoni, 1994.

Farina, Paolo. "Carlo Gozzi 'conservatore rivoluzionario'? Declinazioni dell' anti-illuminismo." *Studi goldoniani* 11.3, n.s. (2014): 67–88. doi: 10.1400/223419.

Fazio, Mara. "Il rinnovamento del Settecento fra attori e autori." In *Breve storia del teatro per immagini*, edited by Luigi Allegri, Roberto Alonge, and Francesco Carpanelli, 161–90. Rome: Carocci.

Feldman, Martha. *Opera and Sovereignty: Transforming Myths in Eighteenth-Century Italy.* Chicago: Chicago University Press, 2007.

Ferrante, Luigi. *I comici goldoniani (1721–1960).* Bologna: Cappelli, 1961.

Ferrone, Siro. "Fortuna di Alfieri nell'Ottocento: Dall'autobiografia al repertorio." *Annali alfieriani* 4 (1985): 52–62.

– *Attori mercanti corsari: La commedia dell'arte in Europa tra Cinque e Seicento.* Turin: Einaudi, 1993.

– "Attori: L'archivio di Molière." In *La passione teatrale. Tradizioni, prospettive e spreco nel teatro italiano: Otto e Novecento. Studi per Alessandro d'Amico*, edited by Alessandro Tinterri, 111–23. Rome: Bulzoni, 1997.

– *La vita e il teatro di Carlo Goldoni.* Venice: Marsilio, 2011.

Ferroni, Giulio. "'Sprezzatura' e simulazione." In *La scena del testo.* Vol. 1 of *La Corte e il "Cortegiano,"* edited by Carlo Ossola, 119–47. Rome: Bulzoni, 1980.

Fido, Franco. "'I portentosi effetti': Delizie della retorica e alibi ideologico del significato." In *Nuova guida a Goldoni*, 63–74. Turin: Einaudi, 2000.

– *Nell'alveare della memoria: Ultimi incontri letterari.* Rome: Aracne, 2012.

Forestier, Georges. *Le théâtre dans le théâtre sur la scène française du XVIIe siècle.* Geneva: Groz, 1981.

Foucault, Michel. *Discipline and Punish: The Birth of the Prison.* Translated by Alan Sheridan. New York: Vintage Books, 1979.

– *Security, Territory, Population. Lectures at the Collège de France, 1977–1978.* Edited by Michel Senellart. Translated by Graham Burchell. Basingstoke, Hants: Palgrave Macmillan, 2009.

Franchi, Saverio. *Drammaturgia romana. Repertorio bibliografico cronologico dei testi drammatici pubblicati a Roma e nel Lazio. Secolo XVII.* Rome: Edizioni di storia e letteratura, 1988.

– *Le impressioni sceniche. Dizionario bio-bibliografico degli editori e stampatori romani e laziali di testi drammatici e libretti per musica dal 1579 al 1800. Ricerca storica, bibliografica e archivistica condotta in collaborazione con Orietta Sartori.* Rome: Edizioni di Storia e letteratura, 1994.

Frantz, Pierre. "Un hôte mal attendu: Goldoni, Diderot, Voltaire." *Revue d'histoire du théâtre* 1 (1993): 55–66. https://sht.asso.fr/revue/goldoni-a-paris/.

– *L'esthétique du tableau dans le théâtre du XVIIIe siècle.* Paris: Presses Universitaires de France, 1998.

Frattali, Arianna, ed. *Alfieri, lo spettacolo e le arti.* Pisa: ETS, 2015.

Fried, Michael. *Absorption and Theatricality: Painting and Beholder in the Age of Diderot.* Chicago and London: University of Chicago Press, 1988.

Friedland, Paul. *Political Actors: Representative Bodies and Theatricality in the Age of the French Revolution.* Ithaca, NY: Cornell University Press, 2002.

Fubini, Mario. *Vittorio Alfieri (Il pensiero-la tragedia).* Florence: Sansoni, 1937.

Fumaroli, Marc. *Héros et orateurs. Rhétorique et dramaturgie cornéliennes.* Geneva: Droz, 1990.

Geraci, Stefano. *Destini e retrobotteghe. Teatro Italiano nel primo Ottocento.* Rome: Bulzoni, 2004.

Gioberti, Vincenzo. *Il gesuita moderno.* Edited by Michele Federico Sciacca. 6 vols. Milan: Bocca, 1940.

Gobbi, Guelfo. "Le fonti spagnole del teatro drammatico di G.A. Cicognini: Contributo alla storia delle relazioni tra il teatro italiano e lo spagnolo del Seicento." *La biblioteca delle scuole italiane* 11, series 3, no. 18 (30 November 1905): 218–22; no. 19 (15 December 1905): 229–31; no. 20 (31 December 1905): 240–2.

Gombrich, Ernst H. *Art and Illusion: A Study in the Psychology of Pictorial Representation.* New York and Princeton: Princeton University Press, 1961.

Goodden, Angelica. "'Un peinture parlante': The *tableau* and the *drame.*" *French Studies* 38, no. 4 (1984): 397–413. https://doi.org/10.1093/fs/XXXVIII.4.397.

Grashey, Ludwig. *Giacinto Andrea Cicogninis Leben und Werke unter besonderer Berücksichtigung seines Dramas La Marienne ovvero il maggior mostro del mondo.* Leipzig: Deichert, 1909.

Greco, Franco Carmelo. "Ideologia e pratica della scena nel primo Settecento napoletano." *Studi pergolesiani* 1 (1986): 33–72.

– "Dal Belvedere al Liveri: La scrittura teatrale nel primo Settecento napoletano." In *Il teatro italiano nel Settecento*, edited by Gerardo Guccini, 205–41. Bologna: Il Mulino, 1988.

Greenblatt. Stephen J. *Sir Walter Ralegh: The Renaissance Man and His Roles.* New Haven, CT: Yale University Press, 1973.

– *Renaissance Self-Fashioning: From More to Shakespeare.* Chicago: University of Chicago Press, 1980.

– "Invisible Bullets: Renaissance Authority and Its Subversion, *Henry IV* and *Henry V*." In *Political Shakespeare: New Essays in Cultural Materialism*, edited by Jonathan Dollimore and Alan Sinfield, 18–47. Manchester: Manchester University Press, 1985.

Guccini, Gerardo. "Dall'innamorato all'autore. Strutture del teatro recitato a Venezia nel secolo XVIII." *Teatro e storia* 2 (1987): 251–93. http://www.teatroestoria.it/pdf/3/Gerardo_Guccini_53.pdf.

– "Introduzione." In *Il teatro italiano nel Settecento*, edited by Gerardo Guccini, 9–73. Bologna: Il Mulino, 1988.

– "*Il teatro San Luca*." In *Il teatro di Goldoni*, edited by Marzia Pieri, 295–313. Bologna: Il Mulino, 1993.

– "Goldoni scenografo. Con alcune considerazioni di carattere storico sulle componenti e le funzioni degli spazi comici." *Studi goldoniani* 10, no. 2 (2013): 11–41. http://digital.casalini.it/2634556.

Guerlag, Susanne. "The *tableau* and Authority in Diderot's Aesthetics." *Studies on Voltaire and the Eighteenth Century* 219 (1985): 183–94.

Gutiérrez Carou, Javier. "Goldoni fra riforma e controriforma: *Il genio buono e il genio cattivo*." *Rivista di letteratura italiana* 25, no. 1 (2007): 57–74. doi: 10.1400/56963.

– *Metamorfosi drammaturgiche settecentesche: Il teatro "spagnolesco" di Carlo Gozzi.* Venice: lineadacqua, 2011.

Gutiérrez Carou, Javier, ed. *Goldoni "avant la lettre": Esperienze teatrali pregoldoniane (1650–1750).* Venice: lineadacqua, 2015.

– "Pregoldoniano." In Gutiérrez Carou, ed., *Goldoni "avant la lettre"*, 17–23.

Gvozdeva, Katja, Tatiana Korneeva, and Kirill Ospovat, eds. *Dramatic Experience: Poetics of Drama and the Public Sphere(s) in Early Modern Europe and Beyond.* Leiden-Boston: Brill, 2016.

Habermas, Jürgen. "Naturrecht und Revolution." In *Theorie und Praxis. Sozialphilosophische Studien.* Frankfurt am Main: Suhrkamp, 1971.

– "Natural Law and Revolution." In *Theory and Practice*, translated by John Viertel, 82–120. Boston: Beacon Press, 1973.

– *The Structural Transformation of the Public Sphere: An Inquiry into a Category of Bourgeois Society*. Translated by Thomas Burger with Frederick Lawrence. Reprint, Cambridge, MA: MIT Press, 1989.
– *Strukturwandel der Öffentlichkeit. Untersuchungen zu einer Kategorie der bürgerlichen Gesellschaft. Mit einem Vorwort zur Neuauflage 1990*. Frankfurt am Main: Suhrkamp, 2001.
Hallamore Caesar, Ann. "Theatre and the Rise of the Italian Novel: Venice 1753–84." *Italian Studies* 67, no. 1 (March 2012): 37–55. doi: 10.1179/174861812X13202431700045.
Hammond, Nicholas. "The Theme of Ennui in Pascal's *Pensées*." *Nottingham French Studies* 26, no. 2 (1987): 1–16. https://doi.org/10.3366/nfs.1987-2.001.
– "'Levez le rideaux': Images of the Theatre in Pascal's *Pensées*." *French Studies* 47, no. 3 (July 1993): 276–87. https://doi: 10.1093/fs/XLVII.3.276.
– *Playing with Truth: Language and the Human Condition in Pascal's "Pensées."* Oxford: Oxford Clarendon Press, 1994.
Harris, Joseph. *Inventing the Spectator: Subjectivity and the Theatrical Experience in Early Modern France*. Oxford: Oxford University Press, 2014.
Hénaff, Marcel, Jean-Louis Morhange, and Marie-Line Allen. "The Stage of Power." Special Issue: Politics on Stage. *SubStance* 25, no. 2 (1996): 7–29. doi: 10.2307/3685327.
Herrick, Marvin T. *Tragicomedy: Its Origin and Development in Italy, France, and England*. Urbana: University of Illinois Press, 1962.
Herry, Ginette. *Carlo Goldoni. Biografia ragionata. Vol. 1: 1707–1744*. Venice: Marsilio, 2007.
Hess, Jonathan M. *Reconstituting the Body Politic: Enlightenment, Public Culture and the Invention of Aesthetic Autonomy*. Detroit, MI: Wayne State University Press, 1999.
Hobson, Marian. *The Object of Art: The Theory of Illusion in Eighteenth-Century France*. Cambridge: Cambridge University Press, 1982.
Hogsett, Charlotte. "Jean-Baptiste Dubos on Art as Illusion." *Studies on Voltaire and the Eighteenth Century* 73 (1970): 147–64.
Hohendahl, Peter Uwe. "Recasting the Public Sphere." *October* 73 (1995): 27–54. https://www.jstor.org/stable/779007.
Hoxby, Blair. *What Was Tragedy? Theory and the Early Modern Canon*. Oxford: Oxford University Press, 2015.
Ianniciello, Felice. *Marchese Domenico Luigi Barone. Commediografo alla corte di Carlo III di Borbone*. Naples: Istituto grafico editoriale italiano, 2011.
Jauss, Hans Robert. "La teoria della ricezione. Identificazione retrospettiva dei suoi antecedenti storici." In *Teoria della ricezione*, edited by Robert C. Holub, 3–26. Turin: Einaudi, 1989.

Joly, Jacques. "*Il genio buono e il genio cattivo,* 'pièce à spectacle' réformée." In *Le désir et l'utopie. Études sur le théâtre d'Alfieri et de Goldoni,* 231–57. Clermont-Ferrand: Association des publications de la Faculté des Lettres et Sciences Humaines de l'Université de Clermont Ferrand, 1978.

Jonard, Norbert. "L'abbé Du Bos en Italie." *Revue de littérature comparée* 37, no. 2 (1963): 177–201.

Jones, James F. "Du Bos and Rousseau: A Question of Influence." *Studies on Voltaire and the Eighteenth Century* 127 (1974): 231–41.

Jordan, Constance. "The Household and the State: Transformations in the Representation of an Analogy from Aristotle to James I." *Modern Language Quarterly* 54, no. 3 (1993): 307–26.

Kastan, David Scott. "Proud Majesty Made a Subject: Shakespeare and the Spectacle of Rule." *Shakespeare Quarterly* 37, no. 4 (1986): 459–75. doi: 10.2307/2870677.

Kavanaugh, Thomas M. *Enlightened Pleasures: Eighteenth-Century France and the New Epicureanism.* New Haven, CT: Yale University Press, 2010.

Kitzes, Adam H. *The Politics of Melancholy from Spencer to Milton.* New York: Routledge, 2006.

Klibansky, Raymond, Erwin Panofsky, and Fritz Saxl. *Saturn and Melancholy: Studies in the History of Natural Philosophy, Religion and Art.* New York: Basic Books, 1964.

Koepnick, Lutz P. "The Spectacle, the 'Trauerspiel,' and the Politics of Resolution: Benjamin Reading the Baroque Reading Weimar." *Critical Inquiry* 22, no. 2 (Winter 1996): 268–91. http://www.jstor.org/stable/1343972.

Kolesch, Doris. *Theater der Emotionen. Ästhetik und Politik zur Zeit Ludwigs XIV.* Frankfurt and New York: Campus, 2006.

Koselleck, Reinhart. *Kritik und Krise. Ein Beitrag zur Pathogenese der bürgerlichen Welt.* Freiburg: Alber, 1969.

– *Critique and Crisis: Enlightenment and the Pathogenesis of Modern Society.* Cambridge, MA: MIT Press, 1988.

Kruger, Loren. *The National Stage. Theatre and Cultural Legitimation in England, France, and America.* Chicago: The University of Chicago Press, 1992.

La Torre, Anna Maria. "Scrittura drammatica e fascinazione del teatro: La Merope." In Gian Paolo Marchi and Corrado Viola, eds, *Il letterato e la citta,* 113–48.

Lattarico, Jean-François. *Venise incognita: Essai sur l'académie libertine au XVIIe siècle.* Paris: Champion, 2012.

Leonelli, Giuseppe. "La regina ha la febbre." *Paragone Letteratura* 30, no. 358 (December 1979): 4–18.

Ley, Graham. "The Significance of Diderot." *New Theatre Quarterly* 11, no. 44 (1995): 342–54. doi:10.1017/S0266464X00009325.

Lombard, Alfred. *L'abbé Du Bos, un initiateur de la pensée moderne (1670–1742)*. Paris: Hachette, 1913.

Lombardi, Marco. "L'educazione del sovrano. Platonismo nello spettacolo francese del Seicento." *Drammaturgia* 2 (1995): 14–47.

Longoni, Franco. "'Ecco il tiranno.' Quale testo della *Merope* maffeiana lesse l'Alfieri." *Studi settecenteschi* 21 (2001): 111–40. https://bibliopolis.it/shop/studi-settecenteschi-21-2001/.

– "*Merope*: Genesi e parabola di un successo." In Gian Paolo Marchi and Corrado Viola, eds, *Il letterato e la città*, 75–112.

Luciani, Paola. *Le passioni e gli affetti. Studi sul teatro tragico del Settecento*. Pisa: Pacini, 1999.

– "Esordi tragici." In *Drammaturgie goldoniane*, 3–19. Florence: Società editrice fiorentina, 2012.

Lukács, György. *Il romanzo storico*. Turin: Einaudi, 1972.

Mamczarz, Irène. "Esperienze e innovazioni di Carlo Goldoni prima della riforma del 1748." *Studi goldoniani* 8 (1988): 7–50.

Mamone, Sara. *Il teatro nella Firenze medicea*. Milan: Mursia, 1981.

Mangini, Nicola. *I teatri di Venezia*. Milan: Mursia, 1974.

– "Alle origini del teatro moderno: Lo spettacolo pubblico nel Veneto tra Cinquecento e Seicento." *Biblioteca teatrale* 5/6 (1987): 87–103.

– "Gasparo Gozzi, cronista teatrale." In Crotti and Ricorda, eds, *Gasparo Gozzi: Il lavoro di un intellettuale nel Settecento veneziano*, 315–29.

– "La polemica Goldoni-Diderot." *Problemi di critica goldoniana* (1994): 261–71.

Maranini, Barbara. "Il comico nel tragico: I drammi per musica di Giacinto Andrea Cicognini." In *Commedia dell'arte e spettacolo in musica tra Sei e Settecento*, edited by Alessandro Lattanzi and Paologiovanni Maione, 185–212. Naples: Editoriale Scientifica, 2003.

Marchi, Gian Paolo. "La vocazione teatrale di Scipione Maffei." In *L'Accademia Filarmonica di Verona e il suo teatro*, 89–111. Verona: Grafiche Fiorini, 1982.

– *Un italiano in Europa: Scipione Maffei tra passione antiquaria e impegno civile*. Verona: Libreria Universitaria, 1992.

– "Voltaire, Lessing e Alfieri di fronte alla *Merope* di Scipione Maffei." *Studi italo-tedeschi* 23 (2002): 141–66.

Marchi, Gian Paolo, and Corrado Viola, eds. *Il letterato e la città. Cultura e istituzione nell'esperienza di Scipione Maffei*. Atti del convegno di studi nel 250° anniversario della morte (Verona, Sala Maffeiana, 21–22 novembre 2005). Accademia Filarmonica di Verona, Verona: Cierre, 2009.

Marin, Louis. *Le portrait du roi*. Paris: Minuit, 1981.

Mariti, Luciano. "La pubblica utilità del teatro. Dall'idea illuminista alla realtà della Repubblica romana." In *Il teatro e la festa. Lo spettacolo a Roma tra Papato e Rivoluzione. Catalogo della mostra realizzata al Museo napoleonico, 13 giugno–30 settembre 1989*, 14–22. Rome: Artemide, 1989.

Mattioda, Enrico. "Machiavelli nei trattati politici." In *Alfieri in Toscana*, Atti del Convegno internazionale di studi, Firenze 19–20–21 ottobre 2000. Edited by Roberta Turchi and Gino Tellini. 2 vols. Florence: Olschki, 2002, 1: 411–26.

– *Teoria della tragedia nel Settecento.* Alessandria: Edizioni dell'Orso, 2016.

Maza, Sarah C. *Private Lives and Public Affairs. The Causes Célèbres of Prerevolutionary France.* Berkeley: University of California Press, 1993.

– "The Theatre of Punishment: Melodrama and Judicial Reform in Prerevolutionary France." In *From the Royal to the Republican Body Incorporating the Political in Seventeenth- and Eighteenth-Century France*, edited by Sara E. Melzer and Kathryn Norberg, 182–98. Berkeley: University of California Press, 1998.

McCormick, John P. "Machiavelli's Greek Tyrant as Republican Reformer." In *The Radical Machiavelli. Politics, Philosophy and Language*, edited by Filippo Del Lucchese, Fabio Frosini, and Vittorio Morfino, 337–49. Leiden and Boston: Brill, 2015.

Melcarne, Nunzia. "Giacinto Andrea Cicognini: Un amico dell'Accademia veneziana degli Incogniti." *Aprosiana. Rivista annuale di studi barocchi*, no. 14 (2006): 34–40.

Merlin-Kajman, Hélène. *Public et littérature en France au XVIIe siècle.* Paris: Les Belles Lettres, 1994.

Miato, Monica. *L'Accademia degli Incogniti di Giovan Francesco Loredan (1630–1661).* Florence: Olschki, 1998.

Michelassi, Nicola. "La 'Finta pazza' a Firenze: Commedie 'spagnole' e 'veneziane' nel teatro di Baldracca (1641–65)." *Studi secenteschi* 41 (2000): 313–53. https://www.olschki.it/riviste/23.

Michelassi, Nicola, and Salomé Vuelta García. "La fortuna del teatro spagnolo a Firenze: Il *Don Gastone di Moncada* di Giacinto Andrea Cicognini." In *Teatri del Mediterraneo. Riscritture e ricodificazioni tra '500 e '600*, edited by Valentina Nider, 19–42. Trento: Editrice Università degli Studi di Trento, 2004.

– "Il teatro spagnolo sulla scena fiorentina del Seicento." *Studi secenteschi* 45 (2004): 67–137. https://www.olschki.it/riviste/23.

– *Il teatro spagnolo a Firenze nel Seicento.* Florence: Alinea, 2013.

Migliorini, Ermanno. "Note alle *Réflexions critiques* di Jean-Baptiste Du Bos." *Atti e memorie dell'Accademia toscana di scienze e lettere* 27 (1962–63): 287–8.

Mineo, Niccolò. "Vittorio Alfieri nella crisi dell'antico regime." In *Alfieri e il suo tempo.* Atti del Convegno internazionale (Torino-Asti, 29 novembre–

1 dicembre 2001), edited by Marco Cerruti, Maria Corsi, and Bianca Danna, 407–44. Florence: Olschki, 2003.

Molinari, Cesare. "Un teatro immaginario per Goldoni." In Goldoni, *Il teatro illustrato nelle edizioni del Settecento*, IX–XL.

Montorfani, Pietro. *Uno specchio per i principi. Le tragedie di Pomponio Torelli (1539–1608)*. Pisa: ETS, 2010.

Mullaney, Steven, and Angela Vanhaelen, "Introduction: Making Space Public in Early Modern Europe – Performance, Geography, Privacy". In Angela Vanhaelen and Joseph P. Ward, eds, *Making Space Public in Early Modern Europe: Performance, Geography, Privacy*, 1–14.

Napoli Signorelli, Pietro. *Storia critica de' teatri antichi e moderni*. 6 vols. Naples: Vincenzo Orsino, 1790.

Orgel, Stephen. *The Illusion of Power: Political Theatre in the English Renaissance*. Berkeley: University of California Press, 1975.

Ortolani, Giuseppe. "Carlo Gozzi ipocondriaco." In *La riforma del teatro nel Settecento e altri scritti*, edited by Gino Damerini, 313–31. Venice: Istituto per la collaborazione culturale, 1962.

Ozouf, Mona. "'Public Opinion' at the End of the Old Regime." *Journal of Modern History* 60 supple. (September 1988): 1–21. https://www.jstor.org/stable/1880368.

Pellegrini, Alessandro. "Alfieri e la tragedia senza coro." In *Dalla "Sensibilità" al Nichilismo*, 97–116. Milan: Feltrinelli, 1962.

Philips, Henry. *The Theatre and Its Critics in Seventeenth-Century France*. Oxford: Oxford University Press, 1980.

Piazza, Antonio. *Gazzetta Urbana Veneta*, n. 6, Wednesday, 21 January 1789.

Pieri, Marzia. *Il teatro di Goldoni*. Bologna: Il Mulino, 1993.

– "Recitare/recitarsi fra Firenze Pisa e Siena: Prove di futuro." In *Alfieri, lo spettacolo e le arti*, edited by Arianna Frattali, 15–30. Pisa: ETS, 2015.

Pii, Eluggero. "Il pensiero politico di Scipione Maffei: Dalla Repubblica di Roma alla Repubblica di Venezia." In *Scipione Maffei nell'Europa del Settecento*, edited by Gian Paolo Romagnani, 93–117. Verona: Cierre, 1998.

Placella, Vincenzo. "La polemica settecentesca della *Merope*." *Filologia e letteratura* 13, no. 3.51 (1967): 309–36 (I part) and no. 4.52: 394–447 (II part).

Pompejano Natoli, Valeria. "La seduzione in tragicommedia. La percezione dell'oriente islamico nell'*Amant libéral*." In *Dalla tragedia rinascimentale alla tragicommedia barocca. Esperienze teatrali a confronto in Italia e in Francia*. Atti del Convegno Internazionale di Studio (Verona-Mantova, 9–12 ottobre 1991), edited by Elio Mosele, 201–21. Fasano: Schena, 1993.

Popkin, Jeremy. "The Concept of Public Opinion in the Historiography of the French Revolution: A Critique." *Storia della Storiografia* 20 (1991): 77–92. https://www.libraweb.net/articoli.php?chiave=199111502&rivista=115.

Potts, D.C. "Pascal's Contemporaries and 'Le Divertissement.'" *Modern Language Review* 57, no. 1 (January 1962): 31–40. doi: 10.2307/3721969. https://www.jstor.org/stable/3721969?origin=crossref&seq=1#metadata_info_tab_contents.

Profeti, Maria Grazia. "Jacopo Cicognini e Lope de Vega: 'attinenze strettissime'?" In *Materiali, variazioni, invenzioni*, edited by Maria Grazia Profeti, 21–31. Florence: Alinea, 1996.

Radden, Jennifer. *The Nature of Melancholy: From Aristotle to Kristeva*. Oxford: Oxford University Press, 2000.

Raimondi, Enzio. "Le ombre sull'abisso." In *Le pietre del sogno. Il moderno dopo il sublime*. Bologna: Il Mulino, 1985.

Rando, Giuseppe. *Alfieri europeo: Le "sacrosante" leggi. Scritti politici e morali–tragedie–commedie*. Soveria Mannelli: Rubbettino, 2007.

Ranzini, Paola. "I canovacci goldoniani per il Théâtre Italien secondo la testimonianza di un *Catalogo delle robbe* inedito." *Problemi di critica goldoniana* 9 (2002): 7–169. http://digital.casalini.it/10.1400/21426.

Ravel, Jeffrey S. *The Contested Parterre: Public Theatre and French Political Culture, 1680–1791*. Ithaca, NY: Cornell University Press, 1999.

Rieger, Dietmar. "Tra Mira de Amescua / Rotrou e Marmontel. La tragicommedia 'Il Belisario' di Goldoni." *Problemi di critica goldoniana* 1 (1994): 233–60.

Ringger, Kurt. "La *Merope* e il 'furor d'affetto': La tragedia di Scipione Maffei rivisitata." *Modern Language Notes* 92, no. 1 (1977): 38–62. www.jstor.org/stable/2907045.

Rosand, Ellen. *Opera in Seventeenth-Century Venice. The Creation of a Genre*. Berkeley: University of California Press, 1991.

Rospocher, Massimo. "Beyond the Public Sphere: A Historical Transition." In *Beyond the Public Sphere: Opinions, Publics, Spaces in Early Modern Europe*, edited by Massimo Rospocher, 9–28. Bologna: Il Mulino; Berlin: Dunker & Humblot, 2012.

Ruffini, Franco. "'Gens de letteres' e 'gens de theatre': Dell'attore nel Settecento." In *Scritti in onore di Giovanni Macchia*. 2 vols. Milan: Mondadori, 1983, 2: 569–95.

Russo, Luigi, ed. *Il gusto. Storia di una idea estetica*. Palermo: Aesthetica, 2000.

Saisselin, Rémy G. *The Rule of Reason and the Ruses of the Heart: A Philosophical Dictionary of Classical French Criticism, Critics and Aesthetic Ideas*. Cleveland, OH: The Press of Case Western Reserve University, 1970.

Salfi, Francesco Saverio. *Saggio storico critico della commedia italiana.* Paris: Baudry, 1829.

Sanesi, Ireneo. *La commedia.* 2 vols. 2nd ed. Milan: Vallardi, 1954.

Sannia Nowé, Laura. "Il 'Tiranno' e la 'Madre' nella 'Merope' alfieriana." In *Vittorio Alfieri e la cultura piemontese fra illuminismo e rivoluzione.* Atti del Convegno internazionale di studi in memoria di Carlo Palmisano (San Salvatore Monferrato, 22–4 September 1983), edited by Giovanna Ioli, 205–23. Turin: Vincenzo Bona, 1985.

– "Introduzione. Il Marchese Scipione Maffei: Un mediatore tra letteratura e spettacolo." In Maffei, *De' teatri antichi e moderni e altri scritti teatrali,* XI–LXXVIII.

Santato, Guido. *Alfieri e Voltaire. Dall'imitazione alla contestazione.* Florence: Olschki, 1988.

Scannapieco, Anna. "Noterelle gozziane ('in margine' al teatro di Antonio Sacco e di Carlo Gozzi): Aggiuntavi qualche schermaglia." *Studi goldoniani* 11.3, n.s. (2014): 101–23. https://www.libraweb.net/riviste.php?chiave=117.

Scaramuzza Vidoni, Mariarosa. *Relazioni letterarie italo-ispaniche: Il "Belisario" di A. Mira de Amescua.* Rome: Bulzoni, 1989.

Scotton, Paolo. "La poetica della *Merope* nella *Drammaturgia amburghese* di Lessing. Pubblico e catarsi." In Zucchi, ed, *"Mai non mi diero i Dei senza un egual disastro una ventura,"* 149–68.

Selmi, Elisabetta. "Alla ricerca di una tradizione moderna: Attraverso le *Meropi* del teatro italiano." In Zucchi, ed, *"Mai non mi diero i Dei senza un egual disastro una ventura,"* 15–47.

Senardi, Fulvio. "Alle origini del dramma borghese: *Merope* di Scipione Maffei." In *Tre studi sul teatro tragico italiano tra manierismo ed età dell'Arcadia,* 83–117. Rome: Edizioni dell'Ateneo, 1982.

Serra, Francesca. "Piazze d'Italia: I teatri del Settecento." In *Dalla Controriforma alla Restaurazione,* vol. 2 of *Atlante della letteratura italiana,* edited by Erminia Irace, 632–4. Turin: Einaudi, 2011.

Silvestri, Giuseppe. *Scipione Maffei europeo del Settecento.* Vicenza: Neri Pozza, 1968.

Sìmini, Diego. "Alcune opere 'spagnole' di Giacinto Andrea Cicognini fra traduzione, adattamento e creazione." In *Teatro, scena, rappresentazione dal Quattrocento al Settecento.* Atti del Convegno internazionale di studi (Lecce, 15–17 maggio 1997), edited by Paola Andreoli Nemola, Giuseppe Antonio Camerino, Gino Rizzo, and Paolo Viti, 305–13. Galatina: Congedo, 2000.

– *Il corpus teatrale di Giacinto Andrea Cicognini. Opere autentiche, apocrife e di dubbia attribuzione.* Lecce and Brescia: Pensa Multimedia, 2012.

Snyder, Jon R. *Dissimulation and the Culture of Secrecy in Early Modern Europe.* Berkeley: University of California Press, 2009.

Sorba, Carlotta. "Teatro, politica e compassione. Audience teatrale, sfera pubblica ed emozionalità in Francia e in Italia tra XVIII e XIX secolo." *Contemporanea. Rivista dell'800 e del 900* 12, no. 3 (2009): 421–46. http://doi.org/10.1409/29969.

– "National Theater and the Age of Revolution in Italy." *Journal of Modern Italian Studies* 17, no. 4 (2012): 400–13. https://doi.org/10.1080/1354571X.2012.690578.

Spera, Lucinda. *Due biografie per il principe degli Incogniti. Edizione e commento della Vita di Giovan Francesco Loredano di Gaudenzio Brunacci (1662) e di Antonio Lupis (1663).* Bologna: I libri di Emil, 2014.

Spini, Giorgio. *Ricerca dei libertini: La teoria dell'impostura delle religioni nel Seicento italiano.* Rome: Editrice Universale, 1950.

Starobinski, Jean. *Histoire du traitement de la mélancolie des origines à 1900.* Basle: Geigy, 1960.

Sterpos, Marco. "La 'nuov'arte del dir molto in poco': La satira *I pedanti* e la poetica tragica alfieriana." In *Alfieri fra tragedia commedia e politica,* 13–55. Modena: Mucchi, 2006.

Stolleis, Michael. *Stato e ragion di stato nella prima età moderna.* Bologna: Il Mulino, 1998.

Strong, Roy. *Art and Power: Renaissance Festivals 1450–1650.* Berkeley: University of California Press, 1984.

Tatti, Mariasilvia. "Bruto secondo." *La rassegna della letteratura italiana* 107 (2003): 748–60.

Tcharos, Stefanie. *Opera's Orbit. Musical Drama and the Influence of Opera in Arcadian Rome.* Cambridge: Cambridge University Press, 2011.

Tedesco, Anna. "'Capriccio,' 'Comando,' 'Gusto del pubblico' e 'Genio del luogo' nelle premesse ai libretti per musica a metà del Seicento." In *Norme per lo spettacolo, norme per lo spettatore. Teoria e prassi del teatro intorno all'"Arte Nuevo."* Atti del seminario internazionale (Firenze, 19–24 ottobre 2009), edited by Giulia Poggi and Maria Grazia Profeti, 345–58. Florence: Alinea, 2001.

Tedesco, Salvatore. "Du Bos fra retorica e antropologia: Huarte de San Juan e François Lamy." In *Jean-Baptiste Du Bos e l'estetica dello spettatore,* edited by Luigi Russo, 45–54. Palermo: Centro internazionale studi di estetica, 2005.

Tikhonravov, Nikolai. *Russkie dramaticheskie proizvedenia 1672–1725 godov.* 2 vols. St Petersburg: Izdanie D.E. Kozancikova, 1874.

Toldo, Pietro. "Se Diderot abbia imitato il Goldoni." *Giornale storico della letteratura italiana* 26 (1895): 350–76. https://search.proquest.com/docview/1310284980?accountid=11004.

Treadwell, Nina. *Music and Wonder at the Medici Court. The 1589 Interludes for La pellegrina.* Bloomington: Indiana University Press, 2008.

Trivero, Paola. "La ricezione settecentesca della *Merope.*" In *Il debito delle lettere. Pomponio Torelli e la cultura farnesiana di fine Cinquecento,* edited by Alessandro Bianchi, Nicola Catelli, and Andrea Torre, 207–20. Milan: Edizioni Unicopoli, 2012.

Turchi, Roberta. "'Un'edizione colta e magnifica': Immagine e testo nella Pasquali." In *Parola, musica, scena, lettura. Percorsi nel teatro di Carlo Goldoni e Carlo Gozzi,* edited by Giulietta Bazoli and Maria Ghelfi, 403–18. Venice: Marsilio, 2009.

– "Spettatori in commedia (1750–1754)." *Problemi di critica goldoniana* 16 (2009): 333–47. doi: 10.1400/130575.

Vamos, Mara. "The Forgotten Book of Pascal's *Pensées.*" *Romanic Review* 62, no. 4 (1971): 262–9. https://search.proquest.com/docview/1290858077?accountid=11004.

Vanhaelen, Angela, and Joseph P. Ward, eds. *Making Space Public in Early Modern Europe: Performance, Geography, Privacy.* London: Routledge, 2013.

Van Krieken, Robert. *Norbert Elias.* London: Routledge, 1998.

Vescovo, Piermario. "Lo specchio e la lente: Il ruolo dello spettatore (1760–62)." In Crotti and Ricorda, eds, *Gasparo Gozzi: Il lavoro di un intellettuale nel Settecento veneziano,* 383–412.

– "L'esperienza del quotidiano nel teatro veneziano tra Goldoni e Gallina." *Esperienze letterarie* 32, no. 3–4 (2007): 289–314.

– "'J'avois grande envie d'aller à Naples.' Goldoni, l'erudito cavaliere Baron di Liveri, e i sistemi di produzione del teatro comico settecentesco." In *Oltre la Serenissima. Goldoni, Napoli e la cultura meridionale.* Giornata di Studio. 9 settembre 2008, edited by Antonia Lezza and Anna Scannapieco, 63–82. Naples: Liguori, 2012.

– "La biblioteca di Carletto Goldoni. Qualche osservazione sul teatro 'pregoldoniano.'" In Gutiérrez Carou, ed, *Goldoni "avant la lettre,"* 667–78.

– *Dei drammaturghi-concertatori: Diderot, Goldoni, Barone.* In Zucchi, *"Mai non mi diero i Dei senza un egual disastro una ventura,"* 131–48.

Villari, Rosario. *Elogio della dissimulazione. La lotta politica nel Seicento.* Rome: Laterza, 1987.

Warner, Michael. "Publics and Counterpublics." *Public Culture* 14, no. 1 (2002): 49–90. Project MUSE, muse.jhu.edu/article/26277.

Weintraub, Jeff. "The Theory and Politics of the Public/Private Distinction." In *Public and Private in Thought and Practice: Perspectives on a Grand Dichotomy*, edited by Jeff Weintraub and Krishan Kumar, 1–42. Chicago: University of Chicago Press.

Wetters, Kirk. *The Opinion System Impasses of the Public Sphere from Hobbes to Habermas.* Ashland, OH: Fordham University Press, 2008.

Whigham, Frank. *Ambition and Privilege. The Social Tropes of Elizabethan Courtesy Theory.* Berkeley: University of California Press, 1984.

Wootton, David. *Paolo Sarpi: Between Renaissance and Enlightenment.* Cambridge: Cambridge University Press, 1983.

Worvill, Romira M. *"Seeing" Speech: Illusion and the Transformation of Dramatic Writing in Diderot and Lessing.* Oxford: Voltaire Foundation, 2005.

– "From Prose to *peinture* to Dramatic *tableau.* Diderot, Fénelon and the Emergence of the Pictorial Aesthetic in France." *Studies in Eighteenth Century Culture* 39 (2010): 151–70. doi:10.1353/sec.0.0055.

Yates, Frances A. *Theatre of the World.* London: Routledge and Kegan Paul, 1969.

Yoch, James J. "The Renaissance Dramatization of Temperance: The Italian Revival of Tragicomedy and the Faithful Shepherdess." In *Renaissance Tragicomedy: Explorations in Genre and Politics,* edited by Nancy Klein Maguire, 115–38. New York: AMS Press, 1987.

Zaccaria, Michela. "Elena Balletti attrice e letterata." In Gutiérrez Carou, ed, *Goldoni "avant la lettre,"* 101–10.

Zagorin, Perez. *Ways of Lying: Dissimulation, Persecution, and Conformity in Early Modern Europe.* Cambridge, MA: Harvard University Press, 1990.

Zaniol, Alessandro. "Per una rilettura storico-filologica delle ultime edizioni goldoniane del Settecento." *Problemi di critica goldoniana* (1994): 189–232.

Zanlonghi, Giovanna. "La tragedia fra *ludus* e *festa.* Rassegna dei nodi problematici delle teoriche secentesche sulla tragedia in Italia." *Comunicazioni sociali* 15, no. 2–3 (1993): 157–240. http://digital.casalini.it/18277969.

Zilli, Luigia. "Fonti italiane della teoria tragicomica." In *Dalla tragedia rinascimentale alla tragicommedia barocca. Esperienze teatrali a confronto in Italia e in Francia.* Atti del Convegno Internazionale di Studio (Verona-Mantova, 9–12 ottobre 1991), edited by Elio Mosele, 51–9. Fasano: Schena, 1993.

Zorzi, Ludovico. *Il teatro e la città.* Turin: Einaudi, 1977.

Zucchi, Enrico. "La figura corale nelle tragedie alfieriane." *Lettere italiane* 4 (2010): 548–83. http://www.jstor.org/stable/26239894.

– "Suddito or giudice? Il contributo della tragedia italiana del Settecento alla definizione del concetto 'popolo.'" *Intersezioni* 36, no. 3 (2016): 343–62. doi: 10.1404/84825.

Zucchi, Enrico, ed. *"Mai non mi diero i Dei senza un egual disastro una ventura." La Merope di Scipione Maffei nel terzo centenario (1713–2013)*. Milan: Mimesis, 2015.

Index

absolutism, 34, 41, 82, 151, 167, 191n36, 222n37
Académie Française, 103, 127, 208n32
Accademia degli Arcadi, x, 63, 198, 201n26
Accademia degli Incogniti, ix, 16, 187n4, 187n7, 188n14
Accademia degli Incostanti, 186n1
Accademia degli Infuocati, 21
Accademia degli Instancabili, 186n1
Accademia degli Intronati, 186n1
Accademia dei Granelleschi, x, 96, 101, 206n11
actor, ix–x, 3, 8–9, 13–14, 20, 33, 37, 41, 48, 53, 55, 57, 59, 65, 67, 69, 81, 85, 107, 109, 117, 120, 125, 127–8, 131–3, 139, 143, 145–7, 169–70, 174–5, 178–9, 186n1, 192n49, 194n75, 197n42, 206n11, 218n58
actress, 199n5
Agamben, Giorgio, 7, 161, 164–5, 176; *Homo sacer. Il potere sovrano e la nuda vita,* 164
Agnelli, Maddalena, 58, 124, 195n12, 197n37, 215n30
Albergati Capacelli, Francesco, 130, 185n2
Alexandre, Denise, 143
Alfieri, Vittorio, x–xii, 5, 13–14, 69, 71, 74, 83, 86, 142–51, 153–6, 159, 161, 163, 165–7, 169–70, 172, 174–6, 178, 181–3, 198n2, 201n26, 202nn38–9, 221nn22–3, 222n35; *Agamennone,* xi; *Agide,* xi, 143–4; *Antigone,* xi; *Il Bruto primo,* xi, 14, 86, 143–4, 147–51, 153, 155–6, 160, 162–7, 174–6, 181, 220n8, 220n13, 221n23; *Il Bruto secondo,* xi, 14, 86, 143–4, 148, 166, 181, 221n23; *La congiura dei Pazzi,* xi; *Don Garzia,* xi; *Filippo,* xi; *Maria Stuarda,* xi; *Merope,* xi, 86, 143–4, 201n26, 202n38; *Mirra,* xi, 159; *Oreste,* xi, 144; *Ottavia,* xi; *Parere sull'arte comica in Italia,* xii, 145; *Parere sulle tragedie,* xii, 202n37, 220n13, 220n20, 223n48; *Polinice,* xi; *Del principe e delle lettere,* xi, 142, 149, 159, 219n3; *Risposta dell'Alfieri al Calzabigi,* xii, 14, 143–4, 156, 220n7, 220n16, 223n45; *Rosmunda,* xi; *Saul,* xi; *Sofonisba,* xi; *Timoleone,* xi; *Della tirannide,* xi, 147, 155, 161, 163,

172, 221n25, 223n42, 223n44, 223n54, 224n70; *Virginia*, xi, 143–4, 182; *Vita scritta da esso*, xii, 14, 142–4, 172, 219nn1–2, 220n5, 220n15, 221n23, 224n71
Alfonzetti, Beatrice, 222n34
Allacci, Leone, 48, 195n16
allegory, 51, 88, 108, 215n25; of debates on the reform of theatre, 92, 104; in eighteenth century, 92; for the Venetian public, 93, 97
ancien régime, 153, 169
L'année littéraire, 129
Apostolidès, Jean-Marie, 33, 192n54
Ariani, Marco, 146
Aristotle, 70, 77, 96–7, 99, 110, 164, 186n1, 194n77, 201n29, 204n53, 207n24; *Poetics*, 70, 186n1; *Politics*, 77, 201n29; *Problems*, 96, 207n24
Asti, x
Aubignac, François-Hédelin d', 211n66
audience, ix, 3–16, 19–21, 23–5, 33, 36, 38–44, 49, 51–3, 56–61, 63–8, 70–2, 75, 81, 84, 87–8, 90–1, 93–5, 97, 101–2, 104–8, 110–15, 118–20, 122–6, 130, 135, 137, 139–42, 144–7, 156, 170, 172, 174, 176–83, 186n11, 188n14, 194n77, 214n14, 215n28, 218n67, 223n62; response, 9, 12, 14. *See also* court, audience; spectatorship
Aufresne (Jean Rival), 218n62

Baglioni, Baccio, 189n21. *See also* Cicognini, Giacinto Andrea: *Il Celio*
Balletti, Elena, x, 70, 199n5
Bargagli, Girolamo, 18; *La pellegrina*, 18
Barone, Domenico Luigi, 13, 131–5, 140, 178, 217nn55–6, 218n58
Baroque, 19, 25, 27, 33–4, 37, 39–40, 50, 53, 79, 97, 138, 152, 191n36, 194n70, 196n31, 202n36, 208n32
Barricelli, Franca, 203n44, 224n3
Basile, Giambattista, 27–8, 206n11; *Lo cunto de li cunti, overo Lo trattenemiento de' peccerille*, 27, 192n43, 206n11
Bazoli, Giulietta, 208n41, 209n49, 214n9
Beaumarchais, Pierre-Augustin Caron de, 197–8n49, 218n62; *Essai sur le genre dramatique sérieux*, 198n49; *Eugénie*, 218n62
Becelli, Giulio Cesare, 199n12, 204n54
Bembo, Pietro, 38
Benjamin, Walter, 7, 51, 79, 82, 97, 99, 202n35, 208n31, 208n36; *Ursprung des deutschen Trauerspiels*, 79, 97, 202n35, 208n31, 208n36
Bettinelli, Giuseppe, ix, 45, 106
Bettinelli, Saverio, 150, 221–2n33
biopolitics, 165, 175
Bloemendal, Jan, viii, 185n9, 199n3
Bologna, vii, 3, 130
Bourbons, 6

Caccini, Giulio, ix, 18; *Euridice*, ix, 18. *See also* Peri, Jacopo; Rinuccini, Ottavio
Caesar, Julius, 27
Calderón de la Barca, Pedro, 22, 46; *Gustos y disgustos son nada más que imaginación*, 22; *La vida es sueño*, 46
Calzabigi, Ranieri de', 143

Caminer, Domenico, 214n10, 215n31
Caminer Turra, Elisabetta, 116
canovaccio, 49, 93. See also *commedia dell'arte* scenario
Capaci, Bruno, 215n24
Caraccioli, Domenico, 133, 218n61
carnival, 19, 57, 199n
Casali, Gaetano, 48, 59, 196n12
Casalpusterlengo, 58
Casanova, Giovanna, known as Zanetta, 197n42
Castiglione, Baldassarre, 30, 35–8, 192n49, 193n69, 194n71; *Il libro del cortegiano*, 30, 38, 192nn48–9, 193n64, 193n69, 194n71
Castro, Guillén de, 22
Cavalieri, Emilio de', ix; *La rappresentazione di anima, et di corpo*, ix
Cavallerino, Antonio, 72; *Telefonte*, 72
Cavalli, Francesco, ix. *See also* Cicognini, Giacinto Andrea: *Il Giasone*
Cecchini, Pietro Maria, 186n1
Cesarea, Procopio di, 49; *La storia arcana*, 49
Chantonnière de Grenaille, François, 196n26; *Bélisaire ou le conquérant*, 196n26
Charles III of Spain, 131
Chiari, Pietro, x–xi, 91–5, 101, 104–6, 112, 116, 122, 205n5, 205nn9–10, 206n11, 207n21, 213n84, 214n6; *Commedie in versi*, 214n6; *Commedie rappresentate ne' Teatri Grimani di Venezia*, 213n84; *Osservazioni critiche sopra* Le Sorelle rivali, 116; *Le sorelle rivali*, 95
Christine of Lorraine, grand duchess, 16, 18
Cicali, Gianni, 215n17
[Cicognini], 11, 47–53, 55–7, 59–61, 63–6, 68, 195n18, 196n28; *La caduta del gran capitan Belissario sotto la condanna di Giustiniano imperatore*, ix, 11, 48, 196n27
Cicognini, Giacinto Andrea, ix, 4, 10–11, 34–48, 53, 55, 57, 59, 63–6, 68, 73, 113, 157, 170, 175–8, 186n1, 187nn4–5, 187n7, 188nn14–15, 189nn21–3, 189n28, 191n34, 194n77; *L'Adamira, overo La statua dell'honore*, 17; *L'amicitia riconosciuta*, 47; *Gli amori di Alessandro Magno e di Rossane*, 17, 46; *Il Celio*, ix, 20, 189nn21–2; *Il convitato di pietra*, 46; *Il Don Gastone di Moncada*, ix, 10, 17, 20–5, 27, 33–4, 36, 40–2, 53, 57, 188n16, 189n20, 189n22, 190n29; *Le gelosie fortunate del principe Roderigo*, 17; *Il Giasone*, ix, 17, 48, 63, 188n14; *L'honorata povertà di Rinaldo*, 46; *L'innocente giustificato*, 17; *La Iuditta*, 17; *La Mariene ovvero Il maggior mostro del mondo*, 17; *Il maritarsi per vendetta*, 46; *La moglie di quattro mariti*, 17; *L'Orontea*, 17; *Il principe giardiniero*, 17; *Il tradimento per l'onore*, 17; *La vita è un sogno*, 17, 46. *See also* Cavalli, Francesco: *Il Giasone*
Cicognini, Jacopo, 186n1; *Il trionfo di David*, 186n1
classes, 8, 87, 150, 182–3; bourgeoisie, 152, 160, 182; elite, 20, 29, 33, 35; lower, 23, 40, 104, 181–2; lower-middle, 20, 23, 64, 181; upper, 9, 23, 60, 187
comedy, x–xi, 9, 12–13, 18, 45, 63, 91–4, 101, 106, 117–18, 121, 124–5, 128, 130, 132, 135,

138–9, 146, 206n13, 215n20, 215n28, 215n31, 216n34, 218n62; bourgeois, 215n34; of character, x; fairy-tale comedy, 13, 91, 124; improvised comedy, 93–4: See also *commedia dell'arte*; *larmoyant*, 105
comedia of the *Siglo de Oro*, 17, 22–3, 46, 49–50
commedia dell'arte, 3, 9, 17, 23, 48, 92, 94, 121–2, 138, 197n45, 215n24, 216n34; *commedia dell'arte* scenario, 48–9
Connors, Logan, 8
Conti, Antonio, 200n13, 222n34; *Giunio Bruto*, 222n34
Corneille, Pierre, 108–9; *Le Cid*, 108–9; *L'illusion comique*, 211n74
Costantini, Antonio, 197n42
Cotticelli, Francesco, 217n55
coups de théâtre, 23, 125, 127
court, 4, 7, 16–18, 20–2, 24–6, 29–42, 50, 52–4, 57, 61–2, 71, 94–6, 115, 131, 133, 142, 191nn36–7, 192n52, 193n64, 194n71; audience, 21, 47; etiquette, 25, 30, 36, 40, 133; life, 21, 61, 142; society, 7, 25, 29–30, 33–4, 54. *See also* court theatre
Crescimbeni, Giovanni Maria, x, 63, 194n78, 198; *La bellezza della volgar poesia*, 194n78
critic, 4, 6–8, 11–13, 56, 66, 69, 89, 92, 105, 113–14, 116, 121, 123–4, 170, 176, 178–9, 211n64
critical: awareness, 12, 68, 82; community, 14; consciousness, 70, 180; force, 142; freedom, 143; judgment, 12, 70, 169; opinion, 69; power, 43, 112
critique, 125, 153
Croce, Benedetto, 131, 200n21, 217n55

Della Porta, Giambattista, 44
De Sanctis, Francesco, 167, 223n62
Desfontaines, Nicolas, 196n26; *Bélisaire*, 196n26
Diderot, Denis, 13, 47, 127–36, 139–40, 178, 216nn39–41, 217nn42–4, 217nn47–8, 217n56, 218nn59–60, 218n62, 218n65, 218n67, 219n75; *Discours de la poésie dramatique*, 129–30, 217n48, 219n75; *Les entretiens sur Le fils naturel*, 127–8, 139, 216nn40–1; *Le paradoxe sur le comédien*, 132–4, 218n59, 218n61; *Le père de famille*, 129, 133, 218n62
DiGaetani, Louis John, 102, 209n47
dissimulation, 22, 34–5. See also *sprezzatura*
divertissement, 97–102, 104, 107, 138, 209n50
dramaturgy, 9, 46, 68–70, 110, 127, 146, 170, 172, 182
drame: bourgeois, 105; *larmoyant*, 71
dramma giocoso, 9, 46
Dubos, Jean-Baptiste, 12, 90, 97, 103–5, 108–13, 204n59, 209n51, 210nn53–8, 211–12n74, 213n83, 213n86; *Réflexions critiques sur la poésie et sur la peinture*, 12, 90, 103, 108, 113, 139, 209n51, 210nn55–6, 213n83, 213n86
Duni, Egidio Romualdo, 130
Durazzo, Giacomo, 134, 218n63
Dürer, Albrecht, 207n25

Elias, Norbert, 7, 25–6, 29–34, 191nn35–8, 192n41, 192nn45–6;

Die höfische Gesellschaft, 29, 192n41, 192nn45–6; *Über den Prozess der Zivilisation*, 25, 191nn35–6, 191nn37–8, 192n45
Elizabeth I, of England, 33
emotion, 9–10, 13, 25–8, 38, 61, 71, 91, 95, 105, 108–11, 113, 126, 128, 139, 172, 178, 191, 194; control of, 26
England, 5, 8, 17, 112, 138
Enlightenment, 7–8, 11, 42, 70, 105, 112–13, 127, 151–3, 155, 161, 164, 167, 175–6, 181, 213n86
ennui, 97, 99–100, 102–5, 208n37, 209n50, 210n53, 213n86
entertainment, 16, 19, 68, 93, 100–1, 105, 110, 166; courtly, 20; theatrical, 12, 18, 101–2, 105
Épinay, Louise Tardieu d'Esclavelles d', 218n62
Euripides, 70–1; *Cresphontes*, 70
Europe, 42, 54, 64, 69–70, 117, 129, 140, 146, 150–1, 177, 180–2, 188n18, 191n36, 199n8, 209n50, 213n86

Fabiano, Andrea, 214n12
Fabrizi, Angelo, 94, 147, 205n11, 220n8
Fagiuoli, Giovan Battista, 46
Favart, Charles-Simon, 134–5, 281n63
Feldman, Martha, 185n7, 188n10
Ferrari, Benedetto, ix, 18; *L'Andromeda*, ix, 18. *See also* Manelli, Francesco
Ferrone, Siro, 188n18, 196n28, 214n9, 220n18
Ficino, Marsilio, 96, 207n25; *De vita triplici*, 207n25
Fido, Franco, 195n10
Fiesole, 21
Florence, ix, xii, 4, 16–18, 20–1, 45–9, 57, 63, 183, 186n3, 188n17, 189n22, 207n25; Florentine Customs office, 20; Palazzo Pitti, 18; Teatro del Cocomero, 21; Teatro degli Uffizi, 18; Teatro della Dogana (also Teatro della Baldracca), ix, 4, 20–1, 48, 188n17, 188n19, 189n21; Uffizi Palace, 20
Foucault, Michel, 7, 54, 148–50, 153, 176, 196n32, 221n30, 222n40
France, xii, 5, 8, 18, 112, 118, 121, 134, 138–9, 148, 186n11, 196n29, 208n32; French Revolution, xii, 8, 181; Revocation of the Edict of Nantes, 208n32; Versailles, 191n36, 192n52
Fréron, Élie Catherine, 129
Fried, Michael, 8, 136–7, 218nn64–6, 219n69
Friedland, Paul, 8
Friedrich Christian, Prince of Saxony, 46
Fubini, Mario, 144, 170, 174, 220n14, 224n68

Galiani, Ferdinando, 133, 218nn60–2
Gandini, Pietro, 197
Gazzetta Urbana Veneta, 214n13
Gazzetta Veneta, 205n6, 209n46
Genoa, 5
genre, 8, 18, 23, 50, 62, 71, 92, 94–5, 105, 110, 117, 120–1, 123, 127, 129, 135, 138, 140, 143, 179, 216n31, 223n64
Germany, 5, 121
Gigli, Girolamo 44, 46

Gioberti, Vincenzo, 172, 224n69
Giraldi, Giovan Battista, 23, 190nn31–3, 194n77; *Discorso intorno al comporre delle commedie e delle tragedie,* 190n32
Goethe, Johann Wolfgang von, 67, 111; *Tagebuch der italienischen Reise,* 198n58, 212n79
Goldoni, Carlo, x–xii, 3–5, 11–13, 44–51, 57–62, 64–8, 91–5, 101, 104–8, 110, 112, 115–26, 128–40, 147, 170, 175–9, 185nn1–3, 195nn1–9, 196n19, 196nn22–4, 197n45, 205n5, 205n10, 206n11, 207n21, 209n49, 211n66, 211n69, 214n12, 214n14, 215n20, 215nn24–5, 215n31, 216n34, 217n47, 217n58, 219n70; *Gli amori di Alessandro Magno,* 46; *Le baruffe chiozzotte,* 67, 198n57; *Il Belisario,* x, 11, 48–9, 57–9, 61–2, 64, 68, 196n20, 196n23, 197n41; *La bella verità,* xi, 3, 185n3; *Le bourru bienfaisant,* xi, 217n48; *Una delle ultime sere di carnovale,* xi, 121; *Don Giovanni Tenorio o sia Il dissoluto punito,* 46; *La donna di garbo,* x; *I due gemelli veneziani,* 214n2; *Enrico re di Sicilia,* 46; *Il festino,* 214n14; *Il filosofo inglese,* 132; *Il genio buono e il genio cattivo,* xi, 13, 117–18, 120–1, 122, 125–6, 128, 130, 134–41, 214n12, 216n31; *Le inquietudini di Zelinda,* 47, 195n11; *La locandiera,* 117, 214n9; *Mémoires,* xii, 48–9, 58–9, 117–18, 120–1, 130, 185n1, 196n2, 196n24, 197nn39–40, 197nn44–5, 214n8, 215n17, 215n26, 216n36, 217n46; *Memorie italiane,* 46, 195nn4–7, 196n23, 197n42, 197n46; *Il Moliere,* 214n14, 215n28; *Momolo cortesan,* x; *I portentosi effetti della madre natura,* 46; *Rinaldo di Mont'Albano,* 46; *La serva amorosa,* 185n2; *Il servitore di due padroni,* x; *La sposa persiana,* 134; *Il teatro comico,* x; *L'uomo di mondo,* x; *Il vero amico,* 46, 129; *Zelinda e Lindoro,* 117
governance, 12, 14, 56, 82–3, 151–2, 156–7
Gozzi, Carlo, x–xii, 5, 12–13, 64, 67, 91–7, 99, 100–13, 115–16, 121–6, 128, 135, 176, 178–9, 205nn8–11, 206n13, 207n21, 207n28, 209nn49–51, 210n58, 210n60, 211n69, 211n73, 215n31; *Amore assottiglia il cervello,* 210n61; *L'amore delle tre melarance,* xi, 12, 91–5, 97, 101, 105, 111, 113, 205n8, 205nn10–11, 206n13; *Appendice al "Ragionamento ingenuo,"* 204n4, 211n63, 211n73; *I due fratelli nimici,* 208n28; *Le fiabe teatrali,* xi, 204n1; *Le gare teatrali,* xi; *Le memorie inutili,* xi, 92, 101; *La più lunga lettera di risposta che sia stata scritta inviata da Carlo Gozzi a un poeta teatrale italiano de' nostri giorni,* xii, 213n82; *La prefazione al "Fajel,"* 101; *Il ragionamento ingenuo, e storia sincera dell'origine delle mie dieci fiabe teatrali,* xi, 67, 91; *La scrittura contestativa al taglio della Tartana,* 205n10; *La tartana degl'influssi per l'anno bisestile 1756,* 205n10; *Il teatro comico all'osteria del pellegrino,* 205n10; *Zeim, Re de' genj,* 211n65, 214n1, 215n31

Gozzi, Gasparo, 92, 102, 110, 205n6, 209n46, 212n77
Gracián, Baltasar, 25, 192nn39–40; *Oráculo manual y arte de prudencia*, 192nn39–40
Grand Tour, 123
Gravina, Gian Vincenzo, x, 62
Greenblatt, Stephen, 7, 33, 39, 192n49, 193nn55–6
Grimani, family, 117
Grimani, Michele, x
Griselini, Francesco, 124, 215n29, 217n53
Guarini, Giambattista, 23, 190n31, 194n77; *Il compendio della poesia tragicomica*, 23, 190n31; *Il pastor fido*, 23, 190n31
Guccini, Gerardo, 137, 185n4, 196n33, 199n6, 219n72
Gutiérrez Carou, Javier, 121–2, 195n1, 205n9, 214n12, 215n18, 215n21, 216n32

Habermas, Jürgen, 5–7, 10–11, 14, 34, 41–2, 69–70, 79, 82, 84–5, 89, 111–12, 120, 149–51, 160, 169, 176, 180, 185nn5–6, 185n8, 186n10, 186n15, 193n58, 194n75, 213n81, 215n18, 221n31, 222nn36–7, 223n64; *Naturrecht und Revolution*, 149, 186n15, 221n31; *Strukturwandel der Öffentlichkeit*, 5, 185nn5–6, 193n58, 215n18
Habsburg, xii, 6
Hallamore Caesar, Ann, 213n84
Hammond, Nicholas, 100, 208nn37–8
Harris, Joseph, 8, 213n86
Henry IV of France, ix, 18
Hobbes, Thomas, 151–2; *Leviathan*, 151
Hoxby, Blair, viii, 8

identity, 11–12, 30, 32, 71, 87–8, 181, 192n49; collective, 70; formation, 4; national, 183, 223n62
illusion, 105–9, 127–8, 132–3, 137, 139–40, 174, 210n61, 211n74
Imer, Giuseppe, x, 48–9, 58–9, 197n42
impresario, x, 20, 131, 181
Ingegneri, Angelo, 194n76; *Della poesia rappresentativa e del modo di rappresentare le favole sceniche*, 194n76
intermedi, 18
intermezzo, 138
Italy, xi, 4–9, 14–16, 19, 35–6, 54, 69–70, 104, 118, 121, 123, 135, 138, 144–6, 176, 178–83, 187n5, 194n77, 199n8, 213n81, 218n62, 220n18; Loss of the Morea, 86; Restoration, 183; *Risorgimento*, 142, 181; Treaty of Campoformio, xii

Jacobins, 181; Jacobin movement, 182; Jacobin propaganda, 181, 183; Jacobin theatre, 182–3
Justinian, Emperor, 49

Koselleck, Reinhart, 7, 150–3, 155, 160, 164–5, 167, 169, 176, 222nn36–8, 223n43, 223n52, 223n63; *Kritik und Krise*, 7, 150–2
Krieken, Robert van, 30, 192n42

law, 16, 40, 74, 78–9, 82, 149, 152, 154–5, 160, 164, 166, 186; moral,

82, 153; of public opinion, 152; state, 152–5
Leonelli, Giuseppe, 89, 198n1
Lessing, Gotthold Ephraim, 69, 74, 116, 201n25, 214n4; *Hamburgische Dramaturgie*, 116
Ley, Graham, 139, 219n76
Liviera, Giovanni Battista, 72; *Cresfonte*, 72
Locke, John, 152, 169; *An Essay Concerning Human Understanding*, 152
London, 118–19, 160; Vauxhall theatre, 120
Longoni, Franco, 69, 199n4
Lope de Vega (Félix Lope de Vega y Carpio), 22, 46, 49, 186, 194n77; *El arte nuevo de facer comedias en este tiempo*, 194n77; *La corona merecida*, 22; *Las pobrezas de Reinaldos*, 46
Luciani, Paola, 57, 62, 197n34, 197n41, 198n51, 200n14, 217n48

Machiavelli, Niccolò, 35–6, 73, 77, 144, 163, 193n62, 200n24, 201n31 220n11; *I discorsi sopra la prima deca di Tito Livio*, 77, 201n31, 223n56; *Il principe*, 35, 193n62
Maffei, Scipione, x–xi, 4, 12, 57, 68–9, 76–9, 82–90, 144, 146, 152, 157, 160, 169, 176, 178, 198nn1–2, 199nn4–5, 199n9, 199nn11–12, 200n13, 200n18, 201n26, 201n32, 201n34, 202nn37–8, 202n40, 204n54, 204n59, 215n28; *Il consiglio politico al Governo Veneto*, 73, 77, 86; *La Merope*, 12, 57, 68–90, 152, 159–60, 169, 198nn1–2, 199n8, 200n13, 200n18, 202n38; *De' teatri antichi e moderni*, xi, 88–9, 146; *Teatro italiano o sia scelta di tragedie per uso della scena*, x
Mamczarz, Irène, 49, 57, 196n22, 197n35
Mamone, Sara, 188n, 214n9
Manelli, Francesco, ix, 18; *L'Andromeda*, ix, 18. *See also* Ferrari, Benedetto
Manzoni, Alessandro, 182; *Adelchi*, 182
Marchi, Gian Paolo, 88, 199n8, 201n32, 203n46, 204n55
Marin, Louis, 7, 34, 193n57
Marivaux, Pierre Carlet de Chamblain de, 121, 215n24; *Arlequin poli par l'amour*, 122
Marliani, Maddalena, 117, 214n9
Marmontel, Jean-François, 196n26; *Bélisaire*, 196n26
Mary, Queen of Scots, 33
mask, 3, 30–1, 35–7, 61, 137, 215n24
Massimo, Innocenzo, 207n28
Medebach, Girolamo, x–xi, 117
Medici, Cosimo III de', 21
Medici, Ferdinando I de', 18
Medici, Ferdinando II de', 21
Medici, Leopoldo de', 20, 189n20
Medici, Maria de', ix, 18
Medici, Mattias de', 189n20
melancholy, 93–7, 99, 101, 104–5, 110, 206n17, 207nn21–2, 207nn24–5, 208n28
Mercier, Sébastien, 198n49; *Du théâtre, ou Nouvel essai sur l'art dramatique*, 198n49
Metastasio, Pietro, 46, 62, 201
Milan, 4, 181, 197n45; Teatro La Scala, 181

Mineo, Niccolò, 159, 223n49
Mira de Amescua, Antonio, 49; *Capitan Belisario, y exemplo mayor de la desdicha*, 49
Modena, x, 69–70, 72, 89, 196n27, 198n2
Molière (Jean-Baptiste Poquelin), 207n21; *Le malade imaginaire*, 207n21; *Le misanthrope*, 207n21
Molinari, Cesare, 138, 218n68, 219n70
Montaigne, Michel de, 208n37
Monti, Tommaso, 197n42
Monti, Vincenzo, 182; *Aristodemo*, 182; *Caio Gracco*, 182
Muratori, Ludovico, x
music, ix–x, 4, 18, 125, 189n21
musical drama, ix–x, 3, 19, 71, 183

Naples, 3, 13, 218n62
Napoleon I, xii; French revolutionary expansion, xii; invasion of Italy, 181; Napoleonic wars, 181
Napoli Signorelli, Pietro, 131, 217n55
Nelli, Jacopo Angelo, 46
Novelli, Pietro Antonio, 137, 219n70

Onofri, Onofrio degli, 50; *Il Bilissario*, 50
opera, ix, 4, 9, 16–19, 117, 138, 143, 182–3, 187nn4–5, 188n10, 191n34; comic, 134; *opera seria*, 138
Orgel, Stephen, 33, 192n53
Osservatore veneto, 212n77

pantomime, 13, 130, 138–40, 178
Pariati, Pietro, 46
Paris, xi–xii, 13, 47, 67, 117–21, 123–4, 126, 128–31, 133–5, 138, 148, 218n61; Comédie Française, xi; Comédie Italienne, xi, 138; *forain* theatres, 138; Opéra Comique, 134, 138
Pascal, Blaise, 97–103, 105, 107, 113, 208nn32–7, 208n39, 209nn49–50, 210nn53–4; *Pensées*, 97, 99–100, 103, 113, 208nn34–5, 209n50
Pasquali, Giambattista, xi, 45–6, 126, 129, 136–8, 195nn4–7, 196n23, 197n42, 197n46
pastoral, 23, 119
Patriarchi, Gennaro, 206n11
Pellegrini, Alessandro, 148, 221n27
Pellegrini, Bertoldo, 198n2
Peri, Jacopo, ix, 18; *Euridice*, ix, 4. *See also* Rinuccini, Ottavio
Petrarch, x
Philip IV of Spain, 193n59
Piazza, Antonio, 117
Pieri, Marzia, 170, 221n22, 224n67
Pindemonte, Giovanni, 182; *I coloni di Candia*, 182
Plato, 95–6, 207n25; *Symposium*, 95
Pompejano Natoli, Valeria, 64, 198n55
power: absolute, 11, 68, 155; aesthetics of, 10, 19, 41–2; economic, 19, 144; figures of, 5; performance of, 85–6; political, 17, 33–4, 43, 72, 152–3, 159; structures, 7, 175
Profeti, Maria Grazia, 186n1
public: counterpublic, 7; debate, 198n3; horizon of expectations, 13, 42; interest, 73, 77; opinion, 6–7, 12, 14, 65, 69, 73, 89–90, 110–12, 149–53, 155–6, 161, 164, 166–7, 169, 175, 177–81, 185n9, 199n3, 212n78, 222n37

public sphere: bourgeois, 6, 10–11, 41–2; representative (performative), 7, 10, 41, 79, 82, 84–5, 155, 157, 180

raison d'état, 17, 73, 149, 153, 163, 187
Rapin, René, 211n66; *Réflexions sur la Poétique d'Aristote et sur les ouvrages des poètes anciens et moderns*, 211n66
Ravel, Jeffrey, 8
Renaissance, 33, 50, 90, 97, 183, 196n31
Riccoboni, Luigi, x, 44, 69–70, 199n5
Rieger, Dietmar, 49, 196n21
Rinaldo I, Duke of Modena, 89
Rinuccini, Ottavio, ix, 18; *Euridice*, ix, 4, 18. *See also* Caccini, Giulio; Peri, Jacopo
Rome, ix–x, 3, 18, 86, 148, 150–1, 153–4, 158, 160–2, 168–9, 173, 182–3
Rosand, Ellen, 187n4
Rossi, Pio, 30, 39, 192n50, 194n72; *Il convito morale per gli etici, economici e politici*, 30
Rotrou, Jean, 196n26; *Bélisaire*, 196n26
Rousseau, Jean-Jacques, 116, 214n3; *Lettre à M. D'Alembert sur les spectacles*, 116, 214n3
royalty, 10, 24, 42, 60
Rutti, Cecilia, 197n42

Sacchi, Antonio, x, 101, 117, 208n41, 214n9
Saffi, Francesco Saverio, 182; *Il General Colli in Roma*, 182
Saint-Évremond, Charles, 192n52
Sambucetti, Adriana, 197n42
Sannia Nowé, Elena, 87, 199n11, 200n14, 203n52, 209n54
Sapiti, Niccolò, 189n21. *See also* Cicognini, Giacinto Andrea: *Il Celio*
Sarpi, Paolo, 35–6, 193n68
Scannapieco, Anna, 205n10
scènes composées, 133–4
Schlegel, Johann, 181
Sciugliaga, Stefano, 125, 216n33
Scotton, Paolo, 70, 199n11
Selmi, Elisabetta, 200n18
Seneca, 23, 190. *See also* tragedy: Senecan
La Serenissima, 19, 111, 187. *See also* Venice
Shakespeare, William, 96, 206n17; *As You Like It*, 206n17
Siena, xii, 144
Siglo de Oro, 17, 22, 205n9
Sografi, Antonio Simone, 182; *Il matrimonio democratico*, 182
Soldini, Fabio, 96, 205n10, 207n28
Sommi, Leone de', 194n77
Sorba, Carlotta, 85, 203n41, 224n2
sovereignty, 4, 7, 10, 12, 19, 21, 23–5, 34, 39, 41–2, 53, 73, 77, 79, 82, 84–7, 97, 105, 157, 159, 164, 180, 185n7, 202n36; popular sovereignty, 86–7, 203n42
spectatorship, v, 4–6, 8–11, 16, 19, 42, 69, 90, 93, 112–13, 142, 177, 179, 181, 183, 213n84. *See also* audience
sprezzatura, 35
stage directions, 125–6, 131
Starobinski, Jean, 94, 206n16
statecraft, 10, 17, 35; statecraft as stagecraft, 11, 17
Stramboli, Francesco, 48, 195
Strong, Roy, 33, 192n53

tableau, 13, 31, 108–9, 125–8, 130, 134–5, 139–40, 178, 183, 212n74, 213n83, 216n39
Tatti, Mariasilvia, 148, 221n26
theatre: commercial, 47, 180, 218n58; court, 10, 13, 16, 19–20, 134, 142, 177, 218n58; *Nationaltheater*, 181; public, 10, 13, 16, 20, 142, 177
theatre reforms, 3, 5, 44, 47, 49, 94, 101, 106, 121–2, 125–7, 131, 135, 144, 170, 175, 181, 216n34; French, 129, 133; of Italian comic theatre, x, 13, 91–5, 117; of Italian tragic theatre, 69–70; Jacobin, 182
theatricality, 33–4, 39–40, 57, 82, 125, 136, 194n70; of power, 22, 39
Tirso de Molina (Gabriel Téllez), 22, 46; *Burlador de Sevilla y Convidado de piedra*, 46; *Cómo han de ser los amigos*, 22
Torelli, Pomponio, 71–2, 74, 78–9, 82–3, 200nn18–19, 200n21, 201n30, 201n34, 202n40; *La Merope*, 71–2, 82–3, 200n18, 200n21
tragedy, 8–9, 12, 19, 21, 23, 46, 49–53, 55, 59–60, 62–3, 65, 69–71, 73–4, 78, 89, 94, 101, 144, 146–8, 150–1, 153–6, 160, 164–7, 169–70, 174–6, 178, 183, 186n14, 190n31, 194n76, 195n18, 198n49, 199n12, 201n26, 202n40, 204n54, 220n8, 220n18, 222n33–4; revenge, 153; Senecan, 23; *tragedia a lieto fine*, 23; *Trauerspiel*, 79, 82, 97
tragicomedy, 9, 23, 46, 49–50, 62–4, 190n31, 197n49
Trissino, Giangiorgio, 49; *L'Italia liberata dai Goti*, 49; *Sofonisba*, 72
Turchi, Roberta, 195nn4–5, 211n66, 214n14

Ulivieri, Giuliano, 21

Vamos, Mara, 209n50
Vendramin, family, xi, 125
Venice, ix–xii, 4, 13, 16, 18–19, 57–8, 63, 67, 70, 95, 104–5, 111–12, 117–19, 121–2, 124–5, 135, 138, 187n4, 188n12, 193n68, 199n12, 209n49, 209n51, 210n58, 213n81, 215n31, 219n69; "myth" of, 19; Teatro Novissimo, ix; Teatro San Cassiano, ix, 18; Teatro San Giovanni Grisostomo, x–xi, 117; Teatro San Luca, xi, 70; Teatro San Moisè, ix; Teatro San Samuele, x–xi, 57, 205n10; Teatro Sant'Angelo, x; Teatro Santi Giovanni e Paolo, ix
Verdi, Giuseppe, 183; *Nabucco*, 183
Verona, x–xi, 58, 70, 199n12, 204n54
Vescovo, Piermario, viii, 131, 195n1, 198n57, 205n7, 206n11, 212n77, 217n58
Vienna, 134
Vitalba, Antonio, 197n42
Voltaire (François-Marie Arouet), 69, 76, 113, 142, 144, 201n28, 219n2, 221n62; *Brutus*, 222n34; *Les lettres philosophiques*, 213n85; *Mérope*, 76, 201n28; *Nanine*, 218n62

Warner, Michael, 179, 185n8, 224n1

Zatta, Antonio, xii, 117–19, 126, 136–8, 197n41, 215n22, 219n70
Zeno, Apostolo, 46, 62, 69, 88
Zucchi, Enrico, 186n14, 220n11

www.ingramcontent.com/pod-product-compliance
Lightning Source LLC
La Vergne TN
LVHW090155080826
844660LV00013B/816/J

* 9 7 8 1 4 8 7 5 0 5 3 5 6 *